Common Ground?
Readings and Reflections on Public Space

"Orum and Neal offer a wonderful collection of readings about public space. Their cogent arguments synthesize literatures and raise key empirical questions for readers to ponder and to further study."
—Robert M. Adelman, Sociology, *University of Buffalo, SUNY*

"This is by far the most comprehensive, focused, and perceptive work on public space to appear in many years, with selections that cover everything from basic concepts to critical theories. It is an essential work for anyone interested in the ongoing debate over the relative virtues of public and private realms in contemporary societies."
—Evan McKenzie, Political Science, *University of Illinois at Chicago*

"This outstanding collection is an important work from many disciplines focusing on critical issues related to public space. It is a perfectly designed book for an advanced undergraduate or master's level seminar related to urban sociology, urban geography, and urban planning."
—Kevin Romig, Geography, *Texas State University*

Public spaces have long been the focus of urban social activity, but investigations of how public space works often adopt only one of several possible perspectives, which restricts the questions that can be asked and the answers that can be considered. In this volume, Anthony Orum and Zachary Neal explore how public space can be a facilitator of civil order, a site for power and resistance, and a stage for art, theatre, and performance. They bring together these frequently unconnected models for understanding public space, collecting classic and contemporary readings that illustrate each, and synthesizing them in a series of original essays. Throughout, they offer questions to provoke discussion, and conclude with thoughts on how these models can be combined by future scholars of public space to yield more comprehensive understanding of *how public space works*.

Anthony M. Orum is Professor of Sociology and Political Science at the University of Illinois at Chicago. In 2007 and 2008, he was a Fulbright Scholar at Fudan University in Shanghai, China where he began his first systematic studies of public spaces. He also has written, among other books, *Introduction to Political Sociology*, the most recent edition (Oxford University Press, 2008) of which was co-authored with John Dale.

Zachary P. Neal is Assistant Professor of Sociology and Global Urban Studies at Michigan State University. In addition to public space, he has written about restaurants as urban cultural markers, the influence of networks among cities on their economic development, and quantitative methodology in the social sciences.

Anthony Orum and Zachary Neal were the Founding Editor and Managing Editor of *City & Community*, a journal of the American Sociological Association. Together, they edit the book series *The Metropolis and Modern Life*.

METROPOLIS AND MODERN LIFE

A Routledge Series
Edited by **Anthony M. Orum, University of Illinois at Chicago**
Zachary P. Neal, Michigan State University

This Series brings original perspectives on key topics in urban research to today's students in a series of short accessible texts, guided readers, and practical handbooks. Each volume examines how long-standing urban phenomena continue to be relevant in an increasingly urban and global world, and in doing so, connects the best new scholarship with the wider concerns of students seeking to understand life in the 21st century metropolis.

Forthcoming

The Gentrification Debates by Japonica Brown-Saracino
Urban Tourism and 21st Century Cities by Costas Spirou

Common Ground?

Readings and Reflections on Public Space

Anthony M. Orum
University of Illinois at Chicago

Zachary P. Neal
Michigan State University

Routledge
Taylor & Francis Group

NEW YORK AND LONDON

First published 2010
by Routledge
270 Madison Ave, New York, NY 10016

Simultaneously published in the UK
by Routledge
2 Park Square, Milton Park, Abingdon, Oxon OX14 4RN

Routledge is an imprint of the Taylor & Francis Group, an informa business

© 2010 Taylor and Francis

Typeset in Sabon by Swales & Willis Ltd, Exeter, Devon
Printed and bound in the United States of America on acid-free paper by
Edwards Brothers, Inc.

Library of Congress Cataloging in Publication Data
Common ground? : readings and reflections on public space / [edited by]
Anthony M. Orum, Zachary P. Neal.
p. cm.—(Metropolis and modern life)
1. Public spaces—Social aspects.   2. City planning—Social aspects.   I. Orum, Anthony M.   II. Neal, Zachary P.
HT153.C594 2008
307.1′216—dc22
2009005964

ISBN10: 0–415–99689–9 (hbk)
ISBN10: 0–414–99727–5 (pbk)
ISBN10: 0–203–87396–3 (ebk)

ISBN13: 978–0–415–99689–1 (hbk)
ISBN13: 978–0–415–99727–0 (pbk)
ISBN13: 978–0–203–87396–0 (ebk)

CONTENTS

Locating Public Space   1

Setting the stage for this exploration of public space, Zachary Neal addresses two questions: (a) What is Public Space and (b) When and Where are Public Spaces? He defines public space as including all areas that are open and accessible to all members of the public in a society, in principle, though not necessarily in practice. The individual pieces of this definition, as well as distinct legal, political, and social conceptions of public space are considered. Then, focusing on the social conception, he examines how different forms of public space have emerged during major historical periods from antiquity through the twentieth century, and how these forms continue to be relevant today.

PART 1: PUBLIC SPACE AS CIVIL ORDER

Introduction   13

Proceeding from the definition of public space developed in "Locating Public Space," Anthony Orum argues that there are three distinct models of public space. Here he defines a model of public space as civil order. This model insists that the constant and regular use of public space for social activities, such as conversations or public gatherings, is absolutely essential to the workings and the social vitality of cities and societies. He provides some firsthand observations on these matters, among them that there are important differences in the ways in which public space is made available and used by residents of cities and suburbs.

The Death and Life of Great American Cities—*Jane Jacobs*   18

This selection is one of the earliest and still most significant writings on the importance of public spaces. Drawing on her own experiences while living in New York City, Jane Jacobs argues that the everyday activity on the streets and sidewalks of neighborhoods is essential to the life of cities and, therefore, that urban areas must be designed to encourage the use of such spaces. She notes, among other things, that such everyday social life promotes trust among neighbors as well as providing for the safety of urban inhabitants, especially young children.

The Social Life of Small Urban Spaces—*William H. Whyte*   32

William Whyte and his associates systematically studied various parks, plazas, and sidewalks in New York City in the 1970s in order to understand how people used them. They found, for example, that people gather in various ways on plazas, and during specific times, such as the lunch hour, many people cluster in small groups, chatting and conversing with one another. They also discovered how people sometimes gather in unconventional sites such as at the edges of sidewalks. Based on the results of this work, Whyte consulted with officials in New York City to improve the placement and design of its parks and plazas.

In a selection that begins by noting that "the fastest growing kind of public space in America is prisons," Sharon Zukin adopts a critical stance toward the transformation of New York City parks into exclusionary and heavily regulated spaces. In the particular case of Bryant Park, she describes how William Whyte's suggestion to make the park more attractive was used as a method of a encouraging some users, while at the same time keeping "the undesirables" out. This approach, labeled Pacification by Cappuccino in reference to the introduction of chic coffee carts, is viewed as problematic because it relies heavily on the interests of private-sector elites.

William Whyte viewed public spaces, and especially city plazas, as important social gathering places. In this selection, Gregory Smithsimon challenges this view by asking why some plazas resemble empty concrete boxes with none of the sociability Whyte described. In some cases, these empty plazas offer no seating, while in other cases they are poorly lit or feature a fountain that keeps things uncomfortably wet; it is as if the plazas were designed to be inhospitable. And, indeed, through interviews with architects, Smithsimon finds that in many instances developers requested designs that would reduce, not facilitate, the social usefulness of their buildings' plazas.

Questions of the use of public space take place not only in the parks, plazas, and sidewalks of Western cities, but in cities around the world. In this selection, Lisa Law examines how local residents use certain central and significant public plazas in Hong Kong. Many recent immigrants, especially female domestic workers, like to use a central downtown area, known as Statue Square, to gather and socialize on Sundays. But the authorities have begun to resist these efforts, and to make it difficult for the women to engage in such gatherings. Law argues that there will be growing pressure on local authorities to make these kinds of spaces available to people, as major metropolitan areas like Hong Kong become the favored destination of immigrants.

PART 3: PUBLIC SPACE AS ART, THEATRE, AND PERFORMANCE

In this introduction to the third and final model of public space, Anthony Orum suggests that people often use public space today for public gatherings during which they engage in various kinds of performances and artistic expressions. In these activities, public spaces furnish a way for their users to affirm and express their own collective identities. In this regard, then, the study of public space provides insight not only into the social activities of people, but also into their cultures. He illustrates these processes with observations from Chicago and Shanghai.

A city's transit centers—bus stops, train stations, etc.—are often some of the most mundane, overlooked, and ugly urban spaces, despite the fact that they are used by hundreds, if not millions, of people. In this pair of essays, the authors describe how art-in-transit programs have begun to change this. Cynthia Abramson provides an overview of such programs, as they have been deployed in London, Los Angeles, Seattle, Stockholm, and New York. Myrna Margulies Breitbart and Pamela Worden then examine the specific case of Boston's Orange Line, and how involving local residents in the design process not only beautified a public space but also provided a venue for collective expression.

Billboards may not be public spaces themselves, but their ubiquity and high visibility make them an ideal canvas for those who want to get their message into public spaces. Usually these messages are of a commercial nature and can be interesting in their own right. But, as Timothy Drescher explores in this selection, they become particularly attention grabbing when graffiti artists have modified the advertisers' original message.

RIGHTS AND PERMISSIONS LIST

PART 3—PUBLIC SPACE AS ART, THEATRE, AND PERFORMANCE

Locating Public Space

Zachary P. Neal

Public spaces are all around us. We encounter them every day as we go about our routine activities. We use public roads and sidewalks to get to work and school. On the way, we stop by a coffee shop to caffeinate ourselves and say hi to the other regulars. At mid-day, we sit in outdoor plazas and mall food courts to enjoy our lunch. On the way home, we might meet friends at a local bar for a drink and to talk politics. And on the weekends, we go to the mall to shop; to the park to relax; to the museum or theatre for fun. We depend on public spaces just to get through our daily lives.

But, although we use public spaces all the time without thinking much about them, they are actually quite complex. Sometimes public spaces provide opportunities to interact with both strangers and acquaintances and to understand our position in the social world. Other times public spaces are sites where the powerful few exert control over others, who respond with protest and resistance. Public spaces can also be places for individuals to express themselves, by painting murals or playing music, or simply by the ways they dress and act. Moreover, in some cases seemingly public spaces aren't quite so public. In gated communities we can only use the roads and sidewalks if we "belong," while coffee shops and plazas aren't particularly inviting spaces to stay and socialize when their operators don't want people lingering and taking up valuable commercial space. But, before we can really understand how public space works, we have to ask first: What is public space?

WHAT IS PUBLIC SPACE?

While there are many different ways to define public space, most agree that public space includes *all areas that are open and accessible to all members of the public in a society, in principle though not necessarily in practice.* Because this definition is actually composed of several distinct ideas, it is useful to consider each part in more detail. Public space includes:

(1) ALL AREAS

Nearly all definitions of public space include such outdoor areas as parks, streets, and sidewalks. Public buildings like schools, libraries, and courthouses are also commonly recognized as public spaces, but their use might be restricted at certain times or to certain groups. In some cases, private buildings like shopping malls or restaurants are considered public spaces as well, though ultimately the owner or operator decides their use. Recently, conceptions of public space have expanded beyond actual, physical places to include virtual locations like Internet chatrooms and social networking websites. In short, any physical or virtual area where individuals and groups can interact with one another is potentially a public space.

(2) THAT ARE OPEN AND ACCESSIBLE

The publicness of public space derives primarily from its openness. That is, individuals and groups are free to come and go, are free to use the space for its intended purpose, and are free to be either active participants or passive spectators. Use of public space is not conditional upon membership in a particular group like a political party or religious community, upon one's income or education, or upon demographic characteristics like age or sex. A public library can be used by anyone, for example, regardless of what they wish to read. Moreover, not only must public space be open, it must also be accessible. This means that the use of public space should not be limited by barriers of language, physical or mental ability, or geographic mobility. For example, if the public library's entrance is at the top of a long flight of stairs, its status as a truly public space is limited because some people will be unable to use it.

(3) TO ALL MEMBERS OF THE PUBLIC IN A SOCIETY

There is, however, one important restriction to this openness: public space is only open to members of the public. This might seem like a trivial observation, but decisions about who is a member of "the public" and thus has a right to use public space is often a culturally and politically contentious issue. In some cases, laws establish formal social classes that identify those for whom public spaces must be open and accessible, as when certain government buildings are open to citizens but are closed to non-citizens. In other cases, cultural practices may require different groups to use separate public spaces, as is common with men's and women's public restrooms. Finally, informal rules may be used to decide who is and is not a member of the public. For example, some may seek to exclude the homeless from using a public park because they are not members of the "tax-paying public."

(4) IN PRINCIPLE THOUGH NOT NECESSARILY IN PRACTICE

In many cases, public spaces that are technically open and accessible fall short of this ideal in reality. For example, the plaza outside a large office building might be a public space to the extent that anyone can cross it, use it as a meeting spot, or eat lunch on it. But, if the lighting is poor or there are no benches, then in practice its openness and accessibility is severely limited. Similarly, a shopping mall may have no established rules excluding young people, but if the security guards employ techniques of intimidation to discourage loitering teens, the space is not practically open.

These can only be, at best, very general criteria for defining what public space is, because public space is by its very nature contested, ambiguous, and uncertain. It is continuously being redefined in terms of what it is, where it is, who may use it, and how. Thus, while we pass through and use public spaces all the time, saying exactly what public space is turns out to be fairly complicated. Beyond this basic definition, there are a number of more specialized conceptions of public space that consider, for example, their specifically legal or political character.

The Legal Limits of Public Space

Although public space is open and accessible to all, this does not mean that the use of public space is completely unrestricted. In the United States, the First Amendment protects citizens' freedoms of speech and assembly, but exactly how open public space is for various sorts of self-expression or gatherings depends on a number of factors.

The decision of the US Supreme Court in the 1983 case of *Perry Education Association v. Perry Local Educators' Association* established the three-tiered legal conception of public space known as the *public forum doctrine*. The Perry Education Association, the union that represented teachers in Perry, Indiana, was allowed by the local public schools to use teacher mailboxes to send information to its members. The rival teachers union, the Perry Local Educators' Association, was not allowed to use these mailboxes, which they claimed was unjust because the mailboxes were a public space. The Court was asked to decide whether teacher mailboxes in public schools were indeed a public space, and thus whether they should be open and accessible to all.

In the majority opinion, written by Justice Byron White, the Court defined three levels of public space that differ by their intended purpose and extent of openness. The most open type of public space, the *quintessential public forum*, includes places like "streets and parks which 'have immemorially been held in trust for the use of the public and . . . have been used for purposes of assembly, communicating thoughts between citizens, and discussing public questions'." These places are, and must always be, open and accessible to all, with expressive activity limited only in very narrow cases. For example, local authorities might prohibit activities in a public park that would place others at risk (e.g. target shooting) or that would prevent others from also enjoying the space (e.g. loud music). But they cannot exclude certain groups from using the space, or prohibit an individual from delivering a speech criticizing the government.

At the opposite end of the spectrum, the least open public space is the *non-public forum*, which includes "public property which is not by tradition or designation a forum for public communication." Who may use these public spaces, and how they may use them, can be restricted to specific groups and activities. For example, because the lobby of a US Post Office was not created to provide an opportunity for self-expression, even though it is a public space in the sense that it is publicly owned and operated, its use can still be restricted to postal employees and customers, and to activities related to sending and receiving mail. The Court decided that public school mailboxes fit into this category, and therefore that the schools in Perry, Indiana were not required to make them open and accessible to all, including rival unions.

Between these two extremes, the Court also defined a third type called a *limited public forum*. This includes public property that, unlike parks and streets, is not traditionally open, but "which the State has opened for the use of the public as a place for expressive activity." It is this legal category of public space that is most often the subject of controversy. Consider the gymnasium of a public school. School officials may decide to allow a religious group to use the space on Sundays. In doing so, the space has been opened to the public, and must be treated as if it were a quintessential public forum; other groups that also want to use the space cannot be excluded. Alternatively, school officials may decide not to allow the gymnasium to be used by the general public but to restrict its use to student athletics, in which case the space is treated as a non-public forum. Controversy often arises in determining precisely how limited a limited public forum is, and whether it should be treated as quintessentially public or as non-public.

Notably, this three-tiered classification only applies to public property. Privately owned and operated spaces are not public in the legal sense, and therefore are not subject to the same protections that ensure their openness and accessibility. However, in many cases we still think of technically private spaces as public spaces. For example, a coffee shop or bar is often used in much the same way as a public park or plaza. This is one place where questions about what public space is, and how public space works, starts to get complicated. What, for example, should we think about a shopping mall that decides to prohibit unaccompanied minors from hanging out in the food court? Further complications arise because the legal protections over activities in public spaces can vary dramatically from time to time, and from country to country.

Public Space and Democracy

Because public space is open and accessible to all members of the public, many theorists have noted that it plays an especially important role in democracy. In a sense, public space is the "where" of democracy and civic engagement; it gives citizens a place to participate in democracy, that is, to be citizens.

Jürgen Habermas (1989) used the term *public sphere* to describe a special, abstract kind of public space. The public sphere is not a physical location, but rather is a conceptual space filled with ideas, opinions, and debates about issues of public interest. This non-physical kind of public space is sometimes referred to as a *discursive space* because it is where political discourse or talk takes place. For Habermas, the public sphere provides individuals with an opportunity to engage in political participation through discussion, forming opinions, and building consensus. The seventeenth century European coffeehouse or salon is often offered as an example, and illustrates the relationship between physical public spaces and discursive public spaces like the public sphere. The coffeehouse itself—the actual place where people can gather, sit, and talk—is an example of a public space. But, the intellectual atmosphere of the political conversations that took place within the coffeehouse is an example of the public sphere. The two—public spaces and the public sphere—often go hand in hand.

Using the term *public realm*, Hannah Arendt (1998) described a similar kind of abstract public space, but one that was not just filled with talk. In her view, the public realm was a discursive sort of public space, but it was also a place for real political action. Individuals not only build consensus, but they also engage in collective political action to pursue mutual goals. Building on this political conception of public space, some theorists have argued that the public realm is not as active as it once was. Richard Sennett (1992), for example, has written about *The Fall of Public Man*, suggesting that in the modern world we live increasingly private lives. We spend more time in private than in public spaces, and as a result are less focused on political engagement. This claim calls attention to the importance of public space: when the availability and use of public space declines, ideals like freedom and liberty are threatened.

A Social Conception of Public Space

While the legal and political characteristics of public space are important, the readings in this book focus on a social conception of public space. They view public spaces as the places where we live out our public lives. They provide a stage to interact with friends and strangers, for struggles between the powerful and the powerless to unfold, and on which we can define who we are to the rest of the world. The key question, then, is: How do public spaces organize our public, social lives? How does public space work?

This book is organized around three different perspectives on how public space works. First, public space can be viewed as a *facilitator of civil order*. The interactions we have with friends in public spaces like neighborhood streets and local restaurants are the foundation of our social networks; the close social bonds we develop in these settings provide a sense of belonging and security. Similarly, the interactions we have with strangers in public spaces help us to understand our position in the world and how society expects us to act when we are "in public." Second, public space can serve as a *site for power and resistance*. Although openness is a definitional part of public space, none of these spaces are ever fully open and egalitarian. As a result, public spaces will always present opportunities for conflict between those who claim the space for their own use, and those who feel they have been unjustly excluded. Finally, public space can function as a *stage for art, theatre, and performance*. It is where we go to see and be seen; where we go to express our unique identities to one another. This expression might take an active form by performing in, or a passive form by listening to, an outdoor concert. It may be formal, like installing a public sculpture commissioned by the city, or informal, like making chalk drawings on the sidewalk. Together, these three perspectives on how public space works combine, in various ways, to reveal the richness of such places in our social lives.

FOR DISCUSSION

How well do the public spaces you encounter on a daily basis fit these definitions, conceptions, or perspectives of public space? How would you define public space?

WHEN AND WHERE ARE PUBLIC SPACES?

Before exploring the details of how public space works, we need to know where to look. And, because the nature of public space changes over time, we also need to know when to look. We must ask, therefore, when and where are public spaces? While public spaces have emerged in various forms throughout the course of human history, certain types of public spaces have come to be iconically associated with specific periods. The archetypal historical forms of public space discussed below, while they do not constitute an exhaustive history of the subject, provide a useful framework for exploring this question. Moreover, it is also useful in each case to consider how historical forms of public space are reflected in the public spaces we encounter today.

Classical Public Space: The Agora

Public space is certainly not an invention of the modern world, but has played a critical role in social life for many millennia. In fact, public space may have reached the pinnacle of its development in antiquity with the construction of such massive and spectacular public works as honorific columns and arches, colonnades and fountains, stadia and amphitheatres. But few public spaces are more closely associated with the classical world than the Agora of Athens. The Agora (literally, gathering place) served as the spatial focal point of public life in ancient Greece, accommodating political, religious, and commercial activities since the sixth century BC. Located at the base of the Acropolis, it was a rectangular open space surrounded by various public structures including temples, covered walkways, and government buildings including the court and mint.

While the Agora was a public space in principle, notions of "the public" were quite narrow. Thus, in practice it was open only to a small segment of the population—male citizens—though non-citizens and lower-class females could be found in servant and shopkeeper roles. This privileged public engaged in a range of activities in the Agora. Legal proceedings including the trial of Socrates took place here, with criminal verdicts rendered by jurors selected among those present in the Agora at the time. The Colonos Agoraios (literally, hill next to the Agora) served as a meeting place for craftsmen, much like a modern convention center or union hall. The Agora was also a center for ancient education and learning; it was the setting for many of Plato's *Dialogues*, and the philosophical school of thought known as Stoicism derives its name from lectures delivered by Zeno from the porch of the Stoa Poikile.

These legal, commercial, and educational activities made the Agora a vibrant place to interact with fellow citizens. But even more than these, the Agora has been associated with an activity that has defined societies and filled leisure time for ages: shopping. In fact, the term Agora is frequently translated as "marketplace." Setting up small shops within the covered open-air walkways called Stoae, craftsmen sold goods of their own creation that satisfied routine needs (e.g. shoes or eating and drinking vessels), while merchants offered luxury goods like textiles and perfume. The scene would not have been much different from another sort of public space that plays a significant role in our own lives: the shopping mall. Both the ancient Agora and the modern mall provide large open spaces to gather and socialize while browsing many small shops, all within a bustling and vibrant, highly social setting.

Medieval Public Space: The Commons

With the collapse of the Roman Empire, much of public life in the West reverted to the constant struggle to satisfy daily needs within a primarily agricultural context. Civic participation and higher education were reserved for such a small, elite segment of the population that these activities, though part of the public life of the ancient Greeks and Romans, became a largely private affair. For most, then, public life and the public spaces where it played out took on a utilitarian character, as places open and accessible to all for gathering life-sustaining natural resources. This was the role of the medieval commons. The commons were an area of land owned by an individual, often the king or lord, but that was open to all for certain purposes, including grazing cattle, fishing, and taking wood or soil for household use. To some extent, the commons and other open spaces in the few small settlements of the time also functioned as marketplaces and festival sites, but as Masschaele (2002) notes, in Medieval England "the existence of a large public space does not necessarily mean that a large number of people will convene." Although the medieval commons were not as socially or civically vibrant a public space as the Agora, they nonetheless served important functions. Namely, their openness and accessibility facilitated the collective pursuit of common goals (e.g. to eat) that would have been impossible using private land alone, and therefore they sustained the public in an otherwise dark age.

While today having a space to graze cattle or collect firewood is a concern for relatively fewer individuals, certain modern public spaces share many of the same characteristics. In 1634 Boston Common was established to provide residents of the town a place to pasture their cows, but in a series of incremental changes the space slowly evolved into what we now think of as a public park. In 1675 the first walkway was constructed through the otherwise agricultural area; in 1728 a tree-lined pedestrian mall was added; the gallows were removed in 1817 and the cattle in 1830; and ultimately a garden was established in 1837. In the early twentieth century, the further transformation from medieval common to modern public park was overseen by Frederick Law Olmstead, who considered the park as "the most valuable of all possible forms of public places" because it provides a space "to which people may easily go after their day's work is done, and where they may stroll for an hour, seeing, hearing, and feeling nothing of the bustle and jar of the streets, where they shall, in effect, find the city put far away from them." Today, Boston Common and the adjacent public garden offer an escape from the city, and rather than cows grazing on grass, provide residents and tourists a space to graze on a range of cultural activities including outdoor Shakespearian theatre and the Boston Pride festival.

Like its predecessor, the medieval commons, the public park is open and accessible to all for a range of activities. Even more recently, some have described the Internet as an electronic version of the commons. However, the openness of the medieval, and indeed modern forms of the commons, did not last. The medieval commons' role as a public space was abridged through *enclosure laws* that, in some cases, physically enclosed the open pastures with fences and hedges, but more generally restricted their use to private owners. The readings in this book from Don Mitchell and Sharon Zukin describe similar restrictions on the use of modern public parks, which like in the earlier medieval case, triggered significant political resistance.

Renaissance Public Space: The Plaza

A revival of classical Greek and Roman thinking fueled a flourishing of art and science during the Renaissance, while at the same time the development of new technologies and renewed interest in public life prompted rapid urbanization. As a result, the archetypal public spaces that emerged during this time were city-focused places that reflected elements of the Agora: the piazza (Italian), platz (German), plaza (Spanish), place (French), or square (English). While there is much variety, most such spaces take a very similar basic form: a large, open, and paved space, anchored at the center by a monument, fountain, or other architectural feature. They are located at the center of the town, often in front of a building of public significance like a courthouse or city hall, and are surrounded by other structures that mark its edges. In many newer cities the space is square or rectangular, fitting into the town's grid layout, while in older cities the space is usually round or oval and accessed by large boulevards that radiate out from the center. The development of the plaza form of public space is typically traced to European urban planning traditions, but Setha Low has argued that in fact it derives from much earlier Mesoamerican architectural practices that were appropriated by Spanish explorers. Indeed, plazas were common forms of public space in Incan and Mayan cities, and even in Spanish American cities well before they appeared in the great European capitals.

These types of public spaces have a number of uses, ranging from the active to the purely symbolic. They served as a place for public gathering, where individuals and small groups could meet and talk, that is, where ideas could be exchanged. They also offered a place for strolling and people watching, which was elevated beyond relaxation to a serious social activity as social status communicated through the pageantry of dress and manner increasingly dictated the flow of public life. And when the rigid social order of the day was transgressed, or became oppressive, the plaza was a site for protest and resistance. In addition to these activities, the plaza as public space served a number of symbolic functions as well. It was often used for ceremonial purposes—parades, coronations, or even Oktoberfest—that enhanced the reputation of the State and fostered civic pride and involvement. Similarly, because the grandiose and imposing spaces clearly took large sums of money to construct, these plazas made architectural assertions about the power and authority of the State.

Many of these Renaissance public spaces remain largely unchanged and are still in use today, while new plazas and squares are built every day following similar designs and with similar purposes. Tiananmen Square, a massive open public plaza established in Beijing in 1949, has been the site of numerous political conflicts, including the 1989 protests that ended in the deaths of an unknown number (perhaps several thousand) of demonstrators. It has also functioned as a symbol of the power of the Communist Party of China, as the site of annual mass military displays. Though also the site of protests and symbols of municipal power, Chicago's Daley Plaza, completed in 1965 and anchored by a 50 foot tall steel sculpture by Pablo Picasso, functions more as a civic gathering space. Throughout the year it hosts a variety of ethnic cultural festivals, farmer's markets, and political rallies.

Enlightenment Public Space: The Coffeehouse

The coffeehouse has, since the fifteenth century, served as an important type of public space throughout the Middle East. When Ottoman merchants introduced coffee to Europe in the seventeenth century, the popularity of the coffeehouse exploded. It offered a more exotic and refined alternative to the pub (shorthand for "public house") for individuals to gather and talk about a range of issues, but it came to be a key location for activity in several domains of public life.

Because they allowed relatively private conversations among close friends, the coffeehouse was a hotbed for political dissent and activism, which led Charles II in 1675 to call for their suppression as "places where the disaffected meet and spread scandalous reports concerning the conduct of His Majesty." The coffeehouse also offered a space for the public transaction of business, and in several cases developed into major public and private institutions. For example, stock and commodity prices were regularly posted and updated at Johnathan's Coffeehouse, which evolved into the London Stock Exchange. Similarly, the coffeehouse operated by Edward Lloyd was frequented by those engaged in the underwriting of ship insurance, and exists today as the global insurance firm, Lloyd's of London. Finally, as a social center, the coffeehouse was a place to discuss cultural trends and to assert one's position in society through the company one keeps. These public spaces gave way, ultimately, to more exclusive and private spaces. But, they retained some of their open and public character as Joseph Addison reported on the events in this more exclusive coffeehouse and salon society in *The Spectator*, a predecessor to the modern tabloid.

The coffeehouse continues to serve as a key public space, but its role in public life has proceeded in waves. Through the 1960s coffeehouses offered a venue for folk music performers like Joan Baez and Bob Dylan, and for such beat generation authors as Jack Kerouac and Allan Ginsberg. The political content of these artistic works connected the modern coffeehouse to its Enlightenment forerunners, but its use as a social gathering place declined through the 1970s and 1980s in favor of speed and convenience. By the 1990s however, Starbucks led the mass revival of the coffeehouse as a public space; they and other chains have focused on more than just serving a hot beverage by reintroducing music, fireplaces, and overstuffed chairs and couches.

Nineteenth-Century Public Space: The Street

The street had always been a sort of public space, but had served the largely utilitarian purpose of getting from one place to another. However, the nineteenth and early twentieth century saw advances in technology—the introduction of pavement and sidewalks, gas and electric illumination—that permitted the street to become a social public space in its own right. Georges-Eugène "Baron" Haussmann, hired by Napoleon in 1852 to modernize Paris, played a particularly central role in this transformation by introducing wide boulevards. The older, narrow streets towered over by buildings were dark and cold, and thus not inviting social spaces. But Haussmann's boulevards allowed sunlight to shine down between buildings, provided space for sidewalks and trees, and connected neighborhoods not just through infrastructure but also socially. These design ideas have served as the basis for subsequent public space development in America, in the form of the City Beautiful movement that aimed to use public spaces to channel civic energy, and in Daniel Burnham's 1909 plan of Chicago that relied heavily upon wide diagonal streets cutting across the city's rigid grid layout.

Along with the pedestrian-friendly boulevards, the development of covered iron-and-glass arcades facilitated the rise of a new kind of social activity in public spaces: *flanerie*. A *flâneur*, or person who engages in *flanerie*, strolls the streets of the city in order to experience it, taking in the sights and sounds as a sort of distanced observer. Walter Benjamin (2002), in his *Passagenwerk* or *Arcades Project*, documented the new public spaces created in Paris and how they fostered a distinct type of public life and street culture that revolved around "people watching." In these public spaces, the *flâneur* played a unique double role, on the one hand as an observer and interpreter of urban social life, but on the other hand as a direct participant in it, being observed and interpreted by others. In this way, Benjamin and other theorists pointed out the role of public spaces in structuring the way we understand ourselves, one another, and the spaces we inhabit. The reading by Mona Domosh in this book provides an opportunity to be a virtual *flâneur* by "reading" images of the nineteenth century streets of New York.

While sidewalks and streetlamps are now common, the street remains an important kind of public space. Despite the rise of high-speed transit and online retailing, many cities still have broad boulevards, often lined with shops, that present opportunities for residents and tourists to stroll, windowshop, see, and be seen: Champs-Elysees in Paris, Michigan Avenue in Chicago, Fifth Avenue in New York, or Rodeo Drive in Los Angeles. The role of the street is so closely connected with American nostalgia, in fact, that it has been memorialized and exported by Disney as Main Street USA. The advent of the pedestrian mall—a street without cars—has pushed the street as public space still further. In 1959 Kalamazoo, Michigan closed two blocks of a major street to automobile traffic, replacing the roads with gardens, fountains, and benches. Several other cities have followed suit, with varying degrees of success in creating public spaces that actually get used. Finally, a street does not have to be a majestic boulevard to be an important public space. Rick Grannis (1998), for example, has recently called attention to the roles of smaller "Trivial Streets" and the "T-Communities" they form.

Twentieth-Century Public Space: Public Accommodations

Many of the forms of public space that emerged in earlier eras are easy to recognize as public space: parks and plazas are built precisely to provide room for the public to gather, while malls and coffeehouses exist to provide a place for the public to spend money. But some public spaces—ordinary public accommodations like schools or libraries—are such mundane parts of everyday life that they can be overlooked as public spaces. In America, the creation of many of these types of spaces were the direct result of Franklin Roosevelt's New Deal, the massive public works program aimed at putting people back to work following the Great Depression. Between 1935 and 1943 the Work Projects Administration was responsible for the construction of, for example, 5,900 new schools, 9,300 new auditoriums and gyms, 1,000 new libraries, 3,085 playgrounds, and even 65 ski jumps. Perhaps one of the most important, yet overlooked, projects was the installation of thousands of public restrooms in parks across the country. Certainly, they do not provide a space to chat with old friends or to hold a grand parade, but they do provide relief that is open and accessible to all, and in doing so make public life possible.

FOR DISCUSSION

How are the public spaces you encounter on a daily basis similar to historical forms of public space? How have the public spaces you use changed over their history? What kinds of public spaces do you think are likely to develop in the future?

THE ORGANIZATION OF THIS BOOK

This collection of readings is organized into three sections. Each section begins with an introductory essay that describes a particular way of thinking about how public space works: (1) as a facilitator of civil order, (2) as a site for power and resistance, and (3) as a stage for art, theatre, and performance. These introductory essays are followed by five readings that illustrate how these perspectives have been used to understand public space. In selecting these readings, we have aimed to provide a mix of seminal theoretical contributions from major figures and current research from emerging scholars. Following these three sections, the book concludes with two essays: a discussion of whether public space is being lost and how it can be "relocated," and a discussion of the strengths of the three perspectives and ways they can be combined to provide a toolkit for exploring public space.

PART 1

*P*ublic Space as Civil Order

Introduction

Anthony M. Orum

The first order of business here is to provide a working definition of public space. There are a variety of definitions, as the introductory essay by Zachary Neal reveals, but they all essentially come down to the same thing: they are those common sites at which people gather in public, such as meeting halls, parks, plazas, streets, sidewalks, public markets and the like and, in the present era, they may even include cyberspaces on the Internet. *Such areas, like all public space, are open and accessible, in principle, to all members of the public in a society.* The significance of those sites can be seen at a moment's notice. If those spaces are open and accessible, then they provide venues and opportunities where the sundry and diverse constituents of a society (or a community, for that matter) can mingle, exchange ideas and socialize with one another. And presumably, the more such sites are actually public, in the sense of being open and accessible to everyone, the more they are working like public spaces should, at least in theory.

But the mystery and the drama of public spaces begin with their very definition: How open are they? To whom are they accessible? And what happens in public space that constitutes a special kind of social activity? If we are able to address these questions in some clear and careful fashion, then, in fact, we will not only have gone some ways towards understanding public space, but, more significantly, we will have understood something about what people do and how they act in public.

The first image of public space is that which conceives of it as though it were the civil order of a society. Many scholars and students of society employ this model, including some of the leading writers of our time. For example, Jane Jacobs, the famous journalist who, despite no formal training in the field, produced some of the most perceptive and powerful writing about cities in the twentieth century; Elijah Anderson, a sociologist who has written classic books about how blacks and whites interact with one another in such public spaces as streets and sidewalks; and, early in the twentieth century, Georg Simmel, the famous German sociologist who gave birth to a number of fruitful ideas and powerful insights into the ways in which people interacted with one another, especially in the large modernizing metropolis.

The model of public space as civil order is fairly straightforward. Writers and thinkers look at public space and focus upon the way that people relate to one another in such space. They are concerned both with the small intimacies of such interaction as, for example, whether people wave, nod, say hello to one another, but also the deeper exchanges, which may occur on benches, sidewalks, even at street corners. They are also concerned with the flow of people in public space, such as sidewalks, and whether there is a regular flow of pedestrian traffic, for example, or whether people just use such space intermittently. Concepts are developed to capture some of the elements of such space that may play a role in social interaction. Jacobs, for example, wrote of "dead end" places, such streets that went nowhere, and she argued that such areas did not promote intense and vital social interaction among people.

One of the most perceptive observers of public space in urban areas is the writer, William H. Whyte. Beginning in the early 1970s, Whyte and his associates conducted extensive studies of public spaces in New York City. They examined parks and plazas, sidewalks and streets, and they assembled a rich body of data through the use of interviews as well as cameras. Whyte found that people tended to gather and chat on the steps outside buildings, on benches if they were provided, but also on the walls that surrounded outdoor gardens. Ultimately his work became instructive and useful for planning in New York City. Based upon his lengthy and detailed observations, the New York City Planning Department implemented a number of very important measures, the major one of which was to encourage developers to build more plazas and similar public spaces in areas adjoining the buildings they constructed.

The theoretical importance of such observations as these about how and why people use public spaces lies in the significance that writers such as Jacobs and Whyte attach to the kind and quality of social interaction that occurs. They believe that such interaction is vital to the life of a city as well as to the life of society in general. Where such interaction, even of the smallest kind, like brief intimacies involving a wave of the hand or soft hello, is absent, the social life of the city is itself diminished. On the other hand, where such intimacies occur, and take place on a regular basis, and where there are plenty of sites at which people can sit, gather or assemble, thus to chat and visit with one another, then the social life of the city is vital and robust.

While Jacobs and Whyte emphasize the natural sites, like parks and plazas, for such social interaction, Ray Oldenburg draws attention to the role of what he calls "third places." Third places in his view are those sites outside of the places of our home and our work where we have an opportunity to meet and exchange ideas with other people. Taverns, bars and even coffee houses are the ideal third place: they are sites where we can expand our intellectual horizons, meeting and talking with people who are different than us, and who, therefore, enable us to develop a broader and richer understanding of the world around us.

A key assumption to this view of public space is that, despite the apparent disorder and disarray, there can be a great deal of order and routine to the visits and chats, even brief exchanges, people have with one another on sidewalks, at corners, or even in bars and coffee houses. One may pass the same people on a regular basis, and say hello everyday; or, may simply pass and say hello to strangers they meet on the street. Nevertheless, out of such daily comings-and-goings, a kind of civil order emerges whereby people develop a sense of community with one another. Hence, in the eyes of figures such as Jacobs and Whyte, the more there is such traffic, the deeper and richer the sense of civil order, or community. Again, where there is a diminished flow of pedestrians, and where that flow tends to be uniform (e.g. all men, all workers, etc.) rather than diverse, the more diminished the sense of civil order that exists, and the narrower and thinner the sense of community.

Beyond the importance of pedestrian traffic and the flow and diversity of such movement, it is the radical differences between the public spaces of areas to which attention often is drawn. In modern America, a number of writers, for example, have highlighted the sharp differences between the civil order in the public spaces of suburbs, on the one hand, and cities, on the other. Jacobs seemed especially incensed by the emptiness of parks and other public spaces she found in suburban areas compared to the full and rich social vitality of the streets and sidewalks in a city such as New York City. As she put it so directly: "Why are there so often no people where the parks are and no parks where the people are?" But she was not the only writer to offer such an observation.

The sociologist, M. P. Baumgartner, in a powerful and penetrating study of the community life of people in an Eastern suburb, argued that among such people there was clearly a sense of a diminished and limited civil order. "Moral minimalism," as she termed it, was found among the residents of Hampton, evident across a wide spectrum of private and public activities. Residents tended to live in their own private worlds, rarely having contact with outsiders. People infrequently encountered one another on streets or sidewalks, and if there were someone new in town, such a person was immediately identified as a stranger, thus subject to unremitting and unfriendly glances or stares.

In my own observations and research on the public spaces of suburbs and cities, the differences in the flow of pedestrian traffic and the seeming quality of civil order are obvious. Living in an affluent suburb for almost twenty years, I was continually surprised by several recurring events: one, the very small number of people that I would regularly encounter on my walks, runs and strolls through the area; two, the uniform and homogenous character of this everyday pedestrian traffic, a reflection of the ethnic homogeneity of the area, plus the absence of many outsiders; and three, the careless disregard that people showed both towards one another as well as towards features of the community/place itself. Even those people who I might pass on a regular basis rarely, if ever, gave a wave of the hand or a small hello to one another. They all seemed to be living tightly enclosed in their own private worlds, and Heaven forbid if someone should try to intrude on such private spaces.

But I was particularly struck by the disregard people showed towards, for lack of a better word, elements of the civil order itself. Almost every day I would pass a metal trash disposal bin in which people could put their refuse, such as paper cups, newspapers and, in my case, the litter bags of my dogs. People like me walked by these disposal bins regularly. Now and then it would happen that the wind would blow them over, or sometimes they would become simply so full of trash that it would spill out and fall across the walking paths. But no one ever stopped to pick up the containers; and rarely, if ever, did anyone clean up the litter. It was as though people were so absorbed by their own interior lives that they had no time to stoop down, return the trash to the container, or even simply to put the container upright again.

A short while ago, I moved from this suburb to a smallish urban area—according to current census figures, this area numbers about 80,000 residents, and lies on the edge of Chicago. Almost immediately I noticed the difference in the quality and flow of pedestrians on the sidewalks and streets of this new area. From almost early morning until late evening, there is a regular flow of people on the sidewalks. Some are on the way to, or coming from, the train into the city; others are simply on their way to shop; and yet still others are going to work at nearby offices and firms. And every day I see people say hello to one another, and I eventually have done so myself. Whether it is an older black man who might be going to work at the nearby pharmacy, or a young Asian woman who is heading to a train destined for downtown Chicago, almost everyone exchanges a smile, or even a small greeting.

People in this new area seem to take note of one another, and, more than that, they seem to relish the small intimacies that can take place on sidewalks. Unlike many of the parks where I previously lived, the parks in this area are often full of people, especially in the summers. Moreover, because this particular small city consists of such a diverse group of people, diversity can be found almost everywhere—on the sidewalks, streets and in other public sites, including nearby plazas that contain seats and benches where people can sit and visit.

Comparing the two settings, the suburb and the small city to which I moved, there is a world of difference in the seeming vitality as well as the breadth and diversity of people. And all of this is evident in the public spaces of the two sites: on close inspection one seems to furnish a diminished sense of community, whereas the other seems to be full and rich, where the social complexion of the place seems to be broad and inclusive.

This disparity between the pedestrian traffic and the flow and intimacies of people in the public spaces of suburbs as compared to cities in recent years has prompted a string of investigations. Most of them concern the reasons for such differences. Are the people who live in the suburbs, some wonder, simply different from those who live in the city? Do suburbanites simply prefer to live in a "morally minimalist" world, as Baumgartner insists? Some observers, of course, argue in the affirmative, claiming that those who live in the suburbs tend to be richer, whiter and different from those who live in cities—though this difference is changing as many suburbanites begin to be lured back into the downtown areas of cities. But there is also something far more important at work—why people do not pass one another on the sidewalks, or see one another in the parks and other suburban public spaces. The culprit—or, more formally, the immediate cause—of such differences is said to be the automobile. Those who live in the suburbs typically do things, like shopping, or going to work, or even carting their children around, by doing it in cars. The car becomes the means of getting around in the suburbs; it is the only way that people can get across the long distances separating them from friends and neighbors as well as from schools and other such facilities. And the byproduct of the car is the absence of the kind of vital everyday street life that Jane Jacobs so much affirms.

Though the students of public space as civil order accentuate the positive, and focus much of their attention on sociability in cities and other areas, they are not naïve about the uses of such space. Indeed, sociability is important not merely for the vitality and sense of community it breeds, but also because it serves as a deterrent to the possibility of violence and crime on the streets. Jacobs is especially insistent on this point, noting that in her neighborhood the local grocer, or the neighbor who regularly sat and watched the comings-and-goings of people, served as a way of providing "eyes" on the street. They watched and observed, noting whether there might be some signs of a fight or a mugging, and they were there to alert others and to help possible victims. It is in this regard that the social relationships, both strong and weak, provide a means for constructing and sustaining the civil order in cities and neighborhoods.

Elijah Anderson, the astute observer of street life in Eastern City, adds to our understanding of the way the civil order may develop in a place. Anderson spent time observing and thinking about the ways in which blacks and whites in two adjacent small communities in Eastern City, Northton and the Village, dealt with one another. Like other places, blacks and whites in this area rubbed shoulders. And as in such places, there always was the potential for some kind of disagreeable behavior or, at the very worst, some kind of crime committed by one group against the other. Those who seemed to come in for special attention, in Anderson's view, were young black males. Whites tended to look away from them on the street, while the young black men often showed their stuff, proudly strutting down the street as though they were kings and princes of the neighborhood.

It was on the street, Anderson says, where young black males ruled, having a sense of power and authority they lacked in other locations. Because of the potential difficulties that blacks and whites had in dealing with one another, Anderson argues that people had to learn the "code of the street," to become "streetwise," and thus to be able to negotiate walking and passing one another on the street. This was especially true in the boundary and border areas of the two very different communities for in these places the expectations for people could come into conflict. Blacks and whites, and people of varying ages, who walked on the sidewalks safely traveled these spaces, especially the most dangerous ones, by negotiating how they walked and greeted one another, if they did so at all. And, in the process of so doing, they helped to sustain the civil order and the viability of the two communities in the face of potentially disruptive and harmful encounters.

Let me conclude this brief introduction on a practical note. Though it would seem that the image of public space as civil order is largely a way of viewing the world, in fact, it also represents a way of designing the world. Some urban planners and architects, like Jan Gehl, take these ideas—of sociability, of the flow and location of people in public spaces—very seriously, using them to design spaces where people can, in fact, chat with one another, and have free and easy access to socialize.

FOR DISCUSSION

Does your own neighborhood feel like those described here, or different? How? Why? If you were to design a new park for your neighborhood, how would you design it and how would you want people to use it?

The Death and Life of Great American Cities

Jane Jacobs

This book is an attack on current city planning and rebuilding. It is also, and mostly, an attempt to introduce new principles of city planning and rebuilding, different and even opposite from those now taught in everything from schools of architecture and planning to the Sunday supplements and women's magazines. My attack is not based on quibbles about rebuilding methods or hair-splitting about fashions in design. It is an attack, rather, on the principles and aims that have shaped modern, orthodox city planning and rebuilding.

In setting forth different principles, I shall mainly be writing about common, ordinary things: for instance, what kinds of city streets are safe and what kinds are not; why some city parks are marvelous and others are vice traps and death traps; why some slums stay slums and other slums regenerate themselves even against financial and official opposition; what makes downtowns shift their centers; what, if anything, is a city neighborhood, and what jobs, if any, neighborhoods in great cities do. In short, I shall be writing about how cities work in real life, because this is the only way to learn what principles of planning and what practices in rebuilding can promote social and economic vitality in cities, and what practices and principles will deaden these attributes.

There is a wistful myth that if only we had enough money to spend—the figure is usually put at a hundred billion dollars—we could wipe out all our slums in ten years, reverse decay in the great, dull, gray belts that were yesterday's and day-before-yesterday's suburbs, anchor the wandering middle class and its wandering tax money, and perhaps even solve the traffic problem.

But look what we have built with the first several billions: Low-income projects that become worse centers of delinquency, vandalism and general social hopelessness than the slums they were supposed to replace. Middle-income housing projects which are truly marvels of dullness and regimentation, sealed against any buoyancy or vitality of city life. Luxury housing projects that mitigate their inanity, or try to, with a vapid vulgarity. Cultural centers that are unable to support a good bookstore. Civic centers that are avoided by everyone but bums, who have fewer choices of loitering place than others. Commercial centers that are lackluster imitations of standardized suburban chain-store shopping. Promenades that go from no place to nowhere and have no promenaders. Expressways that eviscerate great cities. This is not the rebuilding of cities. This is the sacking of cities.

Under the surface, these accomplishments prove even poorer than their poor pretenses. They seldom aid the city areas around them, as in theory they are supposed to. These amputated areas typically develop galloping gangrene. To house people in this planned fashion, price tags are fastened on the population, and each sorted-out chunk of price-tagged populace lives in growing suspicion and tension against the surrounding city. When two or more such hostile islands are juxtaposed the result is called "a balanced neighborhood." Monopolistic shopping centers and monumental cultural centers cloak, under the public relations hoohaw, the subtraction of commerce, and of culture too, from the intimate and casual life of cities.

That such wonders may be accomplished, people who get marked with the planners' hex signs are pushed about, expropriated, and uprooted much as if they were the subjects of a conquering power. Thousands upon thousands of small businesses are destroyed, and their proprietors ruined, with hardly a gesture at compensation. Whole communities are torn apart and sown to the winds, with a reaping of cynicism, resentment and despair that must be heard and seen to be believed. A group of clergymen in Chicago, appalled at the fruits of planned city rebuilding there, asked,

> Could Job have been thinking of Chicago when he wrote:
> Here are men that alter their neighbor's landmark . . . shoulder the poor aside, conspire to oppress the friendless.
> Reap they the field that is none of theirs, strip they the vine-yard wrongfully seized from its owner . . .
> A cry goes up from the city streets, where wounded men lie groaning . . .

If so, he was also thinking of New York, Philadelphia, Boston, Washington, St. Louis, San Francisco and a number of other places. The economic rationale of current city rebuilding is a hoax. The economics of city rebuilding do not rest soundly on reasoned investment of public tax subsidies, as urban renewal theory proclaims, but also on vast, involuntary subsidies wrung out of helpless site victims. And the increased tax returns from such sites, accruing to the cities as a result of this "investment," are a mirage, a

pitiful gesture against the ever increasing sums of public money needed to combat disintegration and instability that flow from the cruelly shaken-up city. The means to planned city rebuilding are as deplorable as the ends.

Meantime, all the art and science of city planning are helpless to stem decay—and the spiritlessness that precedes decay—in ever more massive swatches of cities. Nor can this decay be laid, reassuringly, to lack of opportunity to apply the arts of planning. It seems to matter little whether they are applied or not. Consider the Morningside Heights area in New York City. According to planning theory it should not be in trouble at all, for it enjoys a great abundance of parkland, campus, playground and other open spaces. It has plenty of grass. It occupies high and pleasant ground with magnificent river views. It is a famous educational center with splendid institutions—Columbia University, Union Theological Seminary, the Juilliard School of Music, and half a dozen others of eminent respectability. It is the beneficiary of good hospitals and churches. It has no industries. Its streets are zoned in the main against "incompatible uses" intruding into the preserves for solidly constructed, roomy, middle- and upper-class apartments. Yet by the early 1950s Morningside Heights was becoming a slum so swiftly, the surly kind of slum in which people fear to walk the streets, that the situation posed a crisis for the institutions. They and the planning arms of the city government got together, applied more planning theory, wiped out the most run-down part of the area and built in its stead a middle-income cooperative project complete with shopping center, and a public housing project, all interspersed with air, light, sunshine and landscaping. This was hailed as a great demonstration in city saving.

After that, Morningside Heights went downhill even faster.

Nor is this an unfair or irrelevant example. In city after city, precisely the wrong areas, in the light of planning theory, are decaying.

Less noticed, but equally significant, in city after city the wrong areas, in the light of planning theory, are refusing to decay.

Cities are an immense laboratory of trial and error, failure and success, in city building and city design. This is the laboratory in which city planning should have been learning and forming and testing its theories. Instead the practitioners and teachers of this discipline (if such it can be called) have ignored the study of success and failure in real life, have been incurious about the reasons for unexpected success, and are guided instead by principles derived from the behavior and appearance of towns, suburbs, tuberculosis sanatoria, fairs, and imaginary dream cities—from anything but cities themselves.

If it appears that the rebuilt portions of cities and the endless new developments spreading beyond the cities are reducing city and countryside alike to a monotonous, unnourishing gruel, this is not strange. It all comes, first-, second-, third- or fourth-hand, out of the same intellectual dish of mush, a mush in which the qualities, necessities, advantages and behavior of great cities have been utterly confused with the qualities, necessities, advantages and behavior of other and more inert types of settlements.

There is nothing economically or socially inevitable about either the decay of old cities or the fresh-minted decadence of the new unurban urbanization. On the contrary, no other aspect of our economy and society has been more purposefully manipulated for a full quarter of a century to achieve precisely what we are getting. Extraordinary governmental financial incentives have been required to achieve this degree of monotony, sterility and vulgarity. Decades of preaching, writing and exhorting by experts have gone into convincing us and our legislators that mush like this must be good for us, as long as it comes bedded with grass.

Automobiles are often conveniently tagged as the villains responsible for the ills of cities and the disappointments and futilities of city planning. But the destructive effects of automobiles are much less a cause than a symptom of our incompetence at city building. Of course planners, including the highwaymen with fabulous sums of money and enormous powers at their disposal, are at a loss to make automobiles and cities compatible with one another. They do not know what to do with automobiles in cities because they do not know how to plan for workable and vital cities anyhow—with or without automobiles.

The simple needs of automobiles are more easily understood and satisfied than the complex needs of cities, and a growing number of planners and designers have come to believe that if they can only solve the problems of traffic, they will thereby have solved the major problem of cities. Cities have much more intricate economic and social concerns than automobile traffic. How can you know what to try with traffic until you know how the city itself works, and what else it needs to do with its streets? You can't.

It may be that we have become so feckless as a people that we no longer care how things do work, but only what kind of quick, easy outer impression they give. If so, there is little hope for our cities or probably for much else in our society. But I do not think this is so.

Specifically, in the case of planning for cities, it is clear that a large number of good and earnest people do care deeply about building and renewing. Despite some corruption, and considerable greed for the other man's vineyard, the intentions going into the messes we make are, on the whole, exemplary. Planners, architects of city design, and those they have led along with them in their beliefs are not consciously disdainful of the importance of knowing how things work. On the contrary, they have gone to great pains to learn what the saints and sages of modern orthodox planning have said about how cities *ought* to work and what *ought* to be good for people and businesses in them. They take this with such devotion that when contradictory reality intrudes, threatening to shatter their dearly won learning, they must shrug reality aside.

Consider, for example, the orthodox planning reaction to a district called the North End in Boston. This is an old, low-rent area merging into the heavy industry of the waterfront, and it is officially considered Boston's worst slum and civic shame. It embodies attributes which all enlightened people know are evil because so many wise men have said they are evil. Not only is the North End bumped right up against industry, but worse still it has all kinds of working places and commerce mingled in the greatest complexity with its residences. It has the highest concentration of dwelling units, on the land that is used for dwelling units, of any part of Boston, and indeed one of the highest concentrations to be found in any American city. It has little parkland. Children play in the streets. Instead of super-blocks, or even decently large blocks, it has very small blocks; in planning parlance it is "badly cut up with wasteful streets." Its buildings are old. Everything conceivable is presumably wrong with the North End. In orthodox planning terms, it is a three-dimensional textbook of "megalopolis" in the last stages of depravity. The North End is thus a recurring assignment for M.I.T. and Harvard planning and architectural students, who now and again pursue, under the guidance of their teachers, the paper exercise of converting it into super-blocks and park promenades, wiping away its nonconforming uses, transforming it to an ideal of order and gentility so simple it could be engraved on the head of a pin.

Twenty years ago, when I first happened to see the North End, its buildings—town houses of different kinds and sizes converted to flats, and four- or five-story tenements built to house the flood of immigrants first from Ireland, then from Eastern Europe and finally from Sicily—were badly overcrowded, and the general effect was a district taking a terrible physical beating and certainly desperately poor.

When I saw the North End again in 1959, I was amazed at the change. Dozens and dozens of buildings had been rehabilitated. Instead of mattresses against the windows there were Venetian blinds and glimpses of fresh paint. Many of the small, converted houses now had only one or two families in them instead of the old crowded three or four. Some of the families in the tenements (as I learned later, visiting inside) had uncrowded themselves by throwing two older apartments together, and had equipped these with bathrooms, new kitchens and the like. I looked down a narrow alley, thinking to find at least here the old, squalid North End, but no: more neatly repointed brickwork, new blinds, and a burst of music as a door opened. Indeed, this was the only city district I had ever seen—or have seen to this day—in which the sides of buildings around parking lots had not been left raw and amputated, but repaired and painted as neatly as if they were intended to be seen. Mingled all among the buildings for living were an incredible number of splendid food stores, as well as such enterprises as upholstery making, metal working, carpentry, food processing. The streets were alive with children playing, people shopping, people strolling, people talking. Had it not been a cold January day, there would surely have been people sitting.

The general street atmosphere of buoyancy, friendliness and good health was so infectious that I began asking directions of people just for the fun of getting in on some talk. I had seen a lot of Boston in the past couple of days, most of it sorely distressing, and this struck me, with relief, as the healthiest place in the city. But I could not imagine where the money had come from for the rehabilitation, because it is almost impossible today to get any appreciable mortgage money in districts of American cities that are not either high-rent, or else imitations of suburbs. To find out, I went into a bar and restaurant (where an animated conversation about fishing was in progress) and called a Boston planner I know.

"Why in the world are you down in the North End?" he said. "Money? Why, no money or work has gone into the North End. Nothing's going on down there. Eventually, yes, but not yet. That's a slum!"

"It doesn't seem like a slum to me," I said.

"Why, that's the worst slum in the city. It has two hundred and seventy-five dwelling units to the net acre! I hate to admit we have anything like that in Boston, but it's a fact."

"Do you have any other figures on it?" I asked.

"Yes, funny thing. It has among the lowest delinquency, disease and infant mortality rates in the city. It also has the lowest ratio of rent to income in the city. Boy, are those people getting bargains. Let's see ... the child population is just about average for the city, on the nose. The death rate is low, 8.8 per thousand, against the average city rate of 11.2. The TB death rate is very low, less than 1 per ten thousand, can't understand it, it's lower even than Brookline's. In the old days the North End used to be the city's worst spot for tuberculosis, but all that has changed. Well, they must be strong people. Of course it's a terrible slum."

"You should have more slums like this," I said. "Don't tell me there are plans to wipe this out. You ought to be down here learning as much as you can from it."

This is something everyone already knows: A well-used city street is apt to be a safe street. A deserted city street is apt to be unsafe. But how does this work, really? And what makes a city street well used or shunned? Why is the sidewalk mall in Washington Houses, which is supposed to be an attraction, shunned? Why are the sidewalks of the old city just to its west not shunned? What about streets that are busy part of the time and then empty abruptly?

A city street equipped to handle strangers, and to make a safety asset, in itself, out of the presence of strangers, as the streets of successful city neighborhoods always do, must have three main qualities:

First, there must be a clear demarcation between what is public space and what is private space. Public and private spaces cannot ooze into each other as they do typically in suburban settings or in projects.

Second, there must be eyes upon the street, eyes belonging to those we might call the natural proprietors of the street. The buildings on a street equipped to handle strangers and to insure the safety of both residents and strangers, must be oriented to the street. They cannot turn their backs or blank sides on it and leave it blind.

And third, the sidewalk must have users on it fairly continuously, both to add to the number of effective eyes on the street and to induce the people in buildings along the street to watch the sidewalks in sufficient numbers. Nobody enjoys sitting on a stoop or looking out a window at an empty street. Almost nobody does such a thing. Large numbers of people entertain themselves, off and on, by watching street activity.

In settlements that are smaller and simpler than big cities, controls on acceptable public behavior, if not on crime, seem to operate with greater or lesser success through a web of reputation, gossip, approval, disapproval and sanctions, all of which are powerful if people know each other and word travels. But a city's streets, which must control not only the behavior of the people of the city but also of visitors from suburbs and towns who want to have a big time away from the gossip and sanctions at home, have to operate by more direct, straightforward methods. It is a wonder cities have solved such an inherently difficult problem at all. And yet in many streets they do it magnificently.

It is futile to try to evade the issue of unsafe city streets by attempting to make some other features of a locality, say interior courtyards, or sheltered play spaces, safe instead. By definition again, the streets of a city must do most of the job of handling strangers for this is where strangers come and go. The streets must not only defend the city against predatory strangers, they must protect the many, many peaceable and well-meaning strangers who use them, insuring their safety too as they pass through. Moreover, no normal person can spend his life in some artificial haven, and this includes children. Everyone must use the streets.

On the surface, we seem to have here some simple aims: To try to secure streets where the public space is unequivocally public, physically unmixed with private or with nothing-at-all space, so that the area needing surveillance has clear and practicable limits; and to see that these public street spaces have eyes on them as continuously as possible.

But it is not so simple to achieve these objects, especially the latter. You can't make people use streets they have no reason to use. You can't make people watch streets they do not want to watch. Safety on the streets by surveillance and mutual policing of one another sounds grim, but in real life it is not grim. The safety of the street works best, most casually, and with least frequent taint of hostility or suspicion precisely where people are using and most enjoying the city streets voluntarily and are least conscious, normally, that they are policing.

The basic requisite for such surveillance is a substantial quantity of stores and other public places sprinkled along the sidewalks of a district; enterprises and public places that are used by evening and night must be among them especially. Stores, bars and restaurants, as the chief examples, work in several different and complex ways to abet sidewalk safety.

First, they give people—both residents and strangers—concrete reasons for using the sidewalks on which these enterprises face.

Second, they draw people along the sidewalks past places which have no attractions to public use in themselves but which become traveled and peopled as routes to somewhere else; this influence does not carry very far geographically, so enterprises must be frequent in a city district if they are to populate with walkers those other stretches of street that lack public places along the sidewalk. Moreover, there should be many different kinds of enterprises, to give people reasons for crisscrossing paths.

Third, storekeepers and other small businessmen are typically strong proponents of peace and order themsleves; they hate broken windows and holdups; they hate having customers made nervous about safety. They are great street watchers and sidewalk guardians if present in sufficient numbers.

Fourth, the activity generated by people on errands, or people aiming for food or drink, is itself an attraction to still other people.

This last point, that the sight of people attracts still other people, is something that city planners and city architectural designers seem to find incomprehensible. They operate on the premise that city people seek the sight of emptiness, obvious order and quiet. Nothing could be less true. People's love of watching activity and other people is constantly evident in cities everywhere. This trait reaches an almost ludicrous extreme on upper Broadway in New York, where the street is divided by a narrow central mall, right in the middle of traffic. At the cross-street intersections of this long north-south mall, benches have been placed behind big concrete buffers and on any day when the weather is even barely tolerable these benches are filled with people at block after block after block, watching the pedestrians who cross the mall in front of them, watching the traffic, watching the people on the busy sidewalks, watching each other. Eventually Broadway reaches Columbia University and Barnard College, one to the right, the other to the left. Here all is obvious order and quiet. No more stores, no more activity generated by the stores, almost no more pedestrians crossing—and no more watchers. The benches are there but they go empty in even the finest weather. I have tried them and can see why. No place could be more boring. Even the students of these institutions shun the solitude. They are doing their outdoor loitering, outdoor homework and general street watching on the steps overlooking the busiest campus crossing.

It is just so on city streets elsewhere. A lively street always has both its users and pure watchers. Last year I was on such a street in the Lower East Side of Manhattan, waiting for a bus. I had not been there longer than a minute, barely long enough to begin taking in the street's activity of errand goers, children playing, and loiterers on the stoops, when my attention was attracted by a woman who opened a window on the third floor of a tenement across the street and vigorously yoo-hooed at me. When I caught on that she wanted my attention and responded, she shouted down, "The bus doesn't run here on Saturdays!" Then by a combination of shouts and pantomime she directed me around the corner. This woman was one of thousands upon thousands of people in New York who casually take care of the streets. They notice strangers. They observe everything going on. If they need to take action, whether to direct a stranger waiting in the wrong place or to call the police, they do so. Action usually requires, to be sure, a certain self-assurance about the actor's proprietorship of the street and the support he will get if necessary, matters which will be gone into later in this book. But even more fundamental than the action and necessary to the action, is the watching itself.

Not everyone in cities helps to take care of the streets, and many a city resident or city worker is unaware of why his neighborhood is safe. The other day an incident occurred on the street where I live, and it interested me because of this point.

My block of the street, I must explain, is a small one, but it contains a remarkable range of buildings, varying from several vintages of tenements to three- and four-story houses that have been converted into low-rent flats with stores on the ground floor, or returned to single-family use like ours. Across the street there used to be mostly four-story brick tenements with stores below. But twelve years ago several buildings, from the corner to the middle of the block, were converted into one building with elevator apartments of small size and high rents.

The incident that attracted my attention was a suppressed struggle going on between a man and a little girl of eight or nine years old. The man seemed to be trying to get the girl to go with him. By turns he was directing a cajoling attention to her, and then assuming an air of nonchalance. The girl was making herself rigid, as children do when they resist, against the wall of one of the tenements across the street.

As I watched from our second-floor window, making up my mind how to intervene if it seemed advisable, I saw it was not going to be necessary. From the butcher shop beneath the tenement had emerged the woman who, with her husband, runs the shop; she was standing within earshot of the man, her arms folded and a look of determination on her face. Joe Cornacchia, who with his sons-in-law keeps the delicatessen, emerged about the same moment and stood solidly to the other side. Several heads poked out of the tenement windows above, one was withdrawn quickly and its owner reappeared a moment later in the doorway behind the man. Two men from the bar next to the butcher shop came to the doorway and waited. On my side of the street, I saw that the locksmith, the fruit man and the laundry proprietor had all come out of their shops and that the scene was also being surveyed from a number of windows besides ours. That man did not know it, but he was surrounded. Nobody was going to allow a little girl to be dragged off, even if nobody knew who she was.

I am sorry—sorry purely for dramatic purposes—to have to report that the little girl turned out to be the man's daughter.

Throughout the duration of the little drama, perhaps five minutes in all, no eyes appeared in the windows of the high-rent, small-apartment building. It was the only building of which this was true. When we first moved to our block, I used to anticipate happily that perhaps soon all the buildings would be rehabilitated like that one. I know better now, and can only anticipate with gloom and foreboding the recent news that exactly this transformation is scheduled for the rest of the block frontage adjoining the high-rent building. The high-rent tenants, most of whom are so transient we cannot even keep track of their faces,[1] have not the remotest idea of who takes care of their street, or how. A city neighborhood can absorb and protect a substantial number of these birds of passage, as our neighborhood does. But if and when the neighborhood finally *becomes* them, they will gradually find the streets less secure, they will be vaguely mystified about it, and if things get bad enough they will drift away to another neighborhood which is mysteriously safer.

In some rich city neighborhoods, where there is little do-it-yourself surveillance, such as residential Park Avenue or upper Fifth Avenue in New York, street watchers are hired. The monotonous sidewalks of residential Park Avenue, for example, are surprisingly little used; their putative users are populating, instead, the interesting store-, bar- and restaurant-filled sidewalks of Lexington Avenue and Madison Avenue to east and west, and the cross streets leading to these. A network of doormen and superintendents, of delivery boys and nursemaids, a form of hired neighborhood, keeps residential Park Avenue supplied with eyes. At night, with the security of the doormen as a bulwark, dog walkers safely venture forth and

supplement the doormen. But this street is so blank of built-in eyes, so devoid of concrete reasons for using or watching it instead of turning the first corner off of it, that if its rents were to slip below the point where they could support a plentiful hired neighborhood of doormen and elevator men, it would undoubtedly become a woefully dangerous street.

Once a street is well equipped to handle strangers, once it has both a good, effective demarcation between private and public spaces and has a basic supply of activity and eyes, the more strangers the merrier.

In speaking about city sidewalk safety, I mentioned how necessary it is that there should be, in the brains behind the eyes on the street, an almost unconscious assumption of general street support when the chips are down—when a citizen has to choose, for instance, whether he will take responsibility, or abdicate it, in combating barbarism or protecting strangers. There is a short word for this assumption of support: trust. The trust of a city street is formed over time from many, many little public sidewalk contacts. It grows out of people stopping by at the bar for a beer, getting advice from the grocer and giving advice to the newsstand man, comparing opinions with other customers at the bakery and nodding hello to the two boys drinking pop on the stoop, eying the girls while waiting to be called for dinner, admonishing the children, hearing about a job from the hardware man and borrowing a dollar from the druggist, admiring the new babies and sympathizing over the way a coat faded. Customs vary: in some neighborhoods people compare notes on their dogs; in others they compare notes on their landlords.

Most of it is ostensibly utterly trivial but the sum is not trivial at all. The sum of such casual, public contact at a local level—most of it fortuitous, most of it associated with errands, all of it metered by the person concerned and not thrust upon him by anyone— is a feeling for the public identity of people, a web of public respect and trust, and a resource in time of personal or neighborhood need. The absence of this trust is a disaster to a city street. Its cultivation cannot be institutionalized. And above all, *it implies no private commitments.*

I have seen a striking difference between presence and absence of casual public trust on two sides of the same wide street in East Harlem, composed of residents of roughly the same incomes and same races. On the old-city side, which was full of public places and the sidewalk loitering so deplored by Utopian minders of other people's leisure, the children were being kept well in hand. On the project side of the street across the way, the children, who had a fire hydrant open beside their play area, were behaving destructively, drenching the open windows of houses with water, squirting it on adults who ignorantly walked on the project side of the street, throwing it into the windows of cars as they went by. Nobody dared to stop them. These were anonymous children, and the identities behind them were an unknown. What if you scolded or stopped them? Who would back you up over there in the blind-eyed Turf? Would you get, instead, revenge? Better to keep out of it. Impersonal city streets make anonymous people, and this is not a matter of esthetic quality nor of a mystical emotional effect in architectural scale. It is a matter of what kinds of tangible enterprises sidewalks have, and therefore of how people use the sidewalks in practical, every-day life.

The casual public sidewalk life of cities ties directly into other types of public life, of which I shall mention one as illustrative, although there is no end to their variety.

Formal types of local city organizations are frequently assumed by planners and even by some social workers to grow in direct, common-sense fashion out of announcements of meetings, the presence of meeting rooms, and the existence of problems of obvious public concern. Perhaps they grow

so in suburbs and towns. They do not grow so in cities.

Formal public organizations in cities require an informal public life underlying them, mediating between them and the privacy of the people of the city. We catch a hint of what happens by contrasting, again, a city area possessing a public sidewalk life with a city area lacking it, as told about in the report of a settlement-house social researcher who was studying problems relating to public schools in a section of New York City.

Mr. W—— [principal of an elementary school] was questioned on the effect of J—— Houses on the school, and the uprooting of the community around the school. He felt that there had been many effects and of these most were negative. He mentioned that the project had torn out numerous institutions for socializing. The present atmosphere of the project was in no way similar to the gaiety of the streets before the project was built. He noted that in general there seemed fewer people on the streets because there were fewer places for people to gather. He also contended that before the projects were built the Parents Association had been very strong, and now there were only very few active members.

Mr. W—— was wrong in one respect. There were not fewer places (or at any rate there was not less space) for people to gather in the project, if we count places deliberately planned for constructive socializing. Of course there were no bars, no candy stores, no hole-in-the-wall *bodegas*, no restaurants in the project. But the project under discussion was equipped with a model complement of meeting rooms, craft, art and game rooms, outdoor benches, malls, etc., enough to gladden the heart of even the Garden City advocates.

Why are such places dead and useless without the most determined efforts and expense to inveigle users—and then to maintain control over the users? What services do the public sidewalk and its enterprises fulfill that these planned gathering places do not? And why? How does an informal public sidewalk life bolster a more formal, organizational public life?

To understand such problems—to understand why drinking pop on the stoop differs from drinking pop in the game room, and why getting advice from the grocer or the bartender differs from getting advice from either your next-door neighbor or from an institutional lady who may be hand-in-glove with an institutional landlord—we must look into the matter of city privacy.

Privacy is precious in cities. It is indispensable. Perhaps it is precious and indispensable everywhere, but most places you cannot get it. In small settlements everyone knows your affairs. In the city everyone does not—only those you choose to tell will know much about you. This is one of the attributes of cities that is precious to most city people, whether their incomes are high or their incomes are low, whether they are white or colored, whether they are old inhabitants or new, and it is a gift of great-city life deeply cherished and jealously guarded.

Architectural and planning literature deals with privacy in terms of windows, overlooks, sight lines. The idea is that if no one from outside can peek into where you live—behold, privacy. This is simple-minded. Window privacy is the easiest commodity in the world to get. You just pull down the shades or adjust the blinds. The privacy of keeping one's personal affairs to those selected to know them, and the privacy of having reasonable control over who shall make inroads on your time and when, are rare commodities in most of this world, however, and they have nothing to do with the orientation of windows.

Anthropologist Elena Padilla, author of *Up from Puerto Rico*, describing Puerto Rican life in a poor and squalid district of New York, tells how much people know about each other—who is to be trusted and who not, who is defiant of the law and

who upholds it, who is competent and well informed and who is inept and ignorant—and how these things are known from the public life of the sidewalk and its associated enterprises. These are matters of public character. But she also tells how select are those permitted to drop into the kitchen for a cup of coffee, how strong are the ties, and how limited the number of a person's genuine confidants, those who share in a person's private life and private affairs. She tells how it is not considered dignified for everyone to know one's affairs. Nor is it considered dignified to snoop on others beyond the face presented in public. It does violence to a person's privacy and rights. In this, the people she describes are essentially the same as the people of the mixed, Americanized city street on which I live, and essentially the same as the people who live in high-income apartments or fine town houses, too.

A good city street neighborhood achieves a marvel of balance between its people's determination to have essential privacy and their simultaneous wishes for differing degrees of contact, enjoyment or help from the people around. This balance is largely made up of small, sensitively managed details, practiced and accepted so casually that they are normally taken for granted.

Perhaps I can best explain this subtle but all-important balance in terms of the stores where people leave keys for their friends, a common custom in New York. In our family, for example, when a friend wants to use our place while we are away for a week end or everyone happens to be out during the day, or a visitor for whom we do not wish to wait up is spending the night, we tell such a friend that he can pick up the key at the delicatessen across the street. Joe Cornacchia, who keeps the delicatessen, usually has a dozen or so keys at a time for handing out like this. He has a special drawer for them.

Now why do I, and many others, select Joe as a logical custodian for keys? Because we trust him, first, to be a responsible custodian, but equally important because we know that he combines a feeling of good will with a feeling of no personal responsibility about our private affairs. Joe considers it no concern of his whom we choose to permit in our places and why.

The social structure of sidewalk life hangs partly on what can be called self-appointed public characters. A public character is anyone who is in frequent contact with a wide circle of people and who is sufficiently interested to make himself a public character. A public character need have no special talents or wisdom to fulfill his function—although he often does. He just needs to be present, and there need to be enough of his counterparts. His main qualification is that he *is* public, that he talks to lots of different people. In this way, news travels that is of sidewalk interest.

Most public sidewalk characters are steadily stationed in public places. They are storekeepers or barkeepers or the like. These are the basic public characters. All other public characters of city sidewalks depend on them—if only indirectly because of the presence of sidewalk routes to such enterprises and their proprietors.

Settlement-house workers and pastors, two more formalized kinds of public characters, typically depend on the street grapevine news systems that have their ganglia in the stores. The director of a settlement on New York's Lower East Side, as an example, makes a regular round of stores. He learns from the cleaner who does his suits about the presence of dope pushers in the neighborhood. He learns from the grocer that the Dragons are working up to something and need attention. He learns from the candy store that two girls are agitating the Sportsmen toward a rumble. One of his most important information spots is an unused breadbox on Rivington Street. That is, it is not used for bread. It stands outside a grocery and is used for sitting on and lounging beside, between the settlement house, a

candy store and a pool parlor. A message spoken there for any teen-ager within many blocks will reach his ears unerringly and surprisingly quickly, and the opposite flow along the grapevine similarly brings news quickly in to the breadbox.

Blake Hobbs, the head of the Union Settlement music school in East Harlem, notes that when he gets a first student from one block of the old busy street neighborhoods, he rapidly gets at least three or four more and sometimes almost every child on the block. But when he gets a child from the nearby projects—perhaps through the public school or a playground conversation he has initiated—he almost never gets another as a direct sequence. Word does not move around where public characters and sidewalk life are lacking.

Besides the anchored public characters of the sidewalk, and the well-recognized roving public characters, there are apt to be various more specialized public characters on a city sidewalk. In a curious way, some of these help establish an identity not only for themselves but for others. Describing the everyday life of a retired tenor at such sidewalk establishments as the restaurant and the *bocce* court, a San Francisco news story notes, "It is said of Meloni that because of his intensity, his dramatic manner and his lifelong interest in music, he transmits a feeling of vicarious importance to his many friends." Precisely.

One need not have either the artistry or the personality of such a man to become a specialized sidewalk character—but only a pertinent specialty of some sort. It is easy. I am a specialized public character of sorts along our street, owing of course to the fundamental presence of the basic, anchored public characters. The way I became one started with the fact that Greenwich Village, where I live, was waging an interminable and horrendous battle to save its main park from being bisected by a highway. During the course of battle I undertook, at the behest of a committee organizer away over on the other side of Greenwich Village, to deposit in stores on a few blocks of our street supplies of petition cards protesting the proposed roadway. Customers would sign the cards while in the stores, and from time to time I would make my pickups.[2] As a result of engaging in this messenger work, I have since become automatically the sidewalk public character on petition strategy. Before long, for instance, Mr. Fox at the liquor store was consulting me, as he wrapped up my bottle, on how we could get the city to remove a long-abandoned and dangerous eyesore, a closed-up comfort station near his corner. If I would undertake to compose the petitions and find the effective way of presenting them to City Hall, he proposed, he and his partners would undertake to have them printed, circulated and picked up. Soon the stores round about had comfort station removal petitions. Our street by now has many public experts on petition tactics, including the children.

Not only do public characters spread the news and learn the news at retail, so to speak. They connect with each other and thus spread word wholesale, in effect.

A sidewalk life, so far as I can observe, arises out of no mysterious qualities or talents for it in this or that type of population. It arises only when the concrete, tangible facilities it requires are present. These happen to be the same facilities, in the same abundance and ubiquity, that are required for cultivating sidewalk safety. If they are absent, public sidewalk contacts are absent too.

The well-off have many ways of assuaging needs for which poorer people may depend much on sidewalk life—from hearing of jobs to being recognized by the headwaiter. But nevertheless, many of the rich or near-rich in cities appear to appreciate sidewalk life as much as anybody. At any rate, they pay enormous rents to move into areas with an exuberant and varied sidewalk life. They actually crowd out the middle class and the poor in lively areas like Yorkville or

Greenwich Village in New York, or Telegraph Hill just off the North Beach streets of San Francisco. They capriciously desert, after only a few decades of fashion at most, the monotonous streets of "quiet residential areas" and leave them to the less fortunate. Talk to residents of Georgetown in the District of Columbia and by the second or third sentence at least you will begin to hear rhapsodies about the charming restaurants, "more good restaurants than in all the rest of the city put together," the uniqueness and friendliness of the stores, the pleasures of running into people when doing errands at the next corner—and nothing but pride over the fact that Georgetown has become a specialty shopping district for its whole metropolitan area. The city area, rich or poor or in between, harmed by an interesting sidewalk life and plentiful sidewalk contacts has yet to be found.

Efficiency of public sidewalk characters declines drastically if too much burden is put upon them. A store, for example, can reach a turnover in its contacts, or potential contacts, which is so large and so superficial that it is socially useless. An example of this can be seen at the candy and newspaper store owned by the housing cooperative of Corlears Hook on New York's Lower East Side. This planned project store replaces perhaps forty superficially similar stores which were wiped out (without compensation to their proprietors) on that project site and the adjoining sites. The place is a mill. Its clerks are so busy making change and screaming ineffectual imprecations at rowdies that they never hear anything except "I want that." This, or utter disinterest, is the usual atmosphere where shopping center planning or repressive zoning artificially contrives commercial monopolies for city neighborhoods. A store like this would fail economically if it had competition. Meantime, although monopoly insures the financial success planned for it, it fails the city socially.

Sidewalk public contact and sidewalk public

safety, taken together, bear directly on our contry's most serious social problem—segregation and racial discrimination.

I do not mean to imply that a city's planning and design, or its types of streets and street life, can automatically overcome segregation and discrimination. Too many other kinds of effort are also required to right these injustices.

But I do mean to say that to build and to rebuild big cities whose sidewalks are unsafe and whose people must settle for sharing much or nothing, *can* make it *much harder* for American cities to overcome discrimination no matter how much effort is expended.

Considering the amount of prejudice and fear that accompany discrimination and bolster it, overcoming residential discrimination is just that much harder if people feel unsafe on their sidewalks anyway. Overcoming residential discrimination comes hard where people have no means of keeping a civilized public life on a basically dignified public footing, and their private lives on a private footing.

To be sure, token model housing integration schemes here and there can be achieved in city areas handicapped by danger and by lack of public life—achieved by applying great effort and settling for abnormal (abnormal for cities) choosiness among new neighbors. This is an evasion of the size of the task and its urgency.

The tolerance, the room for great differences among neighbors—differences that often go far deeper than differences in color—which are possible and normal in intensely urban life, but which are so foreign to suburbs and pseudosuburbs, are possible and normal only when streets of great cities have built-in equipment allowing strangers to dwell in peace together on civilized but essentially dignified and reserved terms.

There is no point in planning for play on sidewalks unless the sidewalks are used for a wide variety of other purposes and by a wide variety of other people too. These uses need each other, for proper surveillance, for a public life of some vitality, and for general interest. If sidewalks on a lively street are sufficiently wide, play flourishes mightily right along with other uses. If the sidewalks are skimped, rope jumping is the first play casualty. Roller skating, tricycle and bicycle riding are the next casualties. The narrower the sidewalks, the more sedentary incidental play becomes. The more frequent too become sporadic forays by children into the vehicular roadways.

Sidewalks thirty or thirty-five feet wide can accommodate virtually any demand of incidental play put upon them—along with trees to shade the activities, and sufficient space for pedestrian circulation and adult public sidewalk life and loitering. Few sidewalks of this luxurious width can be found. Sidewalk width is invariably sacrificed for vehicular width, partly because city sidewalks are conventionally considered to be purely space for pedestrian travel and access to buildings, and go unrecognized and unrespected as the uniquely vital and irreplaceable organs of city safety, public life and child rearing that they are.

Twenty-foot sidewalks, which usually preclude rope jumping but can feasibly permit roller skating and the use of other wheeled toys, can still be found, although the street wideners erode them year by year (often in the belief that shunned malls and "promenades" are a constructive substitute). The livelier and more popular a sidewalk, and the greater the number and variety of its users, the greater the total width needed for it to serve its purposes pleasantly.

But even when proper space is lacking, convenience of location and the interest of the streets are both so important to children—and good surveillance so important to their parents—that children will and do adapt to skimpy sidewalk space. This does not mean we do right in taking unscrupulous advantage of their adaptability. In fact, we wrong both them and cities.

Some city sidewalks are undoubtedly evil places for rearing children. They are evil for anybody. In such neighborhoods we need to foster the qualities and facilities that make for safety, vitality and stability in city streets. This is a complex problem; it is a central problem of planning for cities. In defective city neighborhoods, shooing the children into parks and playgrounds is worse than useless, either as a solution to the streets' problems or as a solution for the children.

The whole idea of doing away with city streets, insofar as that is possible, and downgrading and minimizing their social and their economic part in city life is the most mischievous and destructive idea in orthodox city planning. That it is so often done in the name of vaporous fantasies about city child care is as bitter as irony can get.

To generate exuberant diversity in a city's streets and districts, four conditions are indispensable:

1. The district, and indeed as many of its internal parts as possible, must serve more than one primary function; preferably more than two. These must insure the presence of people who go outdoors on different schedules and are in the place for different purposes, but who are able to use many facilities in common.
2. Most blocks must be short; that is, streets and opportunities to turn corners must be frequent.
3. The district must mingle buildings that vary in age and condition, including a good proportion of old ones so that they vary in the economic yield they must produce. This mingling must be fairly close-grained.
4. There must be a sufficiently dense concentration of people, for whatever purposes they may be there. This includes dense concentration in the case of people who are there because of residence.

The necessity for these four conditions is the most important point this book has to make. In combination, these conditions create effective economic pools of use. Given these four conditions, not all city districts will produce a diversity equivalent to one another. The potentials of different districts differ for many reasons; but, given the development of these four conditions (or the best approximation to their full development that can be managed in real life), a city district should be able to realize its best potential, wherever that may lie. Obstacles to doing so will have been removed. The range may not stretch to African sculpture or schools of drama or Rumanian tea houses, but such as the possibilities are, whether for grocery stores, pottery schools, movies, candy stores, florists, art shows, immigrants' clubs, hardware stores, eating places, or whatever, they will get their best chance. And along with them, city life will get its best chances.

NOTES

1. Some, according to the storekeepers, live on beans and bread and spend their sojourn looking for a place to live where all their money will not go for rent.
2. This, by the way, is an efficient device, accomplishing with a fraction of the effort what would be a mountainous task door to door. It also makes more public conversation and opinion than door-to-door visits.

The Social Life of Small Urban Spaces

William H. Whyte

We started by studying how people use plazas. We mounted time-lapse cameras overlooking the plazas and recorded daily patterns. We talked to people to find where they came from, where they worked, how frequently they used the place and what they thought of it. But, mostly, we watched people to see what they did.

Most of the people who use plazas, we found, are young office workers from nearby buildings. There may be relatively few patrons from the plaza's own building; as some secretaries confide, they'd just as soon put a little distance between themselves and the boss. But commuter distances are usually short; for most plazas, the effective market radius is about three blocks. Small parks, like Paley and Greenacre in New York, tend to have more assorted patrons throughout the day—upper-income older people, people coming from a distance. But office workers still predominate, the bulk from nearby.

This uncomplicated demography underscores an elemental point about good urban spaces: supply creates demand. A good new space builds a new constituency. It stimulates people into new habits—alfresco lunches—and provides new paths to and from work, new places to pause. It does all this very quickly. In Chicago's Loop, there were no such amenities not so long ago. Now, the plaza of the First National Bank has thoroughly changed the midday way of life for thousands of people. A success like this in no way surfeits demand for spaces; it indicates how great the unrealized potential is.

The best-used plazas are sociable places, with a higher proportion of couples than you find in less-used places, more people in groups, more people meeting people, or exchanging goodbyes. At five of the most-used plazas in New York, the proportion of people in groups runs about 45 percent; in five of the least used, 32 percent. A high proportion of people in groups is an index of selectivity. When people go to a place in twos or threes or rendezvous there, it is most often because they have decided to. Nor are these sociable places less congenial to the individual. In absolute numbers, they attract more individuals than do less-used spaces. If you are alone, a lively place can be the best place to be.

The most-used places also tend to have a higher than average proportion of women. The male-female ratio of a plaza basically reflects the composition of the work force, which varies from area to area—in midtown New York it runs about 60 percent male, 40 percent female. Women are more discriminating than men as to where they will sit, more sensitive to annoyances, and women spend more time casting the various possibilities. If a plaza has a markedly lower than average proportion of women, something is wrong. Where there is a higher than average proportion of women, the plaza is probably a good one and has been chosen as such.

The rhythms of plaza life are much alike from place to place. In the morning hours, patronage will be sporadic. A hot-dog vendor setting up his cart at the corner, elderly pedestrians pausing for a rest, a delivery messenger or two, a shoeshine man, some tourists, perhaps an odd type, like a scavenger woman with shopping bags. If there is any construction work in the vicinity, hard hats will appear shortly after 11:00 A.M. with beer cans and sandwiches. Things will start to liven up. Around noon, the main clientele begins to arrive. Soon, activity will be near peak and will stay there until a little before 2:00 P.M. Some 80 percent of the total hours of use will be concentrated in these two hours. In mid and late afternoon, use is again sporadic. If there's a special event, such as a jazz concert, the flow going home will be tapped, with people staying as late as 6:00 or 6:30 P.M. Ordinarily, however, plazas go dead by 6:00 and stay that way until the next morning.

During peak hours the number of people on a plaza will vary considerably according to seasons and weather. The way people distribute themselves over the space, however, will be fairly consistent, with some sectors getting heavy use day in and day out, others much less. In our sightings we find it easy to map every person, but the patterns are regular enough that you could count the number in only one sector, then multiply by a given factor, and come within a percent or so of the total number of people at the plaza.

Off-peak use often gives the best clues to people's preferences. When a place is jammed, a person sits where he can. This may or may not be where he most wants to. After the main crowd has left, the choices can be significant. Some parts of the plaza become quite empty; others continue to be used. At Seagram's, a rear ledge under the trees is moderately, but steadily, occupied when other ledges are empty; it seems the most uncrowded of places, but on a cumulative basis it is the best-used part of Seagram's.

Men show a tendency to take the front-row seats, and, if there is a kind of gate, men will be the guardians of it. Women tend to favor places slightly secluded. If there are double-sided benches parallel to a street, the inner side will usually have a high proportion of women; the outer, of men.

Of the men up front, the most conspicuous are girl watchers. They work at it, and so demonstratively as to suggest that their chief interest may not really be the girls so much as the show of watching them. Generally, the watchers line up quite close together, in groups of three to five. If they are construction workers, they will be very demonstrative, much given to whistling, laughing, direct salutations. This is also true of most girl watchers in New York's financial area. In midtown, they are more inhibited, playing it coolly, with a good bit of sniggering and smirking, as if the girls were not measuring up. It is all machismo, however, whether up-town or downtown. Not once have we ever seen a girl watcher pick up a girl, or attempt to.

Few others will either. Plazas are not ideal places for striking up acquaintances, and even on the most sociable of them, there is not much mingling. When strangers are in proximity, the nearest thing to an exchange is what Erving Goffman has called civil inattention. If there are, say, two smashing blondes on a ledge, the men nearby will usually put on an elaborate show of disregard. Watch closely, however, and you will see them give themselves away with covert glances, involuntary primping of the hair, tugs at the ear-lobe.

Lovers are to be found on plazas. But not where you would expect them. When we first started interviewing, people told us we'd find lovers in the rear places (pot smokers, too). But they weren't usually there. They would be out front. The most fervent embracing we've recorded on film has usually taken place in the most visible of locations, with the couple oblivious of the crowd.

Certain locations become rendezvous points for coteries of various kinds. For a while, the south wall of Chase plaza was a gathering point for camera bugs, the kind who like to buy new lenses and talk about them. Patterns of this sort may last no more than a season—or persist for years. Some time ago, one particular spot became a gathering place for raffish younger people; since then, there have been many changeovers in personnel, but it is still a gathering place for raffish younger people.

SELF-CONGESTION

What attracts people most, it would appear, is other people. If I belabor the point, it is because many urban spaces are being designed as though the opposite were true, and that what people liked best were the places they stay away from. People often do talk along such lines; this is why their responses to questionnaires can be so misleading. How many people would say they like to sit in the middle of a crowd? Instead, they speak of getting away from it all, and use terms like "escape," "oasis," "retreat." What people *do*, however, reveals a different priority.

This was first brought home to us in a study of street conversations. When people stop to have a conversation, we wondered, how far away do they move from the main pedestrian flow? We were especially interested in finding out how much of the normally unused buffer space next to buildings would be used. So we set up time-lapse cameras overlooking several key street corners and began plotting the location of all conversations lasting a minute or longer.

People didn't move out of the main pedestrian flow. They stayed in it or moved into it, and the great bulk of the conversations were smack in the center of the flow—the 100 percent location, to use the real-estate term. The same gravitation characterized "traveling conversations"—the kind in which two men move about, alternating the roles of straight man and principal talker. There is a lot of apparent motion. But if you plot the orbits, you will find they are usually centered around the 100 percent spot.

Just why people behave like this, we have never been able to determine. It is understandable that conversations should originate within the main flow. Conversations are incident to pedestrian journeys; where there are the most people, the likelihood of a meeting or a leave-taking is highest. What is less explainable is people's inclination to remain in the main flow, blocking traffic, being jostled by it. This does not seem to be a matter of inertia but of choice—instinctive, perhaps, but by no means illogical. In the center of the crowd you have the maximum choice—to break off, to continue—much as you have in the center of a cocktail party, itself a moving conversation growing ever denser and denser.

People also sit in the mainstream. At the Seagram plaza, the main pedestrian paths are on diagonals from the building entrance to the corners of the steps. These are natural junction and transfer points and there is usually a lot of activity at them. They are also a favored place for sitting and picnicking. Sometimes there will be so many people that pedestrians have to step carefully to negotiate the steps. The pedestrians rarely complain. While some will detour around the blockage, most will thread their way through it.

Standing patterns are similar. When people stop to talk on a plaza, they usually do so in the middle of the traffic stream. They also show an inclination to station themselves near objects, such as a flagpole or a statue. They like well-defined places, such as steps, or the border of a pool. What they rarely choose is the middle of a large space.

There are a number of explanations. The preference for pillars might be ascribed to some primeval instinct: you have a full view of all comers but your rear is covered. But this doesn't explain the inclination men have for lining up at the curb. Typically, they face inwards, toward the sidewalk, with their backs exposed to the dangers of the street.

Foot movements are consistent, too. They seem to be a sort of silent language. Often, in a shmoozing group no one will be saying anything. Men stand bound in amiable silence, surveying the passing scene. Then, slowly, rhythmically, one of the men rocks up and down: first on the ball of the foot, then back on the heel. He stops. Another man starts the same movement. Sometimes there are reciprocal gestures. One man makes a half turn to the right. Then, after a rhythmic interval, another responds with a half turn to the left. Some kind of communication seems to be taking place here, but I've never broken the code.

Whatever they may mean, people's movements are one of the great spectacles of a plaza. You do not see this in architectural photographs, which typically are empty of life and are taken from a perspective few people share. It is a quite misleading one. At eye level the scene comes alive with movement and color—people walking quickly, walking slowly, skipping up steps, weaving in and out on crossing patterns, accelerating and retarding to match the moves of the others. There is a beauty that is beguiling to watch, and one senses that the players are quite aware of it themselves. You see this, too, in the way they arrange themselves on steps and ledges. They often do so with a grace that they, too, must sense. With its brown-gray monochrome, Seagram's is the best of settings—especially in the rain, when an umbrella or two spots color in the right places, like Corot's red dots.

How peculiar are such patterns to New York? Our working assumption was that behavior in other cities would probably differ little, and subsequent comparisons have proved our assumption correct. The important variable is city size. As I will discuss in more detail, in smaller cities, densities tend to be lower, pedestrians move at a slower pace, and there is less of the social activity characteristic of high-traffic areas. In most other respects, pedestrian patterns are similar.

Observers in other countries have also noted the tendency to self-congestion. In his study of pedestrians in Copenhagen, architect Jan Gehl mapped bunching patterns almost identical to those observable here. Matthew Ciolek studied an Australian shopping center, with similar results. "Contrary to 'common sense' expectations," Ciolek notes, "the great majority of people were found to select their sites for social interaction right on or very close to the traffic lines intersecting the plaza. Relatively few people formed their gatherings away from the spaces used for navigation."

The strongest similarities are found among the world's largest cities. People in them tend to behave more like their counterparts in other world cities than like fellow nationals in smaller cities. Big-city people walk faster, for one thing, and they self-congest. After we had completed our New York study, we made a brief comparison study of Tokyo and found the proclivity to stop and talk in the middle of department-store doorways, busy corners, and the like, is just as strong in that city as in New York. For all the cultural differences, sitting patterns in parks and plazas are much the same, too. Similarly, shmoozing patterns in Milan's Galleria are remarkably like those in New York's garment center. Modest conclusion: given the basic elements of a center city—such as high pedestrian volumes, and concentration and mixture of activities—people in one place tend to act much like people in another.

THE STREET

Now we come to the key space for a plaza. It is not on the plaza. It is the street. The other amenities we have been discussing are indeed important: sitting space, sun, trees, water, food. But they can be added. The relationship to the street is integral, and it is far and away the critical design factor.

A good plaza starts at the street corner. If it's a busy corner, it has a brisk social life of its own. People will not just be waiting there for the light to change. Some will be fixed in conversation; others, in some phase of a prolonged goodbye. If there's a vendor at the corner, people will cluster around him, and there will be considerable two-way traffic back and forth between plaza and corner.

The activity on the corner is a great show and one of the best ways to make the most of it is, simply, not to wall it off. A front-row position is prime space; if it is sittable, it draws the most people. Too often, however, it is not sittable and sometimes by an excruciatingly small margin. Railings atop ledges will do it. At the General Motors Building on Fifth Avenue in New York City, for example, the front ledge faces one of the best of urban scenes. The ledge would be eminently sittable if only there weren't a railing atop it, placed exactly five and three-quarter inches in. Another two inches and you could sit comfortably. Canted ledges offer similar difficulties, especially in conjunction with prickly shrubbery.

Another key feature of the street is retailing—stores, windows with displays, signs to attract your attention, doorways, people going in and out of them. Big new office buildings have been eliminating stores. What they have been replacing them with is a frontage of plate glass through which you can behold bank officers sitting at desks. One of these stretches is dull enough. Block after block of them creates overpowering dullness. The Avenue of the Americas in New York has so many storeless plazas that the few remaining stretches of vulgar streetscape are now downright appealing.

As a condition of an open-space bonus, developers should be required to devote at least 50 percent of the ground-floor frontage to retail and food uses, and the new New York City zoning so stipulates. Market pressures, fortunately, are now working to the same end. At the time of our study, banks were outbidding stores for ground-level space. Since then, the banks have been cutting back, and economics have been tipping things to stores. But it does not hurt to have a requirement.

The area where the street and plaza or open space meet is a key to success or failure. Ideally, the transition should be such that it's hard to tell where one ends and the other begins. New York's Paley Park is the best of examples. The sidewalk in front is an integral part of the park. An arborlike foliage of trees extends over the sidewalk. There are urns of flowers at the curb and, on either side of the steps, curved sitting ledges. In this foyer, you can usually find somebody waiting for someone else—it is a convenient rendezvous point—people sitting on the ledges, and, in the middle of the entrance, several people in conversations.

Passersby are users of Paley, too. About half will turn and look in. Of these, about half will smile. I haven't calculated a smile index, but this vicarious, secondary enjoyment is extremely important—the sight of the park, the knowledge that it is there, becomes part of the image we have of a much wider area. (If one had to make a cost-benefit study, I think it would show that secondary use provides as much, if not more, benefit than the primary use. If one could put a monetary value on a minute of visual enjoyment and multiply that by instances day after day, year after year, one would obtain a rather stupendous sum.)

The park stimulates impulse use. Many people will do a double take as they pass by, pause, move a few steps, then, with a slight acceleration, go on up the steps. Children do it more vigorously, the very young ones usually pointing at the park and tugging at their mothers to go on in, many of the older ones breaking into a run just as they approach the steps, then skipping a step or two.

Watch these flows and you will appreciate how very important steps can be. The steps at Paley are so low and easy that one is almost pulled to them. They add a nice ambiguity to your movement. You can stand and watch, move up a foot, another, and, then, without having made a conscious decision, find yourself in the park.

THE "UNDESIRABLES"

If good places are so felicitous, why are there not more of them? The biggest single reason is the problem of "undesirables." They are not themselves much of a problem. It is the measures taken to combat them that is the problem. Many businessmen have an almost obsessive fear that if a place is attractive to people it might be attractive to undesirable people. So it is made unattractive. There is to be no loitering—what a Calvinist sermon is in those words!—no eating, no sitting. So it is that benches are made too short to sleep on, that spikes are put in ledges; most important, many needed spaces are not provided at all, or the plans for them scuttled.

Who are the undesirables? For most businessmen, curiously, it is not muggers, dope dealers, or truly dangerous people. It is the winos, derelicts who drink out of half-pint bottles in paper bags—the most harmless of the city's marginal people, but a symbol, perhaps, of what one might become but for the grace of events. For retailers, the list of undesirables is considerably more inclusive; there are the bag women, people who act strangely in public, "hippies," teenagers, older people, street musicians, vendors of all kinds.

The preoccupation with undesirables is a symptom of another problem. Many corporation executives who make key decisions about the city have surprisingly little acquaintance with the life of its streets and open spaces. From the train station, they may walk only a few blocks before entering their building; because of the extensive services within the building, some don't venture out until it's time to go home again. To them, the unknown city is a place of danger. If their building has a plaza, it is likely to be a defensive one that they will rarely use themselves.

Few others will either. Places designed with distrust get what they were looking for and it is in them, ironically, that you will most likely find a wino. You will find winos elsewhere, but it is the empty places they prefer; it is in the empty places that they are conspicuous—almost as if, unconsciously, the design was contrived to make them so.

Fear proves itself. Highly elaborate defensive measures are an indicator that a corporation might clear out of the city entirely. Long before Union Carbide announced it was leaving New York for suburbia, its building said it would. Save for an exhibit area, the building was sealed off from the city with policelike guards and checkpoints, and in all the empty space around it there was not a place to sit. (There is no surcease in suburbia, it should be noted. Most of the firms that have moved still seem every bit as obsessed with security. New headquarters are often designed like redoubts, with gatehouses, moats, and, in one case, a hillside motor entrance with a modern version of a portcullis.)

The best way to handle the problem of undesirables is to make a place attractive to everyone else. The record is over-whelmingly positive on this score. With few exceptions, plazas and smaller parks in most central business districts are probably as safe a place as you can find during the times that people use them.

The way people use a place mirrors expectations. Seagram's management is pleased people like its plaza and is quite relaxed about what they do. It lets them stick their feet in the pool; does not look to see if kids are smoking pot on the pool ledge; tolerates oddballs, even allowing them to sleep the night on the ledge. The sun rises the next morning. The place is largely self-policing, and there is rarely trouble of any kind.

Paley Park is courtly to people. With its movable chairs and tables, it should be quite vulnerable to vandalism. Here is the record of security infractions at the park since it opened in 1967:

1968 One of the flower urns on the sidewalk was stolen by two men in a van.
1970 The "Refreshments" sign was taken from the wall.
1971 A small table was taken.
1972 A man attempted to carve his initials in one of the trees.
1974 One of the brass lights at the entrance was removed.

In the nine years I have been studying plazas and small parks in New York City, there has been a serious problem in only one, and in the places that are well used, none at all. The exception is a plaza on which pot dealers began operating. The management took away about half the benches. Next, it constructed steel-bar fences on the two open sides of the plaza. These moves effectively cut down the number of ordinary people who used the place, to the delight of the pot dealers, who now had it much more to themselves and their customers.

At many plazas you will see TV surveillance cameras. What they see is a question. For monitoring remote passageways and doors, the cameras can be useful. For outdoor areas, they don't make very much sense. Occasionally, you will see one move from side to side, and it's rather spooky if it's you that the lens seems to be tracking. But it's probably all in play. Down in the control room, some guard is likely twiddling the dials more out of boredom than curiosity.

Electronics can't beat a human being, and it is characteristic of well-used places to have

a "mayor." He may be a building guard, a newsstand operator, or a food vendor. Watch him, and you'll notice people checking in during the day—a cop, bus dispatcher, various street professionals, and office workers and shoppers who pause briefly for a salutation or a bit of banter. Plaza mayors are great communication centers, and very quick to spot any departure from normal. Like us. When we go to a place and start observing—unobtrusively, we like to think—the regulars find us sticking out like sore thumbs. For one thing, we're not moving. Someone will come over before long and find out just what it is we're up to.

One of the best mayors I've seen is Joe Hardy of the Exxon Building. He is an actor, as well as the building guard, and was originally hired by Rockefeller Center Inc. to play Santa Claus, whom he resembles. Ordinarily, guards are not supposed to initiate conversations, but Joe Hardy is gregarious and curious and has a nice sense of situations. There are, say, two older people looking somewhat confused. He will not wait for them to come up and ask for directions. He will go up to them and ask whether he can help. Or, if two girls are taking turns snapping pictures of each other, he may offer to take a picture of the two of them together.

Joe is quite tolerant of winos and odd people, as long as they don't bother anybody. He is very quick to spot real trouble, however. Teenage groups are an especial challenge. They like to test everybody—with the volume knob of their portable radios as a weapon. Joe's tactic is to go up to the toughest-looking person in the group and ask his help in keeping things cool.

Unlike Joe Hardy, guards at most places are an underused asset. Usually, they just stand, and for want of anything else to do tend to develop occupational tics. One might wave his arms rhythmically to and fro, or rock up and down on his heels. Another may bend his knees at odd intervals. If you watch, you'll get mesmerized trying to anticipate

THE SOCIAL LIFE OF SMALL URBAN SPACES | 39

when the next bend will come. The guard's job ought to be upgraded.

The more a guard has to do, the better he does it, and the better the place functions. At Paley Park it was originally expected that special security guards would be needed, in addition to several people to keep the place tidy and run the snack bar. The two men who worked at keeping the place tidy, however, did such an excellent job that no security guards were needed. Similarly, the guards take a proprietary pleasure in Greenacre Park. They are hosts, friendly to everyone, especially to the regulars, who serve as a kind of adjunct force. If someone flouts one of the unposted rules—like wheeling in a bicycle—it is likely as not the regulars who will set him straight.

PROPERTY RIGHTS

Let us turn to a related question. How public are the public spaces? On many plazas you will see a small bronze plaque that reads something like this: PRIVATE PROPERTY. CROSS AT THE RISK OF THE USER AND WITH REVOCABLE PERMISSION OF THE OWNER. It seems clear enough. It means that the plaza is the owner's, and he has the right to revoke any right you may have to use it. Whether or not a floor-area bonus was given, most building managements take it for granted that they can bar activity they believe undesirable. Their definition of this, furthermore, goes beyond dangerous or antisocial behavior. Some are quite persnickety. When we were measuring the front ledges by the sidewalk at the General Motors Building, the security

people rushed up in great consternation; we would have to desist unless we could secure permission from public relations.

This is not one to go to the Supreme Court on, perhaps, but there is principle involved, and inevitably it is going to be tested. The space was really provided by the public—through its zoning and planning machinery. It is true that the space falls within the property line of the developer, and it is equally true that he is liable for the proper maintenance of it. But the zoning legislation enabling the bonus unequivocally states as a condition that the plaza "must be accessible to the public at all times."

What does "accessible" mean? A commonsense interpretation would be that the public could use the space in the same manner as it did any public space, with the same freedoms and the same constraints. Many building managements have been operating with a much narrower concept of accessibility. They shoo away entertainers, people who distribute leaflets, or give speeches. Apartment building managements often shoo away everybody except residents. This is a flagrant violation of the zoning intent, but to date no one has gone to court.

The public's right in urban plazas would seem clear. Not only are plazas used as public spaces, in most cases the owner has been specifically, and richly, rewarded for providing them. He has not been given the right to allow only those public activities he happens to approve of. He may assume he has, and some owners have been operating on this basis with impunity. But that is because nobody has challenged them. A stiff, clarifying test is in order.

The Character of Third Places

Ray Oldenburg

Third places the world over share common and essential features. As one's investigations cross the boundaries of time and culture, the kinship of the Arabian coffeehouse, the German *bierstube*, the Italian *taberna*, the old country store of the American frontier, and the ghetto bar reveals itself. As one approaches each example, determined to describe it in its own right, an increasingly familiar pattern emerges. The eternal sameness of the third place overshadows the variations in its outward appearance and seems unaffected by the wide differences in cultural attitudes toward the typical gathering places of informal public life. The beer joint in which the middle-class American takes no pride can be as much a third place as the proud Viennese coffeehouse. It is a fortunate aspect of the third place that its capacity to serve the human need for communion does not much depend upon the capacity of a nation to comprehend its virtues.

The wonder is that so little attention has been paid to the benefits attaching to the third place. It is curious that its features and inner workings have remained virtually undescribed in this present age when they are so sorely needed and when any number of lesser substitutes are described in tiresome detail. Volumes are written on sensitivity and encounter groups, on meditation and exotic rituals for attaining states of relaxation and transcendence, on jogging and massaging. But the third place, the people's own remedy for stress, loneliness, and alienation, seems easy to ignore.

With few exceptions, however, it has always been thus. Rare is the chronicler who has done justice to those gathering places where community is most alive and people are most themselves. The tradition is the opposite; it is one of understatement and oversight. Joseph Addison, the great essayist, gave the faintest praise to the third places of his time and seems to have set an example for doing so. London's eighteenth-century coffeehouses provided the stage and forum for Addison's efforts and fired the greatest era of letters England would ever see. And there was far more to them than suggested by Addison's remarks: "When men are thus knit together, by a Love of Society, not a Spirit of Faction, and don't meet to censure or annoy those that are absent, but to enjoy one another: When they are thus combined for their own improvement, or for the Good of others, or at least to relax themselves from the Business of the Day, by an innocent and cheerful conversation, there may be something very useful in these little Institutions and Establishments."

The only "useful something" that the typical observer seems able to report consists of the escape or time out from life's duties and drudgeries that third places are said to offer. Joseph Wechsberg, for example, suggests that the coffeehouses of Vienna afford the common man "his haven and island of tranquility, his reading room and gambling hall, his sounding board and grumbling hall. There at least he is safe from nagging wife and unruly children, monotonous radios and barking dogs, tough bosses and impatient creditors." H. L. Mencken offered the same limited view of the places on our side of the Atlantic, describing the respectable Baltimore tavern of his day as "a quiet refuge" and a "hospital asylum from life and its cares."

But there is far more than escape and relief from stress involved in regular visits to a third place. There is more than shelter against the raindrops of life's tedium and more than a breather on the sidelines of the rat race to be had amid the company of a third place. Its real merits do not depend upon being harried by life, afflicted by stress, or needing time out from gainful activities. The escape theme is not erroneous in substance but in emphasis; it focuses too much upon conditions external to the third place and too little upon experiences and relationships afforded there and nowhere else.

Though characterizations of the third place as a mere haven of escape from home and work are inadequate, they do possess a virtue—they invite *comparison*. The escape theme suggests a world of difference between the corner tavern and the family apartment a block away, between morning coffee in the bungalow and that with the gang at the local bakery. The contrast is sharp and will be revealed. The *raison d'etre* of the third place rests upon its differences from the other settings of daily life and can best be understood by comparison with them. In examining these differences, it will not serve to misrepresent the home, shop, or office in order to put a better light on public gathering places. But, if at times I might lapse in my objectivity, I take solace in the fact that public opinion in America and the weight of our myths and prejudices have never done justice to third places and the kind of association so essential to our freedom and contentment.

ON NEUTRAL GROUND

The individual may have many friends, a rich variety among them, and opportunity to engage many of them daily *only* if people do not get uncomfortably tangled in one another's lives. Friends can be numerous and often met only if they may easily join and depart one another's company. This otherwise obvious fact of social life is often obscured by the seeming contradiction that surrounds it—we need a good deal of immunity from those whose company we like best. Or, as the sociologist Richard Sennett put it, "people can be sociable only when they have some protection from each other."

In a book showing how to bring life back to American cities, Jane Jacobs stresses the contradiction surrounding most friendships and the consequent need to provide places for them. Cities, she observed, are full of people with whom contact is significant, useful, and enjoyable, but "you don't want them in your hair and they do not want you in theirs either." If friendships and other informal acquaintances are limited to those suitable for private life, she says, the city becomes stultified. So, one might add, does the social life of the individual.

In order for the city and its neighborhoods to offer the rich and varied association that is their promise and their potential, there must be *neutral ground* upon which people may gather. There must be places where individuals may come and go as they please, in which none are required to play host, and in which all feel at home and comfortable. If there is no neutral ground in the neighborhoods where people live, association outside the home will be impoverished. Many, perhaps most, neighbors will never meet, to say nothing of associate, for there is no place for them to do so. Where neutral ground is available it makes possible far more informal, even intimate, relations among people than could be entertained in the home.

Social reformers as a rule, and planners all too commonly, ignore the importance of neutral ground and the kinds of relationships, interactions, and activities to which it plays host. Reformers have never liked seeing people hanging around on street corners, store porches, front stoops, bars, candy stores, or other public areas. They find loitering deplorable and assume that if people had better private areas they would not waste time in public ones. It would make as much sense, as Jane Jacobs points out, to argue that people wouldn't show up at testimonial banquets if they had wives who could cook for them at home. The banquet table and coffee counter bring people together in an intimate and private social fashion—people who would not otherwise meet in that way. Both settings (street corner and banquet hall) are public and neutral, and both are important to the unity of neighborhoods, cities, and societies.

If we valued fraternity as much as independence, and democracy as much as free enterprise, our zoning codes would not enforce the social isolation that plagues our modern neighborhoods, but would require some form of public gathering place every block or two. We may one day rediscover the wisdom of James Oglethorpe who laid out Savannah such that her citizens lived close to public gathering areas. Indeed, he did so with such compelling effect that Sherman, in his destructive march to the sea, spared Savannah alone.

THE THIRD PLACE IS A LEVELER

Levelers was the name given to an extreme left-wing political party that emerged under Charles I and expired shortly afterward under Cromwell. The goal of the party was the abolition of all differences of position or rank that existed among men. By the middle of the seventeenth century, the term came to be applied much more broadly in England, referring to anything "which reduces men to an equality." For example, the newly established coffeehouses of that period, one of unprecedented democracy among the English, were commonly referred to as levelers, as were the people who frequented them and who relished the new intimacy made possible by the decay of the old feudal order.

Precursors of the renowned English clubs, those early coffeehouses were enthusiastically democratic in the conduct and composition of their habitués. As one of the more articulate among them recorded, "As you have a hodge-podge of Drinks, such too is your company, for each man seems a Leveller, and ranks and files himself as he lists, without regard to degrees or order; so that oft you may see a silly Fop, and a wonder Justice, a griping-Rock, and a grave Citizen, a worthy Lawyer, and an errant Pickpocket, a Reverend Noncomformist, and a canting Mountebank; all blended together, to compose an Oglio of Impertinence." Quite suddenly, each man had become an agent of England's newfound unity. His territory was the coffeehouse, which provided the neutral ground upon which men discovered one another apart from the classes and ranks that had earlier divided them.

A place that is a leveler is, by its nature, an inclusive place. It is accessible to the general public and does not set formal criteria of membership and exclusion. There is a tendency for individuals to select their associates, friends, and intimates from among those closest to them in social rank. Third places, however, serve to *expand* possibilities, whereas formal associations tend to narrow and restrict them. Third places counter the tendency to be restrictive in the enjoyment of others by being open to all and by laying emphasis on qualities not confined to status distinctions current in the society. Within third places, the charm and flavor of one's personality, irrespective of his or her station in life, is what counts. In the third place, people may make blissful substitutions in the rosters of their associations, adding those they genuinely enjoy and admire to those less-preferred individuals that fate has put at their side in the workplace or even, perhaps, in their family.

Further, a place that is a leveler also permits the individual to know workmates in a different and fuller aspect than is possible in the workplace. The great bulk of human association finds individuals related to one another for some objective purpose. It casts them, as sociologists say, in roles, and though the roles we play provide us with our more sustaining matrices of human association, these tend to submerge personality and the inherent joys of being together with others to some external purpose. In contrast, what Georg Simmel referred to as "pure sociability" is precisely the occasion in which people get together for no other purpose, higher or lower, than for the "joy, vivacity, and relief" of engaging their personalities beyond the contexts of purpose, duty, or role. As Simmel insisted, this unique occasion provides the most democratic experience people can have and allows them to be more fully themselves, for it is salutary in such situations that all shed their social uniforms and insignia and reveal more of what lies beneath or beyond them.

Necessarily, a transformation must occur as one passes through the portals of a third place. Worldly status claims must be checked at the door in order that all within may be equals. The surrender of outward status, or leveling, that transforms those who own delivery trucks and those who drive them into equals, is rewarded by acceptance on more humane and less transitory grounds. Leveling is a joy and relief to those of higher and lower status in the mundane world. Those who, on the outside, command deference and attention by the sheer weight of their position find themselves in the third place enjoined, embraced, accepted, and enjoyed where conventional status counts for little. They are accepted just for themselves

and on terms not subject to the vicissitudes of political or economic life.

Similarly, those not high on the totems of accomplishment or popularity are enjoined, accepted, embraced, and enjoyed despite their "failings" in their career or the marketplace. There is more to the individual than his or her status indicates, and to have recognition of that fact shared by persons beyond the small circle of the family is indeed a joy and relief. It is the best of all anodynes for soothing the irritation of material deprivation. Even poverty loses much of its sting when communities can offer the settings and occasions where the disadvantaged can be accepted as equals. Pure sociability confirms the more and the less successful and is surely a comfort to both. Unlike the status-guarding of the family and the czarist mentality of those who control corporations, the third place recognizes and implements the value of "downward" association in an uplifting manner.

Worldly status is not the only aspect of the individual that must not intrude into third place association. Personal problems and moodiness must be set aside as well. Just as others in such settings claim immunity from the personal worries and fears of individuals, so may they, for the time being at least, relegate them to a blessed state of irrelevance. The temper and tenor of the third place is upbeat; it is cheerful. The purpose is to enjoy the company of one's fellow human beings and to delight in the novelty of their character—not to wallow in pity over misfortunes.

The transformations in passing from the world of mundane care to the magic of the third place is often visibly manifest in the individual. Within the space of a few hours, individuals may drag themselves into their homes—frowning, fatigued, hunched over— only to stride into their favorite club or tavern a few hours later with a broad grin and an erect posture. Richard West followed one of New York's "pretty people" from his limousine on the street, up the steps, and into the interior of Club 21, observing that "by the time Marvin had walked through the opened set of doors and stood in the lobby, his features softened. The frown was gone, the bluster of importance had ebbed away and had been left at the curb. He felt the old magic welling up."

In Michael Daly's tragic account of young Peter MacPartland (a "perfect" son from a "perfect" family) who was accused of murdering his father, there is mention of a place, perhaps the only place, in which MacPartland ever found relief from the constant struggling and competition that characterized his life. On Monday evenings, a friend would go with him to Rudy's, a working-class tavern, to watch "Monday Night Football." "It was Yale invading a working-class bar," said the friend. "It was like his first freedom of any kind. He thought it was the neatest place in the world." Mere escape can be found in many forms and does not begin to account for transformations such as these.

CONVERSATION IS THE MAIN ACTIVITY

Neutral ground provides the place, and leveling sets the stage for the cardinal and sustaining activity of third places everywhere. That activity is conversation. Nothing more clearly indicates a third place than that the talk there is good; that it is lively, scintillating, colorful, and engaging. The joys of association in third places may initially be marked by smiles and twinkling eyes, by handshaking and back-slapping, but they proceed and are maintained in pleasurable and entertaining conversation.

A comparison of cultures readily reveals that the popularity of conversation in a society is closely related to the popularity of third places. In the 1970s, the economist Tibor Scitovsky introduced statistical data confirming what others had observed casually. The rate of pub visitation in England or café visitation in France is high and corresponds to an obvious fondness for sociable conversation. American tourists, Scitovsky notes, "are usually struck and often morally shocked by the much more leisurely and frivolous attitude toward life of just about all foreigners, manifest by the tremendous amount of idle talk they engage in, on promenades and park benches, in cafés, sandwich shops, lobbies, doorways, and wherever people congregate." And, in the pubs and cafés, Scitovsky goes on to report, "socializing rather than drinking is clearly most people's main occupation."

American men of letters often reveal an envy of those societies in which conversation is more highly regarded than here, and usually recognize the link between activity and setting. Emerson, in his essay on "Table Talk," discussed the importance of great cities in representing the power and genius of a nation. He focused on Paris, which dominated for so long and to such an extent as to influence the whole of Europe. After listing the many areas in which that city had become the "social center of the world," he concluded that its "supreme merit is that it is the city of conversation and cafés."

In a popular essay on "The American Condition," Richard Goodwin invited readers to contrast the rush hour in our major cities with the close of the working day in Renaissance Italy: "Now at Florence, when the air is red with the summer sunset and the campaniles begin to sound vespers and the day's work is done, everyone collects in the piazzas. The steps of Santa Maria del Fiore swarm with men of every rank and every class; artisans, merchants, teachers, artists, doctors, technicians, poets, scholars. A thousand minds, a thousand arguments; a lively intermingling of questions, problems, news of the latest happening, jokes; an inexhaustible play of language and thought, a vibrant curiosity; the changeable temper of a thousand spirits by whom every object of discussion is broken into an infinity of sense and significations—all these spring into being, and then are spent. And this is the pleasure of the Florentine public."

The judgment regarding conversation in our society is usually two-fold: we don't value it and we're not good at it. "If it has not value," complained Wordsworth, "good, lively talk is often contemptuously dismissed as talking for talking's sake." As to our skills, Tibor Scitovsky noted that our gambit for a chat is "halfhearted and . . . we have failed to develop the locale and the facilities for idle talk. We lack the stuff of which conversations are made." In our low estimation of idle talk, we Americans have correctly assessed the worth of much of what we hear. It is witless, trite, self-centered, and unreflective.

If conversation is not just the main attraction but the sine qua non of the third place, it must be better there and, indeed, it is. Within its circles, the art of conversation is preserved against its decline in the larger spheres, and evidence of this claim is abundant.

Initially, one may note a remarkable compliance with the rules of conversation as compared to their abuse almost everywhere else. Many champions of the art of conversation have stated its simple rules. Henry Sedgwick does so in a straightforward manner. In essence, his rules are: 1) Remain silent your share of the time (more rather than less). 2) Be attentive while others are talking. 3) Say what you think but be careful not to hurt others' feelings. 4) Avoid topics not of general interest. 5) Say little or nothing about yourself personally, but talk about others there assembled. 6) Avoid trying to instruct. 7) Speak in as low a voice as will allow others to hear.

The rules, it will be seen, fit the democratic order, or the leveling, that prevails in third places. Everyone seems to talk just the right amount, and all are expected to contribute. Pure sociability is as much subject to good and proper form as any other kind of association, and this conversational style embodies

that form. Quite unlike those corporate realms wherein status dictates who may speak, and when and how much, and who may use levity and against which targets, the third place draws in like manner from everyone there assembled. Even the sharper wits must refrain from dominating conversation, for all are there to hold forth as well as to listen.

By emphasizing style over vocabulary, third place conversation also complements the leveling process. In the course of his investigations into English working-class club life, Brian Jackson was struck by the eloquence of common working people when they spoke in familiar and comfortable environments. He was surprised to hear working people speak with the "verve and panache" of Shakespearian actors. I observed much the same artistry among farmers and other workers in Midwestern communities who could recite, dramatically, verse after verse of poetry, reduce local cockalorums to their just proportions, or argue against school consolidation in a moving and eloquent style.

In Santa Barbara there is a tavern called The English Department, which is operated by a man who was banished from the English department at the local university for reasons that august body never saw fit to share with him. He'd spent most of his adult life listening to talk. He had listened in seminars, classrooms, offices, and hallways of various English departments. But the tavern, he found, was better; it was *living*. "Listen to these people," he said of his customers. "Have you ever heard a place filled like this? . . . And they're all interested in what they're saying. There's genuine inquiry here." In a moment of candor, a past president of a professional association in one of the social sciences told an audience that it had been his experience that most academic departments effectively "rob their students of their Mother wit." The owner of The English Department had made the same discovery.

In contrast, third places are veritable gymnasiums of Mother wit.

The conversational superiority of the third place is also evident in the harm that the bore can there inflict. Those who carry the despicable reputation of being a bore have not earned it at home or in the work setting proper, but almost exclusively in those places and occasions given to sociability. Where people expect more of conversation they are accordingly repulsed by those who abuse it, whether by killing a topic with inappropriate remarks or by talking more than their share of the time. Characteristically, bores talk more loudly than others, substituting both volume and verbosity for wit and substance. Their failure at getting the effect they desire only serves to increase their demands upon the patience of the group. Conversation is a lively game, but the bore hogs the ball, unable to score but unwilling to pass it to others.

Bores are the scourge of sociability and a curse upon the "clubbable." In regard to them, John Timbs, a prolific chronicler of English club life, once cited the advice of a seasoned and knowledgeable member: "Above all, a club should be large. Every club must have its bores; but in a large club you can get out of their way." To have one or more bores as "official brothers" is a grizzly prospect, and one suggesting an additional advantage of inclusive and informal places over the formal and exclusive club. Escape is so much easier.

Conversation's improved quality within the third place is also suggested by its temper. It is more spirited than elsewhere, less inhibited and more eagerly pursued. Compared to the speech in other realms, it is more dramatic and more often attended by laughter and the exercise of wit. The character of the talk has a transcending effect, which Emerson once illustrated by an episode involving two companies of stagecoach riders *en route* to Paris. One group failed to strike up any conversation, while the other quickly became engrossed in it. "The first, on their arrival, had rueful accidents to relate, a terrific thunderstorm, danger, and fear and gloom, to the whole company. The others heard these particulars with surprise—the storm, the mud, the danger. They knew nothing of these; they had forgotten earth; they had breathed a higher air." Third place conversation is typically engrossing. Consciousness of conditions and time often slips away amid its lively flow.

Whatever interrupts conversation's lively flow is ruinous to a third place, be it the bore, a horde of barbaric college students, or mechanical or electronic gadgetry. Most common among these is the noise that passes for music, though it must be understood that when conversation is to be savored, even Mozart is noise if played too loudly. In America, particularly, many public establishments reverberate with music played so loudly that enjoyable conversation is impossible. Why the management chooses to override normal conversation by twenty decibels is not always obvious. It may be to lend the illusion of life among a listless and fragmented assembly, to attract a particular kind of clientele, because management has learned that people tend to drink more and faster when subjected to loud noise, or simply because the one in charge likes it that way. In any case, the potential for a third place can be eliminated with the flip of a switch, for whatever inhibits conversation will drive those who delight in it to search for another setting.

As there are agencies and activities that interfere with conversation, so there are those that aid and encourage it. Third places often incorporate these activities and may even emerge around them. To be more precise, conversation is a *game* that mixes well with many other games according to the manner in which they are played. In the clubs where I watch others play gin rummy, for example, it is a rare card that is played without comment and rarer still is the hand dealt without some terrible judgment being leveled at the dealer. The game and conversation move along in lively fashion, the talk enhancing the card game, the card game giving eternal stimulation to the talk. Jackson's observations in the clubs of the working-class English confirm this. "Much time," he recorded, "is given over to playing games. Cribbage and dominoes mean endless conversation and by-the-way evaluation of personalities. Spectators are never quiet, and every stage of the game stimulates comment—mostly on the characteristics of the players rather than the play; their slyness, slowness, quickness, meanness, allusions to long-remembered incidents in club history."

Not all games stimulate conversation and kibitizing; hence, not all games complement third place association. A room full of individuals intent upon video games is not a third place, nor is a subdued lounge in which couples are quietly staring at backgammon boards. Amateur pool blends well into third place activity generally, providing that personality is not entirely sacrificed to technical skill or the game reduced to the singular matter of who wins. Above all, it is the latitude that personality enjoys at each and every turn that makes the difference.

The social potential of games was nicely illustrated in Laurence Wylie's account of life in the little French village of Peyranne. Wylie had noted the various ways in which the popular game of *boules* was played in front of the local café. "The wit, humor, sarcasm, the insults, the oaths, the logic, the experimental demonstration, and the ability to dramatize a situation gave the game its essential interest." When those features of play are present, the game of *boules*—a relatively simple one—becomes a full-fledged and spirited social as well as sporting event. On the other hand, "Spectators will ignore a game being played by men who are physically skilled but who are unable to dramatize their game, and they will crowd around a game played by men who do not play very well but

who are witty, dramatic, shrewd, in their ability to outwit their opponents. Those most popular players, of course, are those who combine skill with such wit."

To comprehend the nature of the third place is to recognize that though the cue stick may be put up or the pasteboards returned to their box, the game goes on. It is a game that, as Sedgwick observed, "requires two and gains in richness and variety if there are four or five more . . . it exercises the intelligence and the heart, it calls on memory and the imagination, it has all the interest derived from uncertainty and unexpectedness, it demands self-restraint, self-mastery, effort, quickness—in short, all the qualities that make a game exciting." The game is conversation and the third place is its home court.

ACCESSIBILITY AND ACCOMMODATION

Third places that render the best and fullest service are those to which one may go alone at almost any time of the day or evening with assurance that acquaintances will be there. To have such a place available whenever the demons of loneliness or boredom strike or when the pressures and frustrations of the day call for relaxation amid good company is a powerful resource. Where they exist, such places attest to the bonds between people. "A community life exists," says the sociologist Philip Slater, "when one can go daily to a given location and see many of the people he knows."

That seemingly simple requirement of community has become elusive. Beyond the workplace (which, presumably, Slater did not mean to include), only a modest proportion of middle-class Americans can lay claim to such a place. Our evolving habitat has become increasingly hostile to them. Their dwindling number at home, seen against their profusion in many other countries, points up the importance of the accessibility of third places. Access to them must be *easy* if they are to survive and serve, and the ease with which one may visit a third place is a matter of both time and location.

Traditionally, third places have kept long hours. England's early coffeehouses were open sixteen hours a day, and most of our coffee-and-doughnut places are open around the clock. Taverns typically serve from about nine in the morning until the wee hours of the following morning, unless the law decrees otherwise. In many retail stores, the coffee counters are open well before the rest of the store. Most establishments that serve as third places are accessible during both the on and off hours of the day.

It must be thus, for the third place accommodates people only when they are released from their responsibilities elsewhere. The basic institutions—home, work, school—make prior claims that cannot be ignored. Third places must stand ready to serve people's needs for sociability and relaxation in the intervals before, between, and after their mandatory appearances elsewhere.

Those who have third places exhibit regularity in their visits to them, but it is not that punctual and unfailing kind shown in deference to the job or family. The timing is loose, days are missed, some visits are brief, etc. Viewed from the vantage point of the establishment, there is a fluidity in arrivals and departures and an inconsistency of membership at any given hour or day. Correspondingly, the activity that goes on in third places is largely unplanned, unscheduled, unorganized, and unstructured. Here, however, is the charm. It is just these deviations from the middle-class penchant for organization that give the third place much of its character and allure and that allow it to offer a radical departure from the routines of home and work.

As important as timing, and closely related to it, is the location of third places. Where informal gathering places are far removed from one's residence, their appeal fades, for two reasons. Getting there is inconvenient, and one is not likely to know the patrons.

The importance of proximate locations is illustrated by the typical English pub. Though in the one instance its accessibility has been sharply curtailed by laws that cut its normal hours of operation in half, it has nonetheless thrived because of its physical accessibility. The clue is in the name; pubs are called locals and every one of them is somebody's local. Because so many pubs are situated among the homes of those who use them, people are there frequently, both because they are accessible and because their patrons are guaranteed the company of friendly and familiar faces. Across the English Channel sociable use of the public domain is also high, as is the availability of gathering places. Each neighborhood, if not each block, has its café and, as in England, these have served to bring the residents into frequent and friendly contact with one another.

Where third places are prolific across the urban topography, people may indulge their social instincts as they prefer. Some will never frequent these places. Others will do so rarely. Some will go only in the company of others. Many will come and go as individuals.

The Moral Order of Strangers

M. P. Baumgartner

Compared with large cities, suburbs have few public places where strangers intermingle. For this reason alone, conflict between unacquainted people in Hampton tends to be rare. In addition, predatory behavior by strangers—such as burglary and mugging—is quite infrequent. Even when individuals do encounter unknown offenders, they tend to avoid direct confrontation with them at all costs. The town's larger pattern of moral minimalism finds expression, where strangers are concerned, in an extreme aversion to any personal exercise of social control. Rather, townspeople leave the business of dealing with strangers almost exclusively to officials, most notably the police, and involve themselves very little in the maintenance of public order.

THE PUBLIC REALM

Hampton's social organization prevents many conflicts between strangers from arising in the first place. This is so because it keeps unacquainted people away from one another to a degree not seen in cities, reducing the sorts of friction likely to arise in face-to-face encounters. As a primarily residential town, Hampton contains few public places which draw inhabitants from their private homes. There are a handful of restaurants and an even smaller number of bars, a few dozen retail shops, one library, one

museum, one community pool, one live theater (in the summer), one movie theater, one bowling alley, one athletic club, and little else. Zoning laws cram the great majority of these together onto a strip of land running about four blocks along Main Street. The town's parks—mostly grassy, open spaces—are usually empty. It is this state of affairs, seen in suburb after suburb, which has earned for suburbia its reputation as a boring place.

On their way to and from public locations, most people in the town ride in private automobiles. Indeed, comparatively few walk anywhere except to mail an occasional letter at a corner mailbox, to drop in on a near neighbor, or to exercise a dog; few make use of public transit. Partly because there are no destinations along most roads except private homes, and partly because residents drive when they have errands to do, there is very little street life in Hampton. It is possible to ride in a car for blocks at almost any time of day without encountering pedestrians. Even downtown, the streets are usually quiet.

Once citizens park their cars and emerge into public places, they still remain insulated from strangers to a degree not found in urban environments. For one thing, despite the fact that in this community of over 16,000 it is impossible for everyone to be acquainted with everyone else, people in public places are likely to meet someone they know. This is true along Main Street and even more so within establishments. Not only are those who pump their gas, cut their meat, or check out their library books frequently their acquaintances but so are other patrons and customers. In fact, many technically public places are actually used by the same people over and over again until all become acquaintances, or are commandeered by groups of friends for their own purposes. Thus, for instance, the commuter trains in and out of New York City are filled every day with men (and some women) who know one another by name, save seats for one another, share newspapers, and discuss world and local events. In the town's athletic club, many of those who jog on the track and sit in the sauna together have come to recognize each other and to carry on conversations about nonathletic matters. And at Hampton High School sporting events, which the same people attend throughout the school year, many spectators sit in the same seats time after time beside others who do likewise.

Unacquainted people, when they do meet on Hampton's streets or in shops, are in any case less unfamiliar to one another than urban strangers are. The social role of the stranger is partly defined by relational distance, the sheer absence of intimacy, but also by cultural differences and marginalities of various sorts. Because of the considerable homogeneity of the town's population, maintained with some effort by zoning at the formal level and apparently more informally by real-estate agents and banks, strangeness based on social and cultural differences is not widespread. Striking by their near absence are racial minorities and the very poor. As a result, the town's residents live for the most part in a world of their own.

STANDARDS OF ORDER

The relative isolation of people in Hampton from strangers is not only a fact of social morphology but also a moral expectation. It is one of the major yardsticks by which people measure order in public places on a daily basis and assess the conduct of strangers, so that those who disturb the town's protected world offend its inhabitants by doing so. Thus, for instance, individuals who use the streets or other public places more than is customary, especially for socializing, are seen as deviants. Young people are the greatest offenders in this regard, since they often congregate in public locations to smoke, snack, and talk. Other uses of the street may also arouse unfavorable notice. One young woman of about 18 years of age became known to many as "The Walker" and was seen as "mentally ill" because she was in the habit of strolling with her dog throughout town for hours on end. People responded similarly to an older woman who used to sit on a bench downtown for long periods of time and watch cars and pedestrians pass by.

Residents expect those they encounter in public places to go about their business not only expeditiously but also unobtrusively. Like people in other modern communities, they find grievances in a wide array of situational improprieties which they associate with mental disturbance or rowdiness. Individuals who approach others for no apparent reason, speak loudly to themselves or shout to companions, appear drunk on the streets, run recklessly among pedestrians, and engage in a variety of similar actions are met with disapproval. It is expected that strangers will not impose themselves upon others and will proceed with caution and circumspection, both on foot and in cars.

Simply being in a public place at all can be offensive. Quiet residential streets, and the public parks scattered among them, are used on a day-by-day basis almost exclusively by neighborhood people. If outsiders appear in such locations, they are likely to arouse uneasiness or even alarm. Thus, one woman was disturbed and indignant to notice a man in a strange van sitting at the side of the road by her house. Other people have been singled out as "suspicious" while merely walking along residential streets. Even downtown, those who appear to be outsiders—by virtue of race or unconventionality—may effectively deviate by their very presence.

In many cases of this kind, the citizens of Hampton would explain their disapproval by voicing a fear of "crime"—by which they generally mean predatory behavior by strangers. Burglaries occur often enough to be a possibility for every household, but the chances of such victimization are slim. (During the period of this study there were about 100 burglaries per year—residential and commercial combined—recorded in police statistics, and contact with townspeople suggests that the great majority of such instances are reported.) It would appear that the most successful burglars are those who manage to blend in among the respectable citizens. For example, one pair responsible for several crimes were a middle-aged man and woman who dressed "well" and drove an expensive but "tasteful" car. Aside from burglaries, actions by strangers that would likely be handled as crimes—street muggings, assaults, and robberies, for instance—are virtually nonexistent. By town standards, the occasional exhibitionists who accost school children on the street are major criminals. Despite the low rate of predation, however, citizens are greatly concerned about crime and wary of people who seem out of place. They see strangers as potentially dangerous and anyone who is too conspicuous as alarming.

One final way in which offenders may violate public order in Hampton should be mentioned here as well. Townspeople have standards of cleanliness and aesthetics to which they hold strangers as well as intimates. They are annoyed, for instance, by run-down houses and lots, and also by dirty shops and restaurants. It is difficult to say conclusively that standards of this sort are higher in Hampton than in less suburban places, but such appears to be the case. A single school bus, for example, parked in a municipal lot across from the town hall outraged many people as a visual blight that hurt the appearance of the community. In another instance, a minor furor erupted when one of the town's banks placed new name signs on the outside of its building. The signs were modernistic in design, made of plastic, and had the bank's logo printed in black, orange, and white. Many townspeople vehemently objected to what they claimed were garish and ugly signs, totally out of keeping with the more subdued character of Hampton's downtown areas. After numerous complaints poured into the bank's offices, town officials, and local newspapers, the bank voluntarily removed the signs. Hampton's residents would explain their concern about matters such as these partly as an effort to prevent their town from becoming what they consider nearby cities to be already—hopelessly disorganized and filthy places.

STRANGERS AND CITIZENS

The citizens of Hampton are extremely reluctant to deal with offensive strangers personally. As much as they dislike hostile exchanges with family members or neighbors, they evidence even stronger aversion when unknown persons are involved. This is the most striking fact about the moral order prevailing among strangers in the town, and as a result, very little social control takes place between unacquainted people.

In fact, the immediate response of most individuals to a stranger's deviant action is to do nothing and wait for the offender to move on or for the situation to resolve itself. Sometimes, aggrieved people initiate avoidance by leaving the scene entirely. Even beyond single encounters, the responses of tolerance and avoidance are common. If the offender is someone likely to turn up again, or the offense of a sort likely to persist, people will often decide simply to absorb the deviance or to make efforts to prevent exposure to it in the future. In this way, several eccentric individuals whose behavior has been seen as abnormal have nonetheless escaped most sanctioning altogether. One was an older woman who, until her recent death, walked along the streets daily picking up all the litter she found, even the smallest specks of paper. As she did so, she muttered continually and unintelligibly under her breath. Another person, who recently moved out of town, commonly approached residents on the street and engaged them in meandering conversations which he refused to end. Yet another man frequented public places while drunk until, at some point, he gave up alcohol on his own initiative. In all of these cases, townspeople were remarkably tolerant of the unusual conduct involved, only commenting among themselves about it or seeking to avoid the offenders. They reacted in the same way to "The Walker" and to the woman who liked to sit for hours on a downtown bench. In addition, people similarly tolerate or avoid most "ugliness" or "filth" around the town, the case of the bank signs notwithstanding. They may comment disapprovingly about it to their family members or friends, but usually that is all they do.

Confrontation of any kind between strangers is so rare that this study uncovered only a handful of cases involving it, and just two that contained violence. In one of these intances, two youths in a car pulled into a driveway in front of a middle-aged jogger, who took offense and kicked the car's fender. When the young men got out of the car and found that it had been dented, they set off in pursuit of the jogger. Overtaking him, they demanded to know his name and that of his insurance company, and when he refused to answer them, they struck him with their fists. This case ended up in court, where it was the jogger who received the greater penalty and the sterner lecture. In the only other recorded matter in which violence occurred between strangers, a young man running through town collided with an older pedestrian, who thereupon punched him. When the victim of the blow summoned the police, the other man explained that he had thought he was being mugged. Incidents like these are strongly disapproved of by the public. So far as the townspeople are concerned, those who threaten or even criticize strangers are deviant for doing so. They are apt to be seen as "crazy" or "foolish" people who are "just asking for trouble."

The ease with which people can withdraw into their own private enclaves, leaving problems with strangers behind them, is a dimension of life in suburbia which its citizens appreciate greatly. In the language of animal ethology, it allows "flight" rather than "fight" when tensions arise between those who were previously unacquainted. However, the suburbanites of Hampton do not rely simply on tolerance or avoidance as ways of coping with strangers. Another favorite strategy for dealing with such individuals is to delegate to others the task of monitoring, approaching, and sanctioning them. Suburbanites thus like to leave their problems with strangers in the care of champions or surrogates, people who prosecute the grievances of others as if they were their own and, in so doing, "substitute for another person or group in the management of a conflict, largely or totally relieving a principal of responsibility and risk in the whole affair." In Hampton, these champions are the police and administrative officials. As part of their job, they act upon complaints made by citizens against strangers, the overwhelming majority of which are anonymous or secret. Whereas calling the authorities about relatives or neighbors can mean an escalation in hostility, when strangers are concerned this is generally not the case because the offender never learns the identity of the complainant. For people who value nonconfrontation as much as suburbanites do, the use of champions only becomes appealing under the conditions of anonymity that prevail among strangers. Yet given this anonymity, it provides a way to get something done about grievances without requiring any personal exercise of social control at all. Even more desirable from the suburban point of view, these champions can prevent, uncover, and pursue much misconduct on their own, without even waiting for citizens to mobilize them.

In the view of Hampton's citizens, it is for their contribution in controlling strangers that they employ the police and administrative officers, and they measure the value of these officials by the extent to which they protect residents from unknown offenders. The precise techniques used toward this end are not of special interest, so long as they are effective and do not require citizen participation, since the town's residents do not want to be involved in any way.

SUSPICIOUS PERSONS

Another major focus of police concern in suburbia is the discovery and control of "suspicious persons." In light of what has already been said, it should not be surprising that many suspicious people are young adults. In general, however, this problem is distinct from that represented by unruly youths. Suspicious persons tend to be older, are usually unknown to the police, and are generally found alone or with one or two companions. What distinguishes them from others is that they are out of place—in locations where strangers of any kind are uncommon or where people with their particular social characteristics are rarely seen.

The movements of suspicious persons, like the behavior of young people, seem to arouse more concern in the town than they would in nearby cities, where other matters appear more pressing. Police encounters with suspicious persons arise both from citizen complaints and from police surveillance. Town residents share with the police a belief that people who are out of place are potentially dangerous, and also a firm conviction that ordinary citizens should never approach such individuals themselves but should leave that job to the authorities. Thus, in one case, a woman who noticed a stranger parked in a van along her roadside called the police to deal with him rather than confront him personally. Another citizen telephoned to report that "strange people" were walking through an old estate across the street. A third called to say that a stranger in a car had slowed down alongside her children when they were walking home from school and had then driven off. She gave a description of the man and hoped the police could locate him and question him. In a fourth case, an elderly woman called the police because she heard a man's voice outside her home one evening. Someone else called to report a "prowler" at the home of a vacationing neighbor.

The extent to which people depend on the police to be their champions in confrontations with suspicious persons can be documented through information provided by the police department. Overall, Hampton's police force, staffed by slightly more than 30 officers, receives about 30 calls from citizens per day, or about 1,000 per month. Among these are frequent requests for nonlegal assistance of various kinds (about a third of the total) and calls seeking information from the police or imparting information to them about matters other than offenses— such as when citizens will be out of town (about 10 to 15 percent of the total). Another third allege actual offenses of some kind, while the remainder—accounting for nearly a fourth of all calls—report suspicious persons or circumstances. (The latter might be, for example, an open window in a vacationing neighbor's house.) Domestic disputes and public disturbances together account for less than 3 percent of all calls. By way of comparison, on a single day in 1964 the Chicago police received about 5,000 calls. The overall rate of calls was thus similar to that in Hampton (just under two calls daily per 1,000 people in each place). The substance of the calls was quite different, however, with the citizens of Chicago asking their police to intervene much more frequently in actual confrontations. One-quarter of the calls in Chicago were made about ongoing fights. Fewer callers asked the Chicago police for nonlegal assistance or imparted information about matters other than crimes, and only 4 percent reported suspicious persons.

The physical organization of Hampton—which allows residents to monitor their neighborhoods and to spot outsiders who linger in their areas—in itself may account for the comparatively large number of calls about suspicious persons. In a large city such as Chicago or New York with high population densities and a steady flow of diverse people, it is more difficult to single out a few among the many strangers to label as especially suspicious. At the same time, Hampton's less-burdened police welcome calls reporting suspicious persons and circumstances in a way that inner-city police might not. They even actively solicit such business from citizens in conversations and through articles written periodically by the police chief for the local newspaper.

The police also uncover many suspicious persons on their own. Given the near absence of assaults, muggings, and other events that would take priority in the allocation of police service, officers in Hampton have a great deal of time to search for those who strike them as potential criminals. The kinds of persons they are watching for virtually never materialize, however. Thus, one fear of many townspeople is that poor blacks or Hispanics from New York or other nearby cities will enter the town and prey upon its residents. A couple of well-publicized incidents in which this occurred have helped to convince many that such predation is a serious threat. A person who appeared to be from an urban ghetto would surely arouse police concern

and would quite likely be approached. On a day-by-day basis, however, such people are essentially never seen in Hampton. They have little occasion to be there, and they are probably well aware of how cold their welcome would be. Nonetheless, suspicious persons of other sorts do turn up in the town.

STRANGERS AND MORAL MINIMALISM

This chapter has described the extreme aversion of Hampton's suburbanites to open confrontation with strangers, or indeed to the exercise of any kind of direct social control against them. So thoroughgoing is this sentiment of aversion to open confrontation that the business of regulating strangers and maintaining public order is largely delegated to officials. Citizens view these officials as absolutely essential and support them financially with few questions asked. Should an offender manage to elude them—and to be encountered within the greatly limited range of public life—citizens will usually tolerate or avoid that person, or they may invoke an official in secret. After automobile accidents, they withdraw calmly to file claims with insurance companies.

The sheer insulation from strangers that prevails in suburbia, the rarity of predation by outsiders, and the efficiency and helpfulness of officials all help to make this strategy of disengagement feasible and attractive. There appear to be other dynamics at work, however. Since the comparatively weak and restrained nature of social control between relatives and neighbors in Hampton is largely the result of the atomization, transiency, and autonomy of the town's population, and since it is among strangers that these attributes are most prominent, it is not surprising that there social control is least forcefully exerted by the citizens themselves.

Weak ties and social dispersion among strangers undermine direct and forceful responses to grievances in some of the same ways that they do in other relationships. Partly, they make offenses by strangers less persistent and less bothersome. Thus, the brief duration of meetings between unacquainted persons helps to make the costs of tolerance low, since problems that arise will usually be temporary. Furthermore, since strangers who come together casually in public places know nothing about one another's past histories and reputations, they cannot detect chronic or repeat offenders and react accordingly. In most instances, avoidance or retreat will be readily possible should a stranger prove so annoying that mere tolerance is not an adequate solution. At the same time, atomization and autonomy among strangers also directly reduces the willingness or ability to be forceful. People's many responsibilities or activities in other settings command their attention, leaving them little time or energy to invest in grievances against strangers. At the same time, the mutual independence of people who encounter each other by chance in public places reduces the range of possible sanctions available to them. Violence, though theoretically feasible, is unattractive to isolated people without support groups at hand. Secret recourse to officials is effectively the only option that allows people to do more than simply tolerate or avoid offenders without also requiring a confrontation. What is crucial about this response is that the anonymity prevailing among strangers virtually guarantees that the objects of any complaints will never know who has invoked the authorities against them. Or better yet from the suburban point of view, in many cases officials will discover offensive conduct on their own and move to control it, relieving citizens even of the need to voice their grievances.

Since transiency and atomization are properties of social life between strangers throughout modern societies, and should everywhere have similar effects, it is understandable that moral interaction in public places seems generally minimal and restrained. Many observers have commented on the extremes of tolerance and avoidance seen among strangers in urban America and upon the rarity of open confrontation—even criticism—among them. First of all, people appear to time their movements in public places so as to avoid altogether individuals or situations likely to be annoying or to arouse conflict. Once face to face, strangers seem to have adapted to one another's presence with what one social scientist has described as an ethos of noninvolvement and nonconcern, partly because as isolated individuals each is highly vulnerable to every other. Another researcher has documented the use of studied inattention (something which in practice entails a great deal of tolerance) and flight from unpleasant situations as techniques for the management of offensive or threatening conduct by strangers in urban areas. In a study of social interaction and social control on a crowded beach outside Los Angeles, an investigation has found that tolerance, avoidance, and the delegation of order maintenance to authorities (the police and lifeguards) are the three major means used to prevent and resolve "trouble." The peaceful and pleasant nature of activities on the beach results precisely because people there are isolated from one another and encapsulated in their private worlds.

Yet as weakly as people in the industrialized West are tied to strangers, and as little as they exert moral sanctions against them, to the suburbanites of Hampton it is still too much. If these people were to have their way, ties to strangers would be even weaker. Simply having to deal with socially distant persons—however civil the interchanges—makes them uncomfortable. Correcting the behavior of strangers is much worse. Thus, in the best of all possible worlds, they would exercise no moral authority against strangers whatsoever.

Street Etiquette and Street Wisdom

Elijah Anderson

The streets have a peculiar definition in the Village community. Usually pedestrians can walk there undisturbed. Often they seem peaceful. Always they have an elegant air, with mature trees, wrought-iron fences, and solid architecture reminiscent of pre-war comfort and ease. But in the minds of current residents the streets are dangerous and volatile. Lives may be lost there. Muggings occur with some regularity. Cars are broken into for tape decks and other valuables. Occasionally people suffer seemingly meaningless verbal or even physical assaults. For these reasons residents develop a certain ambivalence toward their neighborhood. On the one hand, they know they should distrust it, and they do. But on the other hand, distrusting the area and the people who use it requires tremendous energy. To resolve this problem, they tentatively come to terms with the public areas through trial and error, using them cautiously at first and only slowly developing a measure of trust.

How dangerous an area seems depends on how familiar one is with the neighborhood and what one can take for granted. Villagers often use the euphemism "tricky." Depending on how long they have lived here and how "urban" they are, the streets may seem manageable or unmanageable.

Most people in the Village, because of their social class as well as the cultural history of the community (which includes a legacy of nonviolence), shy away from arming themselves with guns, knives, and other weapons. A more common "defense" is simply avoiding the streets. Many whites and middle-income blacks use them as infrequently as they can, particularly at night.

Because public interactions generally matter for only a few crucial seconds, people are conditioned to rapid scrutiny of the looks, speech, public behavior, gender, and color of those sharing the environment. The central strategy in maintaining safety on the streets is to avoid strange black males. The public awareness is color-coded: white skin denotes civility, lawabidingness, and trustworthiness, while black skin is strongly associated with poverty, crime, incivility, and distrust. Thus an unknown young black male is readily deferred to. If he asks for anything, he must be handled quickly and summarily. If he is persistent, help must be summoned.

This simplistic racial interpretation of crime creates a "we/they" dichotomy between whites and blacks. Yet here again the underlying issue is class. One may argue that the average mugger is primarily concerned with the trouble or ease of taking his victim's property and only secondarily with race or with the distant consequences of his actions. It is significant, then, that the dominant working conception in the black community at large is that the area is being overrun by well-to-do whites. Not only do the perpetrators of crime often view anonymous whites as invaders but, perhaps more important, they see them as "people who got something" and who are inexperienced in the "ways of the streets."

Middle-income blacks in the Village, who also are among the "haves," often share a victim mentality with middle-income whites and appear just as distrustful of black strangers. Believing they are immune to the charge of racism, Village blacks make some of the same remarks as whites do, sometimes voicing even more incisive observations concerning "street blacks" and black criminality.

That middle-class whites and blacks have similar concerns suggests a social commonality and shared moral community, allowing people the limited sense that all residents of the neighborhood have comparable problems with street navigation. But this assumption ultimately breaks down, affecting neighborhood trust and the social integrity of the community. For in fact the experiences and problems on the streets of a person with dark skin are very different from those of a white person, for several reasons.

First, whereas the law-abiding black possesses a kind of protective coloration, the white man or woman has none. This defense allows the black person to claim street wisdom, which the white person generally does not find it easy to do.

Second, there is a felt deterrent to black-on-black crime because the victim may recognize his assailant later. This possibility may cause the potential mugger, for a crucial instant, to think twice before robbing another black person. Not only may the victim "bump into" his assailant again, but there is a chance he will try to "take care of him" personally. Many a mugger would not like to carry such a burden, especially when there are so many "inexperienced" whites around who may be assumed, however erroneously, to be easier to rob, unlikely to recognize their assailant, and certainly less likely to retaliate.

Finally, the white male does not represent the same threat in the public arena, making him, and by implication whites generally, feel especially vulnerable and undermining respect for his defensive capabilities. Perhaps in response to this cultural truth, some white men take a generalized, exaggerated, protective posture toward white women in the presence of "threatening" black males. One young black man described this scene:

> One evening I was walking down the street and this older white lady was at the middle of the block, and I was walking toward her. It was just me and her. Then all of a sudden this young white man runs across the street and just stands between me and this lady. He just kept watching me, and I stared him down. When I passed him, I turned and kept on looking at him. I know he thought I was gon' mess with that woman or something.

This deliberate confrontation is rare on Village streets. Rather, whites and middle-class blacks are skilled in the art of avoidance, using their eyes, ears, and bodies to navigate safely. Although this seems to work for the residents, however, it vitiates comity between the races. One class of people is conditioned to see itself as law-abiding and culturally superior while viewing the other as a socially bruised underclass inclined to criminality. This perspective creates social distance and racial stereotyping, to which middle-income blacks are especially sensitive. Further, it makes even liberal whites vulnerable to the charge of racism.

Although such prejudice is at work in the Village community, there is a deceptive appearance of an effortlessly ordered and racially tolerant public space. All individuals walking the streets, whether white or black, must negotiate their passage with others they encounter. There are essentially two ways of doing this. One is to formulate a set of rules and apply them in every situation, employing what I call "street etiquette." This requires only a generalized perception of the people one encounters, based on the most superficial characteristics. Because it represents a crude set of guidelines, street etiquette makes the streets feel somewhat comfortable to the user, but it may be a security blanket rather than a real practical help. For many it becomes a learning tool.

Pedestrians who go beyond the simplistic rules of street etiquette develop a kind of "street wisdom," a more sophisticated approach. Those who acquire this sophistication realize that the public environment does not always respond to a formal set of rules rigidly applied to all problems. So they develop coping strategies for different situations, tailoring their responses to each unique event. By doing so they develop a "conception of self" in public that in itself provides some safety; in effect, they learn how to behave on the streets.

STREET ETIQUETTE

A set of informal rules has emerged among residents and other users of the public spaces of the Village. These rules allow members of diverse groups orderly passage with the promise of security, or at least a minimum of trouble and conflict. The rules are applied in specific circumstances, particularly when people feel threatened. Public etiquette is initiated where the jurisdiction of formal agents of social control ends and personal responsibility is sensed to begin. Because crime is a central issue to most residents, their concern for safety leads them to expend great effort in getting to know their immediate area. Potential and actual street crime inspires the social process of mental note taking, which lays a foundation for trust among strangers, dictated by the situation and proceeding by repeated face-to-face encounters. It works to form the basis of public community within the immediate neighborhood.

The process begins something like this. One person sees another walking down the street alone, with another person, or perhaps with a few others. Those seen might be getting out of an unusual car, riding a ten-speed bicycle, walking a dog, strolling on the grounds of a dwelling in the neighborhood, or simply crossing the street at the light or leaving a store carrying groceries. The sight of people engaging in such everyday activities helps to convey what may be interpreted as the usual picture of public life—what residents take for granted.

Skin color, gender, age, dress, and comportment are important markers that characterize and define the area. Depending on the observer's biases, such specific markers can become the most important characteristics determining the status of those being watched, superseding other meaningful attributes. However, the most important aspect of the situation is simply that the observer takes mental note of the other person: a significant social contact, though usually not a reciprocal one, is made. The person seen, and the category he or she is believed to represent, comes to be considered an ordinary part of the environment.

Although the initial observation is important, it is not the crucial element in "knowing about" others and feeling comfortable. Rather, it helps determine the social context for any other meaningful interactions, whether unilateral or bilateral. It gives users of the streets a sense of whom to expect where and when, and it allows them to adjust their plans accordingly.

The significance of the initial encounter is contingent upon subsequent meetings and interactions. If the person is never seen again, the encounter gradually loses significance. But if the observer sees the person again or meets others who are similar, the initial impression may become stronger and might develop into a theory about that category of people, a working conception of a social type. The strength of such impressions— nurtured and supported through repeated encounters, observations, and talk with other residents—gradually builds.

Background information and knowledge

may provide a basis for social connection. A stranger may be seen in one context, then in another, then in a third. In time the observer might say to himself, "I know that person." Certainly he does know the person, if only by sight. He has noticed him many times in various neighborhood contexts, and with each successive encounter he has become increasingly familiar with him and the class he has come to represent. Probably the two are not yet speaking, though they may have exchanged looks that establish the minimal basis for trust. If asked directly, the observer might say, "Yeah, I've seen him around." In this way strangers may know each other and obtain a degree of territorial communion without ever speaking a word. It is quite possible that they will never reach speaking terms.

But there are circumstances where the social gap between visual and verbal interaction in public is pressed and the relationship between incomplete strangers is required to go further. People sometimes feel silly continually passing others they know well by sight without speaking to them. They may resolve their discomfort by greeting to them or by contrived avoidance. If they choose to speak, they may commit themselves to a series of obligatory greetings.

Introductions may also occur when two people who have seen each other in the neighborhood for some time happen to meet in a different part of town; there, despite some awkwardness, they may feel constrained to greet each other like long-lost friends. Perhaps they had not yet reached the point of speaking but had only warily acknowledged one another with knowing looks, or even with the customary offensive/defensive scowl used on the street for keeping strangers at a distance. After this meeting, previously distant Villagers may begin to speak regularly on the neighborhood streets. In this way trust can be established between strangers, who may then come to know each other in limited ways or very well.

Just the fact of their regular presence offers a sense of security, or at least continuity, to their neighbors. Thus, many people walk the streets with a confidence that belies their serious concerns. They use those they "know" as buffers against danger. Although they may still be strangers, they feel they can call on each other as allies when neighborhood crises emerge, when they would otherwise be seriously short of help, or when they must protect themselves or their loved ones. For example, during emergencies such as house fires, street crimes in which someone clearly needs help, or some other event where partial strangers have an opportunity to gather and compare notes with neighbors who seemed out of reach before, they may first provide help and only then reach out a hand and introduce themselves, saying, "Hello, my name is . . ."

This invisible but assumed network of reserve relationships binds together the residents and regular users of the public spaces of the Village. However, the person-specific designations that Villagers make every day are not always conducive to the flourishing of "ideal-typical gemeinschaft" relations. On the contrary, mental note taking like that described above also allows neighbors *not* to become involved in indiscriminate social exchange. For example, lower-income black people are often observed closely by whites who use the streets, perhaps primarily because they remain exotic and sometimes dangerous to many Villagers. Many whites may wish to get closer to the blacks, but for complicated reasons having to do with local history, class etiquette, and lingering racism, they normally maintain their established social distance. Most residents want social contact only with others of their own social class. In public they note the speech patterns of lower-class blacks. They pay attention to how "they" walk and how "they" treat their children, absorbing everything and shaping and reshaping their notions. It is not unusual to see whites, particularly women, observing the ways lower-income black women handle their children in public. The following field note illustrates this:

> On a Saturday morning in May at approximately 11:00, a young black woman was managing a little girl of three, a boy of about five, and a small baby in a stroller. They were standing at Linden Avenue and Cherry Street in the Village, waiting for the bus. Two young white women and a middle-aged black man, apparently from the Village, were waiting for the bus too. The two small children began to fight over a toy. The older child won, and the smaller one began to have a temper tantrum. She wailed and stamped. Her face contorted, the mother cursed at the children, yelling obscenities at them and trying to get them to behave themselves. The white women paid "civil inattention," their actions and words belying their interest. As the woman spanked the three-year-old, one of the white women visibly cringed, as if to say to her friend and anyone else caring to pay attention, "Oh! What a way to treat your child!" Meanwhile, the other white woman didn't say a word. The black man, in silence, simply observed the performance. The woman continued to berate the children. She clearly had her hands full. Finally the bus arrived.

Such critiques are not for the black woman's benefit, nor are they always made openly. Whereas in the gemeinschaft type of community people may become quite openly involved with the lives of their neighbors, trading favors and various kinds of help without keeping an account of who owes what to whom, Villagers generally avoid the responsibilities and social obligations that emerge from deeper forms of interpersonal involvement. Instead of intervening in either a helpful or a critical way, the two white women chose to strengthen the bond between them—their shared values—and to distance themselves from this other "element" of the public community.

TALK

In the Village, as in various neighborhoods of the city, young black males are carefully observed. They are often blamed for crimes when no contrary evidence is available. However, neighborly talk about crime becomes a problem when the age, ethnicity, or other defining attributes of the assailant and victim are introduced. In the Village, the all-too-easy dischotomizing by race into criminal and victim categories is complicated by the friendly, even intimate, relations between some blacks and whites. Neighbors bound by the dominant Village ideology of racial harmony and tolerance risk offending some members of their audience when they make broad racial remarks. Hence neighbors tread lightly, except when they forget themselves or presume they are in "safe" company and can speak freely.

There are many times when whites educate other whites who believe their prejudices are generally shared. A thirty-year-old white man who grew up in an Irish working-class section of the city had this to say:

> I had a small gathering at my house just the other night. Tommy Jones, Charlie, Dave, and some women. Well, Dave started in talking about crime in the streets. And he started to talk about "niggers." And I just said to him, "Whoa, whoa, man. I don't allow that kind of talk in my house. If you want to talk like that, you gotta go outside, or go somewhere else." And I meant it. Yeah, I meant it. You should have seen the look on his face. Well, he didn't use that word no more.

Patterns of information exchange develop where neighbors talk to each other with different degrees of frankness about the alleged or actual attributes of assailants and victims. For instance, a white person might tell his black neighbor a story in which the assailant was believed to be black, but he might politely omit race if he thinks the black neighbor will be offended.

As neighbors come to know one another, fewer offenses are likely to occur; identifications with certain social circles become known, and information exchanges can proceed by neighborhood-specific code words in which race need not be overtly stated but is subtly expressed. For instance, a young couple moving in from the suburbs learns from an upstairs neighbor that the reason Mrs. Legget (white) walks with a cane is not just that she is eighty-five years old. Until a few years ago, she took her regular afternoon walks unaided by the thick wooden stick she now relies on. One afternoon she was knocked to the pavement by a "couple of kids" outside Mr. Chow's, the neighborhood market where black high-school students stop for candy and soda and congregate on their way home from school. In the scuffle, Mrs. Legget's purse was taken. The police took her to the hospital, and it was discovered that she had a broken hip.

Since her injury, Mrs. Legget's gait is less steady. She still takes her walks, but now she goes out earlier and avoids Mr. Chow's at the time school lets out. When the new couple ask her about the mugging, she is unwilling to describe the "kids" who knocked her down. She only smiles and gestures toward the small, low-slung cloth bag in which she now carries her valuables. "This one is mug-proof, they tell me," she says, a playful glimmer in her eye. It is a poignant lesson for the young couple. Purse straps should be worn across the chest bandolier style, not carelessly hooked over the arm, and perhaps Mr. Chow's is worth avoiding at 3:00 in the afternoon. As time goes by the young couple will come to understand the special meaning of the term "kids," which Villagers, particularly whites, often use in stories about street muggings to mean "black kids."

Through neighborly talk, inhabitants of the Village provide new arrivals, as well as established residents, with rules concerning the use of sidewalks at different times of day. Newcomers learn the schedule of the nearby black high school, enabling them to avoid the well-traveled north-south streets when the high-school students are there in force. They slowly learn how the racial and age composition of the clientele at Mr. Chow's varies with time of day, so they can choose safer hours, "working around" those they view as threatening. In addition, they come to recognize other Villagers and frequent visitors from Northton, though they may not always be conscious of the process. The more general color-coding that people in racially segregated areas apply goes through a refinement process because of the heterogeneous makeup of the Village.

When neighbors tell horror stories from the next block over, the shape of the tale and the characteristics of the actors depend on the values that the storyteller and his audience share. In this sense a general moral community is forged each time neighbors get together and talk about crime. A we/they dichotomy often becomes explicit, and a community perspective of "decent" people is articulated:

> While casually sitting in their backyard, Adam and Lisa (a newly arrived white professional couple; he is an architect, she is a school-teacher) and I were discussing their upcoming vacation to California. They were concerned about their house and wanted me to keep an eye on things. They lamented having to be so worried about break-ins but conceded that the Village was "not the suburbs." "If we have a break-in, they wouldn't know what to take; they wouldn't know the value of our things. I just worry about my Sony," Adam said with a laugh. From his tone of voice, his glance, and his nod toward Northton, it was clear that the would-be intruders, at least in his mind, were poor, ignorant, and black.

Coded or not, the collective definitions of "safe," "harmless," "trustworthy," "bad," "dangerous," and "hostile" become part of the Village perspective. Reports of personal experiences, including "close calls" and "horror stories," initiate and affirm neighborhood communion. At social gatherings, dinner parties, and the like, middle-class white Villagers mingle with other city dwellers and exchange stories about urban living. Conversation invariably turns to life in their neighborhoods—particularly its more forbidding aspects. Middle-class people commiserate, casting themselves and others they identify with in the role of victim. Recent stickups, rapes, burglaries, and harassment are subjects that get their attention, and they take note of where certain kinds of trouble are likely to occur and in what circumstances.

This type of communication enables residents to learn more about the streets, adding to what they have gleaned from experience. Though initially superficial, this information and the mental maps it helps form let strangers and residents of various life-styles and backgrounds navigate the Village streets with a reserve of social knowledge and a "working conception," a coherent picture, of local street life.

Neighborhood talk also affirms the belief that "city people" are somehow special, deserving commendation for tolerating the problems of being middle class in an environment that must be shared with the working class and the poor. "I'm convinced," one middle-class woman said while out on her porch fertilizing the geraniums, "that city people are just so much more ingenious." (She was discussing a friend who had moved out to one of the city's posh suburbs.) "We *have* to be," she concluded matter-of-factly.

PASSING BEHAVIOR

Even the deceptively simple decision to pass a stranger on the street involves a set of mental calculations. Is it day or night? Are there other people around? Is the stranger a child, a woman, a white man, a teenager, or a black man? And each participant's actions must be matched to the actions and cues of the other.

The following field note illustrates how well tuned strangers can be to each other and how capable of subtle gestural communication:

It is about 11:00 on a cold December morning after a snowfall. Outside, the only sound is the scrape of an elderly white woman's snow shovel on the oil-soaked ice of her front walk. Her house is on a corner in the residential heart of the Village, at an intersection that stands deserted between morning and afternoon rush hours. A truck pulls up directly across from the old lady's house. Before long the silence is split by the buzz of two tree surgeons' gasoline-powered saws. She leans on her shovel, watches for a while, then turns and goes inside. A middle-aged white man in a beige overcoat approaches the site. His collar is turned up against the cold, his chin buried within, and he wears a Russian-style fur-trimmed hat. His hands are sunk in his coat pockets. In his hard-soled shoes he hurries along this east-west street approaching the intersection, slipping a bit, having to watch each step on the icy sidewalk. He crosses the north-south street and continues westward.

A young black male, dressed in a way many Villagers call "streetish" (white high-top sneakers with loose laces, tongues flopping out from under creased gabardine slacks, which drag and soak up oily water; navy blue "air force" parka trimmed with matted fake fur, hood up, arms dangling at the sides) is walking up ahead on the same side of the street. He turns around briefly to check who is coming up behind him. The white man keeps his eye on the treacherous sidewalk, brow furrowed, displaying a look of concern and determination. The young black man moves with a certain aplomb, walking rather slowly.

From the two men's different paces it is obvious to both that either the young black man must speed up, the older white man must slow down, or they must pass on the otherwise deserted sidewalk.

The young black man slows up ever so slightly and shifts to the outside edge of the sidewalk. The white man takes the cue and drifts to the right while continuing his forward motion. Thus in five or six steps (and with no obvious lateral motion that might be construed as avoidance), he maximizes the lateral distance between himself and the man he must pass. What a minute ago appeared to be a single-file formation, with the white man ten steps behind, has suddenly become side-by-side, and yet neither participant ever appeared to step sideways at all.

In this intricate "ballet," to use Jane Jacobs's term (1961), the movements are patterned to minimize tension and allay fears and yet not openly express a breach of trust between the two parties. This "good behavior" is more conspicuous on the relatively well-defended east-west streets of the Village, where many white professionals tend to cluster and where blacks and whites often encounter each other. Such smooth gestural communication is most evident between blacks and whites traveling alone, especially during hours when the sidewalks are deserted. White Villagers' fears seem to run highest then, for that is when the opportunity for harrassment or mugging is greatest.

However, black male strangers confront problems of street navigation in similar ways. This field note illustrates some of the rules city dwellers must internalize:

At 3:00 Sunday morning I parked my car one street over from my home. To get to my front door, I now had to walk to the corner, turn up the street to another corner, turn again, and walk about fifty yards. It was a misty morning, and the streets were exceptionally quiet. Before leaving the car, I found my door key. Then, sitting in the parked car with the lights out, I looked up and down the street at the high bushes, at the shadows. After determining it was safe, I got out of the car, holding the key, and walked to the first corner. As I moved down the street I heard a man's heavy footsteps behind me. I looked back and saw a dark figure in a trench coat. I slowed down, and he continued past me. I said nothing, but I very consciously allowed him to get in front of me. Now I was left with the choice of walking about five feet behind the stranger or of crossing the street, going out of my way, and walking parallel

to him on the other side. I chose to cross the street.

All these actions fall in line with rules of etiquette designed to deal with such public encounters. First, before I left the safety of my car, I did everything possible to ensure speedy entrance into my home. I turned off the car lights, looked in every direction, and took my house key in hand. Second, I immediately looked back when I heard footsteps so that I could assess the person approaching. Next, I determined that the stranger could be a mugger in search of a victim—one of many possible identities, but naturally the one that concerned me most. I knew that at night it is important to defer to strangers by giving them room, so I established distance between us by dropping back after he passed me. Further, providing for the possibility that he was simply a pedestrian on his way home, I crossed the street to allow him clear and safe passage, a norm that would have been violated had I continued to follow close behind him.

When I reached the corner, after walking parallel to the stranger for a block, I waited until he had crossed the next street and had moved on ahead. Then I crossed to his side of the street; I was now about thirty yards behind him, and we were now walking away from each other at right angles. We moved farther and farther apart. He looked back. Our eyes met. I continued to look over my shoulder until I reached my door, unlocked it, and entered. We both continued to follow certain rules of the street. We did not cross the street simultaneously, which might have caused our paths to cross a second time. We both continued to "watch our backs" until the other stranger was no longer a threat.

In this situation skin color was important. I believe the man on the street distrusted me in part because I was black, and I distrusted him for the same reason. Further, we were both able-bodied and young. Although we were cautious toward each other, in a sense we were well matched. This is not the case when lone women meet strangers.

A woman being approached from behind by a strange man, especially a young black man, would be more likely to cross the street so that he could pass on the opposite side. If he gave any sign of following her, she might head for the middle of the street, perhaps at a slight run toward a "safe spot." She might call for help, or she might detour from her initial travel plan and approach a store or a well-lit porch where she might feel secure.

In numerous situations like those described above, a law-abiding, streetwise black man, in an attempt to put the white woman at ease, might cross the street or simply try to avoid encountering her at all. There are times when such men—any male who seems to be "safe" will do—serve women of any color as protective company on an otherwise lonely and forbidding street.

This quasi "with" is initiated by the woman, usually as she closely follows the man ahead of her "piggyback" style. Although the woman is fully aware of the nature of the relationship, the man is usually not, though he may pick up on it in the face of danger or demonstrable threat. The existence of this "with," loose and extended as it may be, gives comfort and promises aid in case of trouble, and it thereby serves to ward off real danger. Or at least the participants believe it does.

EYE WORK

Many blacks perceive whites as tense or hostile to them in public. They pay attention to the amount of eye contact given. In general, black males get far less time in this regard than do white males. Whites tend not to "hold" the eyes of a black person. It is more common for black and white strangers to meet each other's eyes for only a few seconds,

and then to avert their gaze abruptly. Such behavior seems to say, "I am aware of your presence," and no more. Women especially feel that eye contact invites unwanted advances, but some white men feel the same and want to be clear about what they intend. This eye work is a way to maintain distance, mainly for safety and social purposes. Consistent with this, some blacks are very surprised to find a white person who holds their eyes longer than is normal according to the rules of the public sphere. As one middle-aged white female resident commented:

Just this morning, I saw a [black] guy when I went over to Mr. Chow's to get some milk at 7:15. You always greet people you see at 7:15, and I looked at him and smiled. And he said "Hello" or "Good morning" or something. I smiled again. It was clear that he saw this as surprising.

Many people, particularly those who see themselves as more economically privileged than others in the community, are careful not to let their eyes stray, in order to avoid an uncomfortable situation. As they walk down the street they pretend not to see other pedestrians, or they look right at them without speaking, a behavior many blacks find offensive.

Moreover, whites of the Village often scowl to keep young blacks at a social and physical distance. As they venture out on the streets of the Village and, to a lesser extent, of Northton, they may plant this look on their faces to ward off others who might mean them harm. Scowling by whites may be compared to gritting by blacks as a coping strategy. At times members of either group make such faces with little regard for circumstances, as if they were dressing for inclement weather. But on the Village streets it does not always storm, and such overcoats repel the sunshine as well as the rain, frustrating many attempts at spontaneous human communication.

MONEY

Naturally, given two adjacent neighborhoods representing "haves" and "have-nots," there is tremendous anxiety about money: how much to carry, how to hold it, how to use it safely in public. As in other aspects of Village life, shared anecdotes and group discussions help newcomers recognize the underlying rules of comportment.

Perhaps the most important point of etiquette with regard to money in public places is to be discreet. For example, at the checkout counter one looks into one's wallet or purse and takes out only enough to cover the charge, being careful that the remaining contents are not on display. Further, one attempts to use only small bills so as not to suggest that one has large ones.

When walking on the streets at night, it is wise to keep some money in a wallet or purse and hide the rest in other parts of one's clothing—some in a jacket pocket, some in the back pocket of one's jeans, maybe even some in a sock. In this one way would not lose everything in a mugging, yet the mugger would get something to appease him.

A final rule, perhaps the most critical, is that in a potentially violent situation it is better to lose one's money than one's life. Thus the person who plans to travel at dangerous times or in dangerous areas should have some money on hand in case of an assault:

> It was 9:00 P.M., and the Christmas party had ended. I was among the last to leave. John [a forty-five-year-old professional], the host, had to run an errand and asked if I wanted to go with him. I agreed. While I was waiting, Marsha, John's wife, said in a perfectly serious voice, "Now, John, before you go, do you have $10 just in case you get mugged?" "No, I don't have it, do you?"
>
> Marsha fetched $10 and gave it to John as what was in effect protection money, a kind of consolation prize designed to cool out a prospective mugger. As we walked the three blocks

or so on the errand, John said, "We've come two blocks, and it's not so bad." His tone was that of a nervous joke, as though he really half expected to encounter muggers.

The reality of the Village is that residents can make their lives safer by "expecting" certain problems and making plans to cope with them. The mental preparation involved—imagining a bad situation and coming up with the best possible solution, acting it out in one's mind—may well be a valuable tool in learning to behave safely on the streets.

DOGS

Dogs play an important role in the street life of the Village. Whether they are kept as protectors or strictly as pets, their presence influences encounters between strangers. Many working-class blacks are easily intimidated by strange dogs, either off or on the leash. Such behavior may be related to social class values, attitudes, or past experiences with dogs. As one young black man said:

> I tell you, when I see a strange dog, I am very careful. When I see somebody with a mean-looking dog, I get very defensive, and I focus on him. I make sure, when the deal goes down, I'm away from it. I'll do what I have to do. But white people have a whole different attitude. Some of them want to go up and pet the dog. Some of these white people will come to the situation totally different from me.

In the working-class black subculture, "dogs" does not mean "dogs in the house," but usually connotes dogs tied up outside, guarding the backyard, biting trespassers bent on trouble. Middle-class and white working-class people may keep dogs in their homes, allowing them the run of the house, but many black working-class people I interviewed failed to understand such behavior. When they see a white adult on his knees kissing a dog, the sight may turn their stomachs—one more piece of evidence attesting to the peculiarities of their white neighbors.

Blacks seem inclined to see affection for dogs as reflecting race more than class—as telling something about whites in general. It may be that many working-class whites would be just as astounded to witness such "white" behavior toward dogs and might respond like poorer blacks. But as a general rule, when blacks encounter whites with dogs in tow, they tense up and give them a wide berth, watching them closely.

Sometimes a white person taking his dog for a morning stroll will encounter a black jogger, who may act very nervous when confronted by the pair. The jogger slows down and frowns at the dog's owner, who may be puzzled by this reaction toward his "playful young pooch." What began as a "good faith" meeting (a white man and a dog encountering a lone black male on a public street where the intentions of each party might not normally be thought suspect) evolves into a tense confrontation.

In what may seem to be an innocent situation, one can discern profound meaning. The white person and the black person, after repeated encounters of this sort, know something of what to expect; in effect, they become conditioned. The dog owner understands on some level what his animal means to others. The participants may even cooperate in dealing with the dog, passing easily and going about their business. The dog walker will continue on his route, perhaps feeling less afraid than he otherwise would, since the black person backed off and gave him and his dog a wide berth. These themes are expressed by a young black man from the general neighborhood:

I have this neighbor who lives across from me, he's a brother [black]. And the white girls [living] above me have a big, giant dog. The dog is huge! I don't know how they keep that big dog in their apartment, 'cause he's so huge. He's friendly, but he's huge. Well, my neighbor is very concerned about this dog. Boy, when that dog gets out in the courtyard, he gets very upset. He told me, now. He told me that he stayed inside one day when they brought the dog out. He wouldn't go outside until they got the dog out of the courtyard. He's very uptight about it. And he hates it when he's walking in the courtyard and the dog runs up on him. But the funny thing about it is that even though they kinda try to discourage the dog from jumping up on him, it happens anyway. Now, I ease up a little bit when I see the dog. It doesn't bother me as much as it does him.

It bothers me, 'cause he does jump up on you, and I don't like it, to be honest. I don't like no dog running up on me, even if he is tame, running up to me real fast. Well, Joe, my neighbor, gets very, very uptight about that. And it's funny, 'cause they know he gets uptight, and he knows that they know he gets uptight. And the whole thing just gets played out. In a certain way, they just mess with him, without even meaning anything bad by it, I think. It happens. But with me, they know that I'm not as uptight as he is. Yet for me they control the dog a certain way. They're able to grab him before he sees me. They can stop him. But with Joe, they just let the dog get all up on him. I don't know. They just let it play itself out.

Dog-related incidents become part of community lore. The company of a dog allows residents, particularly whites, to feel more secure on the street and gives them more power in anonymous black-white interactions.

To be sure, many white dog owners want to project a friendly presence on the streets, but in public interactions with blacks they find it difficult to do so. The following comments were made by a white Village woman:

I see how intimidating my dog is. I go out with my dog, and the blacks give me lots of room. I used to walk my son to school, and the children would be flying like leaves in the wind. Oh, the little kids. . . . The kids are hysterically afraid of dogs. For a long time the kids would just scream and run for their mothers, if their mothers were around, and we would have to go through the whole thing about how he was a nice dog. On the other hand, I thought I should not teach them to trust Duke, because where they were coming from, it was not a good thing. Because a lot of people of the community do use dogs to intimidate.

To be sure, defensive motives for owning dogs reflect a concern about crime and violence in the community. When young blacks see someone, white or black, approaching with a dog, they tend to steer wide of them. Some of the whites are amused by such observations; some are mildly ashamed, like the woman quoted above. Still others take advantage of this cultural difference, employing dogs all the more as agents of defense and protection. Some make a point of having their dogs unleashed, allowing the dog to run away and then calling him back, demonstrating control over the animal. They may order the dog to heel, as though he were a ferocious beast that must be controlled. Through such actions they emphasize their advantage in a potentially volatile public situation and thus assert a measure of control over the streets.

Caring for a dog in the city takes much work, but for many residents of the Village the rewards make it worthwhile. Dogs allow their owners to feel secure on the streets and in their homes. With dogs in tow people look smug, even relaxed, as they encounter strangers. White women with dogs tend not to hurry along when a car slows down beside them. With dogs, some residents will more readily greet strange blacks with a hello.

Dog walkers constitute a "use group" of residents who make Village streets safer for all kinds of people during the early morning hours before work, in the evenings before dinner, and late at night. At these times people who have come to "know" one another through their dogs form an effective neighborhood patrol. One can chart their routes and discover what dog walkers consider to be the neighborhood boundaries—what streets one does not cross with or without a dog.

George Lewis, for example, is a veteran white Villager who walks his beloved Irish setter each morning at 8:00. He comes out of his door with the eager dog on a leash and immediately heads for one of the north-south Village streets, for fewer front doors face these streets and residents are less likely to make a scene about where the setter "does his business." Mr. Lewis travels up to but never across or along Bellwether Street, separating Northton and the Village. Nor does he cross Warrington Avenue into the area known as Northton Annex, even to reach the only vacant lot of any size where a dog might be allowed to run. The lot is among a group of run-down buildings, and most Villagers, particularly whites, consider the whole area dangerous. The people who do use the vacant lot are primarily black dog walkers from Northton or the Village. Mr. Lewis is not the only Villager who avoids the vacant lot or any blocks north of Bellwether. Indeed, the general dog-walking route seems to involve very limited travel around two or three of the residential blocks in the heart of the Village.

By not walking their dogs across Bellwether or Warrington, the Villagers themselves help create and enforce lines of division between their own neighborhood and Northton. Although one usually thinks first of stone throwing or other forms of harassment as determining where boundaries are drawn, it is also through daily activities like dog walking that borders are made and remade by people on both sides of the dividing line.

Within the black community, dogs are used mainly as a means of protection, whereas the middle-class whites and blacks of the Village generally see them as pets as well. Some lower-class black dog owners consciously train their dogs to be vicious, thinking that the meaner the animal, the greater protection he affords. For some, viciousness is closely associated with the idea of control:

On Saturday morning at about 11:00, I was walking up Thirty-fourth Street when I saw a young black man accompanied by a full-grown Doberman. I noticed him in part because of his shouts at his dog. "Stop! Stop! You little bastard!" he shouted. He attracted the attention of a few passersby. Then, with fist balled up, he punched the dog in the side. The dog whined and cowered, but the young man continued to hit him, now with a switch. The dog still just whined and cowered.

Two young white women on the sidewalk across the street had stopped to watch. One put her hands to her cheeks in horror but said nothing; they seemed mesmerized by the scene. Others pretended not to notice. After a few minutes of this the man stopped, stood up and pointed to the curbs as he moved across the street. "Stay," he said. The dog was now very alert and stayed, his eyes on his master's every movement. When the man reached the other side of the street and had gone some distance down the next block, he slapped his right thigh. At that the sleek black dog bounded across the street like a shot.

I followed the two for some way, and when they reached the next corner the dog dutifully stopped. The man rubbed and patted the animal. Again the man crossed the street, and this time the dog kept his place until the man gave the signal for him to move. The performance gave meaning to the word masterful. For anyone observing this demonstration, the young man was in full control of his dog. And this was not just any old dog but a "vicious" Doberman. Accompanied by his dog, the young man was hardly someone to approach carelessly.

In this way a dog might be thought of not only as a protector, as an extension of oneself, but even as a potential weapon. The message here is, "I'm in control of my 'mean' dog, and if I tell him to, he will bite you." Consistent with this, such an individual may become upset when others are too friendly with his dog, thereby "spoiling him." This forms quite a contrast to the middle-class people of the Village, who encourage others, particularly children, to get to know animals and to be kind to them. This difference again represents a difference in culture that is influenced, if not determined, largely by the social class of the dog owner, not by skin color.

Recently a popular breed has emerged among those who display dogs aggressively. The pit bull is bred to fight other dogs; it is said that it will fight to the death. Among many young black men, this dog is considered meaner than the Doberman. Both are supposed to be ferocious; to tame such a dog reflects positively on the owner.

That control is important to the motives of the dog owner is not missed by a great number of blacks who see whites with dogs. The following account by a young black attests to this:

Now there's a black fellow who lives in my building. I don't know him at all. I just see him occasionally, we speak. You can see that he's well off, living in the building and all. And he drives like a Riviera. And he has two beautiful boxers. Yeah, they some beautiful dogs! It's funny, when he is outside with them, and they are displaying their obedience to him, sittin', heelin', runnin' back and forth, and listening to his commands. Two of them, now. The response that he gets from young black kids, he's a little older than me [thirty-five], they respect him to a certain extent. They like him. They see him on the streets, they talk to him, respect him, because he's got these animals and these animals will do what he says. And that's appealing to a lot of folks. You know, and he's gettin' a certain response from people 'cause he's got these dogs. He can go wherever he wants to go, long as he has those dogs.

In short, to be able to "control" a dog is often a mark of status on the streets, even among total strangers. Among many young blacks, the "meaner" the dog looks, presumably the more status or regard accrues to the master, particularly when the dog is off the leash. When dogs are used as weapons, the ante is raised in the potentially violent game of street life. The following episode, related by a young black man, illustrates this well:

Once a white guy came with two Dobermans. They don't give a shit about a human. He was walkin' down Bellwether Street. Everybody say, "What's he tryin' to prove?" He stopped at the corner, then walked up the street and came back down and stood on the other side of the corner. "What's up with him? He must be protectin'." So my friend, he go home and get a pistol. He says, "I'm gonna shoot him and both them dogs." That was his way of sayin' that man lookin' for trouble. He'd got beat up by two blacks two nights ago before he came down there. He wanted to see how tough they were when he had his two dogs. They go up to him and say, "What's up?" He said, "What the fuck you mean is up? Two niggers beat me up two nights ago." There was a lady lookin' out the window, she knew there was trouble and called the cops.

Another guy standin' with a rifle. That guy jumped when he saw that. He didn't know what to do then. [The guy with the rifle] said, "I'll kill you and both them motherfuckin' dogs. So why don't you try lettin' the dogs go, so we can kill both their asses, and you better know how to run." So that white man started to back off. You could tell he was scared. My friends had the guy and he was scared when he saw that. Them dogs ain't nothin' with guns. He let them go. He walked away. Then two police cars came up while he walkin' the street.

Somebody told them he come down here and try sic them dogs on people. So cops stopped him and said, "Hold that fuckin' dog." That's what the cop said. He told the cops what happened. [The cop] said, "You recognize any of the guys on the corner?" He said, "No." "Well, why don't you go down and arrest 'em?" He was a white cop, nice cop. But he gettin' to the point. Let's see who's wrong and right. "Where'd it happen?" "Thirty-fourth and Haverford." He wait on Thirty-eighth and Haverford. "What the fuck you doin' on Thirty-eighth and Haverford?" He didn't have nothin' to say. So the cop said, "Why don't you take your dogs and go back where you live at?" He went back to the Village. Cop came back and told us, "Turn 'round." That was all he told us, he just drove away. He knew the guy was wrong. My boy [friend] thanked the officer for bein' under-

standing. That was it. That's the way it is down there. Keep the peace. You got good cops and bad cops.

OTHER SAFETY RULES AND STRATEGIES

Dress is an important consideration when walking the Village streets, day or night. Women wear clothing that negates stereotypical "female frailty" and symbolizes aggressiveness. Unisex jackets, blue jeans, and sneakers are all part of the urban female costume. "Sexy" dresses are worn only when women are in a group, accompanied by a man, or traveling by car.

Village men also stick to practical, non-showy clothing. Most times this means blue jeans or a sweat suit. More expensive clothing is relegated to daytime work hours or, as for females, travel by car.

The safety of cars and things in them is a major worry. Newcomers learn to park on the east-west streets to avoid nighttime vandalism and theft. They buy "crime locks" and hood locks for their cars. They learn, sometimes through painful error, to remove attractive items like tape decks and expensive briefcases, or anything that looks valuable, before they lock up and leave.

Their homes may be similarly barricaded. They sometimes have chains for their bicycles, bars for their first-floor windows, and dead bolts for their back doors. Some install elaborate and expensive burglar alarms or keep dogs for the same purpose. They may build high fences to supplement the quaint waist-high wrought-iron fences from the early 1900s when the wealthy still claimed hegemony in the area.

Watching from the car as companions go into their houses is a standard precaution for city dwellers. The driver idles the motor out front and keeps an eye on the street until the resident has unlocked the door and is safely inside. This common practice has become ritualized in many instances, perhaps more important as a sign of a caring bond between people than as a deterrent of assault. It helps to make people feel secure, and residents understand it as a polite and intelligent action.

But some people are given to overreaction and to overelaboration of "mug-proofing" behaviors and are likely to see a potential mugger in almost anyone with certain attributes, most noticeably black skin, maleness, and youth. A middle-aged white woman told me this story:

> I had a white taxi driver drive me home once, and he was horrified at the neighborhood I lived in. It was night, and he told me what a horrible neighborhood I lived in, speaking of how dangerous it was here. He said, "This neighborhood is full of blacks. You'll get raped, you'll get murdered, or robbed." I replied, "I've lived here for a long time. I really like this neighborhood." He let me out on the opposite side of Thirty-fourth Street. He said, "OK, you go straight to your door, and I'll cover you." And he pulled out a gun. I said, "Please put it away." But he wouldn't. I was scared to death he was going to shoot me or something as I walked toward the house. It was so offensive to me that this man [did this], whom I trusted less than I trusted any of my neighbors, even those I knew only by sight. I felt sick for days.

The woman surmised that the taxi driver "must have been from a white ethnic and working-class background." It is commonly assumed among local blacks that such men feel especially threatened by blacks. But some middle- and upper-middle-class whites within the Village are susceptible to similar situational behavior.

INTERIORS OF PUBLIC SPACES

Public places such as bars, stores, or banks present a special case; the sense of intimidation and fear is somewhat lessened inside them. One might also expect the estrangement from one's fellows to dissipate and the contrived social distance to narrow, but this does not always happen. Generally, people of different races remain estranged, but they take careful mental notes about one another. It may be that the whites, particularly the newcomers, are more interested in the blacks because this integrated neighborhood represents something foreign to their experience. When whites are out in numbers, or when an otherwise forbidding black male is dressed in clothes that are unmistakably middle-class emblems, the whites are put somewhat at ease. In these circumstances they may "move in on" blacks, taking liberties such as asking the time or directions or even bumping into them without a nervous "excuse me."

Inside a business establishment it is easier to assume that others sharing the space, at least while inside, are committed to a certain level of civility. In the worst situation, one might be able to count on "limited warfare." The establishment, particularly if it has an armed guard, helps to ensure this, and customers may then be concerned to be sociable. If there are arguments or disagreements, they are rarely expected to result in violence. Hence the boldness that may be displayed inside, including smart remarks, arguments, and even punches, is not as likely to take place outside. Many such "fights" are ended when one person raises the stakes to a serious level by saying "Let's step outside!" On the street one cannot take civility and goodwill for granted or count on limited warfare.

STREET WISDOM

Those who rely on a simplistic etiquette of the streets are likely to continue to be ill at ease, because they tend not to pay close attention to the characteristics that identify a suspect as harmless. Rather, they envelop themselves in a protective shell that wards off both attackers and potential black allies, allowing the master status of male gender and black skin to rule. Such people often display tunnel vision with regard to all strangers except those who appear superficially most like themselves in skin color and dress.

This is a narrow and often unsatisfying way to live and to operate in public, and many of those who cannot get beyond stiff rules of etiquette decide in the end to move to safer, less "tricky" areas. But most people come to realize that street etiquette is only a guide for assessing behavior in public. It is still necessary to develop some strategy for using the etiquette based on one's understanding of the situation.

Once the basic rules of etiquette are mastered and internalized, people can use their observations and experiences to gain insight. In effect, they engage in "field research." In achieving the wisdom that every public trial is unique, they become aware that individuals, not types, define specific events. Street wisdom and street etiquette are comparable to a scalpel and a hatchet. One is capable of cutting extremely fine lines between vitally different organs; the other can only make broader, more brutal strokes.

A person who has found some system for categorizing the denizens of the streets and other public spaces must then learn how to distinguish among them, which requires a continuing set of assessments of, or even guesses about, fellow users. The streetwise individual thus becomes interested in a host of signs, emblems, and symbols that others exhibit in everyday life. Besides learning the "safety signals" a person might display— conservative clothing, a tie, books, a newspaper—he also absorbs the vocabulary and expressions of the street. If he is white, he may learn for the first time to make distinctions among different kinds of black people. He may learn the meaning of certain styles of hats, sweaters, jackets, shoes, and other emblems of the subculture, thus rendering the local environment "safer" and more manageable.

The accuracy of the reading is less important than the sense of security one derives from feeling that one's interpretation is correct. Through the interpretive process, the person contributes to his working conception of the streets. In becoming a self-conscious and sensitive observer, he becomes the author of his own public actions and begins to act rather than simply to react to situations. For instance, one young white woman had on occasion been confronted and asked for "loans" by black girls who appeared to "guard the street" in front of the local high school. One day she decided to turn the tables. Seeing the request coming, she confidently walked up to one of the girls and said, "I'm out of money. Could you spare me fifty cents?" The young blacks were caught off balance and befuddled. The woman went on, feeling victorious. Occasionally she will gratuitously greet strange men, with similar effect.

A primary motivation for acquiring street wisdom is the desire to have the upper hand. It is generally believed that this will ensure safe passage, allowing one to outwit a potential assailant. In this regard a social game may be discerned. Yet it is a serious game, for failing could mean loss of property, injury, or even death. To prevail means simply to get safely to one's destination, and the ones who are most successful are those who are "streetwise." Street wisdom is really street etiquette wisely enacted.

Among the streetwise, there is a common perspective toward street criminals, those who are "out there" and intent on violating law-abiding citizens. The street criminal is assumed to "pick his people," knowing who is vulnerable and who is not, causing some people to think that victimization is far from inevitable. This belief gives them confidence on the streets and allows them to feel a measure of control over their own fate. Indeed, avoiding trouble is often, though not always, within the control of the victim. Thus the victim may be blamed, and the streets may be viewed as yielding and negotiable. Consistent with this working conception of street life and crime, the task is to carry one-self in such a way as to ward off danger and be left alone. A chief resource is one's own person—what one displays about oneself. Most important, one must be careful.

Typically, those generally regarded as streetwise are veterans of the public spaces. They know how to get along with strangers, and they understand how to negotiate the streets. They know whom to trust, whom not to trust, what to say through body language or words. They have learned how to behave effectively in public. Probably the most important consideration is the experience they have gained through encounters with "every kind of stranger." Although one may know about situations through the reports of friends or relatives, this pales in comparison with actual experience. It is often sheer prox-imity to the dangerous streets that allows a person to gain street wisdom and formulate some effective theory of the public spaces. As one navigates there is a certain edge to one's demeanor, for the streetwise person is both wary of others and sensitive to the subtleties that could salvage safety out of danger.

The longer people live in this locale, hav-ing to confront problems on the streets and public spaces every day, the greater chance they have to develop a sense of what to do without seriously compromising themselves. Further, the longer they are in the area, the more likely they are to develop contacts who might come to their aid, allowing them to move more boldly.

This self-consciousness makes people likely to be alert and sensitive to the nuances of the environment. More important, they will project their ease and self-assurance to those they meet, giving them the chance to affect the interaction positively. For example, the person who is "streetdumb," relying for guidance on the most superficial signs, may pay too much attention to skin color and become needlessly tense just because the person approaching is black. A streetwise white who meets a black person will probably just go about his or her busi-ness. In both cases the black person will pick up the "vibe" being projected—in the first instance fear and hostility, in the second case comfort and a sense of commonality. There are obviously times when the "vibe" itself could tip the balance in creating the sub-sequent interaction.

CRISIS AND ADAPTATION

Sometimes the balance tips severely, and the whole neighborhood reacts with shock and alarm. A wave of fear surges through the community when violent crimes are reported by the media or are spread by word of mouth through the usually peaceful Village. One February a young woman, a new mother, was stabbed and left for dead in her home on one of the well-traveled north-south streets. Her month-old baby was unharmed, but it was weeks before the mother, recuperating in the hospital, remembered she had recently given birth. Word of how the stabbing occurred spread up and down the blocks of the Village. Neighbors said the woman often went out her back door to take out the gar-bage or call in the dog. But to uninitiated new-comers, the brick streets and large yards seem deceptively peaceful. Crises like these leave in their wake a deeper understanding of the "openness" that characterizes this quaint area of the city.

They also separate those who survive by brittle etiquette from those who—despite increased temporary precautions—can con-tinue to see strangers as individuals. Less than half a block away from the scene of the attack, in a building facing an east-west street, a friend of the young mother was overcome with fear. Her husband was sched-uled to go out of town the week after the vicious attack on her friend. She was so frightened that he had to arrange for a neighbor to "baby-sit" with his wife and children at night while he was away.

Security all over the Village was tightened for a time. People who used to go in and out, feeding the birds, shoveling walks, visiting their neighbors and friends, no longer came and went so carelessly. As the news traveled, fear rippled out from the young victim's immediate neighbors to affect behavior in other parts of the Village. One young black man reported that after the attack he was greeted with suspicious stares on his way to Mr. Chow's. "Everyone's looking over their shoulder suddenly," he said. "All black people are suspects."

"It makes you stop and wonder about living here," said one young mother shortly after the stabbing became the main item of conversation. "I've never lived in such a dangerous neighborhood. I run upstairs and leave my back door open sometimes. Like today, I got both kids and took them upstairs, and all of a sudden I said, 'Oh, no! I left the door unlocked!' and I just stopped what I was doing and ran downstairs to lock it." This kind of fear-induced behavior occurs as neighbors work out their group perspective on what is possible, if not probable, in the aftermath of such a crime.

Violence causes residents to tense up and begin taking defensive action again. They may feel uncomfortable around strangers on the streets, particularly after dark. They become especially suspicious of black males. An interview with a young black man from the area sheds some light on how residents react to neighborhood blacks shortly after a violent incident:

People come out of the door and they're scared. So when they see blacks on the streets they try to get away. Even ones who live right next door. All of a sudden they change attitudes toward each other. They're very suspicious. The guy that killed that lady and her

husband down on Thirty-fourth in the Village, he from the Empire [gang]. He tried to rape the lady right in front of the husband—he stabbed the husband and killed him. He'll get the electric chair now; they gave him the death penalty. They caught him comin' out. Wouldn't been so bad, the cops got another call to next door to where he did it at. She was screamin' and the cops heard and came around to the door.

After that happened, you could feel the vibes from whites. When things like that happen, things get very tense between blacks and whites. And you can feel it in the way they look at you, 'cause they think you might be the one who might do the crime. Everytime they see a black they don't trust 'em. Should stay in their own neighborhood.

That's the Village. They paranoid.

In time the fear recedes. Through successive documentations and neighborhood gossip, Villagers slowly return to some level of complacency, an acceptance of the risks of living in the city. Familiar people on the streets are "mapped" and associated with their old places, much as veteran Villagers have mapped them before. Streets, parks, and playgrounds are again made theirs. When these mental notations remain reliable and undisturbed for a time, a kind of "peace" returns. More and more can be taken for granted. Night excursions become more common. Children may be given a longer tether. Villagers gather and talk about the more pleasant aspects of neighborhood life. But they know, and are often reminded, that the peace is precarious, for events can suddenly shake their confidence again. Mr. Chow's gets robbed, or the Co-op, or someone is mugged in broad daylight.

One mugging was especially disturbing, for the victim was a pillar of stability, familiar on the streets. Mrs. Legget, the eighty-five-year-old white woman, was mugged *again*. As she took her usual afternoon walk, coming down one of the well-traveled north-south streets to her own east-west street, at the intersection near Mr. Chow's, several black girls approached her and demanded her money, which Mrs. Legget gave them. News of this crime reverberated throughout the neighborhood. People were shocked, particularly those from the middle-income white and black communities, but also those from other enclaves of the Village. Who would do such a thing? What sort of person would steal from an eighty-five-year-old lady? She was quite defenseless, with her frail body, failing eyesight, and disarming wit. She has been walking the neighborhood streets for years and is the sort of person "everybody knows"—at least by sight.

Neighbors identify with Mrs. Legget. They are aware of her plight and sympathize with her, even if they do not know her personally. Anyone who does any amount of walking in the neighborhood remembers "that frail old lady with a cane." She is a reference point by which many Villagers gauge their own security. If she can walk the streets, then others, visibly stronger (if less streetwise), can feel capable of maintaining the same rights of passage. Mrs. Legget's freedom of movement stood as a symbol of safety.

Now residents think, "If they'll do it to Mrs. Legget, they'll do it to anybody," and thus the mugging becomes an affront to the whole neighborhood. It transforms an amorphous group into a more consolidated community of "decent people." The neighbors begin to talk and ponder their group position in relation to others, particularly the group from which the muggers are thought to originate, the black youths of Northton, the Village, and other ghetto areas of the city.

People became more circumspect again after the attack on Mrs. Legget. Her daily public presence implied that law-abiding residents had at least partial hegemony over some of the streets during the daylight hours. After the attack, Villagers' plans for taking public transportation became more elaborate. One young woman, a tenant in the apartment building where Mrs. Legget has lived for twenty years, changed her plans to take the city bus home from the Greyhound bus terminal. Instead, she drove her car and paid to park it near the terminal, thus assuring herself of door-to-door transportation for her nighttime return from out of town. "There's a lot of crime going on right now," she told a friend. She was embarrassed, for she usually ridicules the block meetings and homeowners' gripes about theft and vandalism. But Mrs. Legget's mugging shook even the firmest believers in street safety.

Yet like the stabbing of the young mother, this incident eventually passed into memory for most Villagers. Time helps people forget even the most perilous incidents. Neighbors talk and socialize about other things. After a period of using the public spaces uneventfully, suspicion and distrust subside, but they never fade completely. Familiarity is rebuilt and a shared trust in the public spaces is gradually restored.

In this way social knowledge of the immediate area becomes assimilated as stories are shared and retold and a more refined group perspective emerges. This rebuilding of trust occurs by testing the public areas through careful walking and greater-than-usual scrutiny of strangers, particularly young black males. But always and inevitably, things gradually return to "normal." Otherwise life would simply require too much energy.

PART 2

Public Space as Power and Resistance

Introduction

Anthony M. Orum

The second model of public space takes an entirely different tack on the nature of such space. Instead of looking at social interaction, it focuses primarily upon the availability and overall structure of such space. It brings into broad relief the whole meaning of public space, questioning how public and how open such space actually is. This is a perspective that takes a darker and more cynical view of public space as compared to the rosy and optimistic view of those who speak of such space as civil order. The public world, in the eyes of those who see it in this manner, is like a battlefield. The lives of people who live in this world are at the mercy of the major social institutions, in particular those of the corporate world and the state. Such major institutions, it is thought, do not automatically serve the interests of the broad body of citizens but instead relentlessly encroach on them.

In most, though not all, cases, the main inspiration for this perspective seems to be Karl Marx. Even though Marx, of course, never wrote about public space, he assumed a deeply critical view of the institutions of the state and modern capitalism. Such institutions, he insisted, do not serve the interests of the public, but rather those of a small class of people. It was left to Henri Lefebvre, who followed in Marx's political and theoretical path, to articulate the ways in which social institutions could produce and thus structure social space. Lefebvre argued that in the modern world space has come to occupy a signature role; in effect, the Marxist problematic of the production of commodities should be replaced by a problematic organized around the production of social space. How cities, and even how dwellings, are constructed, for example, tells us much about the nature of the civilizations and societies that construct them. Moreover, the structure of such space exercises a profound influence on all manner of social activity, from the everyday journeys that people make to work to the ways in which people represent, or think about, their world. And behind such structures lay the legacy of history and the conscious practices by social institutions.

Though Lefebvre is often frustratingly elusive and abstract about how all of this works, he comes closest to providing a clear illustration when he writes of the Spanish-American town:

> The Spanish-American colonial town is of considerable interest in this regard. The foundation of these towns in a colonial empire went hand in hand with the production of a vast space, namely that of Latin America. . . . The very building of the towns . . . embodied a plan which would determine the mode of occupation of the territory and define how it was to be reorganized under the administrative and political authority of urban power. The orders stipulate exactly how the chosen sites ought to be developed. The result is a strictly hierarchical organization of space, a gradual progression outwards from the town's centre, beginning with the *ciudad* and reaching out to the surrounding

pueblos. The plan is followed with geometrical precision: from the inevitable Plaza Mayor a grid extends indefinitely in every direction. Each square or rectangular lot has its function assigned to it, while inversely each function is assigned its own administrative buildings, town gates, squares, streets, port installations, warehouses, town hall, and so on. Thus a high degree of segregation is superimposed upon a homogenous space. (1991: 150–51)

Towns, dwellings, squares, all of these places designed and inhabited by human beings, and their relationship and juxtaposition to one another in space, constitute the social production of such space. And they reveal the clear though often unrecognized practices of major institutions, whether of foreign powers, as in this instance, or of major economic institutions, as in the instance of modern capitalism.

Institutions and their social designs, moreover, play a key role in configuring the nature of public space and how it may be related to private space, Lefebvre observed. He writes that under the Japanese notion of *shin-gyo-sho*, public areas (the spaces of social relationships and actions) are connected up with private areas (spaces for contemplation, isolation and retreat) via "mixed" areas (linking thoroughfares, etc.). The term *shin-gyo-sho* thus embraces three levels of spatial and temporal, mental and social organization, levels bound together by relationships of reciprocal implication. . . . The "public" realm, the realm of temple or palace, has private and "mixed" aspects, while the "private" house or dwelling has public (e.g. reception rooms) and "mixed" ones. Much may be said of the town as a whole. Public space, that area in which people encounter others and engage in social interaction and the formation of social relationships, thus cannot be taken as a given, but rather is constantly created and configured by social designs, plans, representations and, in general, the productive activities of a society, its people and institutions.

By extension, then, this perspective implies that one cannot appreciate the nature of public space only by systematically observing the relationships and activities of people within such space, as those who view such space as civil order assume. Rather, one must examine and disclose the structural determinants of such public space and how it relates to the dominant activities both of the state—a public institution—and of business and commercial interests—the private interests under modern capitalism.

This perspective is also historically situated and conditioned. Public space is always and everywhere contested space—power struggles animate the interests of dominant institutions and of the everyday collective actors frequently aligned in resistance against those institutions. As the modern world has evolved, the interests of private property as well as those of the modern state have come increasingly to dominate the interests of citizens. Institutions take on a life of their own, and they do not serve to advance the interests of all members of society. People of privilege and people of power generally are served best by such institutions. Jane Jacobs, for example, possessed a similar distaste for modern institutions, but mainly those of urban planners, claiming they did not serve the best interests of urban residents. The main difference between her view and that of those who view public space as the site of power is that the latter writers often do not care about, nor are they particularly interested in learning of, the ways that people actually live and reside in the everyday world. Instead, for their evidence they turn to the broad spectrum of history. Indeed, that space which is public, they argue, increasingly has been appropriated by private as well as by state authorities and thus it is diminishing in its availability to the broad swath of citizens in modern society. The modern state, in particular, operates in ways to severely curtail both the boundaries and the availability of such elements as public parks, plazas, sidewalks and streets.

The urban geographer Don Mitchell, for instance, has written persuasively about the ways in which the modern institutions of the state redefine the nature of the "public" and the rights associated with public property. He brings out sharply and clearly the contested nature of public space as well as the political practices by which the state defines space as public, and thus open and accessible to people. However, often the state will consciously not define space in that manner. He maintains that, in principle, all people are entitled to use public space, like parklands, thus echoing Lefebvre who invoked the idea that everyone has "the right to the city." In a sharp and compelling review of recent court rulings, he shows the ways in which rulings on public protests, such as those against abortion clinics, have redefined the nature of public space in such a manner as to diminish its breadth and limit its availability to citizens, in general. Mitchell's greatest attention is devoted to the ways in which the state and local businesses create a new and powerless class of homeless people. He argues that parklands, like that of People's Park in Berkeley, California, must be made available to people who are homeless because, like all citizens, they can claim a basic and fundamental right to home and shelter—a human right. Among the central political struggles, in Mitchell's view, in modern society are struggles over the public space and shelter that homeless people may occupy. His is a view which is rooted fundamentally in the belief that public power today often abuses people who, themselves, are powerless to resist the broad hand of state authority.

Setha Low, Director of the Project on Public Space at City University of New York, has undertaken a number of empirical studies about how people use such sites as parks or plazas. Her argument, similar to that of Mitchell, is that these areas often are inaccessible to members of the public. Along with several associates, she has conducted research on parks and beaches in the United States, and here too she discovers that many public spaces like these are not at all readily accessible to members of the public. Her voice rings with some of the same moral indignation as that of Jacobs, but her claim is that members of various ethnic minorities tend to use the space in public areas differently than other people. Some ethnic minorities tend to congregate around special areas, or assemble in groups, and yet the design of such public spaces, originally done for a largely white population, does not facilitate their gatherings. Low, rather than emphasizing the actual workings of social relationships in everyday life, argues that if spaces are indeed public they must be open, in principle, to all citizens, or at least they must accommodate the special and unique ways that some people use such spaces. She and her colleagues conclude their work by echoing the ideal of the great landscape architect, Frederick Law Olmsted, who believed that parks are the site where democracies are built. "Even more than in Olmsted's day," they write, "large parks and beaches are so important for their ability to bring together diverse groups where, as Olmsted argued, they can encounter each other in an open and inviting atmosphere . . . (because) . . . democracy consists of people engaging with one another to make community" (2005: 210).

The political edge to Low's work is especially evident in her writings on gated communities. Here she extends the path breaking research of the political scientist, Evan McKenzie. McKenzie writes about what he calls "privatopia," the gated communities and other common-interest developments that have arisen in large numbers across America. Such communities emerge, he argues, because wealthy residents want, in effect, to create a fortress between themselves and the rest of the population. And the way they can do that, he insists, is to create a new kind of private community, a community behind high walls and protected by its own private security guards. More and more, as time has passed, such communities are arising across America as well as other parts of the world. At last count, according to the recent book by Edward J. Blakely and Mary Gail Snyder, there are 20,000 such communities in the United States. And, as new communities arise, they develop their own private and exclusive "public" spaces, like parks, green spaces and playgrounds, spaces that are available only to their members and to no one else. They have produced their own version of public grounds and, in so doing, they have effectively seceded from the larger cities and metropolitan areas of which they are a part.

Even those parks, plazas and other public grounds that are open today to the public, and presumably free and accessible, are changing, becoming ever more subject to control by local and state authorities. Mike Davis, in a powerful indictment of modern Los Angeles, observes how various means of surveillance are being increasingly used by public authorities to exercise control over public spaces. Davis insists that Los Angeles, like other major metropolitan areas, has gradually taken on the character of a war-zone, and that the police and other local authorities are gradually reducing the amount of public spaces where people can freely gather. Sharon Zukin, observing changes in Bryant Park in New York City, writes how local security guards have come to control the comings and goings of people in this area. Not only is the area no longer freely accessible and open to people, but it actually now is closed early in the evenings. Both Zukin and Davis believe that the general tendency in the modern city is for public authorities to limit and define where the public—i.e. the citizens and residents— actually can gather. And the net effect, of course, of such carefully defined limits is to reduce the sense of connection, and with it, the sense of a civil community among the inhabitants of the city.

Moreover, it is not only the police and other local authorities that are decisively reshaping the use of public spaces in the downtown areas of major metropolitan sites. It is the private developers of major office and residential towers as well. Gregory Smithsimon, in a follow-up to the work of William Whyte, investigates the use of *bonus plazas* in New York City. Such plazas provide open space to the public. They take their name from the fact that in return for securing permission to construct taller buildings, developers agree to create more open public spaces around their buildings where people can gather. But the problem is, as Smithsimon finds, people rarely are able to use such spaces. As Smithsimon writes in his piece included in this collection, "most (developers) take the opportunity to use designs that exclude users from the spaces."

Those of us who observe public spaces find there is considerable truth to this line of argument. Most recently, the events of September 11, 2001 dramatically changed the way people thought of the city and of their personal safety. Both local and national governments have increased the various measures and implements of security, adding numbers of new police officers, providing new ways of prohibiting access to the city, and taking a number of other steps. Public space, in other words, is actually no longer as open and as available to everyone as it once was. And yet, it is characteristic of those writers who view public space in this manner that they tend to accentuate these darker elements to public life. Theirs is a view with an edge; and while those who view public space as civil order frequently point to the vitality evident in the everyday relationships of people on the streets, those who see public space as exploitation and oppression can only see the cameras, police and other means of surveillance and social control on those very same streets.

In my own recent travels and observations in China, I found many elements in Shanghai and elsewhere that appear to confirm the truth to this view of public space. In Shanghai, for example, as the wealthy and middle-class population has expanded, more and more private, secluded and guarded communities are being built. In South Shanghai, there is one such private gated community. It is occupied by a number of middle-class and upper middle-class residents, including both older ones and many younger ones with children. Vanke Holiday Town satisfies all the usual criteria for what we in America call a gated community. People can only enter by showing their credentials to police who occupy guardhouses. The only individuals who can use the public spaces in the Town—which, by contrast to the rest of their surroundings in nearby Shanghai are quite beautiful and large, including very nice walkways along green areas, a river with benches on its banks, and a number of spaces devoted exclusively to young children—are residents of Vanke Holiday Town. Although the area feels open and unprotected, as a friend and I were walking on the sidewalks, taking pictures, a guard came over to us and wanted to know what we were doing. We were strongly reprimanded by the guard and advised not to take pictures. Later in our walk to the commercial area of Vanke Holiday Town, another guard came over to us to check on what we were doing. Though friendly, he wanted to be certain we were doing nothing wrong. Sites like Vanke Holiday Town are now planned for other parts of Shanghai.

The larger metropolis of Shanghai, like many other cities in China, is filled with a multitude of different kinds of guards, some of the regular military and some that just belong to private security forces. A mall, Wan Da Plaza, was just recently built near to Fudan University where I taught. There are several notable things about Wan Da Plaza. It has a multitude of high-end stores, including furniture and jewelry stores, unusual for Shanghai's outlying areas. But these stores tend to be vacant and empty, in great contrast to the Wal-Mart Store that recently opened in the same area. And everywhere one looks, various private security forces can be found. So, immediately, one might conclude, alas, public space is indeed a space of power and domination, but especially that public space which surrounds newly-emerged private commercial spaces in the People's Republic of China.

However—and here I am compelled to sound a slight discordant note to this otherwise seamless portrait of public space as power and domination—if one looks closely at the behavior of the guards a different sort of picture emerges. The guards, while carrying nightsticks in some instances, do not seem to wield them recklessly. In fact, many of the guards simply stand around; they are armed, but it is not so much their actions as their presence that would seem to be a deterrent on the mall battleground of public space. In the several months that I spent in Shanghai, and in all the many occasions I went to Wan Da Plaza, I never saw any guard engage in any kind of action against a customer, nor, with one exception, any kind of fight or other obvious display of struggle. The security forces were there, present and accounted for, much like the small benches in the plaza of the Mall, as a part of the background. And pedestrians and customers for the most part seemed to ignore them, attending to their own daily comings-and-goings.

There are many public spaces across the world today, it appears, where issues of power and resistance take place, reshaping the character of the public space at the same time as it helps people to create and affirm their own collective identities. Lisa Law writes about the gatherings of Filipina women in Statue Square, a central site in Hong Kong where major political and financial institutions are housed. The women work during the week as domestic workers, but during their free time on the weekends, they gather to chat and talk, and create a small diaspora for themselves. In doing so, they also raise issues of the rights to that space, and public authorities, Law finds, have made it more difficult for the women to gather and use it. Law goes into great detail about how immigrants have begun to transform the social spaces of Hong Kong into political spaces—ones that become contested between the new residents, such as the Filipina women, and the local authorities. These sorts of transformations, and contests over the use of public spaces, are only likely to expand in time as more and more immigrants make their way across national borders from their homelands into their new places of residence and work.

The image of public space as the site of power and resistance shares as great a popular following today as the image of such space as the site of civil order. Indeed, judging from recent writings it may be even more in vogue, and growing ever more so as time passes. Writers such as Mike Davis, Don Mitchell and Sharon Zukin certainly seem to be more fashionable than figures like Jane Jacobs and William Whyte. Yet, we believe, it always remains an open and strictly empirical question whether any instance of public space, say a park or a plaza, is more like a battlefield than a playground, in other words, more like a site of power and resistance than a space wherein civil order is created and sustained over time.

FOR DISCUSSION

Has the amount of public space where you live increased or diminished in recent years? Why? Are there surveillance cameras that are used to monitor public space like parks or street corners? How are different groups, like the homeless or middle-class families, treated when they use public spaces?

The End of Public Space? People's Park, Definitions of the Public, and Democracy

Don Mitchell

STRUGGLING OVER THE NATURE OF PUBLIC SPACE: THE VOLLEYBALL RIOTS

On the morning of August 1, 1991, about twenty activists, hoping to stop a joint University of California (UC) and City of Berkeley plan to develop People's Park, were arrested as bulldozers cleared grass and soil for two sand volleyball courts. By that evening, police and Park "defenders" were battling in the streets over whether work on People's Park could proceed. Rioting around the Park continued for the better part of a week. Police repeatedly fired wooden and putty bullets into crowds and reports of police brutality were widespread (including the witnessed beating of a member of the Berkeley Police Review Commission). But neither did protesters refrain from violence, heaving rocks and bottles filled with urine at the police.[1]

The bulldozers (along with their police reinforcement) represented the first step in a UC and City agreement that, many hoped, would settle conclusively the disposition of People's Park, the site of more than twenty years of continual conflict between the City, UC, local activists, merchants, and homeless people. For those who sought to stop Park development, People's Park represented one of the last truly public spaces in the city— "this nation's only liberated zone," as the People's Park Defense Union called it (Rivlin

1991a:3). Any attempt to develop the land by either the University or the City was seen as a threat to the public nature of the Park.

To be sure, the public status of People's Park has always been in doubt. The property is owned by UC, which had acquired the site through eminent domain in 1967, ostensibly to build dormitories. Although lacking funds to construct the dormitories, the University quickly demolished the houses on the property. For the next two years, the land stood vacant, save for usage as a muddy parking lot. In 1969, an alliance of students, community activists, and local merchants challenged the University and laid claim to the land. Their goal was to create a user-controlled park in the midst of a highly urbanized area that would become a haven for those squeezed out by a fully regulated urban environment (Mitchell 1992a). UC responded to the founding of People's Park by erecting a fence around the Park and excluding those who sought to use it. Activists countered with mass protests that rapidly escalated into the 1969 riots that for many have come to symbolize Berkeley. Park founders argued forcefully and violently for resistance against powerful governmental agencies, police forces, and the expansion of corporate control over the fabric of cities (Mitchell 1992a). And, to a degree, they won. The police and the University were eventually vanquished,[2] and their power over the parcel of land known as People's Park has been minimal ever since.

Nevertheless, the University has maintained ownership of the land, frequently announcing plans for its imminent "improvement." The political reality has been otherwise. People's Park represents for activists an important symbol of political power (Mitchell 1992a), and they have been able to maintain the Park as originally envisioned: as a haven for persons evicted by the dominant society (cf. Deutsche 1990), as a place of political activism, and as a symbolic stronghold in the on-going struggles between university planners and city residents (Lyford 1982). But in 1989, the University, sensing a changing political climate reflected in a moderation of the Berkeley City Council and a remission of activism by UC students during the 1980s, decided that it finally possessed the political strength to take firmer control of the land. Since neither the Berkeley City Council nor Park activists would tolerate a complete elimination of the Park, the University entered into negotiations with the City over plans to build recreation facilities for student use, while retaining portions of the Park for community use. Throughout these negotiations, UC emphasized that it had every intention of maintaining People's Park as a park. But now it would be a park in which inappropriate activities— "the criminal element" in the University's words (Boudreau 1991:A3)—would be removed to make room for students and middle-class residents who, the University argued, had been excluded as People's Park became a haven for "small-time drug dealers, street people, and the homeless" (Lynch 1991b:A12).

To accomplish this goal, the City and UC agreed to a seemingly innocuous development plan. UC agreed to lease the east and west ends of the Park to the City for $1 per year for five years ("on a trial basis") for community use. Meanwhile, the central portion of the Park (the large grassy area where many homeless people slept and the traditional place for concerts and political organizing) would be converted into a recreational area replete with volleyball courts, pathways, public restrooms, and security lights. In exchange for the lease, the City would assume "primary responsibility for law enforcement on the premises." The plan also called for the establishment of a joint City-University "Use Standards and Evaluation Advising Committee" designed to "bring about a much-hoped-for truce, and realization of the place as a park that everyone can enjoy" (Kahn 1991a:28). While these developments seemed modest, all agreed that they portended much greater change. "To be sure," the suburban *Contra Costa Times* (Boudreau 1991:A3) commented, "the one-of-a-kind swath of untamed land will never be the same. And to that extent, an era is ending."

After more than twenty years of riot, debate, controversy, neglect, and broken promises, the end of the era marked by the City-UC agreement seemed long overdue for many in Berkeley and the Bay Area. To critics of the Park in the city government and the university administration as well as in the mainstream national and local press, the need for improvement in the Park was a common theme. "To some park neighbors and students, People's Park, owned by the university, is overrun with squatters, drug dealers and the like" (Boudreau 1991:A3). In the words of UC's Director of Community Affairs, Milton Fujii: "The park is underutilized. Only a small group of people use the park and they are not representative of the community" (*New York Times* 1991a:1.39). Similarly, UC spokesperson Jesus Mena declared: "We have no intention to kick out the homeless. They will still be there when the park changes, but without the criminal element that gravitates toward the park" (Boudreau 1991:A3). For these critics, the evident disorder of the Park invited criminality and excluded legitimate, "representative" users. Illegitimate behavior, coupled with the scruffy appearance of the Park, confirmed that People's Park was a space that had to be reclaimed and redefined for "an appropriate public."

For opponents of the UC-City development plan, however, People's Park constituted one of the few areas in the San Francisco Bay Area in which homeless people could live relatively unmolested (Kahn 1991a:2). For them, People's Park was working as it should: as truly a public space. It was a political space that encouraged unmediated interaction, a place where the power of the state could be held at bay. Activists felt that the accord jeopardized some of the Park institutions that had developed over the years: the grassy assembly area, the Free Speech stage, and the Free Box (a clothes drop-off and exchange). Without these, they felt that People's Park would cease to exist. According to Michael Delacour, one of the founders of the Park in 1969, the defense of People's Park was "still about free speech, about giving people a place to go and just be, to say whatever they want" (Lynch and Dietz 1991:A20). This aspect of the Park—the ability for people "to go and just be"—was inextricably connected to issues of homelessness. For those opposed to the UC-City plan, People's Park since its inception had been regarded as a refuge for the homeless and other streetpeople. Activists feared that the building of volleyball courts struck at the heart of the Park's traditional role. Changes in the Park that led to the removal of homeless people, they surmised, were tantamount to an erosion of public space.

Homeless residents in the Park agreed. In her reply to a reporter who asked her about the UC-City plans, Virginia, a homeless woman living in the Park, voiced the fears of many homeless people in the Park and of Park activists: "You know what this is about as well as I do. It's only a matter of time before they start limiting the people able to come here to college kids with an ID."

When the reporter reminded her that the University promised not to remove the homeless, Virginia responded: "You look smarter than that. A national monument is being torn down" (Rivlin 1991a:27). Oakland Homeless Union activist Andrew Jackson put the struggles over People's Park into a larger context: "They're tearing up a dream.... Ever since I remember this has been a place to come. It's been a place for all people, not just for some college kids to play volleyball or the white collar. It's a place to lie down and sleep when you're tired" (ibid). And for Duane, a homeless man who lived in the Park, the 1991 riots were specifically about the rights of homeless people: "This is about homelessness, and joblessness, and fighting oppression" (Koopman 1991:A13).

Activists considered changes in the Park to be related to changes on nearby Telegraph Avenue, long a center of the "counterculture" in the Bay Area. Activists feared that the Park would become a beachhead for the wholesale transformation of the surrounding neighborhood. "The university says they're not against homeless people," commented homeless activist Curtis Bray soon after the City-UC accord was announced:

> but all the rules and regulations that are coming out for the park are regulations that only affect the homeless community and no one else.... They don't want their students to be faced on a daily basis with what it is like to be poor and in poverty. Once they get the cement courts in, they're going to want to keep the homeless population out as much as possible.
>
> (Kahn 1991a:2, 28)

Bray predicted that the agreement on People's Park was just the beginning. "Once People's Park is off-limits, the homeless are going to go to [Telegraph] Avenue. The university will then say the Avenue is a problem" (ibid). David Nadle, another founder of the Park and an owner of a world-beat dance club in Berkeley, concurred. He denounced the City-UC agreement as a final move toward the total commodification and control of space. "The corporate world is trying to take Berkeley. The park is at the center of that struggle, because the park represents a 22-year struggle over corporate expansion." Berkeley, he claimed, had become "yupped out" (Kahn 1991b:30).

Telegraph Avenue had, in the years since the 1969 People's Park riots, experienced a series of transformations. A popular gathering point for Bay Area teens, the Telegraph Avenue-People's Park area experienced several street disturbances during the latter part of the 1980s. The twentieth anniversary of the 1969 riots, for example, was marked by rock throwing and window smashing (*Los Angeles Times* 1989a:13; *New York Times* 1989a:1.26). But the Avenue also remained a vibrant shopping district, catering to affluent students and young professionals in the 1980s. By the mid-1980s, corporate retail outlets had grown at the expense of locally owned businesses.[3] And upscale bars and restaurants had begun to compete with used bookstores, coffee houses, and businesses catering to students. Coffee bars that appealed to the slumming suburban middle classes replaced the small restaurants and "head" shops that marked an earlier era. Graffiti- and poster-covered walls were partially replaced with pastel colors and tasteful neon.

Moreover, as the boom times of the 1980s turned to the bust of the early 1990s, many students in the South Campus area had little time or patience for street spectacle or street activism. Both the Park and Telegraph Avenue reflected these changes in political and economic climate. "In a city where protesting was once as common as jogging," wrote the *San Francisco Chronicle* (Lynch and Dietz 1991:A1), "there is little tolerance for uprisings." As Park activist Michael Delacour observed, "[t]he students have changed. They know times are tough and they want to survive" (Lynch and Dietz

1991:A20). Time was scarce for activism and the community involvement that make spaces like People's Park possible.[4] Many students simply avoided the "untamed land" of People's Park.

In the early 1990s, some of the chain stores moved out of Telegraph Avenue, and an air of dilapidation permeated this business strip (May 1993:6). While many Avenue merchants attributed decline to the continual hazards posed by People's Park, officials of the Telegraph Avenue Merchants Association conceded that the Park's image was more threatening to business than the realities of rioting and homeless populations. One official, after affirming that crime was not more prevalent in and around the Park than elsewhere in the city, quickly added that perception was much more important than actuality. "If the majority of people think it's unsafe, unclean, why do they think that? Isn't it based on some sort of reality?" (Kahn 1991a:28). For this official, such perceptions were manifested in the declining traffic of what the merchants considered the neighborhood's legitimate public: the shoppers, the students, and the housed.

In their efforts to reverse these perceptions, the City and the University eventually resorted to violence in early August of 1991; Park protesters responded in kind. The papers of that week are filled with reports of street skirmishes, strategic advances by heavily armed police, and the rage felt by many protesters. Police were accused of beating bystanders, roughing-up homeless residents of the Park, and using wood and putty bullets needlessly. Protesters threw rocks and bottles, smashed windows, and lit street fires. By August 6, eight formal complaints of police brutality had been filed with the Police Review Commission and six with the police department itself. A Police Commission member had received fifty statements alleging police abuse and the Commission received another twenty-five calls of complaint. In addition, an unknown number of police were injured in the rioting (Rivlin 1991b: 18).

"We offered to negotiate," club owner David Nadle claimed, "but this is what we got. Militarily, they have commandeered that part of the park"—the center zone with the Free Speech area, the stage, the human services, and the free boxes (Kahn 1991c:11). The occupation had succeeded. Rioting had all but subsided by Saturday night, and Park defenders conceded defeat. At a rally of protestors in the Park on August 4, Park founder and activist Michael Delacour declared: "Basically we've got no choice over what happens in this park anyway" (Auchard 1991:23).

Four days later, the first volleyball games were played in People's Park. Seeking to cement what one Park defender earlier called "dominion, imposing solutions for other people's own good" (*New York Times* 1991c:A8), university officials released student employees from their jobs provided that they would play volleyball in the Park. One of the players, a Berkeley junior and housing office employee, told the *San Francisco Chronicle* (Lynch 1991c:A20): "At first, I thought 'OK, let's go play volleyball.' But then I realized there is more at stake and I got a little scared. But I came out here because I want to see this happen and show my support. People's Park needs to change. I've only been here once before—most people think this place isn't safe." That evening at 7 p.m., despite the absence of "disturbances" since the previous Saturday, police arrested sixteen people for trespassing after the Park—which the University asserted they planned to retain as "open space"—was closed (*ibid*).

ENVISIONING PUBLIC SPACE

The Berkeley housing employee was right. There was a lot more at stake in People's Park than volleyball. Two opposed, and perhaps irreconcilable, ideological visions of the nature and purpose of public space were evident in the words of homeless people, activists, merchants, and city and university officials as they sought to explain the long and sometimes violent struggles over People's Park. Activists and the homeless people who used the Park promoted a vision of a space marked by free interaction and the absence of coercion by powerful institutions. For them, public space was an unconstrained space within which political movements can organize and expand into wider arenas (Mitchell 1992a; Smith 1992a; 1993). The vision of representatives of the University (not to mention planners in many cities) was quite different. Theirs was one of open space for recreation and entertainment, subject to usage by an appropriate public that is *allowed* in. Public space thus constituted a controlled and orderly *retreat* where a properly behaved public might experience the spectacle of the city. In the first of these visions, public space is taken and remade by political actors; it is politicized at its very core; and it tolerates the risks of disorder (including recidivist political movements) as central to its functioning. In the second vision, public space is planned, orderly, and safe. Users of this space must be made to feel comfortable, and they should not be driven away by unsightly homeless people or unsolicited political activity. These visions, of course, are not unique to Berkeley; they are in fact the predominant ways of seeing public space in contemporary cities.[5]

These two visions of public space correspond more or less with Lefebvre's distinction between *representational space* (appropriated, lived space; space-in-use) and *representations of space* (planned, controlled, ordered space).[6] Public space often, though not always, originates as a representation of space, as for example a court-house square, a monumental plaza, a public park, or a pedestrian shopping district (Harvey 1993; Hershkovitz 1993). But as people use these spaces, they also become representational spaces, appropriated in use. This standard chronology was reversed, however, in the case of People's Park. It began as a representational space, one that had been *taken* and appropriated from the outset. Whatever the origins of any public space, its status as "public" is created and maintained through the ongoing opposition of visions that have been held, on the one hand, by those who seek order and control and, on the other, by those who seek places for oppositional political activity and unmediated interaction.

Yet public spaces are also, and very importantly, *spaces for representation*. That is, public space is a place within which a political movement can stake out the space that allows it to be *seen*. In public space, political organizations can represent themselves to a larger population. By claiming space in public, by creating public spaces, social groups themselves become public. *Only* in public spaces can the homeless, for example, represent themselves as a legitimate part of "the public." Insofar as homeless people or other marginalized groups remain invisible to society, they fail to be counted as legitimate members of the polity. And in this sense, public spaces are absolutely essential to the functioning of democratic politics (Fraser 1990). Public space is the product of competing ideas about what constitutes that space —order and control or free, and perhaps dangerous, interaction—and who constitutes "the public." These are not merely questions of ideology, of course. They are rather questions about the very spaces that make political activities possible. To understand, therefore, why the struggles over People's Park turned violent, why people can be so passionate about spaces like these, we need to re-examine the normative ideals that drive political activity and the nature of the spaces we call "public" in democratic societies.

THE IMPORTANCE OF PUBLIC SPACE IN DEMOCRATIC SOCIETIES

Public space occupies an important ideological position in democratic societies. The notion of urban public space can be traced back at least to the Greek *agora* and its function as: "the place of citizenship, an open space where public affairs and legal disputes were conducted ... it was also a marketplace, a place of pleasurable jostling, where citizens' bodies, words, actions, and produce were all literally on mutual display, and where judgements, decisions, and bargains were made" (Hartley 1992:29–30). Politics, commerce, and spectacle were juxtaposed and intermingled in the public space of the agora. It provided a meeting place for strangers, whether citizens, buyers, or sellers, and the ideal of public space in the agora encouraged nearly unmediated interaction—the first vision of public space noted above. In such "open and accessible public spaces and forums," as Young (1990:119) has put it, "one should expect to encounter and hear from those who are different, whose social perspectives, experience and affiliations are different."

Young's definition represents more nearly a normative ideal for public space than an empirical description of the ways that public spaces have functioned in "actuality existing democracies" (Fraser 1990). This normative public space reflects Habermas' (1989) discussion of the aspatial and normative public *sphere* in which the public sphere is best imagined as the suite of institutions and activities that mediate the relations between society and the state (see Howell 1993). In this normative sense, the public sphere is where "the public" is organized and represented (or imagined) (Hartley 1992). The ideal of a public sphere is normative, Habermas (1989) theorizes, because it is in this sphere that all manner of social formations *should* find access to the structures of power within a society. As part of the public sphere, according to many theorists (Fraser

1990; Hartley 1992; Howell 1993), public space represents the material location where the social interactions and political activities of all members of "the public" occur.

Greek agora, Roman forums, and eventually American parks, commons, marketplaces, and squares were never simply places of free, unmediated interaction, however; they were just as often places of exclusion (Fraser 1990; Hartley 1992). The public that met in these spaces was carefully selected and homogenous in composition. It consisted of those with power, standing, and respectability. Here then are the roots of the second vision of public space. In Greek democracy, for example, citizenship was a right that was awarded to free, non-foreign men and denied to slaves, women, and foreigners. The latter had no standing in the public spaces of Greek cities; they were not included in "the public." Although women, slaves, and foreigners may have worked in the agora, they were formally excluded from the political activities of this public space.

Nor has "the public" always been defined expansively in American history. Inclusion of more and varied groups of people into the public sphere has only been won through constant social struggle. Notions of "the public" and public democracy played off and developed dialectically with notions of private property and private spheres. The ability for citizens to move between private property and public space determined the nature of public interaction in the developing democracy of the United States (Fraser 1990; Habermas 1989; Marston 1990). In modern capitalist democracies like the United States, "owners of private property freely join together to create a public, which forms the critical functional element of the political realm" (Marston 1990:445). To be public implies access to the sphere of private property.

Each of these spheres, of course, has been constrained by, *inter alia*, gender, class, and race. By the end of the eighteenth century:

The line drawn between public and private was essentially one on which the claims of civility—epitomized by cosmopolitan, public behavior—were balanced against the claims of nature—epitomized by the family.... [W]hile man *made* himself in public, he *realized* his nature in the private realm, above all in his experiences within the family.
(Sennett 1992:18–19; emphasis in the original)

The private sphere was the home and refuge, the place from which white propertied men ventured out into the democratic arena of public space.[7] The public sphere of American (and other capitalist) democracies is thus understood as a voluntary community of private (and usually propertied) citizens. By "nature" (as also by custom, franchise, and economics), women, non-white men, and the propertyless were denied access to the public sphere in everyday life.[8] Built on exclusions, the public sphere was thus a "profoundly problematic construction" (Marston 1990:457).

For the historian Edmund Morgan (1988:15), the popular sovereignty that arose from this split between publicity and privacy was a fiction in which citizens "*willingly* suspended disbelief" as to the improbability of a total public sphere. The normative ideal of the public sphere holds out hope that a *representative* public can meet, that all can claim representation within "the public" (Hartley 1992). The reality of public space and the public sphere is that Morgan's "fiction" is less an agreeable acquiescence to representation and more "an exercise in ideological construction with respect to who belongs to the national community and the relationship of 'the people' to formal governance" (Marston 1990:450).

As ideological constructions, however, ideals like "the public," public space, and the public sphere take on double importance. Their very articulation implies a notion of inclusiveness that becomes a rallying point for successive waves of political activity. Over time, such political activity has broadened definitions of "the public" to include, at least formally, women, people of color, and the propertyless (but not yet foreigners).[9] In turn, redefinitions of citizenship accomplished through struggles for inclusion have reinforced the normative ideals incorporated in notions of public spheres and public spaces. By calling on the rhetoric of inclusion and interaction that the public sphere and public space are meant to represent, excluded groups have been able to argue for their *rights* as part of the active public. And each (partially) successful struggle for inclusion in "the public" conveys to other marginalized groups the importance of the ideal as a point of political struggle.

In these struggles for inclusion, the distinctions between the public sphere and public space assume considerable importance. The public sphere in Habermas' sense is a universal, abstract realm in which democracy occurs. The materiality of this sphere is, so to speak, immaterial to its functioning. Public space, meanwhile, is material. It constitutes an actual site, a place, a ground within and from which political activity flows.[10] This distinction is crucial, for it is "in the context of real public spaces" that alternative movements may arise and contest issues of citizenship and democracy (Howell 1993:318).

If contemporary trends signal a progressive erosion of the first vision of public space as the second becomes more prominent (Crilley 1993; Davis 1990; Goss 1992; 1993; Lefebvre 1991; Sennett 1992; Sorkin 1992), then public spaces like People's Park become, in Arendt's words, "small hidden islands of freedom," islands of opposition surrounded by "Foucault's carceral archipelago" (Howell 1993:313).[11] In these hidden islands, space is *taken* by marginalized groups in order to press claims for their rights. And that was precisely the argument made by many of the People's Park activists and homeless residents. As the *East Bay Express* (Kahn 1991c:11) observed: "Ultimately, they claim,

this is still a fight over territory. It is not just two volleyball courts; it's the whole issue of who has rightful claim to the land." Michael Delacour argued that People's Park was still about free speech, and homeless activist Curtis Bray claimed: "they are trying to take the power away from the people" (*New York Times* 1991a:1.39). For these activists, People's Park was a place where the rights of citizenship could be expanded to the most disenfranchised segment of contemporary American democracy: the homeless. People's Park provided the space for representing the legitimacy of homeless people within "the public."

THE POSITION OF THE HOMELESS IN PUBLIC SPACE AND AS PART OF "THE PUBLIC"

People's Park has been recognized as a refuge for homeless people since its founding, even as elsewhere in Berkeley, the City has actively removed squatters and homeless people from the streets (sometimes rehousing them in a disused city landfill) (Dorgan 1985:B12; Harris 1988:B12; Levine 1987:C1; *Los Angeles Times* 1988:13; Mitchell 1992a:165; Stern 1987:D10). Consequently, the Park had become a relatively safe place for the homeless to congregate—one of the few such spots in an increasingly hostile Bay Area (*Los Angeles Times* 1990:A1). Around the Bay, the homeless had been cleaned out of San Francisco's United Nations' Plaza near City Hall and Golden Gate Park; in Oakland, loitering was actively discouraged in most parks (*Los Angeles Times* 1989b:13; 1990:A1; *New York Times* 1988b:A14).

In part, the desire to sweep the homeless from visibility responds to the central contradiction of homelessness in a democracy composed of private individuals (see Deutsche 1992; Mair 1986; Marcuse 1988; Ruddick 1990; Smith 1989). The contradiction turns on publicity: the homeless are all too visible.

THE END OF PUBLIC SPACE? PEOPLE'S PARK, DEFINITIONS OF THE PUBLIC, AND DEMOCRACY | 91

Although homeless people are nearly always in public, they are rarely counted as part of *the* public. Homeless people are in a double bind. For them, socially legitimated private space does not exist, and they are denied access to public space and public activity by capitalist society which is anchored in private property and privacy. For those who are *always* in the public, private activities must necessarily be carried out publicly. When public space thus becomes a place of seemingly illegitimate behavior, our notions about what public space is supposed to be are thrown into doubt. Now less a location for the "pleasurable jostling of bodies" and the political discourse imagined as the appropriate activities of public space in a democracy, public parks and streets begin to take on aspects of the home; they become places to go to the bathroom, sleep, drink, or make love—all socially legitimate activities when done in private, but seemingly illegitimate when carried out in public. As importantly, since citizenship in modern democracy (at least ideologically) rests on a foundation of *voluntary* association, and since homeless people are *involuntarily* public, homeless people cannot be, by definition, legitimate citizens.[12] Consequently, "[h]omeless people prove threatening to the free exercise of rights" (Mitchell 1992b:494); they threaten the existence of a "legitimate"—i.e., a voluntary—public.

The existence of homeless people in public thus undermines the ideological order of modern societies. George Will (1987) speaks for many when he argues that: "Society needs order, and hence has a right to a minimally civilized ambience in public spaces. Regarding the homeless, this is not merely for aesthetic reasons because the aesthetic is not merely unappealing. It presents a spectacle of disorder and decay that becomes contagion."[13] For reasons of order, then, the homeless have been eliminated from most definitions of "the public." They have instead become something of an "indicator species" to much of society, diagnostic of the presumed ill-health of public space, and of the need to gain control, to privatize, and to rationalize public spaces in urban places. Whether in New York City (Smith 1989; 1992a; 1992b), Berkeley (Mitchell 1992a), or Columbus, Ohio (Mair 1986), the presence of homeless people in public spaces suggests in the popular mind an irrational and uncontrolled society in which the distinctions between appropriate public and private behavior are muddled. Hence, those who are intent on rationalizing "public" space in the post-industrial city have *necessarily* sought to remove the homeless—to banish them to the interstices and margins of civic space—in order to make room for legitimate public activities (Mair 1986; see also Marcuse 1988; Lefebvre 1991:373).

When, as in Berkeley's People's Park or New York's Tompkins Square, actions are taken against park users by closing public space or exercising greater social control over park space, the press explains these actions by saying that "the park is currently a haven for drug users and the homeless" (*Los Angeles Times* 1991b:A10; see also Boudreau 1991:A3; Koopman 1991:A13; *Los Angeles Times* 1991a:A3; 1992:A3; *New York Times* 1988a:A31). Such statements pointedly ignore any "public" standing that homeless people may have, just as they ignore the possibility that homeless people's usage of a park for political, social, economic, and residential purposes may constitute for them legitimate and necessary uses of public space (Mitchell 1992a:153). When UC officials claimed that the homeless residents of People's Park were not "representative of the community" (Boudreau 1991:A3), they in essence denied social legitimacy to homeless people and their (perhaps necessary) behaviors. By transforming the Park, UC hoped that illegitimate activity would be discouraged. That is to say that the homeless could stay as long as they behaved appropriately—and as long as the historical, normative, ideological boundary between public and private was well patrolled.

PUBLIC SPACE IN THE CONTEMPORARY CITY

Failure to recognize the homeless as part of the urban public; disregard of the fact that new public spaces and homelessness are both products of redevelopment; the refusal to raise questions about exclusions while invoking the concept of an inclusionary public space: these acts ratify the relations of domination that close the borders of public places no matter how much these places are touted as "open and freely accessible to the public for 12 or more hours daily."
(Deutsche 1992:38, emphasis in the original)[14]

. . . *liberty* engenders contradictions which are also spatial contradictions. Whereas businesses tend toward a totalitarian form of social organization, authoritarian and prone to fascism, urban conditions, either despite or by virtue of violence, tend to uphold at least a measure of democracy.

(Lefebvre 1991:319)

As a secular space, the public space of the modern city has always been a hybrid of politics and commerce (Sennett 1992:21–22).[15] Ideally, the anarchy of the market meets the anarchy of politics in public space to create an interactive, democratic public. In the twentieth century, however, markets have been increasingly severed from politics. The once expansive notion of public space that guided early American democratic ideology and the extension, however partial, of public rights to women, people of color, and the propertyless have been jeopardized by countervailing social, political, and economic trends, trends that have caused many to recoil against any exercise of democratic social power that poses a threat to dominant social and economic interests (Fraser 1990; Harvey 1992).

These trends have led to the constriction

of public space. Interactive, discursive politics have been effectively banned from the gathering points of the city. Corporate and state planners have created environments that are based on desires for security rather than interaction, for entertainment rather than (perhaps divisive) politics (Crilley 1993; Garreau 1991; Goss 1992; 1993; Sorkin 1992). One of the results of planning has been the growth of what Sennett (1992) calls "dead public spaces"—the barren plazas that surround so many modern office towers. A second result has been the development of festive spaces that encourage consumption—downtown redevelopment areas, malls, and festival marketplaces. Though seemingly so different, both "dead" and "festive" spaces are premised on a perceived need for order, surveillance, and control over the behavior of the public. As Goss (1993:29–30) reminds us, we are often complicit in the severing of market and political functions. He points to the case of the pseudo-public space of the contemporary shopping mall:

Some of us are . . . disquieted by the constant reminders of surveillance in the sweep of cameras and the patrols of security personnel [in malls]. Yet those of us for whom it is designed are willing to suspend the privileges of public urban space to its relative benevolent authority, for our desire is such that we will readily accept nostalgia as a substitute for experience, absence for presence, and representation for authenticity.

This nostalgic desire for the market Goss (1993:28) calls "agoraphilia"—a yearning for "an immediate relationship between producer and consumer" (see also Hartley 1992).

Such nostalgia is rarely "innocent," however (see Lowenthal 1985). It is rather a highly constructed, corporatized image of a market quite unlike the idealization of the agora as a place of commerce *and* politics (Hartley 1992). In the name of comfort, safety, and profit, political activity is replaced in these spaces by a highly commodified spectacle designed to sell (Boyer 1992; Crawford 1992; Garreau 1991:48–52). Planners of pseudo-public spaces like malls and corporate plazas have found that controlled diversity is more profitable than unconstrained social differences (Crawford 1992; Goss 1993; Kowinski 1985; A. Wilson 1992; Zukin 1991). Hence even as new groups are claiming greater access to the rights of society, homogenization of "the public" continues apace.

This homogenization typically has advanced by "disneyfying" space and place—creating landscapes in which every interaction is carefully planned (Sorkin 1992; A. Wilson 1992; Zukin 1991). Market and design considerations thus displace the idiosyncratic and extemporaneous interactions of engaged peoples in the determination of the shape of urban space in the contemporary world (Crilley 1993:137; Zukin 1991). Designed-and-contrived diversity creates marketable landscapes, as opposed to uncontrolled social interaction which creates places that may threaten exchange value. The "disneyfication" of space consequently implies increasing alienation of people from the possibilities of unmediated social interaction and increasing control by powerful economic and social actors over the production and use of space.

Imposing limits and controls on spatial interaction has been one of the principal aims of urban and corporate planners during this century (Davis 1990; Harvey 1989; Lefebvre 1991). The territorial segregation created through the expression of social *difference* has increasingly been replaced by a celebration of constrained *diversity*.[16] The diversity represented in shopping centers, "megastructures," corporate plazas, and (increasingly) in public parks is carefully constructed (Boyer 1992). Moreover, the expansion of a planning and marketing ethos into all manner of public gathering places has created a

"space of social practice" that sorts and divides social groups (Lefebvre 1991:375) according to the dictates of comfort and order rather than to those of political struggle. But as Lefebvre (1991:375) suggests, this is no accident. The strategies of urban and corporate planners, he claims, classify and "distribute various social strata and classes (other than the one that exercises hegemony) across the available territory, keeping them separate and prohibiting all contacts—these being replaced by *signs* (or images) of contact."

This reliance on images and signs—or representations—entails the recognition that a "public" that cannot exist as such is continually *made* to exist in the pictures of democracy we carry in our heads: "The public in its entirety has never met at all . . ."; yet "the public [is] still to be found, large as life, in the media" (Hartley 1992:1). Hence: "Contemporary politics is *representative* in both senses of the term; citizens are represented by a chosen few, and politics is represented to the public via the various media of communication. Representative political space is literally made of pictures—they *constitute* the public domain" (Hartley 1992:35; emphasis in the original). I will return to this theme of symbolic politics and resistance to it in the material spaces of the city; for now, it is sufficient to note that the politics of symbolism, imaging, and representation increasingly stand in the stead of a democratic *ideal* of direct, less-mediated, social interaction in public spaces. In other words, contemporary designers of urban "public" space increasingly accept signs and images of contact as more natural and desirable than contact itself.

Public and pseudo-public spaces assume new functions in a political and social system in which controlled representation is regarded as natural and desirable. The overriding purpose of public space becomes the creation of a "public realm deliberately shaped as theater" (Crilley 1993:153; see also Glazer 1992). "Significantly, it is theater in which a pacified public basks in the grandeur of a carefully orchestrated corporate spectacle" (Crilley 1993:147).[17] That is the purpose of the carefully controlled "public" spaces such as the corporate plazas, library grounds, and suburban streets critiqued by Davis (1990:223–263) and the festive marketplaces, underground pedestrian districts, and theme parks analyzed by the contributors to Sorkin (1992). It is certainly the goal of mall builders (Garreau 1991; Goss 1993; Kowinski 1985; A. Wilson 1992).

These spaces of controlled spectacle narrow the list of eligibles for "the public." Public spaces of spectacle, theater, and consumption create images that define the public, and these images exclude as "undesirable" the homeless and the political activist. Thus excluded from these public and pseudo-public spaces, their legitimacy as members of the public is put in doubt. And thus *unrepresented* in our images of "the public," they are banished to a realm outside politics because they are banished from the gathering places of the city.

How "the public" is defined and imaged (as a space, as a social entity, and as an ideal) is a matter of some importance. As Crilley (1993:153) shows, corporate producers of space tend to define the public as passive, receptive, and "refined." They foster the "illusion of a homogenized public" by filtering out "the social heterogeneity of the urban crowd, [and] substituting in its place a flawless fabric of white middle class work, play, and consumption . . . with minimal exposure to the horrifying level of homelessness and racialized poverty that characterizes [the] street environment" (Crilley 1993:154). And, by blurring distinctions between private property and public space, they create a public that is narrowly prescribed. The elision of carefully controlled spaces (such as Disneyland, Boston's Fanueil Hall, or New York's World Financial Center) with notions of public space "conspires to hide from us

the widespread privatization of the public realm and its reduction to the status of commodity" (Crilley 1993:153). The irony is, of course, that this privatization of public space is lauded by all levels of government (e.g., through public-private redevelopment partnerships) at the same time as the privatization of public space by homeless people (their use of public space for what we consider to be private activities) is excoriated by urban planners, politicians, and social critics alike.

THE END OF PUBLIC SPACE?

Have we reached, then, the "end of public space" (Sorkin 1992)? Has the dual (though so different) privatization of public space by capital and by homeless people created a world in which designed diversity has so thoroughly replaced the free interaction of strangers that the ideal of an unmediated *political* public space is wholly unrealistic? Have we created a society that expects and desires only private interactions, private communications, and private politics, that reserves public spaces solely for commodified recreation and spectacle? Many cultural critics on the left believe so, as do mainstream commentators such as Garreau (1991) and conservatives like Glazer (1992). Public spaces are, for these writers, an artifact of a past age, an age with different sensibilities and different ideas about public order and safety, when public spaces were stable, well-defined, and accessible to all. But these images of past public spaces and past public spheres are highly idealized; as we have seen, the public sphere in the American past was anything but inclusive—and public space was always a site for and a source of conflict. Definitions of public space and "the public" are not universal and enduring; they are produced rather through constant struggle in the past and in the present. And, in People's Park as in so many other places, that struggle continues.

But these kinds of spaces are dwindling, despite the fact that many cities are increasing their stocks of parks, bicycle and hiking corridors, natural areas, and similar places that are owned or operated in the name of the public. That is certainly the case in Boulder, Colorado, where the preservation of open spaces in and around urbanized areas is one of the most strongly supported city and county initiatives (Cornett 1993:A9). Mountain parks, prairielands, small city blocks, farmlands, and wetlands have all been set aside. But are these public spaces in the political sense?

During the period of rapid suburbanization and urban renewal in the decades after World War II, North American cities: "vastly increased 'open' space, but its primary purpose was different [than public spaces with civic functions], i.e., to separate functions, open up distance between buildings, allow for the penetration of sunlight and greenery, not to provide places for extensive social contact" (Greenberg 1990:324). There are many reasons for the growth of open space —preserving ecologically sensitive areas; maintaining property values by establishing an undevelopable greenbelt; providing places for recreation; removing flood plains from development; and so on. But in each case open space serves functional and ideological roles that differ from political public spaces. It is rare that open spaces such as these are designed or appropriated to fulfill the market and civic functions that mark the public space of the city. More typically, these open spaces share certain characteristics with pseudo-public spaces. Restrictions on behavior and activities are taken-for-granted; prominent signs designate appropriate uses and outline rules concerning where one may walk, ride, or gather. These are highly regulated spaces.

In Berkeley, UC officials recognized this distinction between open space and public space. During various People's Park debates, speakers for the University never referred to the Park as public space, though they frequently reiterated their commitment to maintaining the Park as open space (Boudreau 1991:A3). Berkeley City Council member Alan Goldfarb, an occasional critic of University plans, also traded on the differences between public and open space. Speaking of People's Park, he celebrated the virtues of public space and then undermined them:

> It's a symbol for the police versus the homeless, the have-nots versus the haves, progress versus turmoil, development versus nondevelopment, all of the undercurrents most troubling in the city. You've got pan-handling going on, the business community nearby, the town-gown tensions. You have anarchists and traditionalists. People's Park becomes a live stage for all these actors. For many people around the world, Berkeley *is* People's Park.
> (Kahn 1991a:28; emphasis in the original)

But if "[t]hese things are real and important," he continued, it is more important to make People's Park "a viable open space" that would provide a bit of green in a highly urbanized neighborhood (*ibid*).

CONCLUSION: THE END OF PEOPLE'S PARK AS PUBLIC SPACE?

The University seemed just as clear in its use of precedents. According to an unnamed University employee, Berkeley Chancellor Cheng-Lin Tien "personally rejected" the possibility of further negotiations with activists during the riots "on the grounds that he wanted violence and confrontation to show the regents he is tough. He alluded to Bush's actions in the Persian Gulf; you don't negotiate, you simply attack" (Kahn 1991c:13). Attack was necessary because the occupation of People's Park by homeless people and activists was illegal and illegitimate, and because that occupation had excluded the majority from the Park. Berkeley City Manager Michael Brown promised the City would do all that was necessary to ensure implementation of a more orderly vision of public space. Referring to the homeless residents and activists, Brown told the *New York Times* (1991c:A8): "If they obstruct the majority opinion in a democracy, the city, the university, the county, and the state will apply whatever force is necessary to carry out the law." Brown kept his word. In the midst of the battle between protesters and police, Brown told the press: "We have a serious situation out there. People think this is about volleyball at the park but it is not. It's about a group of people who think they can use violence to force their will on a community, and we won't accept that" (Lynch 1991a:A21). "We almost lost the city," he added later (Kahn 1991c:13); the police and governing institutions of the city, according to Brown, were nearly incapable of quieting the disorderly politics of the street (*ibid*).

The long-simmering, and sometimes white-hot, controversies over People's Park in Berkeley are paradigmatic of the struggles that define the nature of "the public" and public space. Activists see places like the Park as spaces *for* representation. By *taking* public space, social movements represent themselves to larger audiences. Conversely, representatives of mainstream institutions argue that public spaces must be orderly and safe in order to function properly. These fundamentally opposed visions of public space clashed in the riots over People's Park in August 1991. Though the "public" status of People's Park remains ambiguous (given UC's legal title to the land), the political importance of the Park as public space rests on its status as a *taken* space. By wresting control of People's Park from the state, Park activists held at bay issues of control, order, and state power. But for many others, the Park's parallel history as a refuge for the homeless suggested that People's Park had become unmanageable, that large segments of the public felt threatened by the Park's relatively large resident population, and that

the City and University needed to exercise more control over the Park. For more than two decades, these visions of the Park as a public space collided as UC sought to reclaim the Park and to define the Park's appropriate public and what counted as appropriate behavior there.

As the history of People's Park has unfolded, the homeless have become rather iconographic. One of the issues raised by the struggles over People's Park (and one that I have not completely answered), is the degree to which "safe havens" like People's Park address the needs of homeless people themselves.[18] Certainly the provision of "free spaces" for the homeless in cities does nothing to address the structural production of homelessness in capitalist societies. Nor do these "havens" necessarily provide safety for homeless people (cf. Vaness 1993). But, as I have argued, spaces like People's Park are also political spaces. For homeless people, these spaces are more than just "homes." They serve as sites within which homeless people can be seen and represented, as places within which activism on homelessness can arise and expand outward. On the stages of these spaces, homeless people and others may insist upon public representation and recognition in ways that are not possible in the vacuous spaces of the electronic frontier or the highly controlled pseudopublic spaces of the mall and the festival marketplace.

People's Park represents therefore an important instance in the on-going struggles over the nature of public space in America (and elsewhere). The riots that occurred there invite us to focus attention on appropriate uses of public space, the definitions of legitimate publics, and the nature of democratic discourse and political action. By listening to various actors as they assessed their motives in People's Park, we have seen that struggles over public space are struggles over opposing ideologies, over the ways in which members of society conceptualize public space. These public utterances reflect divergent ideological positions, adhering more or less to one of two poles in discourse about public space: public space as a place of unmediated political interaction, and public space as a place of order, controlled recreation, and spectacle. Arguments in behalf of the thesis of "the end of public space" suggest that an orderly, controlled vision of public space in the city is squeezing out other ways of imagining public spaces. The recent history of People's Park suggests that these arguments are, if profoundly important, too simple. Oppositional movements continually strive to assure the currency of more expansive visions of public space. Still, to the degree that the "disneyfication" of public space advances and political movements are shut out of public space, oppositional movements lose the spaces where they may be represented (or may represent themselves) as legitimate parts of "the public." As the words and actions of the protagonists in Berkeley suggest, the stakes are high and the struggles over them might very well be bloody. But that is at once the promise and the danger of public space.

CODA

As for now, an uneasy truce has settled over People's Park. On a sunny but cold Sunday morning in January 1993, some thirty to fifty homeless people sleep, sit on benches, and chat in small groups. The unnetted volleyball courts are idle. The basketball court is also vacant. A new building, already covered with graffiti, houses toilets with no doors on the stalls. During the school term, students may borrow volleyballs and basketballs from a room in this building that looks out over the large grassy center of the Park. According to some Park residents, this room doubles as a police substation. On this particular morning, the shutters are pulled down. Some of the graffiti appears to be gang or individual "tags," but most depicts events of the 1969

and 1991 riots. There are also painted references to Rosebud DeNovo, the Park regular who was killed by police after she broke into the UC Chancellor's house wielding a large cleaver (Fimrite and Wilson 1992:A1; Snider 1992:A1). Police patrol the Park, but on this morning they attract little notice from the homeless people.

By nine in the morning, the arrival of a small group of women for the day's protest serves as a reminder that Park activists continue to use the Park as a staging ground. But their descriptions of political activities are now peppered with tales of police abuse and rumors of homeless women raped by police. While I cannot confirm the truth of these accounts, that they are told at all speaks vividly of the enduring animosity and uneasiness that rules this space. What is certainly true is that UC has brought a series of suits against Park protesters and activists for alleged damages during the 1991 riots. In early 1993, UC offered to settle with the defendants in exchange for a payment of $10,000 and their acquiescence to a permanent injunction that barred them from acts of vandalism and violence against the University and from "interfering with construction on the park." Averring that UC was seeking to silence criticism, the defendants refused the settlement and filed a countersuit claiming that they were victims of a Strategic Lawsuit Against Public Participation (SLAPP) (Stallone 1993:9).[19]

On a beautiful Sunday morning like this one, such matters seem remote to me, but not to the women with whom I speak. They are defendants in the University's suit. As we talk the police spend more and more time watching our activities. The Free Stage and Free Box still stand, but so too do the bright security lights that blaze through the night, illuminating most of the Park. Is this the public space that Park activists envisioned? Is it the open space the University wanted? I am not sure; what I do know is that these issues are far from resolved and that so long as we live in a society which so efficiently produces homelessness, spaces like these will be—indeed *must be*—always at the center of social struggle. For it is by struggling over and within space that the natures of "the public" and of democracy are defined.

NOTES

1. The best reporting of the riots is in the weekly *East Bay Express* (Auchard 1991:1ff; Kahn 1991c:1ff; Rivlin 1991b:1ff) which details incidents of police abuse and the actions of protesters.

2. The details of the 1969 riots are less important here than their effects and meaning. Interested readers may find more detailed descriptions in Mitchell (1992a); Rorabaugh (1989); and Scheer (1969).

3. In the August 1991 riots, the first target for window smashers and looters was Miller's Outpost outlet on Telegraph. Miller's Outpost was one of the earliest corporate chains to expand into the Telegraph shopping district (Auchard 1991:19).

4. The response in Berkeley has been to pioneer a "liberal" anti-homeless campaign. Shoppers and residents are asked to give panhandlers 25¢ vouchers rather than cash. These vouchers may then be exchanged for food or laundry services. They may not be used for alcohol or tobacco. "I don't know that we will discourage panhandling," says Jeffrey Leiter, President of the Down-town Berkeley Association, "but we will encourage good panhandling." The value of the program for a merchant along Shattuck street is that "the truly homeless people will approve. The streetpeople who are just hustling may object. We hope this will help them move on" (Bishop 1991:A10). This program has now been copied in numerous other cities. In each case, the hope that vouchers will separate the "deserving" from the "undeserving" poor is paramount. Marylin Haas, the Director of Downtown Boulder Inc., wonders if vouchers "will make those people [panhandlers] leave. I don't know. But I think this is worth a try, and the timing is good" (George 1993:B4).

5. I recognize that there are potentially many more than two visions of the nature and purpose of public space, and that many people will hold a middle (and perhaps a wavering) ground between them. But these, as we will see, are the predominant ways of seeing public space across a variety of societies and historical periods. I suggest in what follows that by examining these visions, we can begin to see how public space is produced through their dialectical interaction.

6. Lefebvre (1991:39) claims that representational space is "passively experienced" by its users, yet his thesis will not withstand scrutiny. People actively transform their spaces, appropriating them (or not) strategically.

7. At least this is how the separation of spheres was posited, even if in actuality these divisions never precisely existed.

8. Public women in the city, as E. Wilson (1991) suggests, have historically been viewed as suspicious, as prostitutes, deranged, or uncontrolled. Alternatively, stylized representations of women in public—the heroine on the barricades—have often proven ideologically important in political struggles over space.

9. Of course, widening the franchise has never been a guarantee of full political participation—and still is not. Nonetheless, many of the necessary political and legal structures are now in place to guarantee to many traditionally excluded groups at least a fulcrum in the sphere of the public with which to leverage further political advances.

10. This definition of space has been challenged by those who see electronic media assuming the role of public space in modern democracies; see below.

11. "The great difference between Arendt and Habermas," Howell (1993:314) writes, ". . . is that, for Arendt, public space, as distinct from the public sphere, has not lost its geographical significance."

12. Legal definitions of the homeless in English jurisprudence can be traced in Ripton-Turner (1887). For an American example of how citizenship issues and homelessness interact in legal discourse, see Commonwealth of Pennsylvania (1890).

13. This attitude has certainly grown in the years since Will commented on the celebrated Joyce Brown case in New York. This is precisely the type of rhetoric that proved so useful in the recent mayoral campaigns in New York, San Francisco, Los Angeles, and elsewhere. It has guided new laws such as those in Seattle that prohibit sitting or lying down on sidewalks between 7:00 a.m. and 9:00 p.m.; and it intrudes in San Francisco's debate over the size of the "bubble" within which homeless people will be prohibited from standing near automatic teller machines. For a more recent celebration of the need for order in cities, see Leo (1994; also *New York Times* 1989b:A14; 1991b:B1; 1992a:1.40).

14. The quotation from the end of Deutsche's comments is from a Vancouver, BC, Social Planning Department document that defined public space as

places open and accessible for twelve or more hours a day. Obviously, in this rendering, public space has a temporal dimension as well: public spaces *can* be closed.

15. Public spaces have also been places of religious activity in many cities. In the American context, however, the formal relegation of religion to the private sphere—separate from a secular state—has meant that the role of religion has been relatively weak.

16. I am indebted to Neil Smith for helping me to see the distinctions between socially produced "difference" (largely a product of social struggle) and constrained diversity (largely a product of design).

17. Compare Wallace (1989) who argues that the presentation of spectacle in place of history and

society fits well with prevailing corporate conceptions of progress and "democracy."

18. In November 1992, a judge in Miami declared that Dade County would have to establish "safe havens" for homeless people. In these havens, police harassment of aid workers, panhandlers, or those "sleeping rough" would not be tolerated by the court. The court-ordered creation of public space in this instance stands in stark contrast to the dominant trend of closing space to the illegitimate (*New York Times* 1992b:A10; on closing public space to the homeless, see the map and report in the *New York Times* 1989c:E5).

19. An Alameda County Judge has granted a temporary injunction similar to the permanent order sought by UC.

Fortress L.A.

Mike Davis

The carefully manicured lawns of Los Angeles's Westside sprout forests of ominous little signs warning: 'Armed Response!' Even richer neighborhoods in the canyons and hillsides isolate themselves behind walls guarded by gun-toting private police and state-of-the-art electronic surveillance. Downtown, a publicly subsidized 'urban renaissance' has raised the nation's largest corporate citadel, segregated from the poor neighborhoods around it by a monumental architectural glacis. In Hollywood, celebrity architect Frank Gehry, renowned for his 'humanism', apotheosizes the siege look in a library designed to resemble a foreign-legion fort. In the Westlake district and the San Fernando Valley the Los Angeles Police barricade streets and seal off poor neighborhoods as part of their 'war on drugs'. In Watts, developer Alexander Haagen demonstrates his strategy for recolonizing inner-city retail markets: a panoptican shopping mall surrounded by staked metal fences and a substation of the LAPD in a central surveillance tower. Finally on the horizon of the next millennium, an ex-chief of police crusades for an anti-crime 'giant eye'—a geosynchronous law enforcement satellite—while other cops discreetly tend versions of 'Garden Plot', a hoary but still viable 1960s plan for a law-and-order armageddon.

Welcome to post-liberal Los Angeles, where the defense of luxury lifestyles is translated into a proliferation of new repressions in space and movement, undergirded by the ubiquitous 'armed response'. This obsession with physical security systems, and, collaterally, with the architectural policing of social boundaries, has become a zeitgeist of urban restructuring, a master narrative in the emerging built environment of the 1990s. Yet contemporary urban theory, whether debating the role of electronic technologies in precipitating 'postmodern space', or discussing the dispersion of urban functions across poly-centered metropolitan 'galaxies', has been strangely silent about the militarization of city life so grimly visible at the street level. Hollywood's pop apocalypses and pulp science fiction have been more realistic, and politically perceptive, in representing the programmed hardening of the urban surface in the wake of the social polarizations of the Reagan era. Images of carceral inner cities (*Escape from New York*, *Running Man*), high-tech police death squads (*Blade Runner*), sentient buildings (*Die Hard*), urban bantustans (*They Live!*), Vietnam-like street wars (*Colors*), and so on, only extrapolate from actually existing trends.

Such dystopian visions grasp the extent to which today's pharaonic scales of residental and commercial security supplant residual hopes for urban reform and social integration. The dire predictions of Richard Nixon's 1969 National Commission on the Causes and Prevention of Violence have been tragically fulfilled: we live in 'fortress cities' brutally divided between 'fortified cells' of affluent society and 'places of terror' where the police battle the criminalized poor (National Committee on the Causes and Prevention of Violence 1969). The 'Second Civil War' that began in the long hot summers of the 1960s has been institutionalized into the very structure of urban space. The old liberal paradigm of social control, attempting to balance repression with reform, has long been superseded by a rhetoric of social warfare that calculates the interests of the urban poor and the middle classes as a zero-sum game. In cities like Los Angeles, on the bad edge of postmodernity, one observes an unprecedented tendency to merge urban design, architecture and the police apparatus into a single, comprehensive security effort.

This epochal coalescence has far-reaching consequences for the social relations of the built environment. In the first place, the market provision of 'security' generates its own paranoid demand. 'Security' becomes a positional good defined by income access to private 'protective services' and membership in some hardened residential enclave or restricted suburb. As a prestige symbol—and sometimes as the decisive borderline between the merely well-off and the 'truly rich'— 'security' has less to do with personal safety than with the degree of personal insulation, in residential, work, consumption and travel environments, from 'unsavory' groups and individuals, even crowds in general.

Secondly, as William Whyte has observed of social intercourse in New York, 'fear proves itself'. The social perception of threat becomes a function of the security mobilization itself, not crime rates. Where there is an actual rising arc of street violence, as in Southcentral Los Angeles or Downtown Washington D.C., most of the carnage is self-contained within ethnic or class boundaries. Yet white middle-class imagination, absent from any first-hand knowledge of inner-city conditions, magnifies the perceived threat through a demonological lens. Surveys show

that Milwaukee suburbanites are just as worried about violent crime as inner-city Washingtonians, despite a twenty-fold difference in relative levels of mayhem. The media, whose function in this arena is to bury and obscure the daily economic violence of the city, ceaselessly throw up spectres of criminal underclasses and psychotic stalkers. Sensationalized accounts of killer youth gangs high on crack and shrilly racist evocations of marauding Willie Hortons foment the moral panics that reinforce and justify urban apartheid.

Moreover, the neo-military syntax of contemporary architecture insinuates violence and conjures imaginary dangers. In many instances the semiotics of so-called 'defensible space' are just about as subtle as a swaggering white cop. Today's upscale, pseudo-public spaces—sumptuary malls, office centers, culture acropolises, and so on—are full of invisible signs warning off the underclass 'Other'. Although architectural critics are usually oblivious to how the built environment contributes to segregation, pariah groups—whether poor Latino families, young Black men, or elderly homeless white females—read the meaning immediately.

THE DESTRUCTION OF PUBLIC SPACE

The universal and ineluctable consequence of this crusade to secure the city is the destruction of accessible public space. The contemporary opporbrium attached to the term 'street person' is in itself a harrowing index of the devaluation of public spaces. To reduce contact with untouchables, urban redevelopment has converted once vital pedestrian streets into traffic sewers and transformed public parks into temporary receptacles for the homeless and wretched. The American city, as many critics have recognized, is being systematically turned inside out—or, rather, outside in. The valorized spaces of the new megastructures and super-malls are concentrated in the center, street frontage is denuded, public activity is sorted into strictly functional compartments, and circulation is internalized in corridors under the gaze of private police.[1]

The privatization of the architectural public realm, moreover, is shadowed by parallel restructurings of electronic space, as heavily policed, pay-access 'information orders', elite data-bases and subscription cable services appropriate parts of the invisible agora. Both processes, of course, mirror the deregulation of the economy and the recession of non-market entitlements. The decline of urban liberalism has been accompanied by the death of what might be called the 'Olmstedian vision' of public space. Frederick Law Olmsted, it will be recalled, was North America's Haussmann, as well as the Father of Central Park. In the wake of Manhattan's 'Commune' of 1863, the great Draft Riot, he conceived public landscapes and parks as social safety-valves, *mixing* classes and ethnicities in common (bourgeois) recreations and enjoyments. As Manfredo Tafuri has shown in his well-known study of Rockefeller Center, the same principle animated the construction of the canonical urban spaces of the La Guardia–Roosevelt era (Blodgett 1976, Tafuri 1979).

This reformist vision of public space—as the emollient of class struggle, if not the bedrock of the American *polis*—is now as obsolete as Keynesian nostrums of full employment. In regard to the 'mixing' of classes, contemporary urban America is more like Victorian England than Walt Whitman's or La Guardia's New York. In Los Angeles, once-upon-a-time a demi-paradise of free beaches, luxurious parks, and 'cruising strips', genuinely democratic space is all but extinct. The Oz-like archipelago of Westside pleasure domes—a continuum of tony malls, arts centers and gourmet strips—is reciprocally dependent upon the social imprisonment of the third-world service proletariat who live in increasingly repressive ghettoes and barrios. In a city of several million yearning immigrants, public amenities are radically shrinking, parks are becoming derelict and beaches more segregated, libraries and playgrounds are closing, youth congregations of ordinary kinds are banned, and the streets are becoming more desolate and dangerous.

Unsurprisingly, as in other American cities, municipal policy has taken its lead from the security offensive and the middle-class demand for increased spatial and social insulation. De facto disinvestment in traditional public space and recreation has supported the shift of fiscal resources to corporate-defined redevelopment priorities. A pliant city government—in this case ironically professing to represent a bi-racial coalition of liberal whites and Blacks—has collaborated in the massive privatization of public space and the subsidization of new, racist enclaves (benignly described as 'urban villages'). Yet most current, giddy discussions of the 'postmodern' scene in Los Angeles neglect entirely these overbearing aspects of counter-urbanization and counter-insurgency. A triumphal gloss—'urban renaissance', 'city of the future', and so on—is laid over the brutalization of inner-city neighborhoods and the increasing South Africanization of its spatial relations. Even as the walls have come down in Eastern Europe, they are being erected all over Los Angeles.

The observations that follow take as their thesis the existence of this new class war (sometimes a continuation of the race war of the 1960s) at the level of the built environment. Although this is not a comprehensive account, which would require a thorough analysis of economic and political dynamics, these images and instances are meant to convince the reader that urban form is indeed following a repressive function in the political furrows of the Reagan–Bush era. Los Angeles, in its usual prefigurative mode, offers an especially disquieting catalogue of the emergent liaisons between architecture and the American police state.

SADISTIC STREET ENVIRONMENTS

This conscious 'hardening' of the city surface against the poor is especially brazen in the Manichaean treatment of Downtown microcosms. In his famous study of the 'social life of small urban spaces', William Whyte makes the point that the quality of any urban environment can be measured, first of all, by whether there are convenient, comfortable places for pedestrians to sit (Whyte 1985). This maxim has been warmly taken to heart by designers of the high-corporate precincts of Bunker Hill and the emerging 'urban village' of South Park. As part of the city's policy of subsidizing white-collar residential colonization in Downtown, it has spent, or plans to spend, tens of millions of dollars of diverted tax revenue on enticing, 'soft' environments in these areas. Planners envision an opulent complex of squares, fountains, world-class public art, exotic shrubbery, and avant-garde street furniture along a Hope Street pedestrian corridor. In the propaganda of official boosters, nothing is taken as a better index of Downtown's 'liveability' than the idyll of office workers and upscale tourists lounging or napping in the terraced gardens of California Plaza, the 'Spanish Steps' or Grand Hope Park.

In stark contrast, a few blocks away, the city is engaged in a merciless struggle to make public facilities and spaces as 'unliveable' as possible for the homeless and the poor. The persistence of thousands of street people on the fringes of Bunker Hill and the Civic Center sours the image of designer Downtown living and betrays the laboriously constructed illusion of a Downtown 'renaissance'. City Hall then retaliates with its own variant of low-intensity warfare.[2]

Although city leaders periodically essay schemes for removing indigents *en masse*— deporting them to a poor farm on the edge of the desert, confining them in camps in the mountains, or, memorably, interning them on a derelict ferry at the Harbor—such 'final solutions' have been blocked by council members fearful of the displacement of the homeless into their districts. Instead the city, self-consciously adopting the idiom of urban cold war, promotes the 'containment' (official term) of the homeless in Skid Row along Fifth Street east of the Broadway, systematically transforming the neighborhood into an outdoor poorhouse. But this containment strategy breeds its own vicious circle of contradiction. By condensing the mass of the desperate and helpless together in such a small space, and denying adequate housing, official policy has transformed Skid Row into probably the most dangerous ten square blocks in the world—ruled by a grisly succession of 'Slashers', 'Night Stalkers' and more ordinary predators.[3] Every night on Skid Row is Friday the 13th, and, unsurprisingly, many of the homeless seek to escape the 'Nickle' during the night at all costs, searching safer niches in other parts of Downtown. The city in turn tightens the noose with increased police harassment and ingenious design deterrents.

One of the most common, but mind-numbing, of these deterrents is the Rapid Transit District's new barrelshaped bus bench that offers a minimal surface for uncomfortable sitting, while making sleeping utterly impossible. Such 'bumproof' benches are being widely introduced on the periphery of Skid Row. Another invention, worthy of the Grand Guignol, is the aggressive deployment of outdoor sprinklers. Several years ago the city opened a 'Skid Row Park' along lower Fifth Street, on a corner of Hell. To ensure that the park was not used for sleeping—that is to say, to guarantee that it was mainly utilized for drug dealing and prostitution—the city installed an elaborate overhead sprinkler system programmed to drench unsuspecting sleepers at random times during the night.

The system was immediately copied by some local businessmen in order to drive the homeless away from adjacent public sidewalks. Meanwhile restaurants and markets have responded to the homeless by building ornate enclosures to protect their refuse. Although no one in Los Angeles has yet proposed adding cyanide to the garbage, as happened in Phoenix a few years back, one popular seafood restaurant has spent $12,000 to build the ultimate bag-lady-proof trash cage: made of three-quarter inch steel rods with alloy locks and vicious outturned spikes to safeguard priceless moldering fishheads and stale french fries.

Public toilets, however, are the real Eastern Front of the Downtown war on the poor. Los Angeles, as a matter of deliberate policy, has fewer available public lavatories than any major North American city. On the advice of the LAPD (who actually sit on the design board of at least one major Downtown redevelopment project),[4] the Community Redevelopment Agency bulldozed the remaining public toilet in Skid Row. Agency planners then agonized for months over whether to include a 'free-standing public toilet' in their design for South Park. As CRA Chairman Jim Wood later admitted, the decision not to include the toilet was a 'policy decision and not a design decision'. The CRA Downtown prefers the solution of 'quasi-public restrooms'—meaning toilets in restaurants, art galleries and office buildings —which can be made available to tourists and office workers while being denied to vagrants and other unsuitables.[5] The toilet-less no-man's-land east of Hill Street in Downtown is also barren of outside water sources for drinking or washing. A common and troubling sight these days are the homeless men—many of them young Salvadorean refugees—washing in and even drinking from the sewer effluent which flows down the concrete channel of the Los Angeles River on the eastern edge of Downtown.

Where the itineraries of Downtown power-brokers unavoidably intersect with the habitats of the homeless or the working poor, as in the previously mentioned zone of gentrification along the northern Broadway corridor, extraordinary design precautions are being taken to ensure the physical separation of the different humanities. For instance, the CRA brought in the Los Angeles Police to design '24-hour, state-of-the-art security' for the two new parking structures that serve the Los Angeles *Times* and Ronald Reagan State Office buildings. In contrast to the mean streets outside, the parking structures contain beautifully landscaped lawns or 'microparks', and in one case, a food court and a historical exhibit. Moreover, both structures are designed as 'confidence-building' circulation systems—miniature paradigms of privatization—which allow white-collar workers to walk from car to office, or from car to boutique, with minimum exposure to the public street. The Broadway Spring Center, in particular, which links the Ronald Reagan Building to the proposed 'Grand Central Square' at Third and Broadway, has been warmly praised by architectural critics for adding greenery and art (a banal bas relief) to parking. It also adds a huge dose of menace—armed guards, locked gates, and security cameras—to scare away the homeless and poor.

The cold war on the streets of Downtown is ever escalating. The police, lobbied by Downtown merchants and developers, have broken up every attempt by the homeless and their allies to create safe havens or self-organized encampments. 'Justiceville', founded by homeless activist Ted Hayes, was roughly dispersed; when its inhabitants attempted to find refuge at Venice Beach, they were arrested at the behest of the local councilperson (a renowned environmentalist) and sent back to the inferno of Skid Row. The city's own brief experiment with legalized camping—a grudging response to a series of exposure deaths in the cold winter of 1987[6]—was ended abruptly after only four

months to make way for construction of a
transit repair yard. Current policy seems to
involve a perverse play upon Zola's famous
irony about the 'equal rights' of the rich and
the poor to sleep out rough. As the head of
the city planning commission explained the
official line to incredulous reporters, it is not
against the law to sleep on the street per se,
'only to erect any sort of protective shelter'.
To enforce this prescription against 'card-
board condos', the LAPD periodically sweep
the Nickle, confiscating shelters and other
possessions, and arresting resisters. Such cynical repression has turned the majority of
the homeless into urban bedouins. They are
visible all over Downtown, pushing a few
pathetic possessions in purloined shopping
carts, always fugitive and in motion, pressed
between the official policy of containment
and the increasing sadism of Downtown
streets (Davis 1987).[7]

FROM RENTACOP TO *ROBOCOP*

The security-driven logic of urban enclaviza-
tion finds its most popular expression in the
frenetic efforts of Los Angeles's affluent
neighborhoods to insulate home values and
lifestyles. New luxury developments outside
the city limits have often become fortress
cities, complete with encompassing walls,
restricted entry points with guard posts,
overlapping private and public police services, and even privatized roadways. It is
simply impossible for ordinary citizens to
invade the 'cities' of Hidden Hills, Bradbury,
Rancho Mirage or Palos Verdes Estates
without an invitation from a resident. Indeed
Bradbury, with nine hundred residents and
ten miles of gated private roads, is so
security-obsessed that its three city officials
do not return telephone calls from the press,
since 'each time an article appeared ... it
drew attention to the city and the number
of burglaries increased'. For its part, Hidden
Hills, a Norman Rockwell painting behind

high-security walls, has been bitterly divided
over compliance with a Superior Court order
to build forty-eight units of seniors' housing
outside its gates. At meetings of the city's
all-powerful homeowners' association
(whose membership includes Frankie
Avalon, Neil Diamond and Bob Eubanks)
opponents of compliance have argued that
the old folks' apartments 'will attract gangs
and dope' (sic).[8]

Meanwhile, traditional luxury enclaves
like Beverly Hills and San Marino are
increasingly restricting access to their public
facilities, using baroque layers of regulations
to build invisible walls. San Marino, which
may be the richest, and is reputedly the most
Republican (85 per cent), city in the country,
now closes its parks on weekends to exclude
Latino and Asian families from adjacent
communities. One plan under discussion
would reopen the parks on Saturdays only to
those with proof of residence. Other upscale
neighborhoods in Los Angeles have minted a
similar residential privilege by obtaining
ordinances to restrict parking to local homeowners. Predictably, such preferential parking regulations proliferate exclusively in
neighborhoods with three-car garages.

Residential areas with enough clout are
thus able to privatize local public space,
partitioning themselves from the rest of
the metropolis, even imposing a variant of
neighborhood 'passport control' on outsiders. The next step, of course, is to ape
incorporated enclaves like Palos Verdes or
Hidden Hills by building literal walls. Since
its construction in the late 1940s Park La
Brea has been a bit of Lower Manhattan
chutzpah moored to Wilshire Boulevard: a
176-acre maze of medium-rent townhouses
and tower apartments, occupied by an
urbane mix of singles, retirees, and families.
Now, as part of a strategy of gentrification,
its owners, Forest City Enterprises, have
decided to enclose the entire community in
security fencing, cutting off to pedestrians
one of the most vital public spaces along

the 'Miracle Mile'. As a spokeswoman for the owners observed, 'it's a trend in general to have enclosed communities'.[9] In the once wide-open tractlands of the San Fernando Valley, where there were virtually no walled-off communities a decade ago, the 'trend' has assumed the frenzied dimensions of a residential arms race as ordinary suburbanites demand the kind of social insulation once enjoyed only by the rich. Brian Weinstock, a leading Valley contractor, boasts of more than one hundred newly gated neighborhoods, with an insatiable demand for more security. 'The first question out of their [the buyers'] mouths is whether there is a gated community. The demand is there on a 3-to-1 basis for a gated community than not living in a gated community.'[10]

The social control advantages of 'gatehood' have also attracted the attention of landlords in denser, lower-income areas. Apartment owners in the Sepulveda barrio of the Valley have rallied behind a police program, launched in October 1989, to barricade their streets as a deterrent to drug buyers and other undesirables. The LAPD wants the City Council's permission to permanently seal off the neighborhood and restrict entry to residents, while the owners finance a guard station or 'checkpoint charlie'. While the Council contemplates the permanency of the experiment, the LAPD, supported by local homeowners, has continued to barricade other urban 'war zones' including part of the Pico-Union district, a Mid-Wilshire neighborhood, and an entire square mile around Jefferson High School in the Central-Vernon area. In face of complaints from younger residents about the 'Berlin Wall' quality of the neighborhood quarantines, Police Chief Gates reassured journalists that 'we're not here to occupy the territory. This isn't Panama. It's the city of Los Angeles and we're going to be here in a lawful manner.'[11]

Meanwhile the very rich are yearning for high-tech castles. Where gates and walls alone will not suffice, as in the case of Beverly Hills or Bel-Air homeowners, the house itself is redesigned to incorporate sophisticated, sometimes far-fetched, security functions. An overriding but discreet goal of the current 'mansionizing' mania on the Westside of Los Angeles—for instance, tearing down $3 million houses to build $30 million mansions —is the search for 'absolute security'. Residential architects are borrowing design secrets from overseas embassies and military command posts. One of the features most in demand is the 'terrorist-proof security room' concealed in the houseplan and accessed by sliding panels and secret doors. Merv Griffith and his fellow mansionizers are hardening their palaces like missile silos.

But contemporary residential security in Los Angeles—whether in the fortified mansion or the average suburban bunker—depends upon the voracious consumption of private security services. Through their local homeowners' associations, virtually every affluent neighborhood from the Palisades to Silverlake contracts its own private policing; hence the thousands of lawns displaying the little 'armed response' warnings. The classifieds in a recent Sunday edition of the Los Angeles *Times* contained nearly a hundred ads for guards and patrolmen, mostly from firms specializing in residential protection. Within Los Angeles County, the security services industry has tripled its sales and workforce (from 24,000 to 75,000) over the last decade. 'It is easier to become an armed guard than it is to become a barber, hairdresser or journeyman carpenter', and under California's extraordinarily lax licensing law even a convicted murderer is not automatically excluded from eligibility. Although a majority of patrolmen are minority males earning near the minimum wage ($4–7 per hour depending on qualifications and literacy), their employers are often multinational conglomerates offering a dazzling range of security products and services. As Michael Kaye, president of burgeoning

Westec (a subsidiary of Japan's Secom Ltd), explains: 'We're not a security guard company. We sell a *concept* of security.'[12] (This quote, as aficionados will immediately recognize, echoes the boast of Omni Consumer Products' Dick Jones—the villain of Paul Verhoeven's *Robocop*—that 'everything is security concepts ... sometimes I can just think of something and it makes me so horny'.)

What homeowners' associations contract from Westec—or its principal rival, Bel-Air Patrol (part of Borg-Warner's family of security companies, including Burns and Pinkerton)—is a complete, 'systems' package that includes alarm hardware, monitoring, watch patrols, personal escorts, and, of course, 'armed response' as necessary. Although law-enforcement experts debate the efficiency of such systems in foiling professional criminals, they are brilliantly successful in deterring innocent outsiders. Anyone who has tried to take a stroll at dusk through a strange neighborhood patrolled by armed security guards and signposted with death threats quickly realizes how merely notional, if not utterly obsolete, is the old idea of the 'freedom of the city'.

THE FEAR OF CROWDS

Ultimately the aims of contemporary architecture and the police converge most strikingly around the problem of crowd control. As we have seen, the designers of malls and pseudo-public space attack the crowd by homogenizing it. They set up architectural and semiotic barriers to filter out 'undesirables'. They enclose the mass that remains, directing its circulation with behaviorist ferocity. It is lured by visual stimuli of all kinds, dulled by musak, sometimes even scented by invisible aromatizers. This Skinnerian orchestration, if well conducted, produces a veritable commercial symphony of swarming, consuming monads moving from one cashpoint to another.

Outside in the streets, the police task is more difficult. The LAPD, true to its class war background, has always hated certain kinds of public gatherings. Its early history was largely devoted to bludgeoning May Day demonstrators, arresting strikers and deporting Mexicans and Okies. In 1921 it arrested Upton Sinclair for reading the Declaration of Independence in public; in the 1960s it indiscriminately broke up love-ins and family picnics in battles to control Griffith and Elysian Park. Subconsciously it has probably never recovered from the humiliation of August 1965 when it temporarily was forced to surrender the streets to a rebellious ghetto.

Whatever the reasons, the LAPD (and the County Sheriffs as well) continue relentlessly to restrict the space of public assemblage and the freedom of movement of the young. But long before the LAPD and the Sheriffs launched their famous anti-gang dragnets, they were operating extensive juvenile curfews in non-Anglo areas and barricading popular boulevards to prevent 'cruising' (in Hollywood this directly abets the current gentrification strategy). And now, of course, they are sealing off entire neighborhoods and housing projects under our local variant of 'pass law'. Even gilded white youth suffer from this escalating police regulation of personal mobility. In the erstwhile world capital of teenagers, where millions overseas still imagine Gidget at a late-night surf party, the beaches are now closed at dark, patrolled by helicopter gunships and police dune buggies.

A watershed in the dual architectural and police assault on public space was the rise and fall of the 'Los Angeles Street Scene'. Launched in 1978 the two-day festival at the Civic Center was intended to publicize Downtown's revitalization as well as to provide Mayor Bradley's version of the traditional Democratic barbecue. The LAPD were skeptical. Finally in 1986, after the failure of the Ramones to appear as promised, the youthful audience began to tear up the stage. The LAPD immediately sent in a phalanx of one hundred and fifty helmeted officers and a mounted unit. In the two-hour mêlée that followed, angry punks bombarded the police cavalry with rocks and bottles, and fifteen officers and their horses were injured. The producer of the Street Scene, a Bradley official, suggested that 'more middle-of-the-road entertainment' might attract less boisterous crowds. The prestigious *Downtown News* counter-attacked, claiming that the 'Street Scene gives Downtown a bad name. It flies in the face of all that has been done here in the last thirty years.' It demanded 'reparations' for the wounded 'reputation of Downtown'. The Mayor's office cancelled the Scene.[13]

Its demise suggests the consolidation of an official consensus about crowds and the use of space in Los Angeles. Since the restructuring of Downtown eliminated the social mixing of crowds in normal pedestrian circulation, the Street Scene (ironically named) remained one of the few carnival-like occasions or places (along with redevelopment-threatened Hollywood Boulevard and Venice Boardwalk) where pure heteroglossia could flourish: that is to say, where Chinatown punks, Glendale skinheads, Boyle Heights lowriders, Valley girls, Marina designer couples, Slauson rappers, Skid Row homeless and gawkers from Des Moines could mingle together in relative amity.

Until the final extinction of these last real public spaces—with their democratic intoxications, risks and unscented odors—the pacification of Los Angeles will remain incomplete. And as long as this is the case, the various insecure elites, like the yuppie-aliens in John Carpenter's *They Live!*, will never know when some revolt may break out, or what strange guise it may wear. On Halloween eve 1988—a week before the law-and-order climax of the Bush campaign—the LAPD attempted to disperse 100,000 peaceful revelers on Hollywood Boulevard. Police horses charged into crowds while squad cars zigzagged onto curbs, pinning terrified

onlookers against storefront windows. Displaying what the police would later characterize as 'a complete lack of respect for the spirit of the holiday', part of the crowd angrily fought back, tossing bottles and smashing the windows of the Brown Derby. By midnight the rioters, mainly costumed, were looting storefronts. The next morning's *Times* carried the following description, evocative of Nathanael West:

At one souvenir store, the Holly Vine Shoppe, looters smashed windows and took stuffed animals, Hollywood postcards, Hollywood pennants and baseball caps emblazoned 'LAPD'.[14]

NOTES

1. 'The problems of inversion and introversion in development patterns, and ambiguity in the character of public space created within them, are not unique to new shopping center developments. It is commonplace that the modern city as a whole exhibits a tendency to break down into specialised, single-use precincts—the university campus, the industrial estate, the leisure complex, the housing scheme . . . each governed by internal, esoteric rules of development and implemented by specialist agencies whose terms of reference guarantee that they are familiar with other similar developments across the country, but know almost nothing of the dissimilar precincts which abut their own.' (Maitland 1985: 109)

2. The descriptions that follow draw heavily on the extraordinary photographs of Diego Cardoso, who has spent years documenting Downtown's various street scenes and human habitats.

3. Since crack began to replace cheap wine on Skid Row in the mid 1980s, the homicide rate has jumped to almost 1 per week. A back-page *Times* story—'Well, That's Skid Row' (15 November 1989)—claimed that the homeless have become so 'inured to street violence' that 'the brutal slayings of two people within two blocks of each other the night before drew far less attention than the taping of an episode of the television show, "Beauty and the Beast" '. The article noted, however, the homeless have resorted to a 'buddy system' whereby one sleeps and the other acts as 'spotter' to warn of potential assailants.

4. For example, the LAPD sits on the Design

Advisory Board of 'Miracle on Broadway', the publicly funded body attempting to initiate the gentrification of part of the Downtown historic core. (*Downtown News*, 2 January 1989.)

5. Interviews with Skid Row residents; see also Tom Chorneau, 'Quandary Over a Park Restroom', *Downtown News*, 25 August 1986, pp. 1, 4. In other Southern California communities the very hygiene of the poor is being criminalized. New ordinances specifically directed against the homeless outlaw washing oneself in public 'above the elbow'.

6. See 'Cold Snap's Toll at 5 as Its Iciest Night Arrives', *Times*, 29 December 1988.

7. It is also important to note that, despite the crack epidemic on Skid Row (which has attracted a much younger population of homeless men), there is no drug treatment center or rehabilitation program in the area. Indeed within the city as a whole narcotic therapy funding is being cut while police and prison budgets are soaring.

8. Cf. *Daily News*, 1 November 1987; and television interview, Fox News, March 1990.

9. Los Angeles *Times*, 25 July 1989, II, p. 2.

10. Quoted in Jim Carlton 'Walled in', Los Angeles *Times*, 8 October 1989, II, p. 1. The mania for walls has also caught up with the Hollywood Chamber of Commerce who are planning to wall off the base of the famous 'Hollywood Sign' on Mount Lee, as well as installing motion detectors and video surveillance.

11. *Times*, 15 November 1989.

12. Quoted in Linda Williams, 'Safe and Sound', Los Angeles *Times*, 29 August 1988, IV, p. 5.

13. Cf. Los Angeles *Times*, 22 September, II, p. 1, and 25 September, II, p. 1, 1986; and reprint of 'best editorial', 'Trouble at Street Scene', *Downtown News*, 2 March 1987, p. 12.

14. George Ramos, 'Hollywood Halloween: Some Came as Vandals and Looters', Los Angeles *Times*, 2 November 1988, II, pp. 1, 8. Also interviews with eyewitnesses.

Whose Culture? Whose City?

Sharon Zukin

PUBLIC SPACE

The fastest growing kind of public space in America is prisons. More jails are being built than housing, hospitals, or schools. No matter how well designed or brightly painted they may be, prisons are still closely guarded, built as cheaply as possible, and designed for surveillance. I can think of more pleasant public spaces, especially parks that I use in New York City. But is the Hudson River Park, near Battery Park City, or Bryant Park, on 42nd Street, less secure or exclusive than a prison? They share with the new wave of prison building several characteristics symptomatic of the times. Built or rebuilt as the city is in severe financial distress, they confirm the withdrawal of the public sector, and its replacement by the private sector, in defining public space. Reacting to previous failures of public space—due to crime, a perceived lower-class and minority-group presence, and disrepair—the new parks use design as an implicit code of inclusion and exclusion. Explicit rules of park use are posted in the parks and enforced by large numbers of sanitation workers and security guards, both public and private. By cleaning up public space, nearby property owners restore the attractiveness of their holdings and reconstruct the image of the city as well.

It is important to understand the histories of these symbolically central public spaces.

The history of Central Park, for example (Rosenzweig and Blackmar 1992), shows how, as definitions of who should have access to public space have changed, public cultures have steadily become more inclusive and democratic. From 1860 to 1880, the first uses of the park—for horseback riders and carriages—rapidly yielded to sports activities and promenades for the mainly immigrant working class. Over the next 100 years, continued democratization of access to the park developed together with a language of political equality. In the whole country, it became more difficult to enforce outright segregation by race, sex, or age.

By the late 1950s, when Arkansas Governor Orville Faubus failed to prevent the racial integration of Central High School in Little Rock, public parks, public swimming pools, and public housing were legally opened to all of a city's residents. During the 1970s, public space, especially in cities, began to show the effects of movements to "deinstitutionalize" patients of mental hospitals without creating sufficient community facilities to support and house them. Streets became crowded with "others," some of whom clearly suffered from sickness and disorientation. By the early 1980s, the destruction of cheap housing in the centers of cities, particularly single-room-occupancy hotels, and the drastic decline in producing public housing, dramatically expanded the problem of homelessness. Public space, such as Central Park, became unintended public shelter. As had been true historically, the democratization of public space was entangled with the question of fear for physical security.

Streets and parks became camping grounds for mental patients, released from hospitals without access to alternative residential and treatment facilities. Sleeping on the sidewalks alongside them were increasing numbers of drug abusers who had drifted away from their families but were also cut off from other possible support systems. A growing population of homeless families begged for apartments in public housing. A series of lawsuits in various cities made it all but impossible to treat any of these people as criminals. In New York City, a jerry-built system of public shelters offered inadequate, often unsafe beds for a night, hotel rooms for a longer period, and subsidized apartments for persistently homeless families. No government initiatives have yet penetrated the sources of homelessness in poverty and unemployment, hospitals and drug treatment centers, and lack of cheap housing. But homeless people remain a visible presence in public spaces: on the streets, in the parks, on plazas in front of expensive apartment houses, in office building atrium lobbies, in subway cars and stations, in bus stations, in railroad terminals, under bridge and highway entrances.

New York City parks have removed and redistributed the homeless by creating the "defensible spaces" that Oscar Newman wrote about in the 1960s, using the design guidelines prescribed by William H. Whyte in the 1980s. Playgrounds are fenced in for children and their guardians, and parks are closed at night. Tompkins Square Park in lower Manhattan, site of violent confrontations in 1988 and 1991 between the police and neighborhood homeowners, punk activists, and homeless men sleeping in the park— all of whom, or some of whom, opposed gentrification—was closed for two years for extensive landscaping. When the park was reopened, open sight lines permitted children, ballplayers, and elderly bench sitters to keep an eye on each other while using their own spaces.

In 1989, a private organization that manages Central Park, the Central Park Conservancy, demanded demolition of the Naumberg Bandshell, site of popular concerts from the 1930s to the 1950s, where homeless people gathered. Similarly, the Bryant Park Restoration Corporation started cleaning up the midtown business district by adopting the social design principles developed by Whyte. Whyte's basic idea is that public spaces are made safe by attracting lots of "normal" users. The more normal users there are, the less space there will be for vagrants and criminals to maneuver. The Bryant Park Restoration Corporation intended their work to set a prototype for urban public space. They completely reorganized the landscape design of the park, opening it up to women, who tended to avoid the park even during daylight (see Cranz 1982), and selling certain kinds of buffet food. They established a model of pacification by cappuccino.

Central Park, Bryant Park, and the Hudson River Park show how public spaces are becoming progressively less public: they are, in certain ways, more exclusive than at any time in the past 100 years. Each of these areas is governed, and largely or entirely financed, by a private organization, often working as a quasi-public authority. These private groups are much better funded than the corresponding public organization. Design in each park features a purposeful vision of urban leisure. A heightened concern for security inspires the most remarkable visible features: gates, private security guards, and eyes keeping the space under surveillance. The underlying assumption is that of a paying public, a public that values public space as an object of visual consumption. Yet it has become inconceivable in public discussions that control of the parks be left in public hands. When the *New York Times* praised plans to require developers to provide public access to the city's extensive waterfront, the newspaper said that only a public-private partnership could raise the funds to maintain such a significant public space (editorial, October 14, 1993).

A major reason for privatization of some public parks is that city governments cannot pay for taking care of them. Since the 1960s, while groups of all sorts have requested more use of the parks, the New York City Parks Department has been starved of government funds. Half the funding for Central Park is now raised privately by the Central Park Conservancy, which enjoys a corresponding influence on parks policy. Founded by private donors in 1980, the conservancy's original mission was to raise funds in the private sector to offset the park's physical deterioration. But it soon developed an authoritative cultural voice. The conservancy publicly defends the intentions of Olmsted and Vaux, the park's original designers, to create a "natural" landscape for contemplation. Most often, they beautify the park by restoring its 19th century buildings and bridges or setting up a nature program or skating facilities on one of its landscaped ponds. The conservancy has also become an arbiter between groups that want to use the park for sports or demonstrations, thus mediating between the homeless and the joggers, between athletes who come to the park from all over the city and those who come from low-income neighborhoods on the park's northern borders. The conservancy, moreover, has spoken loudly and often in favor of hiring nonunion labor. While Roy Rosenzweig and Betsy Blackmar (1992) show that, historically, the unionization of park employees was an important means of democratizing access to Central Park, the park's public administrator (who is also the conservancy's director) argues that nonunion labor is more efficient and less costly than unionized public employees. By being able to implement its viewpoint on this most central of public spaces, the conservancy has become a more important guardian of public culture than the city's Parks Department.

In midtown, Bryant Park is an even more aggressive example of privatization. Declared a New York City landmark in 1975, the nine-acre park is essentially run by the Bryant Park Restoration Corporation, whose biggest corporate members are Home Box Office (HBO), a cable television network, and NYNEX, a regional telecommunications company. Like the Central Park Conservancy, the Bryant Park Restoration Corporation raises most of the park's budget, supervises maintenance, and decides on design and amenities.

The design of Bryant Park, in 1934, was based on an Olmstedian separation of a rural space of contemplation from the noisy city. By the late 1970s, this was determined to have the effect of walling off the park's intended public of office workers outside from drug dealers and loiterers inside. When the restoration corporation was formed, it took as its major challenge the development of a new design that would visually and spatially ensure security. The wall around the park was lowered, and the ground leveled to bring it closer to the surrounding streets. The restoration corporation bought movable chairs and painted them green, as in Parisian parks, responding to William H. Whyte's suggestion (1980; 1988, 119–23) that park users like to create their own small spaces. Whyte recommended keeping "the undesirables" out by making a park *attractive*. Victorian kiosks selling cappuccino and sandwiches were built and painted, paths were repaved and covered with pebbles, a central lawn was opened up, and performers were enlisted to offer free entertainment in the afternoons. The restoration corporation hired its own security guards and pressured the New York City Police Department to supply uniformed officers. Four uniformed New York City police officers and four uniformed private security guards are on duty all day.

Plainclothes private security guards are also on patrol. A list posted at all entrances prohibits drug use, picking flowers, and drinking alcohol except for beverages bought at park concessions, which are limited to certain seating areas. It states the park's hours, 9 a.m. to 7 p.m., coinciding roughly with the business day. The rules specify that only homeless people connected to a particular shelter in the neighborhood have the right to rummage through the garbage cans for returnable bottles and cans. Unlike Parks Department workers, Bryant Park maintenance workers do not belong to a labor union. Starting salary for a maintenance worker is $6 an hour, half the starting rate of unionized workers in other city parks.

On a sunny summer day at noon, Bryant Park is full of office workers out to lunch—between 1,500 and 6,000 of them. The movable chairs and benches are filled; many people are sitting on the grass, on the edge of the fountain, even on the pebbled paths. Men and women eat picnic lunches singly, in couples, and in groups. Some traditional social hierarchies are subverted. Women feel free to glance at men passing by. Most men do not ogle the women. The dominant complexion of park users is white, with minority group members clustered outside the central green. Few people listen to the subsidized entertainment, an HBO comedian shouting into a microphone; no one notices when she finishes the show. A large sculpture by Alexander Calder stands in the middle of the lawn, on loan from an art gallery, both an icon and a benediction on the space. At sunset in the summer, HBO shows free movies from their stock of old films, a "take back the night" activity similar to those now being tried in other cities. This is a very deliberate exception to the rule of closing the park at night. During lunchtime, at least, the park visually represents an urban middle class: men and women who work in offices, jackets off, sleeves rolled up, mainly white. On the same day, at the same hour, another public

space a block away—the tellers' line at Citibank—attracts a group that is not so well dressed, with more minority group members. The cultural strategies that have been chosen to revitalize Bryant Park carry with them the implication of controlling diversity while re-creating a consumable vision of civility.

The problem of controlling Bryant Park is not new (Biederman and Nager 1981). In 1932, when the park was filled with unemployed people during the Great Depression, private entrepreneurs built a replica of Federal Hall, charged an entrance fee of 25 cents, and installed turnstiles to control access to the park—an early Magic Kingdom until a public boycott forced it to be shut down. In 1944, Mayor Fiorello LaGuardia decreed that anyone caught loitering in the park after 10 p.m. would be arrested.

Since its renovation, Bryant Park has changed character. It has become a place for people to be with others, to see others, a place of public sociability. John Berger (1985) once criticized New Yorkers for eating while walking alone on the street, alienating a social ritual from its proper context. Yet now, in the park, eating becomes a public ritual, a way of trusting strangers while maintaining private identities. Because of the police and security guards, the design, and the food, the park has become a visual and spatial representation of a middle-class public culture. The finishing touch will be a privately owned, expensive restaurant, whose rent payments will help finance the park's maintenance. This, however, is a degree of privatization that has stirred prolonged controversy. First envisioned in the 1980s, the restaurant remained the subject of public approvals processes until 1994.

The disadvantage of creating public space this way is that it owes so much to private-sector elites, both individual philanthropists and big corporations. This is especially the case for centrally located public spaces, the ones with the most potential for raising property values and with the greatest claim to be symbolic spaces for the city as a whole. Handing such spaces over to corporate executives and private investors means giving them carte blanche to remake public culture. It marks the erosion of public space in terms of its two basic principles: public stewardship and open access.

The Central Park Conservancy, a group of 30 private citizens who choose their own replacements, represents large corporations with headquarters in the city, major financial institutions, and public officials. The membership echoes both the new (the nonelected, tripartite Emergency Financial Control Board that has overseen New York City's budget since the fiscal crisis of 1975) and the old (the board of "gentlemen" trustees that originally guided the planning of Central Park in the 1860s). The idea of governing public space in Central Park by a board of trustees was periodically resurrected until the 1930s and again in the 1970s (Rosenzweig and Blackmar 1992, 507). The fiscal crisis of the 1970s, however, inspired a wider institutionalization of local elite control. Overlapping the Carter and Reagan administrations in Washington, D.C., the New York City Parks Commissioner encouraged the formation of private groups to oversee public parks from 1978 to 1983. He also named special administrators for the largest parks, Central Park and Prospect Park. For more than 10 years, the Central Park administrator has also been the president of the Central Park Conservancy. Significantly, while she is one of several people in the Parks Department, including the commissioner, who earn $106,000 a year, her salary is paid by the conservancy. In addition to paying the administrator's salary and expenses, the conservancy raised $64 million during the 1980s (Siegel 1992, 38). According to two political scientists who act as watchdogs over the city's parlous economy, private parks conservancies are one of the few "bright spots" in the Parks Department's budget (Brecher and Horton 1993, 308, 311 ff.).

The Bryant Park Restoration Corporation, a subsidiary of the Bryant Park Business Improvement District, follows a fairly new model in New York State, and in smaller cities around the United States, that allows business and property owners in commercial districts to tax themselves voluntarily for maintenance and improvement of public areas and take these areas under their control. The concept originated in the 1970s as special assessment districts; in the 1980s, the name was changed to a more upbeat acronym, business improvement districts (BIDs). A BID can be incorporated in any commercial area. Because the city government has steadily reduced street cleaning and trash pickups in commercial streets since the fiscal crisis of 1975, there is a real incentive for business and property owners to take up the slack. A new law was required for such initiatives: unlike shopping malls, commercial streets are publicly owned, and local governments are responsible for their upkeep. BIDs were created by the New York State Legislature in 1983; by 1993, 26 were up and running in New York City: 10 in Brooklyn, 9 in Manhattan, 5 in Queens, and 1 each in the Bronx and Staten Island. In 1994, as new BIDs were still being formed, a super-BID was established for an area of lower Manhattan from City Hall to the Battery. One of its "public" functions will be to enhance the area surrounding the World Financial Center and Battery Park City, which are publicly owned but leased to private developers. At the same time, private schools and apartment buildings on the affluent Upper East Side have discussed forming a BID to fight street crime in their area with neighborhood security guards. BIDs have also spread to other states. There are 400 of them in New Jersey.

In New York City, Manhattan BIDs are the richest, reflecting higher property values and business volume. While the entire sum of all special assessments in the 10 Brooklyn BIDs in fiscal year 1993 was a little less than $4 million, 3 BIDs in Manhattan *each* had an assessment over $4 million. These unequal resources enable rich BIDs to do more. A BID in a neighborhood shopping strip in Queens may just be able to buy street cleaning services and put up Christmas lights, but a midtown BID can undertake public works. The Grand Central Partnership, a 53-block organization whose center is on 42nd Street near Bryant Park, employs uniformed street cleaners and security guards, runs a tourist information booth, refashions the illumination of Grand Central Terminal, closes a street in front of the terminal to make a new outdoor eating space, and hires lobbyists to ask the state legislature for supplemental funds from the state budget. Also, while the staffs of BIDs in the outer boroughs worry about working without health benefits and pensions, the executive director of the Grand Central Partnership, who also oversees the Bryant Park Restoration Corporation and the 34th Street BID, earns $315,000 a year—more than double the mayor's salary.

What kind of public culture is created under these conditions? Do urban BIDs create a Disney World in the streets, take the law into their own hands, and reward their entrepreneurial managers as richly as property values will allow? If elected public officials continue to urge the destruction of corrupt and bankrupt public institutions, I imagine a scenario of drastic privatization, with BIDs replacing the city government. As Republican Mayor Rudolph Giuliani said enthusiastically at the second annual NYC BIDs Association Conference in 1994, "This is a difficult time for the city and the country as we redefine ourselves. BIDs are one of the true success stories in the city. It's a tailor-made form of local government" (*Daily News*, November 16, 1994).

The Grand Central Partnership, a midtown BID established in 1988, assumed a key governmental function four years later by issuing its own bonds. At that time, the BID sold $32.3 million worth of 30-year bonds with an A1 rating from Moody's Investors

Service Inc. and Standard & Poor's Corp.; this was a higher rating than that of New York City bonds. In contrast to municipal bonds, which are backed by tax rolls, the BID's bonds are backed by the special property assessment building owners pay annually to the BID. With the proceeds of its bond sales, the Grand Central Partnership plans to rebuild public space in its domain, taking on projects that the city government has neither the will nor the means to accomplish. Traffic is banned from the Park Avenue viaduct while the partnership, acting as a nonprofit developer, creates new space and leases it to a restaurant. Another area across the street will be redesigned as a demonstration district for new lighting, signage, landscaping, street furniture, kiosks, and traffic grids.

We know who defines this image of the city, but who will occupy it? City government agencies have approved the BID's plans, not least because the property owners (including the Philip Morris Corporation) are powerful and their projects promise to create revenue. But the local community board, representing a wide variety of business interests, has challenged the BID's plans because they make traffic more crowded and alter the somewhat rakish, small business character of the area around Grand Central Terminal (Feiden 1992; Wolfson 1992; Slatin 1993). (Creating a pedestrian mall here also makes a taxi ride from Grand Central Terminal to my house more expensive, since cars can no longer turn straight into Park Avenue to drive downtown.) The community board has raised questions about the effectiveness of the BID's "services" for the homeless and the brusqueness of their removal by the BID's security guards (*New York Observer*, January 17, 1994; Community Board 6, March, 1994). These issues were dramatized when the Coalition for the Homeless, an advocacy group, sued the partnership for hiring out the homeless as security guards at below the minimum wage. The partnership was also accused of failing to give homeless people job training and hiring some of them, itself, as low-wage employees (Drucker, 1994). "For years," the coalition stated in a complaint filed February 1, 1995, with the U.S. District Court, Southern District of New York, the Grand Central Partnership and 34th Street Partnership

> have victimized the homeless . . . by tantalizing them with their alluringly named 'Pathways to Employment' ('PET') program, which promises job training and meaningful employment. In fact, the PET program provides neither meaningful job training nor meaningful jobs. Rather, it is bait that lures the homeless to Defendants at illegal, subminimum wages. . . . This cheap, and largely defenseless, labor pool has enabled Defendants to land significant contracts because Defendants' use of a captive, underpaid homeless labor force enables them to underbid competitors who compensate their own employees at lawful rates.

When, in January 1995, the partnership proposed expanding its jurisdiction up Madison Avenue as far as 56th Street, including Sony Plaza, the Coalition for the Homeless offered the only principled opposition.

In their own way, under the guise of improving public spaces, BIDs nurture a visible social stratification. Like the Central Park Conservancy, they channel investment into a central space, a space with both real and symbolic meaning for elites as well as other groups. Like the Central Park Conservancy, the resources of the rich Manhattan BIDs far outstrip those even potentially available in other areas of the city, even if those areas set up BIDs. The rich BIDs' opportunity to exceed the constraints of the city's financial system confirms the fear that the prosperity of a few central spaces will stand in contrast to the impoverishment of the entire city.

BIDs can be equated with a return to civility, "an attempt to reclaim public space from the sense of menace that drives shoppers, and eventually store owners and citizens, to the suburbs" (Siegel 1992, 43–44). But rich BIDs

can be criticized on the grounds of control, accountability, and vision. Public space that is no longer controlled by public agencies must inspire a liminal public culture open to all but governed by the private sector. Private management of public space does create some savings: saving money by hiring nonunion workers, saving time by removing design questions from the public arena. Because they choose an abstract aesthetic with no pretense of populism, private organizations avoid conflicts over representations of ethnic groups that public agencies encounter when they subsidize public art, including murals and statues (*New York Times*, July 17, 1992, p. C22; J. Kramer 1992).

Each area of the city gets a different form of visual consumption catering to a different constituency: culture functions as a mechanism of stratification. The public culture of midtown public space diffuses down through the poorer BIDs. It focuses on clean design, visible security, historic architectural features, and the sociability among strangers achieved by suburban shopping malls. Motifs of local identity are chosen by merchants and commercial property owners. Since most commercial property owners and merchants do not live in the area of their business or even in New York City, the sources of their vision of public culture may be eclectic: the nostalgically remembered city, European piazzas, suburban shopping malls, Disney World. In general, however, their vision of public space derives from commercial culture.

An interesting application of BIDs' taking the opportunity to re-present public culture is the new "community court" in Times Square, which grew out of a proposal put forward in 1991 by officials close to the Times Square BID. The proposal was to dispense immediate justice for local crimes in an unused theater in the area (*New York Times*, November 15, 1991, p. A1). The goal of this unprecedented decentralization—not even envisioned in the city's criminal justice system since the 1960s—was to clean up Times

Square. Prominent city and state government officials in the court system praised the proposal. A neighborhood court, they said, would speed the disposition of cases against minor offenders accused of such crimes as prostitution, shoplifting, trespassing, and running a scam of three-card monte in the street, and enhance community control over quality of life. The theater owner who would donate the use of the theater for a courthouse, who was also the chairman of the Schubert Organization, spoke of the "devastating" impact of crime on a long-delayed Times Square redevelopment plan. The deputy mayor for public safety admitted the proposal for a Times Square court could be criticized as "elitist," but that seemed to be less of a problem than how to finance it. The *Times* printed an editorial in strong support. The only voices of dissent were raised by the Manhattan District Attorney's office, which protested the diversion of time and money to a single branch court, and the Legal Aid Society, which joined the DA's office in criticizing the new pressures on attorneys to run up to midtown from the primary site of the courts in lower Manhattan.

The Times Square court promised to create a new public culture consistent with a historic local identity: "With attentive spectators filling red plush seats, judges and attorneys could be expected to maintain high standards of efficiency and dignity long absent from the Criminal Court. The judges would also be encouraged to use more imaginative and productive sentences than fines or jail time: three-card monte players, for example, might be required to help with street-cleaning" (*New York Times*, November 17, 1991). In fact, once the court was set up in 1994, community service sentences of 10 to 12 days were carried out in the Times Square area. A person convicted by the community court was given a broom by the Times Square BID and told to sweep the sidewalks, not unlike the Grand Central Partnership hiring the homeless to sweep 42nd Street. This is a public culture worthy of Dickens.

Dispersing the Crowd: Bonus Plazas and the Creation of Public Space

Gregory Smithsimon

BONUS PLAZAS

Bonus spaces are the public spaces included in many high-rise building projects in New York and other cities. They include outdoor plazas as well as indoor arcades, sidewalk widenings, public passageways, and a host of other spatial forms. The term *bonus* derives from incentive zoning regulations that give builders additional floor area ratio (FAR), allowing them to build larger, taller buildings in exchange for providing public plaza space at street level. Thus, the bonus FAR and the plaza represent a contract between a developer and the city (and its citizens), in which public access is provided in exchange for private benefits. Unlike other privatized spaces, the city recognizes the public's rights to the space such as the right of anyone to use the space as long as he or she is not disruptive. Because of such requirements, bonus plazas meet common standards for a public space, namely, that people can access it, use it, claim it, and (modestly) modify it (Lynch 1981; Carr et al. 1992; Dijkstra 2000), even though the plazas are not publicly owned.

The bonus-plaza period formally began in 1961, when New York's zoning revision included bonus FAR in exchange for plazas in high-rise districts. Though it was modeled after the landmark tower-in-a-plaza that Mies van der Rohe designed for Seagram in 1958, the new zoning law was more than the institutionalization of modernist aesthetics. The towers offered floor plans that were easier to design, build, and rent than the "wedding cake" buildings dictated by the earlier codes, whose floor plans were set farther back from the street every few stories. Thus the bonus-plaza regime, in theory at least, provided something for everyone: plazas for the public, the latest styles for architects, additional FAR for developers, and rationalized floor plans for tenants.

The bonus plazas that have resulted are significant for several reasons. Not only do they capture the ideal of urban design in the mid-twentieth century, they were the first experiment with private developers building public space to meet planning and zoning objectives. The privatization process that created privately owned public spaces is now widespread, and New York's bonus plazas and incentive zoning regulations have become models for cities across the country and around the world when they pursue public goals with private builders (Kayden et al. 2000; Whyte 1988).

EVIDENCE OF EMPTY BONUS PLAZAS

While there has not been substantial examination of the possible motives of actors involved in the creation of bonus plazas, extensive evidence has documented that the vast majority of the bonus spaces are indeed barren, unusable, and exclusive. In fact, bonus plazas are at times so maligned that they have become, like public housing towers and urban renewal, a symbol of what is wrong with cities and modern urban planning. Three separate bodies of research established bonus plazas as dead space.

First, Whyte's extensive fieldwork in these plazas compellingly documented that most such spaces are not public and "were awful: sterile, empty spaces not used for much of anything" in what were otherwise crowded, busy central business districts (Whyte 1988, 234). Whyte sought to discover the features that would make spaces usable, but his research also identifies numerous spaces that were not. "The evidence was overwhelming. Most of the spaces were not working well—certainly not well enough to warrant the very generous subsidies given for them" (245). Whyte's work, in association with the Department of City Planning, first established that the products of incentive zoning discouraged public use, and framed that shortcoming as a breach of the contract between developers and the public.

The second assessment of bonus plazas is *Privately Owned Public Space* (Kayden et al. 2000). This was the first systematic study of all New York City bonus plazas—prior to its publication, not even the Department of City Planning, a coauthor of the study, knew which spaces in the city were covered by bonus-plaza regulations. The book provides a valuable quantitative assessment of bonus plazas. After assembling an archival record of the spaces from Department of City Planning and Department of Buildings records, with the cooperation of the Municipal Art Society, researchers led by Jerold Kayden evaluated the use and public quality of the spaces. Each space was evaluated and then classified, that is, graded. To assign a classification, every one of the 503 spaces in the study (of which the 291 in midtown and downtown are considered in this article) was visited several times.[1] Classification "relied

on extensive empirical observation and users' interviews, culminating in the exercise of judgment about use or potential use" (Kayden et al. 2000, 51). Researchers focused on how people used the space (including how many people used it, what they did there, which of the provided amenities they used, and who they were demographically) and on design and operation of the space, "with particular attention paid to how it supported or discouraged potential use," including design, actions by the current owner and manager, and compliance with legal requirements governing the space (52). In midtown and the financial district, more than half such spaces were found either to fail to attract people to the space or to actively repel them. This actually understates the original scope of the problem, since in the intervening decades some owners significantly upgraded their spaces, under direction from the Department of City Planning, in exchange for permission to make other changes the owner wanted such as the introduction of retail uses to a space or the closure of a space at night. Furthermore, the grades given by the *Privately Owned Public Space* researchers were particularly generous, because they graded the space primarily on assessments of potential use, not on actual use. Still, the unmatched rigor and thoroughness of the study establishes the survey as an invaluable source against which to compare other findings.

Third, the archives of New York City's Department of City Planning show the agency regularly reached similar conclusions during the 40 years it has been requiring bonus plazas and rewriting regulations in an effort to produce more popular spaces. The commission wrote, in 1975, that "too many have merely been unadorned and sterile strips of cement. These 'leftover' spaces are merely dividers of buildings, windy, lonely areas, without sun or life."[2] The records are also a valuable guide to exclusionary design elements, since as soon as one was identified, the commission sought to prohibit it from future buildings. For example, from the start, plazas could not be elevated too far above or sunken too far below street level, since people would not use them. In 1971, sunken plazas were eliminated entirely. Paving treatment was eventually required to be the same on the plaza as on the adjoining sidewalk, since a granite courtyard next to a concrete sidewalk reads to passersby as a separate, private entity. Indoor spaces had advantages to users because they could be climate controlled and therefore used year-round, but city planners found that a glassed-in space looked to pedestrians like a private lobby; acted as a barrier; and produced a slightly darker, less welcoming space. So signs and large doors were required to signal that those spaces were public.

Throughout the 40 years of the bonus-plaza program, these three sources have consistently found that the spaces are often not public at all and that the city has failed to obtain the types of spaces it had hoped it would gain in exchange for FAR bonuses. But while all three studies considered the state of bonus plazas, none contains careful explanations of why they are so.

WHO EXCLUDES?

Data from this range of sources demonstrate that most bonus plazas were empty and unused because developers did not want them to be used. Developers—not architects or city planners—play the decisive role in creating highly exclusive public spaces. These actions were not simply an effect of the financial motivation to "do the minimum" to get a square-footage bonus, as observers of the bonus-plaza program have often suggested. Nor were they the result of architects blinded by the glitter of architectural modernism, as others believed. Instead, exclusion was a goal of its own.

City planners with extended, firsthand knowledge of the process of creating bonus plazas identified developers as the actors responsible for exclusionary spaces. Jonathan Barnett, who was director of urban design for the New York City planning department from 1967 to 1971, took this position: "Spaces are often inhospitable, not because their designers were stupid but because the owners of the buildings . . . deliberately sought an environment that encouraged people to admire the building briefly and then be on their way" (Barnett 1982, 179). One current city planning staffer concurred. "Well, everything pointed in that direction, which is why we changed the regulations so many times. The client [i.e., the developer] wanted the space to be private, as private looking as possible, as private feeling as possible."

City planners often explicitly see themselves as advocates for more usable spaces and recognize that this role can put them in opposition to developers and architects. Philip Schneider, who has been with the Department of City Planning since the 1970s, called his office's emphasis on public accessibility "a general tension" in the development process. This could lead outside observers to wonder if their accounts were biased by seeing themselves in opposition to developers. But architects who worked closely in cooperation with developers actually paint a more critical picture than city planners, and assign responsibility with less reservation. Richard Roth, whose firm Emery Roth designed a quarter of the bonus plaza buildings in midtown and downtown, gave this explanation:[3]

Roth: The plazas got bleaker and bleaker and bleaker—less people oriented.
GS: Why do you think that happened?
Roth: Because, again, the owners of the buildings didn't want a lot of people sitting in those spaces. Why do you never have seats in a lobby of an office building? Because they didn't want people sitting there. . . .

GS: How did they make them bleaker and bleaker?

Roth: Because they kept putting less and less in. The client kept saying. "No, I want it as minimal as possible." (interview, June 1, 2003)

Roth also provided specific examples of developers' instructions. Paramount Plaza, at 50th Street and Broadway, is notorious for having two unused sunken sections, even though sinking plazas below street level is known to keep people out of them. In the 2000 catalog of bonus plazas, Jerold Kayden et al. (2000) wrote,

> Successor owners to the original developer of this Broadway office tower have faced an inherently problematic site condition at their full blockfront special permit plaza ... two square holes punched into its north and south ends creating sunken spaces. ... Neither offered a reason to stay, lacking functional seating and other public amenities. ... Sunken spaces have always presented difficulties and their pathology is not hard to discern. Compared with street-level spaces, sunken spaces require greater effort on the part of the public to reach them. They are frequently dark and cold, lacking sunlight more available at street level. Without the eyes and ears of pedestrians, they can be downright scary. Without usable amenities and supportive retail uses, they can be dead. ... The empirical record of sunken spaces in the city is not a happy one. (p. 148)

While they succinctly describe the well-known problems of this and other sunken plazas, Kayden et al. restrict themselves to discussing the space passively, as if it were a natural feature. The sunken plazas are "an inherently problematic site condition," but why would the plaza be in this condition? Roth explains much more actively why that space was built as it was:

Roth: When we designed Paramount Building. I mean, again, it was Uris, and they didn't want anybody on the plaza. That's why we had the two sunken areas on either side. It took them forever to rent those [storefronts at the edges of the] sunken areas. One side was a restaurant, the north corner was a restaurant. On the south corner, they never got, I mean, and it was a perfect thing [for potential use] because it was connected to subways, but Percy and Harold [Uris] didn't want people.

GS: So when you come to work on that project, what do they say to you about the plazas?

Roth: We want something that people walk across and not stay there. You know what your parameters are.

Did the Urises, who developed the site, understand that their goals of excluding people from this privately owned public space could be achieved through design? In yet another example, Roth makes clear they did, and that they were committed to that goal:

GS: So developers did understand that there were things they could put in as well?

Roth: Right. Exactly. Oh yeah. I remember when we were doing 55 Water Street. I got Larry Halprin from the West Coast to do the plaza for the building. And Larry Halprin was very people oriented, to the point where his plazas became "people" places. And when Percy and Harold Uris saw this people place that Halprin had created, he was fired!
Now Larry Halprin happened to be a first cousin of the Urises, which I didn't know when I got Larry involved.

Saky Yakas strongly agreed that spaces would be designed to be unusable by people on the developer's instruction. He suggested that the goal, in more recent plazas, was not total, but filtered, exclusion.

> Although the intent of these is to be public, a lot of the design is geared towards making people think before they use them. I mean, you know, a lot of people don't know that these are public spaces. I think a lot of developers like them to not know they're public spaces. And one of the ways is how you do your fencing or how you change the grade, how you situate them in relationship to the buildings, how you use your cameras. They want them to be used, but you want a feel of exclusivity.

From the early period Roth discussed to the more recent buildings Yakas designed, the influence of developers remained constant.

It is possible, of course, that architects are simply creating this explanation after the fact to assign blame to developers rather than themselves. But while this role of developers has not been established in public discussions, it is consistent in the accounts of different architects. Furthermore, Roth at least remains on good personal terms with developers he worked with, and it is unlikely he would inaccurately slight them to make himself look better.[4]

Archival interviews of architects corroborate these accounts. William H. Whyte's interview with a midtown architect affirms that exclusion was not accidental but intentional. Edward Durell Stone, architect of GM Plaza, explained that in a plaza already lacking benches, sitting was difficult because "the owner didn't want people loitering and thus the railings were not designed for comfort" (Conversation with Architect 1972). (It bears repeating here that a larger, more profitable building was permitted by the city in exchange for the benefits the public was to derive from this public space.) Stone's plaza had already been widely derided as among the worst of the worst; architecture critic Ada Louise Huxtable described it as an "insidious kind of destruction" (Huxtable 1970). What such critics did not realize, or

suggest, was that Stone had designed such an unusable plaza on purpose and at the behest of his client, and that for decades it served its intended purpose quite well.

Finally, comments by developers themselves are consistent with those of planners and architects, and support the finding that exclusion was developers' goal. "Building plazas usually have few if any seating accommodations," explained a sympathetic profile in the real estate section of *The New York Times* about Edward Sulzberger, president of the Sulzberger-Rolfe real estate firm.[5] "One of the biggest problems of buildings' security, Mr. Sulzberger points out, is loitering on the premises. . . . Builders therefore do not seek to make their plazas more comfortable to encourage passers-by to spend time resting there" (*New York Times* 1969). This developer thus redefined the pre-requisite to using public space—spending time there—as a "security problem," responded with design choices to prevent people from sitting down, and would have been quite disturbed to find anyone actually using the space he provided for the public. Unusable, barren, empty public space devoid of seating or other basic amenities was not an accident of design; it was by design.

The case of developer Melvyn Kaufman, though exceptional in the types of buildings he produced, illustrates the centrality of the developer. Kaufman is recognized for his distinctively whimsical plazas, which encourage public engagement and rely on lively street life for their impact. Rather than shirking the public, Kaufman's designs invite people in and entertain them with large swinging benches, human-size chess pieces, Wizard of Oz-reminiscent winding brick paths, abstract 20-foot-high clocks, and unconventional lobbies in a 1970s science fiction aesthetic. His spaces are also, by the grades of *Privately Owned Public Spaces*, exceptionally public places. In a survey where 56% of plazas received grades of only 1 or 2 (5 being the highest on the scale), and where even counting only a building's best space (some have more than one), the average grade was 2.52. Kaufman's average of 3.50 was the highest for any developer who had more than one building. Not only was his average high, but his scores were more consistent than almost any other developer.

Roth took credit for getting Kaufman interested in plazas, but not intentionally. According to Roth, he invited Kaufman to visit an architecture class he was teaching in the 1960s, where Kaufman became interested in the ideas and energy of the students. From then on, he wanted to reflect this energy and enthusiasm in his plazas. But Roth makes clear these spaces were different than those he designed for clients such as the Urises or the Fishers because of the explicit instructions and social goals each developer had for the plazas.

Architect Peter Claman agrees that developers influenced the quality of a plaza. "It's a question of basic attitude [on the part of a developer]. . . . The plaza was not made for the developers' benefit, it was made for the public's benefit: That was tough to sell to certain developers." Unlike city planners, who, records show, advocated consistently for public space, or architects, who designed more or less accessible spaces depending on their client, developers decided whether their plaza would be usable or not.

ALTERNATE EXPLANATIONS FOR EXCLUSION IN PUBLIC SPACE

Given the regularity during the past 40 years with which developers built plazas that did not attract people, it is surprising how often this outcome is considered accidental. Contrary to the evidence presented above, previous studies have treated barren public plazas as unintended consequences of unrelated priorities. They are thought to be the products of developers' drive to save money (and miscalculations regarding the returns of investing in public spaces), architects' romance with modernism, or building managers' urge to lighten their workload by keeping plazas empty. Some (though not all) of these play roles, but none are as influential as suggested by the literature. Here I will assess the relative strength of each proposed influence. I consider these explanations because they dominate the discussion of unusable public spaces. Doing so is crucial to the study of the social significance of public space, because it further establishes that the social effects of public space are more often intentional than incidental, the desired outcome and not the side effect of other choices.

DOING THE MINIMUM AND MINDING THE BOTTOM LINE

A common assumption is that developers' actions were simply motivated by their drive to maximize profits. By this logic, developers "do the minimum" required to get the square-footage bonus. But consideration of the actual expenses of a plaza actually casts doubt on whether developers were doing the minimum, whether economic considerations alone would have driven them to do so, and whether this would have led inevitably to unusable spaces.

Philip Schneider voices a common conclusion when he says that "they were interested primarily in getting the bonus and doing whatever they had to do to get past city planning. They would look to do the minimum." Whyte (1988) similarly believed developers did the minimum to gain the bonus. Jonathan Barnett of the Department of City Planning took this position and pointed out two specific costs developers attended to: insurance and maintenance.

Barnett's experience with builders of public plazas and his firsthand observation of their work allowed him to distinguish the priorities of building owners more finely than most. He explained that the actual priorities for a privately owned public space depended on what kind of organization owned the building. Buildings owned by corporations are run by facilities managers, who run them much as they do shopping malls. They are hired to keep the place clean and are therefore interested in keeping maintenance easy and inexpensive. The fewer people to clean up after, the fewer plants to water, the better. Entrepreneurs operating their own building want to squeeze as much money out of it as possible, so if they can find a retail tenant or a café interested in paying for the privilege of spreading their chairs into the plaza, so much the better. Only if they "get it," concluded Barnett, would an owner try to make a plaza a lively, public place. Thus, while for Barnett the financial concerns dictate the quality of plazas, who is minding the bottom line determines the specific effect it will have on the space.

There is some evidence for this "cheap-developer" argument. Consistent with Whyte's findings, when given free reign, from 1961 to 1975, developers failed to build a single space of even decent quality, according to the *Privately Owned Public Space* survey. After the passage of regulations specifying what amenities must be provided, in 1975, the record has been much better. But other changes occurred in the city during those periods. And while earlier spaces were poor, that is not to say that they were cheaply built or that keeping building costs low was the primary consideration.

After all, doing the minimum may, in some cases, have been more costly. Richard Roth provided the example of the banal pay phone. Telephone booths paid the highest rent per square foot of any use an office building could have. They were, said Roth, "a very big source of income." But booths in the lobby also brought outsiders into the building and might create nuisances if the space were damaged, vandalized, or misused. By the beginning of the bonus-plaza period,

developers stopped putting booths in their lobbies.

Furthermore, plaza costs were not generally significant. Yakas observed that "it's not a lot of money when you think of what he's spending on each tower; it's really a very small percentage of each project." West, though he said he had worked with a wide range of clients during the past 10 years, had never been on a project that could not afford to hire a landscape architect for the plaza. Peter Claman estimated the cost of a good versus barren plaza at $10 per square foot, which would be $40,000 for an average-size plaza on a building worth many hundreds of millions of dollars.

A more significant challenge to the economic sense of doing the minimum comes from comments by developer Mel Kaufman. Kaufman suggested that popular plazas could actually be an asset to a building. Whyte reported that in a 1972 conversation, Kaufman "confided, as if top secret, that the fun plaza [is] a big selling point. Rented out 77 Water St. much faster than next building. At 747 3rd Avenue, doing better than the competition" ("Talk with Mel Kaufman" 1972). The accuracy and generalizability of this statement still needs to be determined. Roth recalls Kaufman's buildings having been very difficult to rent (though it is not clear plazas were the cause). Others have suggested that Kaufman was successful in his niche but that the approach would not have worked for all kinds of tenants. Still, his example shows that hewing to the profit motive would not in all cases have led developers not to invest money in their plazas. Interviews with architects of more recent buildings add further support for this argument. David West took it for granted that in the buildings he designed from 1995 to the present, the developer wanted a plaza to "succeed," he said, because an attractive, well-used, well-maintained plaza added to the appeal of the building.

A more detailed consideration of one

bonus plaza helps demonstrate that while cost was something developers always attended to, it is too simplistic to think only this would lead to unadorned and therefore unused spaces.

Consider the Alliance Capital building at 1345 Sixth Avenue. The space is notable for the effectiveness of its exclusion. Built in 1969, before stricter design requirements were imposed, it does a remarkably good job of keeping people off the public space: At lunch hour, the sidewalks abutting the space are so packed with people that it is difficult to get through. Yet the plaza is empty—only a half dozen people are seated on its 10,000 square feet to eat lunch. A closer examination suggests why. Though the plaza stretches a full city block from West 54th to West 55th streets, there are only three benches; even on a calm day, two of them are intermittently sprinkled by a fine mist from one of the two fountains. The fountains themselves are remarkable: While the fountain ledges that run along the public sidewalks are crowded with people sitting, eating, and talking, the fountains have been designed such that within the plaza, they actually have no ledges, preventing even that improvised, but popular, seating option. The immense fountains also effectively put half of the plaza's area off-limits by putting it under water. And unlike other, similar front plazas that use some of their space for a park-like cubby of trees and benches, the remaining half of the plaza space is a barren, dark, stone-paved expanse leading to the entrance. Considering that the entrance consists only of three revolving doors, it seems unlikely that the entire 200-foot-wide granite plane needs to serve only as an entrance.

But as interesting as Alliance Capital's plaza is as a demonstration of antipublic public space, it also serves as evidence against doing the minimum. For as Jerold Kayden et al. explained, water features such as fountains are notoriously costly and troublesome to maintain, which is why he found that

several of those mandated in post-1975 spaces had been surreptitiously decommissioned (2000). They need to be constantly cleaned, they are mechanical features that break and require maintenance, and some are further complicated by water heaters to allow year-round operation. The property manager of an east midtown tower estimated the annual costs of a much smaller fountain on his plaza at $7,500 per year. This is not a large sum of money when compared to the annual costs of maintaining a large New York City building, but it is considerably more than the cost of people-friendly amenities such as benches.

Fountains have other ongoing costs. They are a liability 24 hours a day that can cause people to slip on wet stone pavement or even drown. If they are operated year-round, they have to be heated. And since Manhattan plazas are almost never built over solid ground but rather above several basement floors, leakage is a costly risk ("Plazas, Nice for Strollers" 1969). With each of these characteristics, fountains add to the leading developers' worries identified by Barnett— maintenance and insurance, which owners have paid throughout the building's 30-year existence. But they also achieve the developers' goal Barnett identified: encouraging people to admire the space briefly and then be on their way.

Roth, whose firm designed the Alliance Capital building for the Fisher Brothers, described a design process that incurred still greater costs. Roth had admired a fountain shown in a photograph from Australia. "I loved it," he said, "and I presented it to Larry Fisher, who also loved it." But efforts to locate the designer in Australia turned up nothing. Ultimately, he commissioned a fountain consultant to recreate the dandelion-shaped fountain. The fountain was popular enough, said Roth, that the consultant made and sold smaller copies of it.

To call such developers too cheap to invest in their plaza is unfair. To attribute the emptiness of the plaza to capitalists' penny-pinching rationality would be just as inaccurate. Most plazas are empty, but not because making them useful was too costly.

ARCHITECTS AND MODERNISM

Arguing that developers, not architects, have a decisive influence on design contradicts the conventional aesthetic presentation of architecture fostered by glossy articles about landmark buildings in architecture magazines that suggest the form is an expression of the architect's artistic vision. Blame for architects came from other sources as well. Herbert Gans points out, for instance, that Jane Jacobs blamed empty public spaces on "unknown architects (she called them planners) who were designing International Style public housing projects" (Gans 2006, 214). Such architects were simultaneously building International Style office buildings and private apartment towers in New York, but the usability of the towers proves not to have been a result of their aesthetic preferences.

David Brain's examination of the profession of architecture stresses that architects have far less autonomy than imagined. "The autonomy of the architect is hemmed in on all sides: The client controls the budget; building technology is controlled by builders, engineers, and industries that produce materials and equipment; the construction industry is an intersection of several markets" (Brain 1991, 263). Design is hardly in the architect's hands alone.

Regarding the influence of modernism itself, it is unlikely that the style or conventions of modernism affected the public quality of the spaces. While architects did admire the Seagram Building, the inspiration for New York's bonus-plazas program, the absence of amenities such as seats or even ledges in plazas was explained clearly enough by developers' expectations, without reference to aesthetic movements. Nor were all plazas'

architects conventional modernists: Edward Durell Stone, who explained the developer's desire that there be nowhere to sit in the GM Building's plaza, also designed 2 Columbus Circle. That building, celebrated by Wolfe as a departure from barren modernism, is full of the ornamentation modernism eschewed. But Stone's plazas were as barren and unusable as any (Hales 2004).

Other influences on the design of a building played a much greater role than architectural style. Interviews for this study and the account of the development process provided here both argue strongly against the possibility that architects had such a free and decisive role that a trend as large as the quality of bonus plazas is a result of their initiative or the modernist fashions of their profession.

CONCLUSION

While critics have long bemoaned the exclusivity of most bonus plazas, there has been little consideration and no agreement about who is responsible. The most popular explanations—that unusable plazas are the unintended result of architects' infatuation with modernism or of developers' parsimoniousness—are not supported by a close study of bonus plazas.

Evidence from diverse sources indicates that developers play a decisive role in shaping bonus plazas, and that most take the opportunity to use designs that exclude users from the spaces. Analysis of data from *Privately Owned Public Spaces* showed that developers exercised more control over plazas than architects, who were more often blamed for the state of plazas. Interviews with planners, as well as architects who were still on good terms professionally and personally with developers, confirmed that developers ordered plaza designs that would discourage use. These accounts were consistent even though they were at odds with the conventional explanation that plaza problems were incidental to other concerns. When developers have discussed plazas at all, they have made similar points: that they had the power to determine usability and that most chose to discourage people from using public plazas.

Understanding the decisive role developers play in shaping plazas provides insight into this persistent failure of urban design and the source of one of urbanists' and planners' long-standing frustrations. A more accurate account of barren plazas could also help urbanists improve plazas, public-space incentive zoning, and other privately owned public space to prevent more unusable space from being built.

The widespread tendency to build exclusive bonus plazas cannot simply be explained in economic terms. Particularly given the low relative cost of a plaza, the fact that less exclusive designs could have been built for comparable cost, the potential economic advantages of an attractive space, and the high social impact of a plaza, it is clear that social considerations, not economic ones, are responsible for exclusionary designs. While respondents here described control in broad, class-based terms, that does not rule out the possibility of racially motivated public-space control proposed by Davis (1990, 224, 226), Zukin (1995, 25), and others. In fact, the coincidence of the construction of the worst plazas with the era of White flight suggests bonus plazas may be further physical manifestations of the period of White abandonment of urban space. If so, developers would have been the actors through which larger historical processes of exclusion were reproduced in public space.

Developers' privatizing intentions have had significant effects on public spaces. Since the bonus-plaza program, cities seeking more public space have increasingly turned to public–private partnerships. In the absence of actual democratic control, spaces are most public, most used, and most accessible when control and design of the space is retained by groups with a long institutional history of commitment to public access. In New York, the Department of City Planning and the Department of Parks and Recreation have both shown such a commitment. In a similar vein, though they are rarely presented as ideal examples of public spaces, the parks of the Battery Park City Parks Conservancy are much more successful than bonus plazas. Like plazas, those parks are funded by private development, but they are run by a parks conservancy with a strong institutional commitment to public use of the spaces. In contrast, planned waterfront development in Greenpoint, Brooklyn, will rely on a model much more like the bonus-plaza approach: Individual developers will be expected to build and maintain waterfront public spaces. On the basis of the findings here, those spaces are likely to be much less public and much less widely used than their counterparts in Battery Park City. This study suggests that incentives to build privately owned public spaces are not enough: Even with regulations and interventions, developers often create a public realm that is unusable and undesirable.

The history of city planning regulation of bonus plazas suggests a more varied role for the state when public space is privatized. While in other studies the state has been found to be an agent of privatization, here archival records and regulatory revisions show that planners in local government regularly opposed efforts to create exclusionary designs. This apparent contradiction is part of the more variegated portrait found in this study: Most developers built inaccessible plazas, but there were exceptions such as Melvyn Kaufman. Similarly, while most studies have found government complicity with privatization, there are elements within New York City's government with different agendas. If so, there is at least the potential for advocates for public space to find allies in some segments of city government.

Of course, some state actors do create

exclusionary public spaces. New York State agencies, after all, built Harlem's Adam Clayton Powell State Office Building and 1 Police Plaza, towers with public spaces that bear many similarities to bonus plazas. Were these publicly designed plazas also intentionally made inaccessible? The actors are structurally different than those who built bonus plazas, and so the answer would require different empirical evidence. But this study of private developers demonstrates that exclusion doesn't happen accidentally, but intentionally, suggesting exclusionary public space in state projects is also intentional. Such a finding would be consistent with the body of public-space research that presumed government reflects business interests; now that there is direct evidence of what business interests are in public space, it will be that much easier to test that proposition.

Over nearly 45 years, bonus plazas have gained advocates who seek to defend and expand the usability and public access of bonus plazas. Indeed, much of the research on plazas has been done to further those goals. Until now, bonus-plaza advocates have ignored the possibility that such spaces are intentionally rendered unusable, perhaps believing that their case was made rhetorically stronger by presuming everyone wanted "good" public space. But the decades-long record shows that when private actors can develop space without significant public input, there are unlimited ways in which a space can be made inaccessible. Recognizing that the same actors who are entrusted with creating public space in our densest and most valuable downtowns contravene public objectives is a vital first step in restoring the broad public participation necessary to create successful, widely used public spaces.

NOTES

1. My study is of the 291 spaces at 219 buildings in midtown and downtown. Some buildings had multiple bonus spaces, such as a plaza and an arcade, which were counted and graded separately.

2. From bonus-plaza zoning archives of the City Planning Commission, April 16, 1975. In possession of Philip Schneider.

3. Emery Roth & Sons' long list of achievements includes being the architect of record for all seven buildings of the World Trade Center. Minoru Yamasaki was the architect.

4. On Roth's ongoing relationship with developers: Roth is retired, and I interviewed him during one of his twice-yearly visits to New York from the Bahamas. During the interview, he suggested I talk to developer Melvyn Kaufman, saying he would put in a word for me since "I have to call Mel anyway." In a second interview, he mentioned writing a letter of condolence to a developer after the passing of his brother.

5. Sulzberger is evidently not related to the Sulzberger family that runs the *Times*. John T. McQuiston. "Edward Sulzberger Is Dead at 80; President of Real Estate Concern" (obituary). *The New York Times*, July 1, 1988, p. B8.

Defying Disappearance: Cosmopolitan Public Spaces in Hong Kong

Lisa Law

INTRODUCTION

In Western, capitalist democracies much attention has been directed towards the gendering of cities along public–private lines, the demise of public spaces as sites of democratic politics and the emergence of psuedo-public spaces of corporate interest and consumption (see, among others, McDowell, 1999; Fraser, 1992; Mitchell, 1995; Zukin, 1991). These issues are also important throughout many parts of urban Asia as economies and societies transform. The implications for city life of widespread inclusion of women into the labour force and the rapid development of shopping malls and other spaces of mass consumption are only two pertinent cases in point. Yet the meanings attached to public space and the anxieties associated with its disappearance are mediated through cultural politics that can be quite distinct from those that unfold in places such as Europe or North America. This paper examines how contemporary anxieties about public space in Hong Kong are difficult to disentangle from the post-colonial moment.

The specification of Hong Kong is deliberate and signifies the importance of defining the ways in which public spaces in different cities are understood and used.[1] Public spaces are often conceived as 'social spaces' that are produced and appropriated by different groups (for example, the state, capitalists,

various identity groups, counter-cultures, etc.). In some cases, it might be useful to understand public spaces as 'cultural landscapes', however, and re-imagine them as material manifestations of an "ongoing *relationship* between people and place" (Mitchell, 2000, p. 102). In Central Hong Kong, the key site of this research, attention to the post-colonial helps to keep these social-cultural perspectives of public space in productive tension. On the one hand, the social relations of Central Hong Kong help us to understand the production and appropriation of this public space through its colonial and recent history. These relations further illuminate the transforming meanings through which Central's landscape is known and used. On the other hand, a focus on Central as a cultural landscape— with more explicit attention to its architecture, buildings, open spaces—might help to explain its enduring political meanings that extend beyond any particular social milieu.

DISAPPEARING PUBLIC SPACE

In the face of the Placeless landscape of power and the Anonymous urban vernacular, we might ask where, then, are the erotic spaces of pleasure and encounter, the heterotopic spaces of contestation, the liminal spaces of transition and change? There are not many examples that come to mind [in Hong Kong], and even those that do are somewhat *ambiguous*.

(Abbas, 1997a, p. 86; emphasis added)

In his 1997 analysis of (post)colonial Hong Kong, Ackbar Abbas takes on the enormous task of theorising the politics of cultural space in a city anticipating the hyphenated experience of 'one country, two systems'. The major focus of his writing is the celebrated visual realm of architecture and film—from the urban semiotics of the Hong Kong and Shanghai Bank to the wide-ranging films of Wong Kar-wai. Despite arguing that architecture has a crucial role to play in generating a critical discourse about urban space, Abbas appears resigned to the conviction that it is architecture—and the symbolic order it imagines—that upholds the colonial space of Hong Kong (Abbas, 1997a, p. 65). Indeed, it is the 'placeless' landscape of global capital and the 'anonymous' built form it generates that denies pleasure, contestation and change. Rather than taking up Appadurai's (1996) notion of global flows as facilitating new cultures characterised by the disjunctive 'scapes' of people, technology, finance, ideology and the media, Abbas (1997a, p. 65) pursues a more reductive route and contends that architecture "has the dangerous potential of turning all of us, locals and visitors alike, into *tourists* gazing at a stable and monumental image".

Why architecture, and the city space it reflects and produces, cannot offer the critical possibilities of film rests at least partly on Abbas' notion of 'disappearance'. Hong Kong is a city known through the *cliché* of frenetic rebuilding, where the old is swiftly demolished to make room for the new. To put his sophisticated analysis of disappearance into rather crude form, even Hong Kong's most recently constructed buildings are always threatened with demolition; what appears permanent is very often quite temporary. When buildings are preserved, like the conversion of Flagstaff House into

a museum of Chinese teaware, such conservation is premised on a disappearance of history. Built in 1840, primarily for British military uses, its current use suggests a "harmonious accommodation of Chinese culture in colonial architecture" (Abbas, 1997a, p. 68). The gunboat diplomacy of the British and the historical associations between tea and the Opium Wars, he argues, disappear in a showcase of Chinese culture. Hong Kong is a city where what emerges as new—including a unique local identity—is always intertwined with the conditions of its disappearance. This feeling was particularly acute in the years following the signing of the Sino–British Joint Declaration in 1984, when uncertainty as to what might disappear as Hong Kong 'entered the Chinese fold' became most apparent.

Even the monumental site of Statue Square—the public square in front of the Hong Kong and Shanghai Bank—does not escape the lens of Abbas' critique. He reads the semiotic relation between the Hong Kong and Shanghai Bank (British) and the Bank of China Tower (Chinese) as a political allegory, claiming yet another disappearance: a hyphenated experience disappears into an internationalist architectural system. In this overdetermined landscape of post-colonial politics, Abbas neglects to see Statue Square's dynamic potential—or at least what might escape his Hegelian interpretive grid. Indeed, directly following his comments on ambiguous spaces of pleasure, contestation and change (quoted above), Abbas directs our attention to Statue Square. Despite being taken over by thousands of Filipino domestic workers each Sunday, who gather to shop, gossip, eat Filipino food and enjoy their day off, Abbas suggests that this gathering-space is 'ambiguous' since no real 'contest' has taken place. Statue Square is merely a respite from everyday employer–employee relations, reversing social hierarchies for only one day a week. Elsewhere, I have argued that a visual register cannot capture the important role of the several senses in mediating the space of Central for Filipino women on Sunday, where they disrupt the naturalised representations of the social relations of domestic work (for example, employer–employee, dominant–subordinate) (Law, 2001). Here, however, I shall remain with Abbas' notion of cultural space—dominated, as it is, by the visual—in order to read these spaces with different eyes.

Continuing the theme of 'ambivalent' public spaces, but mobilising a different sense of space from that of Abbas, Cuthbert and McKinnell (1997) contend that Hong Kong's public spaces are disappearing as a result of the on-going corporatisation of development. This process is entwined with the historical merging of the 'knowledge class' with the bureaucracy—a colonial phenomenon that created a powerful class of 'leaselords' (Cuthbert and McKinnell, 1997, p. 299). They demonstrate how Hong Kong's planning and building ordinances have become riddled with ambiguous semantics that give developers much control over the properties they develop. Through this history and practice, euphemistically known as 'positive non-intervention', social spaces in the city now tend to reflect a 'laissez-faire' philosophy (p. 295). This produces 'ambivalent' public spaces where corporate power has control over the activities that occur in them (p. 309). Using detailed case studies of Jardine House and the Hong Kong and Shanghai Bank (among others), they demonstrate how the ownership and control of supposedly public space are invested in these projects: "the public is only permitted to pass over the space, and to be evicted from it if any [undesirable] form of behavior is deployed" (Cuthbert and McKinnell, 1997, p. 302). The 1972 deed of dedication for Jardine House proclaimed

> The company shall be entitled to exclude from the dedicated area any persons causing a nuisance or loitering or sleeping therein or hawking or carrying on any business or activity therein, except bona fide use thereof for the purposes of passage.
> (cited in Cuthbert and McKinnell, 1997, p. 301)

Cuthbert and McKinnell also register disappearance, although in a slightly different discourse from Abbas

> Given the nature of urban development in the context of Hong Kong, history is slowly extinguished, rights are lost, urban space becomes increasingly subject to surveillance and policing, human activities become restricted and the public realm loses its clarity as a symbol of civil society.
> (Cuthbert and McKinnell, 1997, p. 296)

Like Abbas, they also make short mention of the Sunday gathering of Filipino domestic workers, in this case in the area around Jardine House. Jardine House is only one of many properties developed by Central's largest land-holder, Hong Kong Land. There is an extensive network of covered walkways connecting Hong Kong Land's properties in the Central district, some of which are used by Filipinas to gather on their day off. In 1989, Jardine's taped up several pedestrian access points to prevent crowds of Filipinas from gathering—a weekly policing ritual which continues to the present day.[2] What interests Cuthbert and McKinnell is that

> the extensive system of walkways traversing the central area was both paid for and maintained by Jardines. The overall effect was to monopolise and control not merely the land, buildings and associated spaces, but in addition to build pedestrian routes so that they serviced Jardines properties ... This situation was compounded even further by lease conditions, which in allocating plot ratio benefits to developers for 'public space', then returned the space to developers to manage on behalf of the Hong Kong government.
> (Cuthbert and McKinnell, 1997, p. 300)

Here we can see the problematic quite clearly. When public spaces are developed, maintained and surveyed by developers, they lose their status of 'public' spaces. Filipinas *might* be allowed to 'pass over' this space, but precious little else.

These two examples illustrate contemporary anxieties about public space in Hong Kong, despite their mobilisation of different —although in many ways complementary— meanings of space. For Abbas, public spaces are the spaces of culture produced by architecture, encoding relations of power and constituting colonial subjects. For Cuthbert and McKinnell, public spaces are sites of state politics and market forces, but should potentially be separate from both the state and the economy in order to be enjoyed by 'the people'. This latter view suggests the problem of a shrinking public sphere—in Habermas' (1991) sense—where public spaces should be an important realm of democratic politics that are, theoretically at least, open to everyone (see also Calhoun, 1992). Both studies also suggest that public space, as an open space surrounding buildings, can become "a controlled and orderly *retreat* where a properly behaved public might experience the spectacle of the city" (Mitchell, 1995, p. 110). Such sentiments are expressed in Cuthbert and McKinnell's notion of a consumer circulating in elevated shopping landscapes and through Abbas' notion of a colonial subject of architecture. Both subjects gaze at the city with unfulfilled desire.

One might query whether or not these landscapes are so authoritative or encompassing. Winchester *et al.* (forthcoming), for example, suggest that landscapes must be understood through the overlapping concepts of power and resistance. On the one hand, landscapes of power are the artifacts of the powerful: of state planners, of corporate power and of global capital. Often these forces work together, so that capital and state power intersect with social identity issues such as class, race, ethnicity and gender.

Together, they produce landscapes replete with ideological sentiments that in turn mediate everyday lived space in part through defining 'insiders' and 'outsiders' in public space. On the other hand, the exertion of power is never complete and landscapes of power are always subject to resistance. Resistance can be understood as overt conflict as well as symbolic strategies and tactics that can invert or transgress the social relations reflected by landscapes. But because power is exercised rather than possessed, they argue, it can also be subverted.

In Central Hong Kong's public spaces, we see these elements of power and resistance intermingling. The landscape is dominated by both local and global capital, whether by Hong Kong Land's interconnected network of commercial buildings or by the British investment in what was the most expensive building in the world in 1985. Furthermore, the history of urban planning has created favourable conditions for developers, which in turn has encouraged the commodification of landscape. Public spaces are not incorporated into development projects for democratic ideals: they increase the flow of commodities in the city. The result is an urban space that reflects the views of the powerful, with local residents merely traipsing over these spaces as passive subjects. But, on Sundays, Filipino domestic workers disrupt the orderly visual space of Central and engage in 'undesirable' activities such as sitting on straw mats in public spaces, getting haircuts and manicures, and hawking goods from home. This is also a site where migrant worker organisations launch protests to critique policies affecting migrant labour, indicating this space is also a "site of oppositional social movements" and "a political site separate from, and often critical of, the state and the economy" (Duncan, 1996, p. 130). Perhaps it is better to argue that Central is a "multicoded" landscape where shoppers, tourists, office workers and migrant groups are " 'reading' and 'writing' different languages in the built environment" (Goss, 1988, p. 398). Indeed, there is more going on in Central than the archetypal binary of power and resistance.

Rather than rearticulate these prophecies about the demise of public space, it might also be important to underline the significance of Central not just as a gathering-place for domestic workers, but also as a densely political site where the politics of domestic work are brought to the public. Refusing to see these people, activities and the area's dynamic potential is yet another way of keeping domestic workers in Hong Kong invisible. Furthermore, political rallies suggest the existence of 'counter-publics' or 'alternative' public spheres, but they might also help repoliticise the notion of Hong Kong's public sphere "into a multiplicity of *heterogeneous* publics" (Duncan, 1996, p. 130; emphasis added). Migrant workers are, after all, not citizens of Hong Kong/China although they do engage in public debates. Because "public spaces and public spheres often do not map neatly onto one another" (Duncan, 1996, p. 130), it might be difficult for Abbas and for Cuthbert and McKinnell to see the significance of Statue Square on Sunday. It is a transnational space, falling outside traditional interpretations of public space that mobilise an outdated conception of a homogeneous civil society struggling against the state. Statue Square is connected to both Hong Kong and Philippine national imaginaries; a public space that defies routine analysis.

LITTLE MANILA: DEFYING DISAPPEARANCE

As Hong Kong joined the ranks of east Asia's 'miracles' in the 1970s, the number of women joining the workforce increased significantly. Women began taking up employment in the rapidly expanding service and industrial sectors, and many families began to rely on two

incomes. There was a simultaneous increase in demand for live-in domestic help and a decrease in the number of women prepared to provide this service. While women from the mainland had traditionally fulfilled this role, they were now attracted to the more autonomous and financially lucrative service and industry jobs that were increasingly becoming available. If they did continue in domestic work, it was on a live-out, part-time basis. In 1975, 1000 Filipino women arrived in Hong Kong on government-approved domestic worker contracts to help fill the gap. Many were well educated and conversant in English and were conveniently being encouraged to work abroad by President Marcos' administration.[3] This trend continued and, by 1998, domestic workers from the Philippines numbered 140 500—a sizeable foreign community.

Since the mid 1980s, domestic workers have gathered in Central on Sundays, transforming its status as the heart of finance and commerce to a home away from home called 'Little Manila'. In Statue Square and its environs, thousands of domestic workers cast off the cultural conventions of their Chinese employers for one day a week and eat Filipino food, read Filipino newspapers and magazines and purchase products from Filipino specialty shops. The queues for the phone booths and at the post office are enormous and, when domestic workers are not posting letters or chatting long-distance, they are writing and reading letters to and from distant loved ones. Little Manila is now a spectacle of modern life in Hong Kong and, somewhat unexpectedly, Hong Kong Land had a role to play in facilitating its appearance.

In 1982, Hong Kong Land proposed that Chater Road be closed to traffic to encourage pedestrian shopping. At that time, and as in many cities around the world, the Central district was deserted at weekends: it was a 'dead public space' (Sennett, 1992). Although the interconnected walkways facilitated access to Hong Kong Land's properties during the working week, at weekends this financial and commercial centre did not attract the crowds. Chater Road was closed on Sundays as an attempt to revive the area. The crowds did arrive but were not the clientèle that Hong Kong Land had in mind. Rather than attracting local shoppers to The Landmark—an up-market mall of branded items—migrant Filipinas came to shop at the down-market World Wide Plaza. Although they did spend their hard-earned wages in the area, they were certainly not Hong Kong Land's idea of the 'right' patrons. Furthermore, they did not come to shop alone—Statue Square was fast becoming an important and symbolic place to meet friends and gossip. Without a private residence to retire to on days-off, thousands of Filipino domestic workers began to make Central a second home. By 1989, Jardine House was taping up walkways and pedestrian access points in the area (as discussed above) and, in 1992, local shops were lodging numerous complaints about noise, litter and illegal street hawking. Hong Kong Land made the suggestion of re-opening Chater Road and encouraging Filipinos to congregate in underground car parks (!), but there was resistance to this from domestic worker organisations, the broader Filipino community and portions of the Chinese community who stood to benefit financially from their presence (Constable, 1997). Chater Road remains closed on Sundays and Filipinos continue to gather by the thousands.

If Filipinas have breathed new life into Central on Sundays, and are therefore using the space in ways intended by urban planners, how are we to consider their use of this public space? Consider the views put forward by Tony Henderson, Chairman of the Humanist Association of Hong Kong, who wrote to the *South China Morning Post* regarding this issue.

At the Megacities 2000 conference ... a somewhat surprisingly close interest was taken in the appearance of the Filipino community in Central on Sundays. It was noted ... with some horror, that the Government's hawker control teams were seen chasing sellers of clothing and foodstuffs as if those people were thieves. It was suggested that the phenomenon created by the Filipino community is an integral part of Hong Kong's cultural heritage ... [and] beyond that, the assembly was seen in a very positive light as something of interest to visitors, something that adds to Hong Kong. Also, that it filled a gap of the inner city—a problem seen worldwide—that is used simply as a business district that shuts down after business hours and over weekends, leaving a desert of dust-blown buildings ... The Hong Kong Bank was given special mention, as having its ground floor as an intended gathering-place by the buildings architect. It was designed to be a public space. Therefore it is appropriate that it is being used in accordance with the designers' wishes by Filipinos. Many buildings in Central have inhibiting streamers preventing anyone sitting near their hallowed walls. Even on weekdays would-be diners are chased from fountains by alert security guards. What a shame ... The Government and the owners of these buildings and precincts should pause to reflect on their next visit to places such as Piccadilly Circus or the parks and fountains of Paris, Rome and other European cities and bring back some of that democratic access and those simple freedoms to help ease the plight of Hong Kong where there is everything on offer, except the right attitude.

(Henderson, 2000)

Although Filipino domestic workers have breathed new life into Central on Sundays, the heavy policing of the area suggests that their presence in the public realm is contested. In an everyday sense, this is evidenced through "hawker control teams" and "inhibiting streamers" that prevent women from hawking home cooking or other goods from home on the one hand, or from doing anything but 'passing over' these public spaces with the aim of consumption on the other. Filipino women gather to chat, gossip, read and write letters, relax, etc., rather than circulating through elevated walkways with the aim of spending their modest income on branded items in Central's malls and boutiques. This form of gathering is common in public spaces in the Philippines and women do not necessarily understand their Sunday activities as resistance: gathering in Central is a respite from a long working week.

It is important to stress that, for most migrants, transnational migration seems to inspire a heightened sense of national identity. In Hong Kong, domestic workers become negatively aware of their identity as Filipinos, particularly since the identity Filipino is usually synonymous with domestic worker. In this sense, gathering in Central is about feeling a positive sense of community and culture in a city where they live with their own stigmatised foreignness on a day-to-day basis. While this collective feeling of 'our place' may not fall within the classic understanding of resistance, it does help to create an alternative public sphere/ space for self-expression. It is also in Central that women have the opportunity to discuss and remember life in the Philippines. Many conversations are about how to pay school fees for their children back at home, how to start small businesses with their remittances, or how to save enough money eventually to go home. This dreaming of a better life, for themselves and for their children, is a creative way of re-imagining the Philippines. So not only is Little Manila a way to make sense of life in Hong Kong, it is a way to imagine a different life at home upon their return. Many women dream of a Philippines that does not export workers and a government that provides enough jobs to keep families together. While this discursive activity does not reach the reifying forms of political rhetoric, it is a form of national imagining that is now part of everyday life.

The appropriation of Statue Square on Sundays is also important because it enables more overt political forms of mobilisation, such as the rallies launched by migrant labour activist organisations in the area. While not all domestic workers formally participate in these events, their very presence in Central gives rallies a high level of visibility. Little Manila and a political presence are producing a new kind of public space in Central—one where both Philippine and Hong Kong politics are interpreted and argued over. There is a need for a different way to understand this production and use of public space so that it does not 'disappear' or remain 'ambiguous' in terms of its use as a site of democratic politics.

There are dozens of non-government organisations (NGOs) in Hong Kong whose aim is to improve the living and working conditions of domestic workers in the city (and region). These NGOs offer a variety of services including: counselling for those in distress; legal advice on working conditions, immigration requirements and the termination of contracts; and temporary shelter for women who are between jobs and therefore without a place to live. Some NGOs have initiated 'savings groups', which are collectives of domestic workers, usually from shared places of home residence, that pool their savings to invest in small businesses at home (Gibson et al., 2001). Harnessing the creative energy of these women, other NGOs publish magazines that feature articles writen by domestic workers about their problems, fears and desires. Most NGOs are involved in data collection and research, which is distributed widely through political networks —either by e-mail, list-serves or by more traditional means such as printed newsletters. Indeed, new print and electronic media have opened new spaces of communication for both domestic workers and their advocates (Law, 2000). The visibility of domestic workers in Statue Square has enabled NGOs to recruit and engage with these women, and magazines and other print media have helped to generate a set of social and political issues.

Together, these factors have enabled more overt political action and NGOs collectively challenge policies that adversely affect labour migrants in the city.

It would be impossible to give a detailed list of rallies that occur in Statue Square. There are simply too many to catalogue. But it is significant that NGOs became a politicised and vocal force in 1982, when the Philippine government instituted Executive Order 857, an order that forced overseas contract workers to remit 50 per cent of their earnings through Philippine banks. NGOs in Hong Kong were infuriated by this infringement on the rights of overseas workers and, by 1984, had formed an alliance of 10 organisations called United Filipinos Against Forced Remittance (Constable, 1997). The alliance was instrumental in having the Executive Order revoked and, with such success to their credit, the coalition renamed itself United Filipinos in Hong Kong (UNIFIL). UNIFIL remains an umbrella organisation for NGOs that monitor the working and living conditions of domestic workers in Hong Kong, but is now joined by many other NGOs that work for domestic workers from countries other than the Philippines.[4] The Coalition for Migrants Rights and the Asian Migrant Co-ordinating Body are two examples of solidarities being forged between NGOs from the Philippines, Indonesia, Thailand, Nepal and Sri Lanka. These affiliations spearhead many campaigns addressing the protection of migrant workers rights and some of their concerns include excessive consulate fees, wage issues, immigration laws and the violation of employment contracts. Below are described two demonstrations that occurred in Central recently, one about the protection of maternity leave for domestic workers and the other about minimum wages.

The first campaign was a response to a proposed legislative amendment in which special conditions were set out for maternity leave for domestic workers. In Hong Kong, unlike other parts of east and south-east Asia, domestic workers have been accorded equal treatment under the Employment Ordinance with regard to maternity benefits. In 1999, however, an amendment was put forward that appeared to remove maternity protection. It proposed that domestic workers and their employers could 'mutually agree' to terminate a contract if a domestic worker was pregnant and if a severance amount was paid. Due to the unequal relationship between employer and employee, however, and because the policy could be abused, migrant advocates sought to quash it. On 29 August 1999, the Coalition for Migrants Rights took to the streets to protest against what was seen as an infringement of the rights of domestic workers. The rally occurred in Statue Square, where NGOs read out public statements against the proposal and collected thousands of signatures for a petition addressed to the Labour Department and Chief Executive Tung Chee Hwa. The Coalition marched to the Central Government Offices—the new site of Beijing's control, just up the hill behind the Hong Kong Bank—to deliver the petition and then returned to Statue Square where politicised entertainment followed. One performance dramatised the issue by including domestic workers dressed up as pregnant women, with balloons bulging out from baggy dresses, lending an air of carnivalesque to the event.[5] As a result of the public attention brought to the issue, the legislative amendment has been shelved.

The second campaign relates to minimum wages in Hong Kong. In August 1998, Hong Kong's Provisional Urban Council put forward a proposal to cut the wages of domestic workers by 20 per cent. At that time, domestic workers earned the minimum wage of HK$3860 (US$497) per month. It was suggested that these measures were a response to the local economic downturn and, although the Asian financial crisis was stated as the impetus for these proposals, it was also insinuated that migrant worker remittances had increased due to higher exchange rates. In response to the proposal, the Coalition for Migrants Rights and the Asian Migrant Co-ordinating Body delivered a petition to government officials and launched a 6000-strong rally in Statue Square and Chater Garden to protest against the cuts. The financial crisis played an important role in bringing these organisations together, since their status as labour-sending countries to Hong Kong brought to light how migrant workers were collectively being affected by the crisis.[6] The rally was not successful in terms of obstructing the cuts to domestic workers' minimum wages, but their efforts saw the amount of the cut reduced to 5 per cent.

That these rallies usually take place around Statue Square is good evidence for understanding the area as a public space where debates about policies, rights and working conditions are on-going. Not only are domestic workers creating a shared sense of community which is lacking in their everyday life, but also political organisations are maintaining advocacy programmes to keep the issue of the domestic workers on the political agenda. They also influence the outcome of government policies. What is also interesting is that even though Beijing's Central Government Offices are now the new site of political control—rather than the Legislative Council (Legco) Building that abuts Statue Square—the decade-long habit of organising in Statue Square remains. Activists may march petitions up the hill to the Beijing offices for delivery, but the social and material heart of political rallies maintains a focus on the Square. The cultural landscape that reflects the political symbolism of pre-1997 politics has been rewritten by the symbolism of the Square that accords it an unofficial status as a space of migrant worker demonstrations.

COSMOPOLITAN PUBLIC SPACE?

The appropriation, use and redefined symbolism of Statue Square raises interesting questions about the production and use of public space in the city. It also raises questions about the political efficacy of conceiving this space as a cultural landscape. On the one hand, Statue Square could be understood as a diasporic public sphere where struggles over the meanings and policies of domestic work are always about the politics of labour migration from the Philippines. These struggles are for equity and respect by an overseas Filipino community that witnesses its nationals circumscribed by gendered and racialised images abroad. On the other hand, attention has been deliberately drawn to Statue Square's history and emerging uses to suggest that identifying it as purely diasporic might be limited in scope. Central Hong Kong is a multicoded, cultural landscape whose sites and symbols are being constantly read and written over by a variety of groups. It is therefore useful to consider the possibilities of the term 'cosmopolitanism' in the context of the more heterogeneous meanings of this space and landscape. These issues will be taken in turn.

> The notion of a 'public' has traditionally been conceived as an arena of discourses and exchanges outside state control, but [nonetheless] bounded by the borders of the nation.
> (Ong, 1997, p. 193)

Scholars that deploy this notion of the public, or public space more generally, tend to conform to Habermas' (1991) theories of the creation of civil society. There is widespread acknowledgement that this conception of civic space is a utopian ideal, however, and that the contemporary public sphere is a different kind of place created through new forms of governance, capital flows and technology. Furthermore, the accepted wisdom of a homogeneous civil society has been called into question by feminists (see Fraser, 1992; Duncan, 1996) and by scholars in post-colonial and cultural studies who have drawn attention to the creation of new 'publics' and 'public spheres' through transnational migration (for example, Ong, 1997; Werbner, 1998; Appadurai, 1996). It would thus be a rather partial examination of gathering and rallying in Statue Square that was only evaluated in terms of the Hong Kong polity because the issue is saturated with the politics of labour migration, ethnicity and citizenship, and how the situated histories of Hong Kong and the Philippines intersect.

What is needed is a different way to conceptualise these politics and how they gain visibility in a more complicated public sphere. If diasporic public spheres are

> space(s) [where] different transnational political imaginaries are interpreted and argued over, [and] where political mobilisation [is] generated in response to global social dramas.
> (Werbner, 1998, p. 12)

then this might be a more useful way to understand the public sphere generated by migrant workers and their advocates in Hong Kong. Statue Square is a space where Hong Kong and Philippine political imaginaries are juxtaposed and where the integrity of the modern Chinese family and the naturalness of labour export from the Philippines are challenged. Migrant organisations seek to bring these issues into a public sphere that is both within and beyond Hong Kong. This public sphere cannot be reduced to Hong Kong or the Philippines and, although it is important to highlight those different spheres of debate, it is also important to move away from dichotomised notions of public spheres by paying attention to how domestic workers and their advocates re-imagine spaces in the city.

One might also consider the multiple uses of the Square since Filipinos are not the only

city residents to use these spaces for political purposes. Indonesian domestic workers, refugees from China, environmentalists and the anti-smoking lobby also gather here to air their concerns. Chater Garden was used for 'millennium worship' at the turn of this century, a significant event for Christians in the city, and is annually used by the Jewish community for Chanuka where a 12-foot menorah is kindled. Chater Road and Garden have also been used to protest against more sensitive political issues, such as remembering the 1989 Tiananmen massacre or commemorating the anniversary of the mass Falun Gong protest in Beijing. Although there might appear to be a seductive idealism in this roster, one might also ponder why so little emphasis has been placed on the actually existing public spaces, and so much on their immanent disappearance. Central Hong Kong, particularly the area around Statue Square and Chater Garden, remains a significant political site.

In a thoughtful edited volume cleverly titled *Cosmopolitics: Thinking and Feeling beyond the Nation* (Cheah and Robbins, 1998), the authors suggest that the term 'cosmopolitan' could usefully be rethought to address issues pertaining to a complicated political sphere variously inhabited by hybrid identities, transnationalism, exile, immigration, colonial history and a host of other issues to do with what is sometimes naively called a post-national condition. What is innovative about the volume is its commitment to a scaled-down, plural and particular version of 'actually existing cosmopolitanism' (Robbins, 1998), rather than a universal nostalgia for past ecumenical movements. Under this new rubric, cosmopolitans are no longer Christians, intellectuals or aristocrats, and include "merchant sailors, Caribbean au pairs in the United States, Egyptian guest workers in Iraq, [and] Japanese women who take *gaijin* lovers" (Robbins, 1998, p. 1). This more encompassing definition is able to capture the heterogeneous meanings of the politically motivated cosmopolitanisms of migrant organisations, pro-democracy movements, environmentalists and others who gather to air concerns in Central. The loosening of the hyphen between the nation and the state does not mean that these groups are eschewing nationalism; in many cases, this is quite the contrary. But the public spaces they generate are no longer comprehensible through notions such as 'civil society'.

Conceiving Statue Square as a cosmopolitan landscape is not without its problems, however. Consider Clifford's point of view

> Discrepant cosmopolitanisms guarantee nothing politically. They offer no release from mixed feelings, from utopic/dystopic tensions. They do, however, name and make more visible a complex range of intercultural experiences . . . These cosmopolitical contact zones are traversed by new social movements and global corporations, tribal activists and cultural tourists, migrant worker remittances and email. Nothing is guaranteed, except contamination, messy politics and more translation.
> (Clifford, 1998, p. 369)

It is with these difficulties in mind that it might also be possible to re-imagine the Hong Kong public—a public that Abbas' (1997b, p. 303) suggests is constituted of "migrants, immigrants and urban nomads" —and thus public spaces in the city. Perhaps it is in this way that Statue Square can be re-imagined as a hybrid architectural expression of a special administrative region that is simultaneously constituted through the traces of different histories; a place of vexed relations with China and the West. Statue Square is a public space not only dedicated to 'the Queen' in 1901, it is also essential to the healthy *feng shui* of the Hong Kong and Shanghai Bank. It is a site where a new wave of migrant workers gather and reflect on life in Hong Kong and where Tiananmen can be remembered. It is in this cosmopolitical contact zone that we might find unexpected

voices that are helping to shape new meanings for the cultural landscape of Central.

CONCLUSION

It is important to give consideration to new forms of public space that are being produced in response to global forces or transnational capital. And there is a need to theorise them so that the efforts of people to make sense of, or change, their own lives are not subsumed by an understanding of power that neglects a transformative potential. The critical respatialisation of Statue Square into Little Manila, no matter how temporary or how often authorities attempt to remove these women, has altered the space of Central. As Hershkovitz notes in relation to Tiananmen Square

> The tension between the domination of public space and its appropriation as a (temporary) platform from which to communicate alternative or oppositional political messages is part of the social process that continually produces and transforms social space. No matter how temporary the appropriation, or how permanently its traces are eradicated, the very fact of its existence, the memories and associations it evokes permanently changes the face of the place in which it occurred.
> (Hershkovitz, 1993, p. 416)

Little Manila, in this way, transforms social space. But this space is not only social: it is simultaneously a material manifestation of the on-going relationship between people and place. And it is useful to re-present Central in this way, as legible cultural landscape, for a number of reasons. First, because Little Manila takes place only once a week, it is difficult to imagine this temporary enclave as having an urban, material basis. In presenting migrants' reading and use of icons and symbols, however, I hope to have given the Sunday phenomenon a material underpinning. Secondly, and importantly, Little

Manila does have a materiality that is bound up in the historical processes that Abbas (1997a) and Cuthbert and McKinnell (1997), in very different ways, describe. Little Manila has been enabled both by the development of a miracle economy that required women's labour and, somewhat ironically, by the closing of Chater Road in a bid to create more pedestrian shopping. Rather than corroborate prophecies of the enduring colonial subject or the demise of public space, however, I would see those processes as engaging with—but never overdetermining—Central's landscape. Marginal groups can always read and write different meanings into those spaces and, more than this, help us to see landscape as an on-going relationship between multiple groups that interact without a clearly defined 'core'. These sorts of theoretical moves help to decentre the 'social' and give more agency to 'meaning' and architectural expressions that, in Hong Kong especially, produce effect. And it is precisely this sort of politics that helps Central to remain, for lack of a better word, political.

It is unlikely that concerns about the public spaces of democratic politics in Hong Kong will disappear in the near future. As I write, pro-democracy protesters at Hong Kong's Fortune Global Forum are filing lawsuits against police for excessive violence. But the pre-Tiananmen march went off without incident this year and, a few days ago, 4000 Indonesian domestic workers took to the streets to discuss issues relating to their employment contracts. On a good day, for those of us who see consensus as a struggled-over reality, all seems hopeful.

NOTES

1. See Drummond (2000) and Yasmeen (1996) for two examples of how practices of public and private might be differently imagined in Asia (Vietnam and Thailand respectively). This paper does not question the public–private boundary in that it only deals with rather formal public spaces, although I explicitly share their concerns about local specificity.

2. It is, of course, ironic that Jardine, Matheson used to employ Filipino guards in the 1840s (Morris, 1997, p. 105).

3. For a review of labour migration history from the Philippines, see Gonzalez (1998). See also Constable (1997) and Law (2002) for this history in relation to Hong Kong.

4. It is difficult to obtain current statistics, but in 1993 there were approximately 101 000 Filipino domestic workers, 7000 Thai domestic workers, 5000 Indonesian domestic workers and smaller numbers of Sri Lankan, Indian, Malaysian, Burmese, Nepalese and Vietnamese domestic workers (Constable, 1997, p. 3). The figures for Thai and Indonesian workers have increased substantially since this time and the number of Indonesian and Thai labour migrants stood at 46 000 and 6000 respectively in 2000. There are also approximately 18 700 migrant workers from Nepal, although this figure includes British ex-army (Gurkha) workers (AMC and MFA, 2000).

5. See Yeoh and Huang (1998) for a similar deployment of the term 'carnivalesque' in relation to domestic workers in Singapore.

6. For a discussion of the relevance of this event in fostering a sense of community among migrant organisations, see Law (2002).

PART 3

Public Space as Art, Theatre, and Performance

Introduction

Anthony M. Orum

The third model of public space emphasizes cultural designs and symbols. It explores the ways that such space embodies and represents the culture of a community or society, and how those designs themselves provide a way to achieve as well as to sustain the collective identity of people in public space.

This model is especially tailored to emphasize the features of public space in modern and modernizing societies. As many societies, particularly in the West, have moved well beyond the creation simply of industrial space, and are now engaged actually in the creation of post-industrial, or as some would prefer, post-modern space, the cultural and artistic features of such space have become more visible and salient. Local political authorities may engage in the creation of such spaces, such as in the manufacture of museums—the most prominent being Frank Gehry's Guggenheim Museum in Bilbao, Spain—but this effort at creating a sense of public community and manufacturing collective identities often occurs more spontaneously among specific and particular segments of a local population. There are many instances of such efforts to employ art and symbols, in general, to create identities. In Latino areas across America, for example, local citizens often use wall murals as a means of signifying both their cultural roots and their own identities. In this regard, they draw on the strong and vibrant tradition of such murals, and the *muralistas*, originating in the early twentieth century in the works of figures like Diego Rivera and David Orozco.

Local authorities, of course, are not entirely oblivious to the ways in which the production of cultural public spaces can be important both for their own tenure in office and for the larger project of creating a broad and diverse city. Over the course of the past three decades in America, for example, more and more cities are setting time as well as public space aside for the celebration of the roots and collective identities of their inhabitants. Cities now routinely run a variety of parades celebrating this or that ethnic identity, whether Latino, Irish, or even more specific national identities. And the point of such celebrations and parades is that the cities provide public spaces precisely in which the various groups can celebrate themselves, and local authorities can sit back and take credit for the diverse and democratic political community over which they rule.

For all its glamour and significance, however, this model of public space is so new and underappreciated that the deeper and more analytic elements remain to be isolated. Most social scientists that have looked at the cultural elements of public space, in fact, have seen them not for what they represent but rather for the economic purposes and ends they seem to advance. Today there is a growing number of writers who are interested in the ways that cities employ symbolic elements in order to attract more paying visitors. Hence, scholars like

Dennis Judd and Susan Fainstein now speak of the "tourist city"—as opposed to the industrial city of the past—to single out the economic purposes that local authorities have in mind when they develop particular programs and set aside public space for new ventures. And there are certain cities that stand out for the single-minded and intense devotion to using such cultural attractions in order to lure visitors, and money, to them, the most visible in America, of course, being that of Las Vegas, Nevada.

But I strongly believe that it is a serious mistake to somehow think of the cultural features of such cities, and their efforts to set aside public space for these ventures, as simply another wrinkle to the development of capitalism. It is not simply a matter of how, or even why, authorities develop such projects, but it is the elements and contents of such projects themselves that are of central significance, especially to those groups of people who enact and perform them. Why this kind of art, for example, rather than another kind of art? Why on Saturday nights in Barcelona do groups of older people gather to engage in their collective dances at that particular time? And why do some of these celebrations get positioned in central areas of a metropolis rather than in more peripheral areas? In other words, as the anthropologist, Clifford Geertz once wrote in responding to the Marxist analysis of the world, it is the cultural displays and projects, themselves, that are important to understand and to portray, not the so-called forces they are claimed to represent.

The perspective of public space as art, theatre, and performance thus focuses its attention squarely on the symbolic elements that are performed and enacted by people in the public spaces of cities and towns. Such elements, when seen in terms of the scripts people enact and the performances of those who enact them, reveal much about the cultural templates of people. Take, for instance, the wall murals of the Pilsen area in the city of Chicago. Formerly occupied by Czech and Polish immigrants to the city, in the 1960s it became home to growing numbers of immigrants from Mexico. Today, virtually all of its residents have come from Mexico, though they represent different generations of Americans. Like other Mexican areas in the United States, Pilsen displays a variety of various wall murals. Such murals, when examined closely, provide representations of the way the people in the community think of themselves, and also the ways they want others to think of them. There is a mural, for example, set above the outside of an important church in the area that shows the members of a family gathered around a book on either side of which there are the symbols of Mexico—an eagle on one side, a bear on the other. There is another mural set on a wall adjacent to a parking lot which expresses much about the desires, yet everyday failures of people in Pilsen: it is a mural of a dove around which is written the word "Peace."

Perhaps the most famous and powerful mural is that of a line of warriors, each slightly different from the other—one with tears streaming down his face, another red with anger. This mural, created in 1975 by a group of immigrant Mexican artists, is set at the northern boundary of Pilsen. Its location and its representations say quite plainly: This is our area, and these are our warriors who are standing guard, protecting our residents from the powerful forces that lie just outside our area.

One can find these sorts of cultural performances and displays in public spaces across the world. In my time recently in China, for example, I worked with several students to examine the public spaces in Shanghai. The local government has over the course of the past several years made a greater and greater effort to create such public spaces in the form of public parks where citizens of various ages and different genders can gather. Some of these parks provide the same kinds of public spaces as parks in America or England: people can be found there flying kites, or playing ball, or engaged in other cultural activities with one another.

Yet there is one park that is very special and which, like many public spaces across the world, provides an open and accessible area to where people can engage in their own cultural performances. It is called Lu Xun Park, named after a famous Chinese writer of the nineteenth century. Almost every day, but especially on weekends, various groups of people go there and they celebrate different elements of their culture. There are ballroom dancers, for example, who can be found there every Sunday, in good weather, of course. They are members of classes of dancers who have been meeting for years. But there are also people, mainly men, who draw old Chinese poems and stories in calligraphy on the pavement, and they do so with water and large pens. Then there are various singers: couples, accompanied by people on Chinese instruments, who perform Peking operas; large groups of men and women, separated by gender and facing one another, who sing the songs of Mao and the Chinese Revolution. In my travels across the world, to England, France and other places, I have never encountered before a cultural space—a space of performance, a space of art—quite like that of Lu Xun Park.

What one attempts to achieve with this perspective on public space is more challenging and complex than in the case of the two other models, that of civil order, and that of power and domination. There are at least three levels of meaning that can be mined. One, of course, is the nature of the cultural performance, itself. This descriptively is the nature of the dance, or the artwork, or the theatre in which people engage. Another is the broader social significance of those acts. In the case of the residents of Pilsen, by virtue of their murals they were telling themselves and outsiders: this is who we are (this is our identity); this is our place and our public space; and this is how our space is bounded, where we can distinguish between the inside of our space, and those who lie outside of it. In the case of the dancers and other performers in Lu Xun Park, they clearly were telling themselves as well as others who they, as Chinese, were—what the nature of their culture was, what elements were important and what were not.

Yet there is a third manner in which one can also read these cultural enactments, though the analytical vocabulary for such work remains to be developed. It concerns such spatial features as the *centrality* of the particular cultural performance in which people engage, a clue to the social importance attached to the acts performed in specific public spaces. For example, in Lu Xun Park, the large band of choral singers who sang the songs of Mao and the Chinese Revolution could routinely be found in a central area of the Park, near one of the two main gates. In contrast, however, there was a group of people, almost all of whom were men, who met at what was called "complainers corner." These were people who met to discuss the problems in China, and most of them complained about the loss of their jobs and employment. They, like the choral singers, met on a regular basis. However, while they occupied a public space regularly in the Park, they were effectively hidden away from view. I had heard of them for many weeks, but it took me a number of Sundays and some searching to discover where they were to be found. And, of course, once I found them, being the only obvious Westerner there, they effectively stopped talking and asked my companions who I was and what I wanted.

The public space that serves as cultural space provides opportunities then for residents to tell outsiders who they are by virtue of their performances, their actions, in public. But, perhaps more importantly than that, they also tell themselves who they are: they furnish the means through which people can disclose and affirm their own collective identities. The ballroom dancers, for example, in Lu Xun Park have met regularly for years, as their director and teacher told me. There are many of them, and it is clear, from watching their movements and eyeing their expressions and faces, that ballroom dancing is something that is enormously important to them. Some of them come from many miles away just to engage in this dancing, especially on Sunday mornings. Likewise, the calligraphers who draw in water on the pavement come regularly and have become well-known by the people who regularly walk through the Park. I met, and spent some time talking to, through translators, one old man who is 98 years old, reputed to be one of the oldest calligraphers in this particular area. He takes his calligraphy and writing very seriously, and he wrote several poems for me both on the pavement and on two long sheets of paper that he gave me.

This sort of cultural production by the people who are its agents thus serves to provide an identity for them. It tells them, and us, who they are collectively. The fact that in Lu Xun Park there are so many activities all taking place at the same time and in the same public space reveals the great diversity in such cultural displays. Moreover—and this is perhaps a central point of significance—it provides a means of telling the performers not only who they are, but also *who they were*. Indeed, through my conversations it became clear that the recent explosion of this kind of performance art in China is one of many efforts to recover a past, a past that was obliterated during the Cultural Revolution and is only now being restored.

It is sometimes difficult, if not impossible, to disentangle the local from the extra-local or global forces that shape public space. This is certainly the case with the model of public space as civil order and, to a lesser extent, with the model of public space as the space of power and domination. But when one looks at public space as art, theatre, and performance here one sees the local and global made visible. In the mural art in Pilsen, for example, the residents not only identify their community through such art but they also recover, remake, and retrieve their own cultural roots and forms of expression from Mexico. So, too, it is with the many celebrations and parades of various and diverse ethnic groups, whether in New York City, London, or elsewhere. Performance space is precisely the point at which the local and the global intersect; and the more global forces prevail across our world, in the form of new immigrants and immigrant organizations, for instance, the more the global elements will also begin to reshape the representations of local public space and with it, local institutions as well.

THE READINGS

Because this model of public space is still developing, identifying readings that clearly illustrate it proved challenging. In this section, we rely on writings from a more diverse range of sources and authors than in the other sections, partly because seeing public space as a place for art, theatre, and performance is a perspective that has emerged piecemeal from many different fields.

Public art administrators Cynthia Abramson and Pamela Worden, together with geographer Myrna Margulies Breitbart, describe how public art installations have been used in many cities' public transit facilities to create more appealing public spaces. Moreover, they describe how these artistic additions to the space also provide members of the community with opportunities to participate in the creative planning process, and serve as a spatial outlet for individual and group self-expression.

Timothy Drescher considers a slightly different, more subversive form of artistic engagement with public space. In his short essay, originally written for the catalog that accompanied an exhibit at the Institute of Contemporary Art in Philadelphia, he explores how graffiti can be used to transform ordinary public space into expressive public space. When treated like an artist's canvas, but notably one that is highly visible in many public spaces, billboards provide individuals with an opportunity to convey their own messages to wide audiences.

Caroline Levine writes about perhaps the most formal way that public art and public space come together, through an official commission to an artist to produce a work of art for public display. But, by focusing on the case of artist Richard Serra's *Tilted Arc* sculpture, she uncovers the struggles and controversies that can arise when artist and public disagree about what counts at "art" and the extent to which public space should be available for avant-garde expressions.

While painting and sculpture are increasingly common in public spaces, active performances like those considered in the final two readings constitute an artistic use of public space that is particularly unavoidable. Taking a historical view, Mona Domosh describes how such seemingly inconsequential things as how individuals dress and carry themselves while in public spaces can itself constitute a performance. As the behavior of others in public space contributes to the streetscape, Tong Soon Lee discusses how when they are engaged in formal or informal music making, they also contribute to a soundscape that further shades the character of places.

FOR DISCUSSION

Are there any public spaces in your local area that are used for performances such as dancing, or where you find murals and other forms of artwork? Who is participating in these activities and creating these displays? How do public performances and the public display of art make you feel about a place?

Art and the Transit Experience/Creating a Sense of Purpose: Public Art and Boston's Orange Line

Cynthia Abramson, Myrna Margulies Breitbart, and Pamela Worden[1]

As more and more cities build or modify their transit systems, interest has grown in art-in-transit programs, which generally commission works of art for or engage artists in the design of transit systems. Supporters of these programs believe that they can "integrate creative values into such places ... where thousands of people circulate and encounter each other every day"—thereby improving these environments for users and enticing riders back to public transportation (Mara 1981: 201).

Transit art projects have been both decorative and functional. While they can contribute to the cultural life and profile of a city, they also can help shape the experience people have of using a transit system as they move through a city.

The art projects featured here respond to the special nature of traveling through a city on public transit. They celebrate acts of arriving and departing, times when we move not only between different places but also different states of mind. They mediate between local communities and the region to which the transit system connects them, helping passengers understand their place within the region and revealing and strengthening the identity of local communities. And they increase passengers' feelings of safety, comfort and orientation in systems that are often unfamiliar and disorienting.

PLACEMAKING

Landmarks and gateways can help create a sense of place in a city, both for residents and visitors. The ability of transit stations to function as both is illustrated by the art nouveau glass and wrought iron entrances French architect Hector Guimard created for more than 200 Paris Metro entrances between 1900 and 1913. Their stylish design dignifies and elevates the act of traveling by Metro. Guimard's shelters have become synonymous with the Metro and with the city of Paris itself and serve as local landmarks in the neighborhoods where they still stand.

Contemporary artists have created thematic artworks and designed system elements that help establish connections between municipal transit systems and the communities they serve. Often, these projects make reference to a site, landmark, historic person or event that is meaningful to an area served by a transit stop, or they evoke the character of a nearby district.

Metrorama '78, Jean-Paul Laenen's dramatic photomural in Brussels' Aumale Station, recorded both the destruction of the Anderlicht neighborhood and the life that had existed there for more than half a century before metro construction began. The mural literally envelopes riders, wrapping around the upper section of the station walls.

Richard Dragun's vitreous enamelled steel mural in London's Underground marks the place of the Charing Cross station by creating a continuum of visual images—from the National Galleries above to the station below—and by reminding passengers of nearby landmarks in the city.

Recent projects also follow this strategy. In Los Angeles, Francisco Letelier's murals in the Westlake/MacArthur Park station celebrate the culture of the Latino neighborhood above; sculpture in the Aviation and El Segundo stations evoke the dynamism of the aerospace and defense industries nearby.

Other projects celebrate transit environments as places of their own. Jack Mackie's array of green and orange utility poles in a bus staging area next to Seattle's Convention Place Station lend a sense of theatricality to this otherwise workaday space.

HUMANIZING THE METRO ENVIRONMENT

In most cities, the transit system is used by more people than any single building. Yet concerns for passenger comfort seem to have been ignored in the design of transit environments, particularly in older systems. This is especially true for underground lines, where sometimes only minimal lighting and ventilation are provided. While some argue that transit environments are experienced less deliberately than other architectural spaces (International Union of Public Transport 1988), one could also argue that transit environments are experienced more intensively than most other places, and passenger comfort therefore demands extraordinary consideration.

The Stockholm Metro provides some of the best examples of how art has been be used to humanize transit environments, to make them more comfortable and interesting for passengers. There, designers have endeavored to introduce light and color into the underground in order to counteract the effect of Scandinavian winters on passengers.

Gunnar Larson's "Transformation in the Sky," at the Farsta Centrum station, seeks to create a warm and summery atmosphere in what is basically a cold and windy place where passengers both buy tickets and wait for trains. Ulrik Samuelson's Kungsträdgarden station recreates the gardens above—featured are waterfalls with lichens and moss growing on the walls, cast architectural features, statuary and sculptures from different times and a variety of buildings, terrazzo floors and Venetian water vases.

The designers of the Santa Monica/Vermont station on Los Angeles' Red Line realized that Angelenos, with little tradition of using underground spaces and a long tradition of earthquakes, might be fearful of using that city's new subway. Their design for the station entrance includes skylights that allow natural light to reach the station platforms.

At the Douglas/Rosencrans Station, artist Renee Petropoulos notes that people passing through are marking an important transition in their day—moving from work to home or vice versa. Words set in the risers of the station stairway echo the thoughts that might be going through a passenger's mind.

Vicki Scuri's Seattle bus tunnel counters the disorientation and discomfort travelers often feel in dark, claustrophobic tunnels. Bright lighting and vivid graphics help riders see their place in the tunnel and orient themselves to the streets above.

SAFETY, WAYFINDING, CIRCULATION AND ORIENTATION

The connections between different transportation lines or modes present particular challenges for passengers and designers. They are places where people might find themselves momentarily disoriented or where people moving in different directions conflict. Transit artists also have addressed these problems of circulation and wayfinding.

New York City's subway is renowned for

the bas reliefs that adorn its earliest stations and helped identify them to non-English-speaking immigrants—among them are a sailing ship for Columbus Circle and a steam paddlewheeler for Fulton Street.

Nicholas Munro's ceramic murals depicting mazes and the game "Snakes and Ladders" for London's Oxford Circus station were controversial because they parodied the labrynthine passages, corridors, escalators and staircases that characterize many Underground stations. Some critics argued that Munro succeeded only in reinforcing the chaos and complexity of the subway environment.

Ake Pallarp and Enno Hallek adopted a more direct approach to solving the problem of wayfinding at the Stockholm Metro's Stadion station. Using rainbow-colored wooden arrows and pointing fingers, they created lively signage to direct passengers to the College of Music and Stadium.

Gates can serve important functions in metro stations as well, directing passengers towards a particular station entrance or exit and preventing people from crossing the tracks. But they also can be one of the most unwelcoming elements of the transit environment.

The gates in the Stockholm subway, however, include the ornamental ironwork of Britt-Louise Sundell's gate at the Mariatorget station, Sivert Lindblom's sculpted iron platform dividers at Västra Skogen which serve to separate waiting areas for inbound and outbound trains, and the child-like drawings and scribblings of cartoonist Elis Eriksson and Gosta Wallmark on the white wooden fences in the track arches at the Hallonbergen station.

SUBWAY POSTER ART PROGRAMS

The London Underground is famous for its subway posters. The earliest posters, dating back to the early 1900s, were selected by Frank Pick, publicity director of the London Passenger Transport Board. They depict a myriad of desirable destinations that could be reached by "tube." Their emphasis on the connection between public transport and leisure travel developed as a response to dwindling ridership caused by the growth in popularity of the private car.

The most well-known poster artist was Edward Johnston who, in 1916, created the non-serif lettering and logo design which revolutionized the field of topography. Other noteworthy artists used cubist and abstract idioms to idealize the historic events of the time, stir the patriotism of the British citizenry and expose the public to modern art.

The current poster art program is funded out of London Regional Transport's marketing budget. These funds cover both the design and production of the artwork and artist fees. Between 300 and 400 posters are displayed at a time, depending upon the amount of existing unsold advertising space, throughout the Underground. They stay up for six to eight months, and are produced in runs of 6,000. The original paintings from which the posters are made become the property of the London Underground and are added to their fine art collection.

The use of fine art posters on station platforms has been adopted by other cities, most recently New York. The Metropolitan Transit Authority's (MTA) poster art program began in 1990, also with the goal of encouraging recreational use of public transportation and to celebrate the neighborhoods of New York City. Four artists are commissioned every year and charged with creating a vision of a particular neighborhood. Recent posters have depicted the New York Harbor, Brooklyn's Fulton Mall, the farmer's market at Union Square and various cultural institutions. The original artworks, which range from oil paintings to collage, are added to the MTA's fine art collection.

Posters are hung for approximately three months at a time, and printed in runs of three to four thousand. Like in London's Tube, they are displayed in the unused advertising panels throughout the system's 469 stations. The posters, which enjoy tremendous popularity, are funded out of the MTA's marketing budget, with the Arts-in-Transit program paying all artist commissions and fees. Like London's poster art program, the New York MTA's posters function as both aesthetic enhancement and public relations tool.

CREATING A SENSE OF PURPOSE: PUBLIC ART AND BOSTON'S ORANGE LINE

During the 1980s, throughout the U.S., public art policy and funding focused on the big names and singular visions of a handful of artists. Their products, even when performed or installed in publicly accessible places, were often conceived and realized in isolation from the users of those places. Public reaction, as often as not, was one of disinterest, dismay, even rage (Reynolds 1993).

In Boston, during this same period, a very different kind of public art engendered very different reactions. *Arts in Transit: The Southwest Corridor* officially began in 1984. But its true beginnings go back to the sixties, when work crews began to slash their way through the heart of many of Boston's oldest neighborhoods to make way for an extension of a major highway, Interstate 95. As the inexorable destruction continued, outraged citizens took to the streets.

In 1970, in the midst of a recession that might have been eased by the many jobs provided by the project, Governor Francis W. Sargent declared a moratorium on the planned highway construction. In 1975, Sargent's successor, Governor Michael S. Dukakis, responded to the continued protests of citizens, and, for the first time in U.S. history, abandoned a major highway project in favor of alternate uses.

These uses would include relocating one of the city's four major subway lines (the Orange Line), constructing new commuter rail and Amtrak lines, creating a park that would provide critically needed open space and natural and recreational resources for communities located along the 4.7-mile length of the project (the Southwest Corridor) and a comprehensive public art initiative.

The project directly affected more than one quarter of Boston's population, including the ethnically diverse neighborhoods of Chinatown, South Cove, South End, Back Bay, Fenway, Mission Hill, Fort Hill, Roxbury and Jamaica Plain. Economic hardship and racial tension in many of these neighborhoods had been aggravated by the lengthy and disruptive process of this enormous construction project. Even after the highway was abandoned, citizens' fears of land speculation, displacement and negative economic impact motivated many to actively monitor critical land use, urban, park and station design decisions.

Public art came on late in the design process, after construction was already underway.[2] When UrbanArts, a small non-profit agency, came on board to administer *Arts in Transit*, community expectations were high while the transit agency's tolerance for additional community input was low. The Metropolitan Boston Transit Authority (MBTA) was eager for a quick and easy fix to the community's latest demand, this time for public art. If there were to be art, its role would be to enhance the beauty of its stations, reduce vandalism and help erase memories of the past mistakes of urban renewal. Art might also revive images of a more prosperous past and generally improve the MBTA's public image.

Southwest Corridor residents wanted the permanent installations to help create a sense of place within each neighborhood. They also hoped to incorporate citizen participation and public education into the art program so that public art could help achieve the goal of reducing tensions that had long existed in many Southwest Corridor communities, tensions that often were the result of racism and the negative impacts of economic restructuring.

UrbanArts developed a multidisciplinary program. Working with community representatives, the agency lobbied the MBTA to expand community involvement in the selection process for permanent works and public art in each of the new transit stations. In an effort to further community participation, UrbanArts also invited artists and neighborhood groups to develop ideas for temporary and off-site art projects.

The permanent art program, based on established federal guidelines, called for a professional arts panel to select artists to be commissioned to create work for the new stations. UrbanArts expanded this process to include a standing 10-member site committee of community representatives who served as the client for each station's art program, often meeting for several months to develop a community profile and give direction.

Professional arts selection panels, chosen for demographic representation and their ability to offer professional perspective and expertise, worked with information provided by the community to site committees to select artists to develop proposals. When artists finally presented their proposals at a joint meeting of the site committee and arts panel, there was typically a high level of consensus regarding the most appropriate artwork for each site.

The final artworks reflected Southwest Corridor communities in a variety of ways. Some, like Susan Thompson's banners, "Neighborhood," represented a specific community's history in a traditional, literal, narrative way. Others, like Dan George's "Transcendental Greens" and John Scott's "Stony Brook Dance," expressed material relevant to the community in relatively abstract ways.

Concurrent with the selection process, UrbanArts requested and received proposals from artists and community agencies for a series of temporary and off-site projects. Funding for the implementation of these projects initially came from the private sector.

The first of these, a photography project called "The Artist's Lens: A Focus on Relocation," documented the changes taking place as the old elevated Orange Line along Washington Street gave way to the newer transit system along the Southwest Corridor, some distance away. Professional photographers, paired with high school students from the Hubert H. Humphrey Occupational Resource Center in Roxbury, formed teams that worked together for more than a year to capture the architecture, people and feel of "The El" prior to its demolition.

Increasingly, some team members committed themselves to the politics of change, using their images to encourage people to think about the impact the upheaval would have on their own lives. As bonds between artists and residents grew, so often did public debate regarding the social and economic needs of neighborhood residents and the fear of imminent displacements associated with the Southwest Corridor project.

While "The Artist's Lens" used visual documentation to express community history and to engage people in discussion of the future, a second project, "Boston Contemporary Writers," used the written word to capture diverse authors' experience of urban life. In 1986–87 UrbanArts held a statewide competition to solicit works in poetry and prose that would be inscribed in granite and permanently installed in the new Orange Line stations and adjacent parkland. This anthology of work by urban writers went far beyond the expectations of the MBTA for its art program. A large community advisory group had worked with UrbanArts to launch this project and had helped with extensive outreach in established as well as informal literary circles. The selection panel conducted a blind review of manuscripts, and there was no way to know whether authors were male or female, black or white, young or old.

In the end, the 18 selected authors reflected the diversity of the Southwest Corridor's residents as well as a range of literary experience. For one author, Jeanette DeLello Winthrop, her work on granite was the first piece she had ever published. For others, like Gish Jen, the project represented a unique opportunity for her to have her work read and experienced by people for whom it had particular resonance. Jen's prose lines the long entry corridor into the South Cove station in Chinatown. It is a piece with humor, sympathy and understanding for all of us who are engaged in the struggle between individual behavior and cultural expectations, a struggle that is particularly poignant to the recent Asian immigrants who often use this station.

Finally, UrbanArts launched an oral history project, called "Sources of Strength," in collaboration with Roxbury Community College. The program offered students and residents an opportunity to learn the techniques of collecting oral histories and provided a way to interview and collect stories from Southwest Corridor residents.

People were pleased to talk about their lives, often sensing that their stories might help to break down the isolation many felt within their urban neighborhoods. Some felt that the extraordinary quality of many ordinary lives might put to rest the unremitting, negative stereotypes of urban America generated by the media.

I was my father's favorite, growing up – the oldest, smartest, most morally upright of the children, perfect except that I should have been my brother. So cruel a confusion! It was as if in some prenatal rush, we had been dressed in one another's clothes. With the direst of consequences for him, certainly: In the China of 1948, a scholar's son could bring honor to a family, or else shame, nothing else; there was no room in that small country for a good-natured boy with a fondness for duck noodles.

And as for his brainy sister, who would marry me?"

Gish Jen, from "The Great World Transformed," n.d.

The stories were an inspiration to artists and became the material for new work. "Sources of Strength" was produced as a theatrical performance at Massachusetts College of Art hosted by Northeastern University in 1988, using oral history text for the script. In 1991, an exhibition of text, accompanied by photographic portraits of the story tellers, was hosted by Northeastern University. In both the theatrical performance and the exhibition, the presentations were greeted with "Oh, that's you, isn't it" or "I remember that" and clearly had resonance for their audiences.

Nearly 800 people participated actively in the design, production and presentation of *Arts in Transit* projects. Each person came with different objectives. Together, advisors and panelists, interviewers and story tellers, scriptwriters, photographers, students, artists and administrators, created a unique snapshot of a particular place at a particular time in history. Their contribution established a foundation for a public art program that reflected the special character of many Boston neighborhoods without compromising artistic integrity. Many participants also forged a partnership that led to ongoing efforts to rebuild and determine the future of their communities.

PROCESS OVER PRODUCT

Public art is rarely, if ever, subjected to environmental impact studies to determine how it affects the public. When an interdisciplinary study group[3] began its assessment of *Arts in Transit* in the summer of 1991, we discovered how few methodologies there were to accomplish this task and how many choices of focus could be made. We soon concluded that evidence of the effectiveness of the project in meeting community goals would best be understood if the focus of analysis shifted from an assessment of the permanent installations to the methods of their selection and to the impact of accompanying off-site educational programs.

> By defining their individual and cultural identities as well as producing end products, ... collaborators and audiences are neither consumers of the works produced nor merely protestors of the wrongs they might want to right. Their creative process catalyzes reclamation and repossession of self, in art/work and the building of community.
>
> Raven 1989: 10

Arlene Raven's observation that certain forms of public art can begin to empower communities by opening up a dialogue and inviting critical as well as creative imaging to take place, is shared by many practitioners.[4] When members of our study group met with participants from the *Arts in Transit* project, we discovered that many felt more invested in their community through their participation in the selecting and planning for art to be installed, especially because these are neighborhoods that rarely get to see their environments enhanced. As one resident observer of the Orange Line art declared, "We deserve are just as much as anyone else." This is especially the case when, as poet Sam Allen eloquently observed, urban residents are surrounded by pathology and need so desperately to create counter forces that "revive their spirit and feed their humanity."[5]

The photographic documentation and oral history projects also actively stimulated residents' awareness of the changes that had been introduced historically into Southwest Corridor communities and were continuing to be introduced by economic and political forces beyond residents' control. When our study group listened to *Arts in Transit* participants describe these learning experiences, we sensed the effect they had on motivating an even deeper interest in pursuing new research endeavors and forms of artistic expression.

The content of the information uncovered through personal stories as well as the many techniques utilized by Southwest Corridor residents to research their communities may finally have had a more sustained impact on a process of community development than the permanent installations themselves.

CHOOSING A PAST, CREATING A FUTURE

Involving the general public in sharing memories and feelings about their neighborhood surroundings through art does not necessarily evoke happy or soothing themes. Nor does it necessarily generate consensus on how that community wants to be represented (Raven 1989: 26).

In the Southwest Corridor, mass transit stations with spaces predicated on motion provided challenging sites from which to begin to establish any enduring vision of the present or future of the surrounding community. High unemployment, racism and the accumulated effects of years of unequal treatment also restrained hopes for creating a more liveable environment.

Given these obstacles, our study group wondered whether, and if so, how, local site committees managed to "choose a past," in Kevin Lynch's words, so that they might "construct a future"?[6] Did Southwest Corridor neighborhoods use the public art process to re-present themselves to the larger public in the community profiles, which focussed on diversity and history?

Using an art program to begin a process of healing and regeneration in diverse neighborhoods that were experiencing differing measures of political and social conflict was not easy. Most site committees discussed the cultural diversity of their neighborhoods and the difficult transitions they went through over time. Rather than emphasize the conflicts, however, they chose to emphasize the melting pot qualities and residents' common goals or shared values. The stress on common themes suggests that site committees were, perhaps, more interested in constructing an alternative future than in resurrecting these past struggles, and that they deliberately chose one past from many possible pasts to attain that goal.

Most of the Orange Line site committees described their past communities as vibrant places in which to live and work. They emphasized the multitude of contributions made by ethnic groups through work and community life. Though the negative effects of urban renewal, highway construction and recent gentrification were discussed, site committees chose to remind the public of an earlier time when Southwest Corridor communities provided many positive working and living experiences for their residents.

The juxtaposition of a vibrant past with a more problematic present could have been utilized as a call to activist arms for neighborhood residents. The themes, which spark nostalgic memories and emphasize the positive aspects of diversity in the present, however, are benign rather than provocative. Or so they seem.

Current residents, however, may share an interest in this skewed presentation. Negative depictions of the area focussing on crime and violence already receive enormous attention in the media and have justified public intervention in the past (e.g. urban renewal) that displayed residents without addressing their problems. Many *Arts in Transit* participants believed that those outside their neighborhoods ought to be presented with a view of Southwest Corridor life that was more balanced. The picture that site committees presented to the arts panels thus contrasted with that offered by the media or the more multidimensional perspectives portrayed through oral history and photographic imagery.

The political intentions of the site committees are, however, apparent and highly correlated with the destruction wrought in the past by urban renewal and gentrification. Their aim was to be the autonomous creators of a sense of place in order to avoid having one created by others with more questionable intentions for the future of their communities.

MULTIPLE SENSES OF PLACE WITH A SINGULAR PURPOSE

As participants describe it, their involvement in *Arts in Transit* project and search for ideas to inform the content of the art selection was not a search for a special theme to represent each neighborhood. Rather, it was a search for a sense of efficacy and purpose, of thereness. Residents were less concerned about the content of themes represented through the permanent art than they were about whether the art communicated—to the broader public—that they were there, alive, important and very interested in staying on.

Permanent public art installations created through a participatory selection process, together with participatory projects involving residents in seeing their neighborhoods in new ways through theater, literature, history, and photography, generated a sense of ownership of place, the right on the part of residents to define and redefine themselves, and, most especially, to project their existence into the future.

Though multiple senses of place exist within each community surrounding the Orange Line stations, every neighborhood expressed (through its participation in the art selection and oral history, photography and literature programs) a common desire to lay claim to its space and to control its future as well as to record its past. Such a vision could never have been expressed through the placement of a single art product in a public space, even one as central as a train station. It could only be defined through a process of community building such as that initiated through the many education projects that accompanied UrbanArts' art selection process.

CONCLUSION

Several months after *Arts in Transit* was completed, our interdisciplinary study group invited participants to convene to discuss the project and its impact. The large turnout confirmed the community's continuing interest in the project; conversation, however, tended to focus on the future, not the past.

The artists and residents who gathered that evening suggested a wealth of ideas for arts projects they wanted to see happen: community art publications, theater productions, arts journals, neighborhood architectural tours, ongoing history projects, afterschool programs in creative writing and visual arts, and the creation of cultural centers. People also talked about the connections between these activities and potential future economic development. Dozens of projects have grown directly from the *Arts in Transit* experience; among these is a major initiative to reclaim Blue Hill Avenue as Boston's Avenue of the Arts.

For many, the underlying message of the *Arts in Transit* project became clear that evening: the arts and humanities could serve a larger community agenda for neighborhood revitalization. The installation of the public art, literature, oral histories, theatrical performances and exhibitions that had been part of *Arts in Transit* helped give form to that agenda. Because of the "force of its imagination" (Miles 1989: 7), participation in creating art had helped residents to reclaim the cultural meaning of their lives. Having reclaimed abandoned spirits, residents felt more secure in their efforts to reclaim abandoned spaces and address other critical needs.

This focus on the future suggests new possibilities for public art. It also raises questions. How can public art move beyond the simple enhancement of public space to realize a more far-reaching role in the social and economic revitalization of urban neighborhoods.

What lessons can be drawn from *Arts in Transit*?

One lesson may be that public artists and arts administrators cannot assume the pre-existence of a public; instead, citizen participation must be invited and sustained. The project also suggests new indices for evaluating the success of cultural activity in public space. Instead of only asking "Do I like it?" we may begin to ask more of our public art projects. How much discussion does it generate in the community? Is it ongoing? Can it sustain local involvement even after the project is completed? How many additional arts activities does it spawn? Is the art, and the process of its selection, responsive to change? Does it ensure community ownership, not only of the art, but of the community itself? Can that sense of ownership be sustained to prevent gentrification and displacement in neighborhoods upgraded through arts activity?

Along Boston's Southwest Corridor, many of these questions remain unanswered. It will take years to assess the true impact of *Arts in Transit*. That the questions were raised at all, especially by residents deeply affected by their engagement in the project, speaks to the reality that public art has gone beyond the elusive task of creating a sense of place. Public art in Boston has also helped engender a sense of purpose.

NOTES

1. Additional research by Todd W. Bressi, Hanan A. Kivett and Jill Slater.
2. Policies established during the Carter administration encouraged local transit authorities to set aside a portion of construction funds for public art, but Boston's Massachusetts Bay Transporta-

tion Authority (MBTA) was slow to exercise this option for the Orange Line. Pressure from the community forced the bureaucracy to implement an art program that would reflect the diverse cultural identities represented in the communities along the Southwest Corridor.

3. This interdisciplinary study group of scholars, artists, practitioners, and community residents was funded by the Massachusetts Foundation for the Humanities, the Boston Foundation for Architecture and the Rowland Foundation.

4. Lucy Lippard, for example, believes that art for social change must encourage people to become involved in "the making of their own society and culture." See Lucy Lippard, "Moving Targets/Moving Out," in Raven.

5. Sam Allen as quoted in Holton et al. (1993: 43).

6. Kevin Lynch as quoted in Hayden (1988: 45).

The Harsh Reality: Billboard Subversion and Graffiti

Timothy W. Drescher

Daily, more than one hundred thousand vehicles pass the beginning of eastbound Interstate 80 at the western approach to the San Francisco-Oakland Bay Bridge. Rarely is this approach tagged with graffiti, because of the physical danger and its location beyond the purview of most tagging, which tends to be neighborhood oriented. Billboard space viewable from the bridge approach rents for more than $120,000 a year. One billboard, removed in the fall of 1999, faced away from the approach, pushing cigarettes, liquor, and other products to slow-moving street-level traffic heading toward, or under, the massive bridge. This is normal enough, and is repeated untold thousands of times throughout the United States, as advertisers seek to expose their products to the public by controlling a segment of public visual space, but there are two sides to this routine—to this and all other billboards.

On the reverse side of this particular billboard, a piece of spray-can writing remained for several years. It depicted a perplexed businessman—identifiable by his necktie and the assortment of pens in his shirt pocket—beneath the large, ambiguous caption, "The harsh reality." There is no way of telling whether the caption referred to the bewildered expression of the figure, to the recognition that "it's a tough world out there," or to something else. When the location is taken into consideration, however, and when viewed from a snail-paced commuter crawl,

the meaning becomes clearer. One thing is certain: Having to use the reverse side of a billboard to express a message that does not sell products, but that offers an observation about the complexity of daily life for the hundreds of thousands of drivers passing by, is a harsh reality.

There was something delightful in both the character's bemused expression and that he existed in such an unlikely place. His presence signaled a spark of life and a moment of opposition to the mundane, arrogant imposition of billboard advertisements. In this example's location, style, and audacity, spray-can writing[1] meets the growing practice of billboard correction.[2] Writing and correcting both question the nature of life in our urban society, such as who controls public visual space, and who is able to contest that control. The ambiguity of any answer to such questions makes consideration of corrections and graffiti an appropriate lens through which to view public visual art at the start of the twenty-first century.

Graffiti has been around for centuries, yet in the last few years it has begun to receive serious analytical attention. Because billboard corrections are a relatively recent phenomenon, it is useful to sketch some of corrections' basic characteristics before observing some of the similarities, but also significant differences, between graffiti and billboard corrections.

Billboards are vulnerable targets on many

fronts. They may be subjected to attack, ad-blind appropriation (using the space for one's own message, regardless of the ad),[3] a prankster aesthetic (changing boards because it is fun; the changes may or may not have a message beyond the alterations themselves),[4] correction, or total appropriation. Allied with these are fauxvertising (creation of fictitious ads for fictitious products) and sign correction.[5] Of these, correction and ad-blind graffiti are the most pertinent here; they have the clearest ties with the graffiti tradition. Ad-blind appropriation simply uses the advertising space for graffiti. Correction takes that a step further, utlizing the ad design for an alternative, "corrected" purpose.

Billboard corrections represent *unofficial* responses to the public presence of advertisements; they also represent a lack of control by advertisers and government. This lack of control, these illegal, public intrusions into the "proper" bailiwick of paid ownership of public visual space, disturbs corporate and governmental power. Their response is framed most often in legal terms, as in "It is not legal (or moral) to appropriate space someone else has paid for." This is certainly true, and correctors recognize it, but in their admission that billboard improvement is "slightly" illegal lies another, more problematic, truth: While it may be improper to "bomb" paid-for space, that act may be morally, socially, or politically appropriate to highlight the greater impropriety (moral and social, if not legal) of buying public visual space and then subjecting mute viewers to advertisements that offer, for a price, products that ostensibly provide whatever is absent from those viewers' lives. Billboard corrections, by virtue of altering corporate advertisements themselves, indirectly point out the complicity of the advertising process in making peoples' lives seem incomplete. The economic necessity for advertising trumps the social and invidual needs for a noncommodified public visual space. In billboard corrections, the public sphere, which is the sociopolitical realm where private interests are discussed and expressed, garners its feeble assertions in the face of corporate-governmental dominance.

Few billboard corrections consciously strive for such analytical expressions; in fact, the vast majority of corrections are responses to particular ads, albeit some with greater political awareness than others. Whether or not the correctors are aware of the larger ramifications of their acts is, on one level, irrelevant, because the very act of altering a billboard challenges the corporate privilege of controlling public visual space. A Marlboro alteration—putting into the horse's mouth the words "Poo! This macho stinks"—on the surface says nothing about the public sphere or the carcinogenic properties of tobacco, but it does exemplify an alternative use for public space, and in that suggests, however subliminally, a critique of the status quo.

Probably the greatest number of corrections have been made to liquor and tobacco advertisements. Cigarette ads become cancer ads, beer celebrates cirrhosis, and so forth. An Australian correction changed a beer ad for the "Silver Bullet," referring to the color of the can, to the "Liver Bullet," and added the question, "Is your liver shot?" But changes are not limited to medical advice. A tequila ad proclaiming "Two fingers is all it takes" was modified with the addition of "bend over." A Camel cigarette ad showing an adventurer taking a smoking break was elegantly altered by simply erasing his head, suggesting that smokers are mindless.

Some alterations incorporate the spirit of graffiti more than others. For instance, some literally use graffiti, adding spray-paint comments to otherwise unaltered ad designs (the tequila and liver bullet examples). These have a different feel than corrections employing design and artistic skills. A recent antidrug billboard—"Just because you survived drugs, doesn't mean your children will"—was corrected, utilizing the identical typeface and letter-size, by replacing "drugs" with "Bush."

A Bank of America ad, whose text read "Banking on America," was altered in the identical typeface by replacing "banking" with "feeding".

There are many *graffiti* locations and lettering styles, but not much range of content. *Billboard alterations*, because they are responses to a muliplicity of ads, have a wide range of content and location, but "style" refers to the impressiveness of the correction, including its location, size, visibility, cleverness, as well as artistic flair. Sometimes, the two intersect in unexpected ways. In San Francisco, a graffiti crew, whose tag was MGV, obtained a key for a bus-shelter ad case and removed a beer ad for Miller Genuine Draft—a photo looking down on myriad beer bottles with "MGD" printed on the tops. The crew changed the Ds to Vs, thus proclaiming the crew's presence, and returned the ad to its locked case (they didn't want it accessible to vandals, of course). A couple of weeks later, the crew noticed an advertising company worker changing the altered ad. They followed him and watched as he exchanged it for another ad in another bus shelter. That way, the advertising company participated in getting up the graffiti crew's tag throughout San Francisco.

In some ways, the most artistic (in traditional terms) billboard corrections are complete replacements of ads with prepainted corrections. Ron English is the foremost perpetrator of such corrections. He designs replacement billboards and executes them on large rolls of paper. With a highly trained group of accomplices, he covers entire billboards with his "ad," and is gone in seven minutes.

Billboard companies are fully aware that some of their ads are more susceptible than others to corrections. Chiat Day, for instance, knew that its "Think different" campaign for Apple computers would become graffiti magnets; instead of the normal thirty percent overprinting, it printed fifty percent more ads than were contracted for so that replacements would be readily available when the ads were tagged or corrected. Jill Posener, the author of *Spray It Loud*, a book on British graffiti-altered billboards, was informed by an advertising executive that they deliberately designed ads to provoke attacks, because the changes drew greater attention to the products and therefore were beneficial. Aware of this possibility, the Billboard Liberation Front has considered invoicing Chiat Day and other advertisers for enhancing their billboards and increasing their impact.

Billboard activists rework privately owned public spaces targeting potential consumers. Graffiti tags and throw-ups sometimes do this, but are generally less discriminative in location choice. With tags, the goal is to "get up" as often and as widely as possible, period, but the idea with all writing is to gain exposure and, thus, prestige. The assumed audience is mostly fellow writers, with occasional courageous (and, sometimes, famous or infamous) forays into more public realms, such as buses, public buildings, even billboards. Civic representatives, property owners, merchants, and other bourgeois interests despise graffiti. The official response to it is couched in the language of crisis management, which associates spray-can writing with crime, anarchy, violence, and obscenity. Sometimes, these are accurate characterizations. Spray-can writers, in turn, frequently describe themselves as reclaiming public space taken by private owners, city officials, or zoning commissions, often with such comments as "Capitalism sucks, so I can do anything I want," as if this illogic creates a politically progressive defense of tagging. As a species of graffiti, billboard improvement usually places more emphasis on corporations, billboard businesses, advertising companies, and attitudes. Writers and correctors both challenge the commonly accepted roster of who is authorized to speak in the public sphere by speaking, whether or not they are authorized. (Barry McGee, Stephen Powers, and Todd James's invitation to the Institute of

Contemporary Art's "Wall Power" show, in which they were given three properly rented billboards for their outdoor work, is delightfully ironic.)

Graffiti and billboard alteration are illegal and are executed by people who disagree with the structural biases of capitalism and with the institutions that control public visual space, although disagreement is not necessarily a critique. Correctors are somewhat less naive about such issues than writers, because their work is more public and deals more overtly with profit and image-conscious guardians than mere property owners. With a few notable exceptions, graffiti writing is an egocentric pastime, seeking individual prestige. Correcting billboards requires collective planning, preparation, and the organized participation of several people—police lookouts, drivers, people manning communications equipment, and so on. While writing celebrates the individual's tag, billboard-correcting groups remain focused on the changes, not the changers, who become known only by word of mouth among fellow participants or trusted initiates.

When their work is taken collectively, graffiti writers are sometimes hailed as "the voice of the ghetto." Their anguished, Krylon cries are seen as an attempt to assert themselves against establishment policies designed to maintain the (commercial) status quo from which they are excluded. Thus, the writers become romanticized public decorators. Their work may make it onto a website, for electronic perusal by anonymous multitudes. A very few gain gallery representation, yet, this in no way conflicts with the egocentrism of their more public expressions. Billboard correctors remain more anonymous than graffiti writers; only one or two dare to make their works, or, more accurately, photographs of their works, available for sale to the public. Websites proliferate for both forms of expression, but desired anonymity is always protected, even while their expressions gain wider currency.

Writers and correctors share the spectre of violence. There are several possibilities for violence in these practices, especially physical danger to both correctors and writers when they expose themselves to dangerous situations, often high above the ground. In the late nineties, risk became a significant criterion among writers, whose works turned up in extraordinarily dangerous locations.[6] There is also a real danger from police, not merely of arrest but, as any tagger will attest, of being roughed up or beaten if caught in the act.

Shifting from violence done *to* practitioners to violence done *by* them, perhaps most important are the ways in which these activities are considered symbolic violence. Graffiti is presented (accurately) by mass media and politicians as attacks on private property, although writers rarely view their activities in this light—and there is rarely any official condemnation of urban renewal projects that obliterate blocks of property and people's communities. Very little writing is collective or has a social, let alone a political, focus. Billboard alteration, however, is necessarily focused on major institutions, but is rarely decried in the same vein in which taggers are attacked. This is largely because billboard hackers' work does not have the same immediate impact "on ground level," within neighborhood communities. City officials and local residents may feel some responsibility toward their own areas, but no one feels any particular responsibility toward advertising billboards. The "violence" of corrections is not directed toward local residents, but at a disembodied, probably distant, corporation's advertisements. The challenge to this symbolic economy is nonetheless significant, and, depending on the nature of the correction, is more or less quickly undone by billboard companies.

Graffiti writers often battle with each other for prominent locations, and writers themselves decide who has "won" the contest, who is "the best." Within the community of writers, standards are set, expression is evaluated, and a sense of freedom is attendant among writers and their surrounding culture. But this freedom is constrained by the larger society—"We don't much care what you do, as long as you do it in your own neighborhoods"—and by the competitive aspects within their own culture that tacitly accept the hegemony of atomized individualism. Claims that youth are "communicating" their views are accurate to a limited extent, but should not be confused with the notion of free public discourse. There is, nevertheless, a working-out of opportunity for heretofore marginalized voices to express themselves. In the case of spray-can writers, the discourse is largely self-contained, because few outsiders pay any attention to the specifics of the graffiti. But billboard alterations are big and public. Since they suddenly and ironically change the expected messages, they necessarily impinge on the larger society and declare the active existence of someone opposed to the commodification of their existence.

Put another way, some argue that such illegal activities as graffiti and billboard improvement signal an excluded group fighting for its identity in today's impersonal society. Others argue that the goal is freedom or autonomy. It makes more sense to recognize the existence of multiple, simultaneous discourses (parts or subsections of the public sphere), some trying to establish a self-determined identity (spray-can writing), some trying to use or expose, or, perhaps, challenge, dominant attitudes (billboard improvements). Both graffiti and billboard alteration are means by which a more participatory space is being worked out within public forums, although it is important to use such terms carefully. In either case, although billboard attacks are political, and graffiti rarely is, both exemplify oppositional voices making public declarations. However they are defended or criticized, both graffiti writing and billboard improving *are* assertions

by marginalized citizens of often critical perspectives not otherwise given airtime or official credence in U.S. society.

A key difference is the surface—that is, billboards vs. mere buildings. This makes billboard corrections, whatever else they may be, even if they are "just havin' fun" in an urban playground, a challenge to outdoor advertising, to the corporate control of public visual space. This aspect of corrections can be viewed in a larger context as signifying a final whimper of a dying (strangled) public sphere trying to "speak to power," to articulate public opinion vs. the seamlessly intertwined interests of big business and government.

At the start of the twenty-first century, it is perhaps significant that community murals—ancestors of billboard correction—have lapsed into bureaucratized civic decoration, with occasional exceptions. The incisive spirit that marked many of the earliest murals, their relationship to tensions widely held in marginalized communities, is largely absent. Oppositional attitude, however, is resurrected in the (mostly) antagonistic relationship of billboard corrections to their targets. Whereas community murals articulated such social issues as race, gender, landlord exploitation, etc., those foci have been replaced by a politically safe celebration of cultures. Billboard corrections, incisive in their irony, delightful in the surprise and humor they offer, always highlight and protest the commodification of genuine cultures, as we are all viewed as mere numbers in corporate profit-seeking demographics.

NOTES

1. All forms of spray-can work—tags, throw-ups, and 'pieces—are called "writing," so in this essay "writers" refers to spray can users. "Tags" are initials or nicknames, and are usually what people have in mind when they refer to graffiti. "Throw-ups" are larger, balloon-lettered tags, usually done in two or three colors. "Wildstyle" refers to calligraphic tags, often so arcane that no one, not even

other writers, can decipher them without coaching from the artist. "Pieces" is short for "masterpieces," and refers to mural-like spray can works, some permissable, often nonpermissable (Cooper and Chaifant 1984: 27).

2. "Billboard correction" refers to any alteration of an advertising billboard. In its most sophisticated form, the change reverses the message of the ad so that, ironically, it "shoots itself." Other terms substituted for "correction" include alteration, change, editing, improvement, etc.

3. I am indebted to Sarah Drescher for this nomenclature.

4. The term used by Billboard Liberation Front member Jack Napier to describe that group's motivation.

5. A similar taxonomy was suggested in a panel discussion at the "Art of Midnight Editing" show, in San Francisco, on March 14, 1999, by Craig Baldwin: paint ball, graffiti, elision, addition, substitution-linguistic, visual overlay (both linguistic and visual), and surplus creativity.

6. This, of course, is an extension of the seventies New York phenomenon of sneaking into the heavily guarded, often electrified, razor-wire-surrounded subway train yards during the night.

The Paradox of Public Art: Democratic Space, the Avant-Garde, and Richard Serra's "Tilted Arc"

Caroline Levine

For the past hundred years, democratic governments have had to grapple with a range of thorny public policy questions that emerge from the arts. Setting aside more general problems of free speech, injurious influence, and copyright restriction—issues which pertain to many kinds of speech—I want to suggest that policy-makers have had to confront some specifically artistic questions that have arisen in the wake of the modernist avant-garde. The avant-garde was a set of late nineteenth and early twentieth century artistic movements that were proud of their rejection of both officially sanctioned academic art and mass culture, assigning the highest moral and aesthetic value to the art that satisfied the smallest audience. They claimed authenticity only for the art that challenged familiar and conventional tastes. "Public art" became something of an oxymoron in a context where art deliberately flouted public approval. Yet Western governments continued to exhibit, protect, and commission works of art throughout the twentieth century, citing the value of art for national edification, identity, and pride. Thus art policy found itself continually split. If artists insisted that the only genuine art was that which defied public expectations, democracies had to reconcile an official respect for art with an art world that deliberately resisted the tastes and preferences of both state institutions and the voting majority.

This vexing paradox is perhaps most troubling in cases of art commissioned for public spaces. In public spaces, democratic procedures frequently—and perhaps necessarily—come into conflict with an institutionalized artistic defiance. In public spaces, a community's right to use, inhabit, and move through a space in ordinary and utilitarian ways typically clashes with the role of art as that which disrupts and critiques the status quo. And more disconcertingly still, in debates over public art, the deliberately divisive avant-garde exposes conflicting constituencies that compete to claim their rights to public spaces—revealing fissures and contradictions in our conceptions of the public itself.

My example here is the famous history of *Tilted Arc*, a monumental sculpture created by Richard Serra in 1981 for Federal Plaza in Manhattan. The funds for the piece came from the General Services Administration (GSA), a government office which has a policy of commissioning works of art for new federal buildings, allocating one half of one percent of the costs of construction to a prominent American artist. This Art-in-Architecture program, as it is called, has been responsible for both controversies and successes—including Alexander Calder's *La Grande Vitesse* in Grand Rapids, Claes Oldenburg's *Bat Column* in Chicago, and George Segal's *Restaurant* in Buffalo. In 1979, the GSA asked the National Endowment for the Arts to set up a panel of art experts to nominate an appropriate sculptor for the Federal Building in New York. Presented with an array of proposals, the committee chose Richard Serra, believing that his work was monumental enough to stand in the shadow of Manhattan's skyscraping monoliths—including what were then the relatively new World Trade Center towers. Serra's project, the committee agreed, would not "be overwhelmed by a city of skyscrapers and such miracles of engineering as the Brooklyn Bridge," while it was exciting enough to "capture the energy, enterprise, and fast movement of the city's inhabitants."[1] Serra was also a perfect candidate for this prominent public arts program since many saw him as "the most important sculptor of his generation."[2]

Commissioned by the GSA, Serra set to work on his piece by studying the passage of pedestrians through and across the plaza. He aimed to build a work that would draw attention to the way that people moved through the space, and to this end he planned a long, curving wall made out of red Cor-Ten steel to bisect the area. It would stretch to a length of 120 feet and stand 12 feet high. The GSA in New York asked for a detailed study of the impact of *Tilted Arc* on the environment, including safety, pedestrian traffic, lighting, drainage, and law enforcement.[3] Serra altered his proposal to take their concerns into account, and it was approved in 1980.

Even before the work was complete, complaints began to stream in. Initial petitions demanding *Tilted Arc*'s removal boasted thirteen hundred signatories, many of them workers in the adjacent federal building. Chief Judge Edward D. Re was particularly vocal about his dislike of the *Arc*. He circulated petitions and protested vehemently against the "rusted steel barrier" while it was still in the process of construction. The furor later died down, only to be whipped up again three years later, perhaps deliberately by Re, who certainly helped to launch the letter-

writing campaign to Washington. In the first four years of *Tilted Arc*'s life, the GSA reported forty-five hundred letters and appeals urging its removal, lamenting the ugliness, the inconvenience, the incomprehensibility, and the intimidating bulk of Serra's sculpture.

In March of 1985, the GSA's New York Regional Administrator, William Diamond, convened a panel to decide whether or not the *Arc* should be relocated. He held an open public hearing which lasted three days.[4] Those who testified included not only local residents and workers, but art experts, curators, dealers, politicians, arts administrators, sculptors, playwrights, painters, and performance artists. In all, 180 people spoke at the hearing, 122 for preserving *Tilted Arc* in the newly renamed Jacob Javits Plaza, 58 for its removal. By the end of the hearing, the voices raised against the work had persuaded the panel, and *Tilted Arc* was dismantled and taken away. Now it sits in storage, in pieces, no longer a public object. Today there are no traces of Serra's monumental work in Jacob Javits Plaza.

If Serra's public sculpture prompted immediate and vociferous outcry, the reasons for the uproar are striking. The work was not obscene, violent, or offensive on grounds of race, religion, sex, or sexuality. It could not be said to cause injury, corrupt the innocent, endanger the community, or threaten the stability of government. It could not be said to be about harm. What was at stake was a matter of style, of aesthetic preference, of taste. Public outcry revolved around what we might simply call "dislike."

And dislike, as it turned out, was complex indeed. In keeping with the legacy of the avant-garde, many voices in the art world actually argued for the desirability of displeasing the public, citing "dislike" as an appropriate aim of public art. Art's purpose was to unsettle and to upset. Others insisted that the majority was capable of appreciating the most esoteric works, that it was important to educate the public out of their dislike. Some politicians acknowledged the necessity of placating irritated voters, but many also refused to grant majority rule, insisting that it would be absurd to call a referendum on aesthetics. Yet, without a referendum, the debate then ran into the problem of gauging the extent and depth of public "dislike": who would speak for the public? Was it the press, the local government, the artistic community, the courts? Even more troubling, which public mattered most? Was it the people who used the space daily—who had to maneuver around the work in order to conduct their ordinary affairs—or was it the whole nation? Was it only the taxpayers who had paid for the work, or did the public include international visitors and future generations? Exposing the difficulties of identifying the proper boundaries and constituents of the public in a pluralist democracy, this critical and disruptive work of art uncovered the question mark at the heart of the very definition of democratic public space: namely —which public?

AVANT-GARDE PUBLIC SPACE

Up to this point, I have proposed three conclusions: first, that the avant-garde's defiance of public taste has lasted into our own time; second, that its logic poses an awkward, ongoing problem for democratic governments; and third, that the avant-garde challenges the logic of democracy by presenting an alternative, future-oriented notion of the public to counter political attempts to measure the status quo. It is in this context, I want to suggest, that we can begin to unravel the peculiarities of battles over contemporary art commissioned for public spaces. Since it is the avant-garde's desire to transform the public, what does it mean when this push toward the future takes place in a public space? If art's role is to maintain its independence from the world, is it appropriate for it to

locate itself in the midst of worldly activity? And what might such avant-garde disturbances entail for a public who habitually puts their space to use?

In the case of *Tilted Arc*, Serra's work of art deliberately disordered the architectural space it inhabited. In good avant-garde fashion, his champions gave Serra credit for this disruption. One advocate made the case that *Tilted Arc*'s contrast with its surroundings revealed the visual shortcomings of the neighboring buildings: "This appropriately scaled wall of hot, curved steel [looks] like an incredibly polite and human critique of a stiff and inelegant and pretentious architecture."[5] Another Serra supporter argued that the work actually changed the character of a purely utilitarian space, making it into an aesthetically interesting one: "The sculpture's scale and moving form transforms what is essentially a desolate, open space without any distinguishing characteristics into an exciting perceptual encounter."[6] For yet a third witness, *Tilted Arc* drew attention to the alienating quality of the urban setting: the buildings "are inhuman in their scale, boring and tedious, and the sculpture makes you confront that issue every time you walk by it."[7] This was avant-garde site-specificity at its best, celebrating the fact that the art object did not simply sit in a location as a thing in itself, but rather turned attention back on the surroundings, reshaping and critically reinterpreting the space.

Tilted Arc's supporters suggested that what the public should really be complaining about was not the sculpture but the urban status quo—the buildings and space around the work of art. And as the hearing made clear, this was no small gesture. After all, the public spaces we inherit—from parks and plazas to buildings, streets, and highways—organize our movements and structure our experience. Since these spaces are mostly there for their use-value, since they accumulate piecemeal, and since the map changes slowly over time, there are few opportunities to question the extent to which the overall design of public space controls and orders daily life. But surely public space is as important to critique as the art commissioned for it? In the hearing on *Tilted Arc*, more than one witness suggested destroying not the art work but the building and plaza that had been confronted and exposed by the art work:

This federal office building has got to be one of the ugliest buildings in the lower Manhattan skyline—a clear insult to and a distraction from such elegant neighbors as the Federal Courthouse, the Municipal Building, the Woolworth Building, and police headquarters. I don't suggest this merely in jest . . . If by your actions you indicate that there is a legitimate process available for the public to initiate the removal of a work of public art, then why shouldn't the same process be available for the removal of a public building? . . . Maybe you are really onto something. Think of all the problems this new idea could solve: how about all the dull, useless plazas, including this one, that allow developers to build ugly buildings bigger?[8]

Should we be focusing our political attention on the massive scale and hideous style of existing skyscrapers rather than attacking the lone work of art that challenges their existence? The artist Keith Haring thought so: "If . . . people were really concerned about altering the beauty of the urban environment, they would be trying to stop the [construction] of huge, ugly office buildings which change the entire neighborhood."[9]

But of course, there was another side to the story. Those who wanted to remove Serra's *Arc* also credited him with transforming the existing space, but they opposed that transformation, praising the original space as beneficial to the community. One worker explained that it was precisely the unremarkable nature of the plaza that had given it its value: "Until 1980 I regarded it as a relaxing reflective space, where I could walk, sit and contemplate in an unhurried manner."[10]

Representative Theodore Weiss agreed: "*Tilted Arc* rends the serenity of the plaza."[11] Before the *Arc*, Federal Plaza was notable for its insignificance, and its absence of excitement and stimulation were helpfully soothing in the busy city.

On one point, there was again little dispute between Serra's supporters and his detractors: all agreed that Serra had managed to dislocate the original space. One witness who spoke out against the *Arc* testified that it "violate[d] the very spirit and concept of the plaza,"[12] but this comment could just as easily come from one of his supporters. The question was not whether the *Arc* managed to throw its surroundings into crisis, but which was more damaging to the neighborhood: the spirit and concept of the original space or the critical reconception of the space by Richard Serra.

Of course, if this was a dialogue between two designs, Serra was not the only designer. An architect, Robert Allen Jacobs, had carefully planned the plaza, shaping the site to suit its community and surroundings. As one Serra opponent put it, "if we are talking about artists' rights, what about the rights of the artist who designed the square?"[13] Even more pointedly, "the plaza is a site-specific work of art incorporating a geometric paving design, now disrupted . . . Mr. Serra's work, according to him, was deliberately designed to change, alter, and dislocate someone else's artistic creation. This is wrong."[14]

Did the architectural work of Robert Allen Jacobs deserve the same protection and respect and offer the same public value as Richard Serra's *Arc*? The two sides in the debate clearly thought not, since Serra's supporters regularly proposed to destroy the site and his opponents just as consistently defended it. No one argued that all designs were equally sacrosanct. But what exactly was the difference between the two works?

Site-specific sculpture is not the same as architecture, and although the distinction between the two art forms is not absolute, it may be helpful to point to an important difference. Architecture is the shaping of space for *use*. Thus it can be evaluated according to how well it performs its tasks. Does the building house sufficient numbers of workers? Is it structurally sound? Does the space allow for the smooth movement of workers and visitors? By contrast, since the emergence of the avant-garde, art is defined by the fact that serves no immediate practical purpose: in fact, for customs purposes the United States Government defines art as distinct from "articles of utility" (Rowell 1999: 112–113). Art is therefore evaluated by strictly non-utilitarian criteria: its creative energy, its sensuous appeal, its potential to disrupt established norms and habits. In this sense, art seems far more expendable than architecture: surely we can do without sculpture but wouldn't we struggle to function and survive if all buildings, squares, and streets disappeared?

Witnesses who wanted to remove *Tilted Arc* frequently bemoaned the uselessness of the sculpture, pointing to the fact it thwarted more constructive activities and services. "Utilization of the plaza is now severely limited, preventing use by the occupants, and the neighboring community, for ceremonies, cultural attractions, and other recreational activities."[15] With the *Arc* out of the way, a whole range of cultural activities *other* than monumental visual art would come to the plaza. "We will be able to bring cultural shows here. We will have bandstands, and we will have performances. We will have food here sold to people. We will have greenery, landscaping."[16] Scholar James Dickinson explains that Serra's art has always courted controversy precisely because it "interferes with planners' and administrators' ideas about the way public space should be used: for passive enjoyment, strolling, sitting, eating, and watching" (Dickinson 1998: 51). Art is not only useless itself: it precludes other meanings, other expressions, and other functions. Art, we might say, gets in the way.

But if we are to believe the avant-garde, that is precisely the point. Serra's site-specific art was there in part to invite challenge and critique: it called on viewers to reflect on their movements, to contemplate the dehumanizing nature of their surroundings, even to imagine pulling down most of the buildings in downtown Manhattan—in short, to stop in their tracks. At its most successful, the critical art object should be capable of interrupting ordinary life. Richard Serra and his defenders claimed that his art work did not absolutely interfere with other functions: "It is only necessary to plan with the sculpture rather than against it to involve the *Tilted Arc* in the 'increased public use' contemplated by its opponents."[17] But this was not quite the whole story. After all, Serra's side also claimed that the work deliberately disrupted other, more utilitarian uses of space. It hinted at a liberation from the pressure of ordinary duties and obligations:

> Serra's work ... challenges the loss of critical function contained in bureaucracy and retains the critical function which is essential to any genuine art. It stands outside of the homogenization of bureaucracy, forcing an active relationship between the passerby and the space of the plaza, and necessarily the space of the building behind the plaza. The space is no longer vacant, but occupied, organized. There is an opposition in the space of the plaza. This opposition reflects the true oppositions in our society which bureaucracies seek to deny; therefore, it has a critical function.[18]

Skeptical of the ordinary workings of commerce, politics, and labor, *Tilted Arc* revealed the alienation at the heart of contemporary urban life. In this light, it offered a non-utilitarian perspective capable of challenging the uses to which human beings and their spaces are habitually put.

If the aim of art is to question habits and conventions, it makes sense for public art to seek to transform public space so that it is no longer totally absorbed into the utilitarian uses of both labor and leisure. For art to achieve its unsettling aims, its separation from the rest of life—its very uselessness—should feel inescapable. If it is in a public space, that means that it might do well to take over the space, halting and transforming the ordinary utility of public spaces by insisting on an impractical, critical hiatus, an interruption of daily affairs. Avant-garde works of art, we might say, function most successfully when they suppress the routines of ordinary usage, reshaping useful public spaces so that they are subsumed by the critical inutility of art. As art becomes site-specific, then, public sites become art-specific.

To put this in its most perverse formulation: public space, disrupted by the avant-garde, must become the museum. The avant-garde intends to disrupt habitual routines and expectations in favor of unsettling critique. Conventionally, such critical, reflective moments are fostered in spaces designed for critical, reflective purposes—not only museums and galleries, but universities, theaters, and performance spaces. But these are all voluntary spaces, spaces that paying customers choose to enter. If the avant-garde's visionary power is going to reach beyond the walls of such voluntary spaces, to break through to the wider public it intends to provoke, it must disturb the ordinariness of ordinary life, to take its critical practice outside of the sphere of voluntary activity. Art's critical uselessness must therefore enter into and interrupt spaces that are otherwise put to use. Thus it is the dream of the avant-garde to turn the world into a museum.

Clear opposition to such a conclusion came from government officials, who did their best to put *Tilted Arc* back inside the walls of a literal museum. They proposed what they saw as a sensible compromise: to move the art object out of a space where the community did not like or understand it into space where it would find an admiring and knowledgeable audience. "Very likely," Dwight Ink wrote, "the *Tilted Arc* would be

far better appreciated by those who had the free choice of viewing it than those in the Federal Building who find the plaza physically curtailed, and whose view is obstructed by the *Tilted Arc* as they arrive in the morning and as they leave the building at noon and after work."[19] No one should be forced to experience the avant-garde, and thus the art object should go back where it properly belonged: a space made for art lovers.

Levelheaded as this proposal might seem to its proponents, Richard Serra and his supporters argued passionately against such a shift. They claimed that to move *Tilted Arc* would not be a relocation, but a destruction of the work of art. The close interconnection of work and site, they claimed, was integral to Serra's brilliant site-specificity, the work's particular engagement with a local context of buildings, streets, and pedestrians. These arguments for a sophisticated interweaving of art object and environment are surely convincing—and might perhaps seem harmless enough. But the logic of the avant-garde suggests that government officials were right to fear the power implied by *Tilted Arc*'s location. After all, if art works are there to challenge the habits and preferences of a mainstream culture, to do so with any force they cannot be contained in museums. They must disturb spaces that are habitually put to use. For the avant-garde to achieve its grandest purposes, its challenges must take place in public space.

DIVIDED PUBLICS AND FRACTURED PUBLIC SPACE

Flouting local traditions and contemporary tastes, celebrating its status as outsider and innovator, boasting of its cosmopolitan, transnational sophistication, and imagining itself projected out of a hostile present into a welcoming future, the avant-garde rejoices in its difference, its otherness. But public art not only sits in public spaces; it also makes some claim to represent the community or the nation, producing an image of the public that is then broadcast to the world and future generations. The work of art not only sits in a public space and gathers its support from public funds: it comes to stand for the public. So, can avant-garde public art possibly accomplish both of its missions—simultaneously celebrating the margins and representing the mainstream, at once flouting the majority and conveying it to the world?

Numerous witnesses in the *Tilted Arc* hearings worried about the work's representative character. What would the art object say to the world about their government, their nation, themselves? One local resident mentioned the many visitors who came to the plaza to apply for citizenship at the Immigration and Naturalization Service. Surely *Tilted Arc* would represent a hostile America to them: "[W]hen they enter the building from which they hope to emerge with hope and promise for a freer and better future for themselves and their families, they cannot help but be reminded by *Tilted Arc* of the iron curtains from which they escape."[20] A supervisor in the Bureau of Investigations who worked in the plaza was concerned that *Tilted Arc* indicated that America had abandoned its aesthetic traditions. He imagined revolutionary war hero Nathan Hale looking at *Tilted Arc* and asking, "What did I give up my life for if this is what they descend to in these days?"[21] Thus a work that was neither indecent nor violent nor politically partisan nonetheless generated the most heated of controversies in part because the public felt that *Tilted Arc* revealed and implicated them.

Witnesses who supported the *Arc* were equally impassioned about the ways that it represented the public. But they put their emphasis on the art work's very non-conformity, seeing it as proof of America's commitment to freedom of expression. "I am here," said one, "because of my concern for our own image as a great city, a great country, and a remarkable society dedicated to

individual freedoms, including the freedom of expression."[22] For Jacob Javits, "art in our society [is] the symbol of what freedom means in the world."[23] Art historian Irving Sandler argued that the only way for a democratic society to "achieve a valid public art" was to allow a variety of artists to express themselves freely.[24] In this view, art can only be a valid expression of democracy if it communicates marginal and unorthodox perspectives to prove the society's commitment to tolerance and diversity.

Although *Tilted Arc* was abstract and non-representational in itself, its status as public art made it seem to offer up an image of contemporary life, an image to be displayed to the local community, to the nation, to the world, and to the future. On the one hand, witnesses expressed distress about an America revealed as divided, split from its central values and mainstream traditions, and on the other they gave praise for a complex nation enriched by its plurality. Which of these was the right gesture in a public space? Did public art serve democracy by representing the majority, the weighty single voice of a culture's dominant traditions? Or did it serve it better by emphasizing the marginalized voice, the dissenting view, the challenge to convention and tradition?

I want to close with a vote for avant-garde marginality—and thus a vote for the value of avant-garde public art in a democracy. Setting itself up always as eccentric, uncooperative, and unsettlingly alternative, the artistic avant-garde seems anti-democratic in its defiance of the mainstream, but it is quintessentially democratic in one crucial way—its insistence on plurality, on heterogeneity, on otherness. Deliberately disorderly, the avant-garde public art object asks whether public space is serving the margins as well as it serves the mainstream, whether it encourages challenges as well as conformity. Indeed, if the arrangement of urban space in blocks and squares organizes movement and experience, crucially shaping the possibilities of use, habit, and exchange, how successfully can it also foster and accommodate heterogeneity? Does the organizational and utilitarian character of public space compel assimilation, uniformity—sameness? The avant-garde insistently pushes us to address the tension between a celebration of pluralism and a desire for uniformity and harmonious collectivity.

It is in the tension between unity and fractured plurality that conflicts over public art emerge again and again. If the avant-garde always favors dissent, it sustains a pressure to acknowledge difference. And this, I would argue, is valuable for all of us. As Cass Sunstein writes, censorship does not pose the only threat to the freedom of expression; equally dangerous is the increasingly effortless act of filtering—the decision to expose oneself only to sources and kinds of information selected in advance. Filtering is perilous for democratic societies to the extent that it allows citizens to make the decision to expose themselves only to what they already know: to listen only to like-minded people, to come across only topics of prior interest, to encounter only views already held in advance. Filtering works against the "unplanned, unanticipated encounters" that are crucial to a recognition and understanding of plurality (Sunstein 2001: 8). Sunstein asks us to consider "the risks posed by any situation in which thousands or perhaps millions or even tens of millions of people are mainly listening to louder echoes of their own voice" (Sunstein 2001: 16).

In this context, we can rethink the discomfort that avant-garde art offers to its spectators. The discomfort it offers is the distress not of menace or injury but of unfamiliarity, of incomprehensibility and surprise. What it brings into public space is the disquiet of skepticism, the turmoil of possibility. In a world where dominant groups hear their voices in every medium, and minorities turn to niche channels and servers

to air and reaffirm dissenting views, the avant-garde public art project puts fragmentation itself at the heart of public discourse. Though it cannot be said to harm bodies or minds, the avant-garde launches what are indeed significant challenges, asking us to confront differences between majorities and minorities, self and other, utilitarian habit and critical thought, present and future. And when it generates conflicts—as, by definition, it strives to do—avant-garde public art points us to a recognition of competing notions of the public itself, inviting a recognition of the difficulties of representing a complex and often disunited historical group like America.

NOTES

1. These are the words of Suzanne Delahanty, member of the NEA panel that had nominated Serra. These comments come from her testimony in the hearings about *Tilted Arc*. See *The Destruction of Tilted Arc: Documents*, eds Clara Weyergraf-Serra and Martha Buskirk (Cambridge, MA and London: MIT Press, 1991), 83.
2. Art critic Douglas Crimp, *The Destruction of Tilted Arc*, 221.
3. Later Serra's critics would complain about the sculpture as a shield for drug-dealers and terrorists, but the official body responsible for commissioning the sculpture was satisfied that it would cause no harm.
4. Testimony from these hearings is collected in two recent volumes, *The Destruction of Tilted Arc*, already cited, and *Public Art, Public Controversy: Tilted Arc on Trial* (New York: American Council for the Arts, 1987). Neither text offers a complete transcript of the hearings; both make representative selections. The testimony overlaps to a significant degree, but both are necessary to grasp a full sense of the arguments.
5. Steven Davis, in *Public Art, Public Controversy*, 102.
6. Joyce Schwartz, in *Public Art, Public Controversy*, 63.
7. Ronald Feldman, in *Public Art, Public Controversy*, 75. Some witnesses even suggested that perhaps the controversy itself had come about precisely because *Tilted Arc* had taught viewers to question their environment.
8. Roberta Brandes Grantz, in *Public Art, Public Controversy*, 70–1.

9. Keith Haring, in *Public Art, Public Controversy*, 103.
10. Joseph I. Liebman, in *The Destruction of Tilted Arc*, 113.
11. Theodore Weiss, in *The Destruction of Tilted Arc*, 115.
12. William Toby, in *The Destruction of Tilted Arc*, 119.
13. Jessie Gray, in *The Destruction of Tilted Arc*, 122.
14. Margo Jacobs, in *The Destruction of Tilted Arc*, 124–5.
15. Norman Steinlauf, in *The Destruction of Tilted Arc*, 112.
16. Interview with William Diamond (15 March, 1989), in *The Destruction of Tilted Arc*, 271.
17. Coosje van Bruggen, in *The Destruction of Tilted Arc*, 79.
18. Joel Kovel, in *The Destruction of Tilted Arc*, 94.
19. Dwight Ink, in *The Destruction of Tilted Arc*, 171.
20. Shirley Paris, in *The Destruction of Tilted Arc*, 126.
21. Harry Watson, in *The Destruction of Tilted Arc*, 120.
22. Halina Rosenthal, in *Public Art, Public Controversy*, 117–18.
23. Marion Javits, reading a statement by Jacob Javits, in *The Destruction of Tilted Arc*, 98.
24. Irving Sandler, in *Public Art, Public Controversy*, 82–3.

Those "Gorgeous Incongruities": Polite Politics and Public Space on the Streets of Nineteenth Century New York

Mona Domosh

Ellen Olenska, the heroine of Edith Wharton's novel *The Age of Innocence* (1968), is immediately marked as an outsider to New York society when she returns from Europe and strolls on Fifth Avenue with Julius Beaufort, a man of questionable virtues. Mrs. Welland, a prominent social figure in the city, thinks to herself: "It's a mistake for Ellen to be seen, the very day after her arrival, parading up Fifth Avenue at the crowded hour with Julius Beaufort" (1968: 32). This first social faux pas defines her character irrevocably, since Ellen Olenska could have declared her impropriety no more extensively than by her transgression on Fifth Avenue, the most public thoroughfare in middle-class New York, on the day after her arrival in the city. Similarly, Lily Bart, the tragic heroine of Wharton's *The House of Mirth* (1984), positions herself outside the bounds of decorum when she is seen on the wrong street in New York, at the wrong time of day, and is forced to lie about her destination, a lie that ultimately leads to her destruction. Edith Wharton saw the streets of New York as a public stage, where the intricate scripts of bourgeois behavior were played out each and every day. And as public stages, the scripts were monitored closely.

Wharton's streets of nineteenth-century New York seem to bear very little resemblance to the images of streets created by recent scholarship on modernizing cities. Scholars lamenting the loss of public space in the postmodern city depict the streets of the nineteenth century as the preeminent sites of "democracy and pleasure" (Sorkin 1992: xv). Michael Sorkin, for example, speaks of the nineteenth-century city as a "more authentic urbanity," comprised of "streets and squares, courtyards and parks." He counterposes this "authentic urbanity" of the past with the cities, or "theme parks," of the present, places that have lost their traditional moorings in space and time (Sorkin 1992: xv). In drawing these conclusions, Sorkin is pulling together different threads of recent cultural criticism and political theory that posit connections between the decline of the democratic, public sphere and the disappearance of public spaces.[1] Other urban scholars, such as Mike Davis (1991) and Edward Soja (1989), suggest similar scenarios, particularly as they describe a Los Angeles that has lost any connection to real communities, and whose public spaces have become "militarized"—that is, fenced-in and controlled by private interests.

Yet analyses of behavior in the public spaces of nineteenth-century American cities suggest that these spaces too were often controlled by private interests, and were not necessarily any more democratic in the sense of tolerating deviant behavior than are our postmodern "theme parks" (Davis 1986; Domosh 1996; Abelson 1989). Edith Wharton's characters were not free in their behavior on the streets of New York; they were intensely guarded in their displays, aware all the time of how their public behavior communicated their identities. This, then, is a different sense of "public," where public space refers to places under public scrutiny, removed from the privacy of the domestic.[2] In these public spaces, a governing set of social norms controlled behavior, and therefore it is difficult to suggest that these spaces contributed to a completely democratic public sphere, where people were free to express themselves.

Through an analysis of three select images of street life in mid-nineteenth-century New York City, I provide case studies of how social norms were embodied in the everyday, public actions of people on the streets. I also suggest that those social controls were never completely hegemonic. I argue that socially controlled street spaces could serve as sites of political and social transgressions, but in ways different from those suggested by Sorkin and others. It is only by looking carefully at the often hidden codes of social performance that such slight transgressions can be made apparent. Our recent conceptual frameworks for analyzing the nature of public space seem to direct our attention elsewhere. By providing this analysis of the streets of a nineteenth-century city, I hope to show that the democratic potential of public spaces may still be possible, even in our contemporary "theme parks," if we direct careful attention toward slight, everyday transgressions.

THE STREETS OF NEW YORK

New York City's population at the close of the Civil War was a little less than a million people, of whom 85 percent lived less than two miles from the city's population center, Union Square, where Broadway crossed 14th Street. That density of population reflected the economic growth of a city that would become the capital of capitalism in its next

quarter century, and, of course, the relative lack of intraurban transportation systems. All movement of people, goods, and animals took place on streets designed, as the Commissioner of Public Works said in the 1870s, to "impede rather than to facilitate travel" (quoted in Mandelbaum 1965: 12). On those streets all types of people could be found, although not in the same proportion, time, or manner. New York in the 1860s was a city characterized by extremes in wealth and poverty, by ethnic and racial diversity, by economic elites competing for political power, and by an unstable social-class system. As public spaces, then, the streets provided not only transportation corridors, but also sites for the displays of social class and political power.

The three images analyzed here depict scenes on Broadway and Fifth Avenue. By mid-nineteenth century, these two streets had become important icons for portraying the city and, with the additions of Wall Street, constituted the range of symbolic streetscapes that were usually highlighted in contemporary accounts (Spann 1981; Domosh 1996; Rosenzweig and Blackmar 1992). Already by 1860, Wall Street had come to symbolize the economic power of the city. The commercial dominance of the country that New York attained by the 1840s was translated into financial dominance on the eve of the Civil War (Hammack 1987). And that control over the nation's capital was forcibly expressed in the tight clusters of banks, insurance offices, and financial traders that surrounded the exchange buildings on Wall Street, "the great financial centre of America" (Martin 1868: 141). In the small, often cramped offices of financial institutions along Wall Street, the business of America was conducted. The symbolism of Wall Street as the capital of finance was so powerful that as early as 1850 it was known simply as "the street"—home to the "favored and powerful individuals who exert this immense control over society and the world" (Foster 1850: 224).

Broadway was the grand boulevard of display, extending the whole length of the island, and therefore carrying along its edges an incredibly diverse array of people and activities. Below Wall Street, it was home mainly to business offices, particularly shipping, while farther north were the offices of realtors, insurance companies, and bankers. Beyond City Hall, on Broadway at Chambers Street, were the beginnings of the retail district, centering in 1860 on Stewart's Store, just north of City Hall. This retail area, surrounded on sidestreets by wholesalers, extended almost to 14th Street and Union Square, where businesses were taking over what had been a residential area. At that time, the built-up area of Broadway extended to about 23rd Street, at its intersection with Fifth Avenue. Along this path, and particularly on the stretch of businesses south of 14th Street, throngs of New Yorkers passed daily. And those New Yorkers were a diverse lot: "Every class and shade of nationality and character is represented here. America, Europe, Asia, Africa, and even Oceania, has each its representatives here. High and low, rich and poor, pass along these side-walks . . . Fine gentlemen in broadcloth, ladies in silks and jewels, and beggars in squalidness and rags, are mingled here in true Republican confusion . . . From early morning till near midnight this scene goes on" (Martin 1868: 46). This account may not have been exaggerated. In 1850, almost 60 percent of New Yorkers were foreign-born (Spann 1981: 24). The largest group of the foreign-born were the Irish, who constituted about thirty percent of the city's population in the 1850s (Spann 1981). In distinction, the proportion of people with known African heritage was relatively low—1.6 percent of the total population in 1860 (Scheiner 1965: 6). Their population was centered in the lower west-side, particularly along the narrow streets of Greenwich Village (Bernstein 1990). Although there was a small "social aristocracy" within the black community, most

African-Americans were poor. According to a state census of 1855, the unemployment rate among blacks was almost 60 percent, and those who were employed worked largely in services, with domestic servants as the primary occupation (Freeman 1994). Historian Rhoda Freeman (1994) argues that the small numbers and relatively low social status of the pre-Civil War black community prevented it from wielding any form of political or economic power within the city. Yet all these groups inhabited the sidewalks and main thoroughfare of Broadway. It connected their tenements in the lower east side and west side with the factories, offices, warehouses, and homes of the wealthy farther north, where they worked.

Fifth Avenue was the center of the upper-class residential district of New York in the 1860s, as "Wall Street" was "constantly sending fresh 'stars' to blaze on Fifth Avenue" (Martin 1868: 80). The upper classes of the city had been on a northward march throughout the nineteenth century, seeking refuge from the expanding commercial areas below 14th Street and particularly, the immigrant and working-class neighborhoods of the lower east and west sides (Scherzer 1992; Lockwood 1976). By the 1850s, after several prominent New Yorkers built brownstone mansions there, Fifth Avenue became the new fashionable area. It was lined with costly private residences, private clubs, and churches, the magnificence of which increased as one moved farther north. When Alexander Stewart built his mansion on the corner of Fifth Avenue and 34th Street in 1864, he hastened the movement north to this newest of fashionable areas in the city. The street, with its displays of wealth, was the symbolic center of "society"—the space where people could exhibit their good taste, both in fashion and culture. It was the preeminent site of promenades, rivaling the retail areas of Broadway for ladies parading their new fashions:

Nowhere else in America are there such fine opportunities for the display of dress as in New York. Where else in the broad world can there be found such a magnificent week-day promenade as Broadway, or such a Sunday morning strolling-place as Fifth Avenue? ... The spacious sidewalks [of Fifth Avenue], bowered in the most luxurious of foliage, make it a tempting place to walk in the fashionable season, especially on a bright and sunny Sunday morning.

(Ellington 1869: 34–35)

As public spaces, therefore, these two streets were highly scripted arenas for social display.

Scobey (1992) positions the era from the late 1850s to the 1860s as a "threshold-moment" in New York's economic and social history, a moment that was embodied both in the masses of immigrants and natives who comprised the urban street crowds, and in the rituals of respectability that dictated bourgeois behavior on the streets. New York's mid-century economic boom created great social anxieties. By the mid-1850s, New Yorkers had secured for themselves a dominant position in the national economy, as wealth from national and international trade, from the gold rush in the West, and from investments in transportation systems and real estate, began to accumulate in the city (Spann 1981). This wealth was in the hands of a new class of merchants, not those who guarded the mercantile coffers of the late-eighteenth and early-nineteenth centuries (Jaher 1982). Not only did these new moneyed classes seek means to express their identities, but, even more profoundly (and partly as a result of these new identities), the constant social and economic fluidity that characterized the mid-nineteenth century served to question the very basis of a bourgeois solidarity—how would respectable New Yorkers recognize each other as a consolidated class? As Scobey states: "It [social and economic fluidity] rendered problematic the very basis of bourgeois

identity: the capacity of the propertied and powerful to recognize one another as constituents of a moral collectivity" (1992: 212). Under threat both from the masses on the streets, and from constant social mobility, New York's bourgeoisie participated in ritualistic behavior, in a cult of manners, that was enacted at balls, in visits and church-going, and, most important in terms of outward display, on the streets—that is, in the "promenade." Elaborate codes operated here,[3] as small gestures took on great meanings, and where the only norms were those of respectability, worked out in salons and parties, later written into manuals.[4] And it is this use of the streets, as a way of performing identities, and at times challenging those identities, to which I now turn my attention.

IMAGES OF THE STREETS

All three of the images examined here are from *The New-York Illustrated News*, a weekly newspaper modeled after *Harper's Weekly* (Mott 1957).[5] I use these illustrations as a means of "seeing" and perhaps understanding some of the tactical transgressions that created, in Scott's terms, the "barrier reef" on which eventually the "ship of state runs aground" (1985: 36). As an outside observer, both in terms of space and time, what I offer as an interpretation is based on my understanding of the specific spatial, economic, political, and social context of mid-nineteenth-century New York City. With these images as entry points, I attempt here a plausible account of some of the tactical transgressions on the public streets of nineteenth-century New York. The first one appeared in January 1860, showing the crowds on Broadway at different times of day (Figure 1). The captions are telling: "at 7am—laborers, shop boys, and factory girls, begin the moving panorama of the day"; "at 9am—merchants and clerks hurrying to their place of business"; "from

Figure 1 "A Photograph of Broadway." *New-York Illustrated News*, January 21, 1860, p. 148. Collection of the New York Historical Society.

12–3pm—beauty and fashion on the promenade"; "at 6pm—general rush for home"; "midnight revelry in Broadway." An almost total segregation of classes is evident in the first three images—including the working classes, the middle and aspiring middle classes, and the leisured class, particularly the bourgeois women who are allowed to parade in their fashions while window-shopping at the new dry-goods stores along Broadway. As indicated by an 1869 description of Broadway, this temporal segregation was apparent to many:

> Broadway, which leads alike to the banker's offices with their thousands of gold, the large mercantile houses with their immense stocks of goods, leads also to the working places of the working women. At early morn these poor females walk down the great Vanity Fair; later still, the working men; then the shop-boys; then the young clerks; then the junior partners. Later still, the heavy members of the firm roll down in their magnificent carriages; and by noon the wives and daughters, who spend the money their husbands and brothers make, will be out in large numbers promenading and patronizing the various stores. What a contrast between five and six a.m., on Broadway, and twelve noon!
>
> (Ellington 1869: 579)

Yet in the fourth and fifth images, both working and middle classes are commingled—merchants and laborers, factory girls and fashionable women, prostitutes and male consumers. Look carefully at the faces in the fourth image. The very depiction of certain facial features was, at least in the nineteenth century, enough to indicate to a general audience the particular class and type of a person. According to Mary Cowling (1989), this systematic connecting of physical and mental attributes was part of a belief in physiognomy—the "science" of classifying people according to physical characteristics—that was widespread in nineteenth-century England and America. Physiognomy formed an important part of nineteenth-century anthropology, borrowing methods of classification developed by natural historians. In this system, such features as a large jaw and face in proportion to the forehead and head (where the so-called higher faculties reside) indicates people of a lowly, possibly criminal sort. Other lowly signs were a convex chin, "a long, flat upper lip and coarse formless mouth" (Cowling 1989: 297). We can see in this image, then, attempts to depict members of what were considered the lowest class in New York, most likely the new Irish immigrants, mingling in the crowds with members of several other classes. Indeed, all five of the images can be read as excursions into an anthropology of the modern city, depicting for those at home the various specimens of human life. According to Cowling, this was a fairly common form of imagining the nineteenth-century city, creating and then satisfying the curiosity of the middle classes about how their new industrial cities looked and functioned.

And Broadway was the perfect site for such imaginings, since it formed, as I have already shown, one of the most heterogeneous corridors in 1860s New York. It was also the preeminent site of streetwalkers: "Broadway is their favorite resort—their principal time of going out, at night. The gas lights are no sooner lighted than they come forth. It is fit that they should walk on Broadway. The street is broad, and on its pavements how many thousands have been led to destruction God only knows" (Ellington 1869: 298).

But, like Wharton's Lily Bart, fashionable women found on Broadway at the wrong time of day were in danger of losing their bourgeois status—even more so, of course, if they were seen on the street at midnight, when different classes and sexes mix in the revelry of "dark" Broadway. From most accounts of the lives of middle-class New York women in the 1860s, it is indeed true that they rarely ventured out alone to walk after four in the afternoon.[6]

And yet in this image there are fashionable, middle-class women to be found in the crowds of late afternoon. They were, in Cresswell's terms (1996), "out of place." At certain times, then, Broadway brought together different classes of people. And that diversity was frightening—it presented a challenge to nineteenth-century bourgeois life, where each group was meant to inhabit their own places.[7] As historian Scobey says of the promenade, it was "the bourgeois woman who figuratively condensed the class requirements and sexual risks of polite sociability. Like the proverbial canary in the coal mine, her presence marked what had to be protected in and from public exposure" (1992: 214–15). To see a bourgeois woman on Broadway beyond what he calls the "canonical" hour (11 a.m.–3 p.m.) was a breach of "respectability" (215). But such breaches occurred often. As Elizabeth Wilson states, the most frightening aspect of the streets "was the crowd—the promiscuous mingling of classes in close proximity on the street. The gentleman and, worse still, the gentlewoman were forced to rub shoulders with the lower orders and might be buffeted and pushed with little ceremony or deference" (1991: 29). So although throughout much of the day, the purported publicness of Broadway was highly scripted and acted out according to prescribed norms, at other hours, a "dangerous" mingling of the crowd was possible.

In fact, it was the very "publicness" of Broadway that allowed such behavior. Because it was so open to public scrutiny, any threat of potential evil behavior could be assuaged. An entire genre of urban guidebooks written in the mid-nineteenth century focused on the moral and political threats of the hidden city, those areas beyond public view. With such titles as "New York by Gas-Light," "Lights and Shadows of New York Life," and "Sunshine and Shadow in New York," these tracts, aimed at the mostly rural audience of middle-class America, presented a view of the evils of the city residing in the hidden spaces of the city—the basements of oysterhouses, the closed doors of brothels and dancehalls, the dark streets of lower Manhattan (Foster 1850; McCabe 1872; Smith 1868). In Stuart Blumin's assessment of this genre, "much of the immorality of the city occurs underground, in oyster cellars and in basement-level gambling dens and dance halls, reached only through well-guarded and labyrinthine passageways. Above-ground debauchery occurs upstairs, behind deceptive facades, in brothels and gambling houses . . ." (1990: 49–50). Yet, within the surveillance of the bright lights of public scrutiny, immoral behavior was less likely. The bourgeois codes of the street could be violated, at times, if those violations occurred within the purview of the public.

The second image, from January 1863 (Figure 2), was accompanied by a caption and an explanation in the text:

Our best society—A scene on Fifth Avenue, the fashionable promenade on Sunday afternoons. From a sketch taken opposite the (blank) club, 15th Street and Fifth Avenue. Our city readers will not fail to recognize the faithfulness of the picture on page 196, having probably experienced the difficulty that attends a stroll through this fine avenue any pleasant Sunday afternoon.

Our influential Colored Citizens have recently taken this magnificent promenade under their supervision, turning out on Sundays and holidays, with a degree of splendor and enthusiasm quite startling to a reflective mind. The gorgeous incongruities of costume, and the highly intellectual countenances (as seen in the illustration) which proudly sail by the humble white pedestrians, are enough to make a sorrowful man laugh.

The air of satisfaction and nonchalance that characterizes our friends on these occasions, is irresistible. The way they ignore the privileges of their white brethren is not, however, so agreeable.

The scene of our sketch lies in the vicinity of one of the fashionable club-houses. If the reader imagines, for a moment, that our artist

Figure 2 "Our Best Society"—A Scene on Fifth Avenue. *New-York Illustrated News,* January 31, 1863, p. 196. Collection of the New York Historical Society.

has yielded to his satirical propensities, we beg that skeptic to make a pilgrimage through Fifth Avenue the next unclouded Sunday afternoon.
(*New-York Illustrated News,* Jan. 31, 1863: 196)

Certainly this image is in some senses a satire of proper, white society and its discomfort with those who are "in," yet "out of place" in their space. But I believe that it also tells us about a world where such displacements were possible and probable. To situate this point, recall that Fifth Avenue was the most prestigious residential address in 1863, and that the area between Union and Madison squares was home to several upper-class men's clubs and fashionable churches. The Sunday morning fashion promenade had become a standard activity for middle-class New Yorkers—after Sunday morning services at the Presbyterian or Episcopal churches on Fifth Avenue, families paraded

in their finest up and down the Avenue. As a contemporary commentator noted:

There is the Sunday stroll, with pensive face and prayerbook in hand, on Fifth avenue ... The time will be immediately subsequent to morning service. The scene may be scarcely appropriate, following so soon upon the religious exercises that have preceded it, but it is very fascinating in its freaks of worldly frivolity ... all the extremes of the latest fashions mingle in one vast stream of wealth and luxury.
(Ellington 1869: 35)

This image certainly represents a freak of worldly frivolity. A relatively large group of African-Americans are walking up Fifth Avenue on their Sunday promenade. At first glance, they seem appropriately middle-class and fitting to the scene. The central figures form a traditional family unit, dressed in what seems the latest fashions. Their grouping fits the norms of the Victorian family—the woman's arm is resting on her husband's, she is leaning toward him in a diminutive manner, and their daughter walks along the mother's side.

Yet middle-class and fashionable "colored citizens" upset and shock their white counterparts. First of all, there were, of course, no African-American churches on Fifth Avenue, nor did any blacks live there. They have come to Fifth Avenue purposely and solely to promenade—to show off. According to Rhoda Golden Freeman, there was indeed a "social aristocracy" (1994: 317) of blacks in New York at this time, as concerned about their dances, parties, social visits, clothes, and promenades as their white "brethren." Her reading of African-American newspapers suggests that "ladies of the Negro community were as concerned with fashion and elegant attire as were their white counterparts" (1994: 318). It is not difficult to imagine, for example, Lucy Gibbons Morse and her family walking along Fifth Avenue in her Sunday finery. She was the daughter of a wealthy and prominent black family who lived within walking distance of the scene depicted here.[8] In terms of their ability to parade in their finery on New York's display avenues, members of this socially elite class were on a par with other upper-class residents of the city. As Scobey says, this was indeed the point of the promenade—to disengage from any sort of personal or concrete relationships in order to engage in a ritualized behavior whose raison d'etre was the performance: "Not only private sentiments, but also social affiliations, material interests, indeed all concrete grounds of relationship were to be disengaged from the performance of respectability itself. As one expert put it, the 'passers in the street know no difference in individuals' " (1992: 217). The family may be black, but they are completing the performance. Yet even the tightness of behavioral codes that governed the promenade cannot prevent some obvious disruptions,

such as staring. Look particularly at the white women's faces. Clearly, a violation of sorts is taking place here. The most obvious violation is that the African-Americans have taken over the sidewalk, and are pushing their "white brethren" onto the street. Notice the positioning here, as a black woman walks ahead while the white couple bend to keep their balance on the sidewalk—obviously white "privileges" are being ignored. The literal space of the promenade, then, is being appropriated by African-Americans.

There are other, less obvious violations here. The clothing of the African-Americans is telling—most are depicted with clothes a bit over-the-top, some quite literally, with hats that are more ornate and unusual than their white counterparts'. The couple in the center are certainly dressed in their finest and have outdone the whites. The woman's skirt is heavily flounced, her cape is edged in fur, her bonnet is topped with flowers, and she completes her outfit with a parasol, quite an unnecessary item in January in New York, and particularly so for a black woman. The man's fully displayed white vest is topped with an elaborate cravat, and his hat is decorated with a wide band. He carries his walking stick out from his body, resting its end against his face. Both are wearing white gloves. Fancy clothes, white gloves, parasol, walking stick—all items completely dedicated to fashion, to leisure, without function on a cold winter's day. Scholars of African-American culture have documented the importance of clothing to both slaves and freed blacks in distinguishing the "hours of work from the hours of leisure and, in the case of those still enslaved, the master's time from the slave's" (White 1991: 195). As signifiers of status, then, clothes were extremely important to freed blacks. To see African-Americans in clothes clearly unsuited to work must have seemed particularly threatening to whites, who had difficulty fathoming a leisured black class.

But the "gorgeous incongruities" alluded to in the text get more to the heart of the issue. It is the juxtaposition and contrast between, on the one hand, black skin (with all the racist meanings this carried to white culture), and, on the other, top-of-the-line fashions and middle-class family structure, that apparently shocked not only the viewers depicted here, but also the lithographer of this scene. This juxtaposition represents an inversion of the "natural order," and when the world is thrown upside down in this way, dire consequences were sure to follow. Such dire consequences seemed just around the corner in January of 1863—this image appeared in print four weeks after the Emancipation Proclamation was signed, abolishing slavery in America. Most "emancipation" images that appeared in New York newspapers carried a much less threatening message—one of freed blacks as good laborers for the American industrial powers, often depicted as laborers barely above animals in the evolutionary chain. But in this image, the fear of freed, leisured blacks marching north to New York (as they are here walking up the Avenue), promenading in white space, pushing whites out on the street, is given form and voice. Six months later, in July of 1863, New York City experienced the most violent civil disorder in nineteenth-century America, when protests against the Conscription Act for the Civil War turned into riots. The major targets were black laborers, many of whom were hung on the streets, and a large percentage of the rioters were Irish workers who felt threatened by black labor and feared the consequences of a large labor supply if freed slaves moved north (Ignatiev 1995).[9] The Draft Riots, as they were called, differed from other instances of racial violence in New York City, suggesting, in the words of historian Iver Bernstein, a "citywide campaign to erase the post-emancipation presence of the black community" (Bernstein 1990: 5). But on Fifth Avenue, polite society stopped, stared and, at least for the moment, allowed the parade to continue. To do otherwise would have upset the script far too much.

A week later, the image shown in Figure 3 appeared, with the short caption "Club house, Fifth Avenue and Fifteenth Street, New York"—a scene just across the Avenue from the previous one. The men of the Manhattan Club are staring intently at the fashionable crowd passing in front of their plate-glass window. We could argue that the image illustrates the powers of the bourgeois male flaneur of the modern city, surveying the scene, choosing which delights he will indulge in. One of the women on the street is looking back at the men, as is the child, but for the most part, the women are passing without acknowledging the men in the window, without returning the gaze. They are the objects to be consumed, the men are the subjects who decide. In New York society this type of street scene was common: an 1868 description of Fifth Avenue mentions "The numerous clubhouses, filled with young men engaged in flattening their noses against the french plate-glass windows" (Ellington 1869: 35). But that description continues, saying that these men watching add "to the attractions of the walk, so far as the display of dress is concerned." This suggests a more active role for these women as decision-makers in their own right—since what good is a fashionable outfit in nineteenth-century New York unless you can display it to wealthy men? In other words, the male flaneur is in some ways the object of these women's active display.

This inversion of the expected order is more apparent in the text that accompanies the illustration:

the reader is now called upon to respectfully admire, at a distance, some of the approved types of "our best society" as they languidly lounge at the Club House window, ogling the pretty women, who, we are bound to say, do not always seem sufficiently impressed with the honor done them.

Figure 3 "Club House, Fifth Avenue and Fifteenth Street." *New-York Illustrated News*, February 7, 1863, p. 212. Collection of the New York Historical Society.

Mesdames! take your revenge, and look them out of countenance—in our picture! Without a blush, Miss Crosspatch, without so much as a drop of your eyelash, behold Tittlebat Tittlmouse in his element! behold the elegant Adolphus; and the famous Fitz-Clarence, (as carefully gotten up as a venerable ballet-dancer), and close behind him, observe Sir Loin Beef, the young English baronet, who carnt se, for the life of him, why we 'aven't such fine women in this blasted country as he has been in the 'abit of meeting at 'ome. Behold them all—those pretty hot-house plants, native and exotic, as they faintly bud and bloom, and languish in their plate-glass conservatory.

(*New-York Illustrated News*, Feb. 7, 1863: 212)

The caption suggests how the image in some ways subverts social and spatial norms. First, several of the women seem in no way "impressed" by the men in the window, in other words, they are not participating in the expected rituals of the fashion parade. They are simply getting on with their business. Second, the men are inside the house, the women outside on the street. This spatial reversal is echoed in the reversal of gender roles. As occupiers of the interiors, the men here are emasculated. Think of the words and images used to describe them: languid, pretty, ballet-dancer, hot-house plants, exotic, buds and blooms—these are undoubtedly feminine descriptors. These clubmen are decorative objects, as delicate as hot-house flowers in a conservatory, as useless and silly as titled English aristocrats. After all, real (bourgeois, American) men work.

This association with the English nobility might be of more than passing interest. The Manhattan Club was the center of the upper-class Democrats of the city, whose loyalty to America was being questioned by Republicans who held the White House. Many Confederacy sympathizers, who fashioned themselves after the English nobility, were Democrats whose loyalty to the Union was often under suspicion during the Civil War. For a complex set of reasons, they also sided with the Irish immigrants in the city, thus setting up an image of themselves as more European and less American (Bernstein 1990). So the Democrats are pictured as emasculated foreigners, to be laughed at by women.

Yet it is difficult to read the reversal of roles and spaces in the image as subversive in and of itself, for as a signifier of the feminine, the relative subordinate positioning of the domestic in society is simply reinforced— even when occupied by men, it serves a denigrating function. So the men are made fun of precisely because they occupy women's subject position. In this sense, the image does not suggest resistance to the status quo, but supports traditional beliefs by using the idea of the feminine to denigrate a certain group of men. Yet smaller, tactical transgressions are also evident. Women in the image are both watched and watching, but so are the men. The caption is directed at the women readers of the newspaper, who are given the final authority as observers. They are being invited to view these men at a distance and, with a long and accurate gaze, to see them for what they really are—mere fops who would wilt in the cold February air. The women are conducting the important business of the streets, while the men attend to decorative matters. Again, this presents an inversion of the natural order. In the public space of Fifth Avenue, women were, in some senses, in control of the business of life, as they ventured out daily to participate in the commercial city, paying bills, visiting stores, eating at the new restaurants set up for them. In fact, just a block south of the site of this image was Delmonico's, the most fashionable, although exclusively male, restaurant in town. When the first women's club was organized in New York in 1868, it held its meeting at Delmonico's, in direct and conscious chal-lenge to the status quo (Blair 1980). The club's membership was limited to professional, middle-class women, but these women used their access to these new spaces of the city to renegotiate their identities. Because they could walk on the streets unescorted (at certain times), and could participate in the commercial life of the city (albeit in limited ways, usually as consumers), their identities as bourgeois women expanded beyond the domestic, into the public spaces and activities of the city. And the women viewers of this image, who are directly addressed in the caption, are invited to take "revenge," to stare back, to become the "looker"—in other words, to take advantage of what the modern city allows, to switch identities, however intermittently or ambivalently. So the image suggests the possibilities of transgressions at the same time that it supports existing power relationships. Some women could stare back and gain power. Although for some their relegation to the domestic sphere meant that their power was annihilated, they nonetheless could, on the streets, at least for a brief time, "take revenge."

CONCLUSION

These last two images are particularly ironic, as they consciously juxtapose bourgeois norms of behavior with depictions of actual behavior that run counter to those norms. Whether that irony is apparent only to us or was intended by the artist is impossible to determine. But what we can say is that these images point to how the public streets of nineteenth-century New York were neither the "democratic" spaces of an authentic urbanity nor completely manipulated and exclusionary. A more nuanced analysis suggests that the metaphor of theater might be more appropriate, but a theater where scripts could be manipulated. Even in the heart of middle-class space, on Broadway and Fifth

Avenue, classes mingled, different "races" fashionably paraded, and gender roles could be reversed.

A polite politics was possible on these publicly guarded streets of 1860s New York, but not one immediately apparent from our historical record (although, as I have argued, the cumulative effects of such slight transgressions often are apparent, i.e., the appropriation of Delmonico's by a women's group). Nor was it a politics that corresponds to notions of an "authentic urbanity" of democratic possibilities. It was a politics made possible by the conditions of social surveillance, not surveillance by the state or institutions using technological means, but one constituted of minute activities of seeing and being seen. Because bourgeois norms of behavior encouraged people to parade in their finery up Fifth Avenue, and because that space was heavily surveyed, African-Americans too were allowed to engage in the promenade. Their behavior disrupted at the same time as it supported bourgeois standards. Because Broadway was the most public thoroughfare of the city, the mingling of different classes was tolerated when it took place in the "light" and out of the "shadows." And middle-class women could be as much the subject of the gaze as the object because social norms positioned some men as displays in the windows of Fifth Avenue, similar to the frocks and corsets seen in other plate-glass windows.

Edith Wharton's Lily Bart was eventually destroyed by her transgressions, not by violent struggles where the "stakes are high," but by the accumulative effects of a social system that tolerated certain "polite" forms of transgressive behavior and punished those who pushed the borders of politeness too far. Like the images analyzed here, Wharton's *The House of Mirth* (1984) is in some sense a satire of the mores of New York's upper classes, and as such casts that "reality" into stark relief. Lily Bart's transgressions were tactical, as she never positioned herself in

opposition to the status quo. Indeed, she is presented to us as the embodiment of the cult of manners, the woman who will make her way by knowing all the rules and playing by them. Yet her social miscues are obvious to those who matter around her, and each small step positions her in spaces further removed from polite society. Her fatal error, if we can call it that, was refusing to marry the "appropriate" man (the wealthy and well-positioned Percy Gryce) and to seek instead her own individual fulfillment. Her "micropolitics," then, was transgressive to the established norms but was evident only in the smallest of ways, and only to those who understood the complex and contextual script of polite performance.

If we know how and where to look, it seems we will find similar "polite" politics being enacted everyday in our "theme parks" that we now call our cities. As Jon Goss recently reminded us, even spaces considered the most manipulated and controlled, such as festival marketplaces, can be sites of alternative politics, since their "universalist rhetoric" opens them to unintended effects and transgressive readings (1996: 232). But our theories of public space and oppositional politics blind us to their potential force. Broadening our definitions of politics to include a "micropolitics" of complex and contextual agency should direct our attention to the "tactics" that many of us, who cannot afford the emotional and spatial distance required of an oppositional politics, embody in our everyday transgressions.

ACKNOWLEDGMENTS

This paper has benefitted greatly from the comments and suggestions of colleagues, particularly Stephen Daniels, Richard Dennis, Peter Goheen, Don Mitchell, Joan Schwartz, and several anonymous referees. I am grateful to Nick Fyfe for organizing a session on "the street" at the Glasgow Institute of British Geographers meeting, where I presented a paper containing the kernel of the ideas expressed here, and to the participants' comments at seminars in geography departments at Queen's University in Kingston, Ontario, Royal Holloway College of the University of London, University of Vermont, and Middlebury College. Thanks are also due to Barbara Hutchings for her cartographic skills. The research for the paper was funded by the National Science Foundation, Anthropological and Geographic Sciences, #9422051.

NOTES

1. Sociologist Bruce Robbins aligns this scenario of decline with a more general "myth of general decline" about the role of the academy, and argues that like all myths, it is a "defense of a very particular group—in this case, perhaps, white, male, native-born intellectuals who once had something of a monopoly of American 'public' discourse but since the 60s, when the universities in fact became more 'public' by letting some new people in, no longer do" (Robbins 1990: 258).
2. For a very interesting and useful assessment of the importance of private space as a political possibility, see Squires (1994).
3. Scobey provides numerous examples of these codes, drawn mostly from etiquette manuals (1992). A proper woman on the promenade was to faintly smile and present a formal bow to a male acquaintance, while a gentleman was to bow, but not speak, to a female acquaintance. If a man wanted to accord a woman a certain distinction of affection, he should dip his hat at least ninety degrees from its resting place.
4. For example, see *How to Behave: A Pocket Manual of Republican Etiquette* (New York, 1872), *Rules of Etiquette and Home Culture* (Chicago and New York, 1893), *Decorum: A Practical Treatise on Etiquette and Dress of the Best American Society* (New York, 1878) and Margaret Cockburn Conkling (pseud.), *The American Gentleman's Guide to Politeness and Fashion* . . . (New York, 1857). For a more thorough analysis of these etiquette manuals, see Kasson (1990).
5. *The New-York Illustrated News* tried unsuccessfully to compete with *Harper's Weekly* but was only published for four years. It would seem from an analysis of its articles and images that the newspaper was Republican in leaning (see Mott [1957]). My method is informed here both by Robert Darnton's incredibly rich book, *The Great Cat Massacre* (1984), where singular depictions of what seemed to Darnton "odd" behavior in seventeenth-century France were explored in all their complexities in order to gain insight into the social history of the past, and by Mary Poovey's book *Uneven Developments* (1988), where she claims that the richest of insights come from exploring "border cases"—those that do not quite fit into what we expect of the past—and following wherever they lead us. These three images struck me as the most interesting I had seen in several weeks of examining mid-nineteenth-century illustrated newspapers, and I knew that there were insights to be gained from a close examination of them.
6. This generalization is based on my reading of the unpublished diaries of five New York women written between the years 1854 and 1898, and from secondary accounts by Abelson (1989), Boyer (1985), and Smith-Rosenberg (1985). Three of the diaries, by Sophie C. Hall, Elizabeth W. Merchant, and Caroline A. Dunstan, are at the New York Public Library. The other two, by Mrs. George Richards and Clara Burton Pardee, are at the New York Historical Society.
7. For analyses of the class dimensions of street culture in New York City, see Boyer (1985), Scherzer (1992), and Rosenzweig and Blackmar (1992).
8. Her recollections of the Draft Riots of 1863 are the only known contemporary document written by an African-American. She and her family lived on West 29th Street, between 8th and 9th avenues, surrounded by white people. See "Recollections of the Draft Riots of 1863 New York City" by Lucy Gibbons Morse, New York Historical Society, Miscellaneous Manuscripts, 1927.
9. Ignatiev situates New York's Draft Riots within the context of how the Irish "took up arms for the White Republic" and became "white," whether they were fighting in the U.S. Army or in the streets of New York. Their desire to become "white" was rooted in the very American context of a racism born of miserable economic conditions (see Ignatiev [1995]).

Soundscape and Society: Chinese Theatre and Cultural Authenticity in Singapore

Tong Soon Lee

Simply put, the term "soundscape" refers to an area defined by specific sounds. In this essay, the concept of soundscape is modelled after Murray Schafer's *The Soundscape: Our Sonic Environment and the Tuning of the World* (Schafer [1977]1994). Schafer's work predates Arjun Appadurai's five notions of "-scapes" in his well-known essay, "Disjuncture and Difference in the Global Cultural Economy":ethnoscapes,mediascapes,technoscapes, financescapes, and ideoscapes (Appadurai 1990). A music composer, Schafer emphasizes the importance of understanding sound in spatial terms, and how sounds, including music, intersect with our everyday lives, and how we may expand our understanding of our physical and social environment by exploring sounds. Appadurai, a cultural anthropologist, coined his concept of "-scapes" as a framework to understand contemporary cultural flows through the global intersection of people, media, technology, finance, and ideologies, particularly useful in the context of changing power relations between former colonisers and colonies, Euro-America and Asia, us and them. Schafer demonstrates how sounds have the potential to mark acoustic spaces that generate specific sets of social meanings and values. Appadurai proposes a conception of space defined by different interactions of social practices across conventional demarcations of geographical and/or political boundaries.

Music is both a form of sound and a form of social practice that enacts a space, in other words, a soundscape. The meanings and values of this soundscape are located within its broader social settings, just as it simultaneously generates and shape new meanings and values in society. In this chapter, I draw on Schafer and Appadurai's works to examine how music defines culture through its interactions with a specific physical and social space in Singapore, and how emerging notions of culture from this soundscape intersect with broader social contexts in post-independence Singapore.[1] I focus on a Chinese street opera performance series that took place between 1996 and 1998 in Clarke Quay to explore the ways through which culture is shaped through the intersection of music, public space, and politics in contemporary Singapore. Understanding the Chinese street opera tradition in the context of cultural tourism at Clarke Quay requires us to reconsider the multiple meanings of authenticity, especially when it impacts upon the meanings and values of local cultures.[2] Although this performance series no longer exists, similar performances continue in Clarke Quay and in other venues throughout Singapore—issues emerging through this case study continue to be applicable to the understanding of music, social space, and culture in Singapore.

CLARKE QUAY AS A MODERN HISTORICAL SITE

Clarke Quay is a historical site along the Singapore River, within walking distance from Chinatown. In the last two decades or so, it has been reconstructed into a bustling area with pubs, restaurants, cafés, antique shops, among many other attractions, mainly for tourists and middle/upper-class Singaporeans.

Historically, Clarke Quay was one of two major sites (the other is known as Boat Quay) for the import and export of goods such as rice, gambier, and pepper from the nineteenth to twentieth centuries. Cargo ships berthed at the bay area (now known as Marina Bay) and smaller vessels would then carry the goods and manoeuvre through the Singapore River to Boat Quay and Clarke Quay. Chaozhou and Fujian people formed the dominant communities in this area.[3] In fact, Clarke Quay was (and still is) known colloquially in the Chaozhou dialect as "Cha Jung Tau," which literally means "harbour [or jetty] for ships carrying firewood" (Oral History Department 1990: 30). The area is named after Singapore's second governor, Sir Andrew Clarke. A special feature along both Clarke Quay and Boat Quay are the rows of two-storey houses that were originally used to house immigrant labourers who worked along the river. Some of these houses were also used as "godowns", a term referring to warehouses for storing goods. These labourers were known as "coolies" and the houses were referred to as "coolie quarters" or "ducking beds" (ibid.: 31). Today, these coolie quarters have been renovated and refurbished, and the majority have been leased out as pubs, cafés, and restaurants. In terms of cultural activities, both Clarke Quay and Boat Quay have historically been important locales for Chinese opera performances, especially for Chaozhou operas (ibid.: 29–34), in addition to other street entertainment such as storytelling (Wang 1990: 190–198).

In modern Singapore, Clarke Quay refers specifically to the area surrounded by Clarke Quay, North Boat Quay, and River Valley Road. Two main thoroughfares cut across the area, perpendicular to each other: Clarke Street and Read Street. At the end of Clarke Street and in the middle of North Boat Quay is Gas Lamp Square, where the Chinese street opera series was presented in the late 1990s.

According to the visitor's brochure, Clarke Quay is packaged and marketed as a "riverside festival village." Clarke Street, for example, has a merry-go-round at one end and a pavilion known as the Gazebo in the middle (located in the middle of Clarke Quay, known as Central Square), which sometimes features music performances. Along the street, there are outdoor game stalls and retail stalls in the form of huge pushcarts, where souvenirs, paintings, and other local artefacts are sold. Indeed, the section between the merry-go-round and Central Square is locally renamed "Carnival Street," probably to reflect the carnivalesque atmosphere the management tries to create; on official street maps, however, the whole street is known as Clarke Street. There are foreign food joints, local food venues such as Hawkers Alley, and numerous shops selling antiques, handicrafts, and designer apparel. Musically, there are pubs that feature blues, jazz, and rock music, as well as discotheques and Cantonese opera performances.

One of the most significant details in the entire spectacle at Clarke Quay is the emphasis on traditional and historical features of old Singapore. The site itself, an important area in the history of the Chinese community in Singapore, is a juxtaposition of historical reality, nostalgic sentiments, and contemporary popular culture, the conversion of the historic "coolie quarters" into modern amenities being a case in point. Along North Boat Quay, for example, some shops are modelled on historical interior architecture, and restaurants are built on large traditional wooden boats known as "tongkang" or bum boats, which are replicas of traditional Chinese sailing ships used by Chinese immigrants to Singapore. The Chinese opera stage itself, a simplified version of the traditional make-shift stage still used by professional Chinese opera troupes today, symbolizes the persistence of a traditional Chinese cultural form, reinterpreted in order to ensure its continuity in a changing contemporary context.

Perhaps the foremost tribute to old Singapore is the Clarke Quay Adventure. The entrance to the building that houses Clarke Quay Adventure is similar to that of other buildings. However, the inside is decorated with replicas of historical items, such as old radio sets, wine bottles, and pictures. The highlight of the adventure is a ride on a boat-like carrier on flowing waters that run through the building. The ride begins with the image of Singapore as a forested, fishing village, and journey through the entire history of Singapore until modern times, depicted aurally and visually using life-size figures of human, animals, and other artefacts.

CHINESE STREET OPERA
IN SINGAPORE

A "Traditional Chinese Street Opera" series at Clarke Quay began on August 1, 1996, and was performed by the Chinese Theatre Circle twice a week on Thursday and Friday evenings "to bring Cantonese opera to both Singaporeans and tourists" (*Straits Times*, July 30, 1996).[4] This performance situates itself in traditional concepts of Chinese street opera, and at the same time, helps shape and define new meanings and values of Chinese street opera in Singapore. At Clarke Quay, the concept of Chinese street opera is recontextualized and redefined within a framework of cultural tourism, where tourism is seen to develop the cultural resources that it feeds on (see Picard 1996).

Chinese street opera in Singapore refers to Chinese opera performed along the streets and in open areas. Traditionally, this is performed by professional troupes whose members have been trained in the tradition since they were young. These troupes are professional in the sense that they are profit-oriented organizations whose members make a living by performing Chinese opera. Since the 1970s, Chinese street opera performances by professional troupes have largely been limited to ritual and customary purposes, supported by Chinese temples and private religious organizations that serve as patrons. Interestingly, a new tradition of Chinese street opera performance began in the 1970s, presented by amateur troupes that are formed by members who perform Chinese opera for leisure. They are amateurs in the sense that they do not make a living from Chinese opera performance; indeed, many of them pay to join amateur opera troupes in order to practice Chinese opera. Chinese street opera performances by amateur troupes are secular and generally presented in public spaces as a form of cultural performance supported by the government and other arts and culture institutions. Clarke Quay's "Traditional Chinese Street Opera" series is one such example.

"TRADITIONAL CHINESE STREET
OPERA" IN CLARKE QUAY

The Chinese opera stage was positioned in Gas Lamp Square. Gas Lamp Square is strategically located in the middle of North Boat Quay, where it is visible to people walking along the street, or coming from the Boat Quay area situated further south of the river. In addition, it can also be seen from the major road junction between River Valley Road and New Bridge Road. Furthermore, tourists and Singaporeans travelling between Clarke Quay and Boat Quay on the river taxis (half-covered wooden boats propelled by an engine) embark and disembark right behind the Chinese opera stage. In other words, the stage is positioned conspicuously as a major attraction in Clarke Quay. The street leading from the Gas Lamp Square through the centre of Clarke Quay and right through to the other end of the area is significant because it constitutes a central space for public performances and entertainment.

Clarke Street is one of two central avenues in Clarke Quay, the other being Read Street. I suggest that the use of the stretch of space along Clarke Street is an important strategy in defining Clarke Quay culture, that is, the construction of Clarke Quay as a festival village. This stretch of space is framed by a major entrance/exit point near the merry-go-round and an embarkation/disembark-ation point at the other end near the river, where the stage is situated, spanning a distance of approximately 200 metres (650 feet). Visitors entering the Clarke Quay area from the entrance near the merry-go-round will experience different forms of entertainment as they walk straight ahead along Clarke Street towards the other end. Lining the streets are outdoor booths for various types of games, arcade games in indoor, air-conditioned halls, and large wooden push-carts reconstructed as stalls selling food, drinks, and souvenirs. At Central Square where the Gazebo is located, there are cafés and restaurants, and an ample outdoor seating area for al-fresco dining around the pavilion, where music performances by local groups and comic acts by buskers are presented. Further on, Clarke Street continues to be dotted with stalls selling local crafts. Whenever there is a Chinese opera performance, it would be audible just beyond the Gazebo. As one approaches the source of the music, Clarke Street opens into Gas Lamp Square, a junction that is often crowded with people eating and drinking, tourists queuing up for the river cruises, shoppers browsing around, and others standing in front of the opera stage.

The merry-go-round, the central Gazebo, and the Chinese opera stage demarcate a space that constitutes different forms of entertainment. The lane stretching from the entrance at the merry-go-round to Gas Lamp Square may be seen as a microcosm of the entire Clarke Quay. It constitutes a continuum of public entertainment, from the Western concept of a merry-go-round to performances in a pavilion in the form of a bandstand, and a Chinese opera performance at the opposite end by the river. This particular space is symbolic of the overall concept of Clarke Quay as a riverside festival village that embodies Asia and the West, high and popular cultures, the exotic and familiar, traditional and modern.

Gas Lamp Square is located in the centre of the North Boat Quay thoroughfare, the only avenue running parallel to the river. It is named after the unique and historical gas lamps that used to line the paths in Clarke Quay. Today, the original gas lamps can still be seen along the streets of Clarke Quay. While these lamps used to be lighted manually, they are now electronically controlled. The Square, which is closer to the shape of a pentagon, is approximately the size of a basketball court and the opera stage takes up about half of it.

In the late 1990s, the opera stage faced the Wild West Tavern with its outdoor seating extending into Gas Lamp Square. The space between the stage and the perimeter of this outdoor seating section is approximately 9 metres by 6 metres (30 feet by 20 feet), and is used by the audience and by the ensemble accompanying the opera performance. Excess audience space may extend into the outdoor seating areas of the Wild West Tavern or other nearby eateries, where diners have their meals and drinks, and watch Chinese opera at the same time.

The stage is about 9 metres by 5 metres (30 feet by 16 feet). The structural framework is constructed out of timber poles and planks, and it is covered on the sides and the top with large pieces of canvas. The stage is significantly smaller than the usual makeshift stage used by professional opera troupes for their daily street performances. In addition, the stage at Clarke Quay is only large enough for a performance area and therefore does not have a backstage, although two partially covered areas house the sound system, stage props, and costumes. These two areas are concealed from the audience by two whitewashed wooden planks, each of about 2 metres (6 feet) wide, with the following inscription:

CLARKE QUAY
SINGAPORE

TRADITIONAL CHINESE STREET OPERA
EVERY WEDNESDAY, THURSDAY, & FRIDAY
TIME: 7:45 PM—8:30 PM
CHINESE THEATRE CIRCLE
presents

From the audience's perspective, the panel on the right displays the English text while the left panel contains the Chinese version. In the Chinese version, the phrase "Traditional Chinese Street Opera" is presented differently. Since the Chinese Theatre Circle performs solely Cantonese opera, the Chinese version reads "jietou yueju," literally meaning "street Cantonese opera." Below the word "presents" is an empty space for the projection of the English synopsis of the play on the right panel, with the Chinese script projected on the left.

Two small walkways on either side of the stage lead to boats known as "river taxis". At specific times during the day, groups of tourists can be seen along the walkways, either embarking on or disembarking from their cruises on the Singapore River. Standing immediately behind the stage is one of the main gateway structures (the only gateway via the river) to Clarke Quay. Visitors arriving at Clarke Quay by river during opera performances often join the audience before proceeding to other attractions. Thus, Gas Lamp Square is a strategic location for a

cultural show—it is the river gateway to Clarke Quay, positioned in the middle of the North Boat Quay thoroughfare (which stretches along the river), and it is part of the Clarke Street entertainment locus. Whenever there was a performance, an average of eighty people gathered at Gas Lamp Square to watch Chinese opera, drawing the largest crowd of any outdoor performances at Clarke Quay.

A typical performance began at 8 pm, with a make-up demonstration by one of the performers beginning at 6:30 pm. As with traditional Chinese opera performance, the show began with an instrumental prelude, and was followed with an English introduction by Leslie Wong, Chairman of the Chinese Theatre Circle:

[Introduction]
    Good evening ladies and gentlemen, welcome to Clarke Quay Festival Village. The Chinese street opera is brought to you by Clarke Quay Singapore, with the support of the Singapore Tourist Promotion Board, and performed by the Chinese Theatre Circle. It is customary to precede the show with a piece of music. The music you've just heard is a very popular piece called "The Sorrow of Two Stars." You notice that the orchestra is put on the stage this evening, and traditionally, this is the layout of the orchestra of a Chinese opera stage: the percussion on your left and the string and wind instruments on your right.

[Main Section]
    The Chinese street opera was a very popular street entertainment. It used to be a common sight in old Clarke Quay, especially during religious festivals. And with much bustling activities during festivals in this area, Clarke Quay thus became known as the Festival Quay. In the past, families gathered in front of the opera stage with their own wooden benches to watch the shows. The audience would also peep behind backstage to watch the performers put on their elaborate makeup. The face colours and costumes adorned by the

performers symbolize different types of characters and personalities.

The opera tonight is performed by the Chinese Theatre Circle, Singapore's premier Cantonese opera group, a professional arts company. Established in 1981, its aim is to preserve and promote Chinese opera, drama, dance, and music. Since then, it has put [on] over one thousand shows in Singapore and overseas. It is certainly the most widely travelled troupe in Singapore, having performed in fifteen countries, spanning across five continents, countries including Australia, Belgium, Canada, China, Egypt, England, Germany, Italy, Japan, Malaysia, New Zealand, Romania, Scotland, Turkey, and United States of America. It has also participated in the prestigious Edinburgh Festival. The troupe has won many honours and awards throughout the years, including the most recent "Excellence for Singapore" award from the Singapore government. The Chinese Theatre Circle is also responsible for organizing the annual Chinese Opera Festival in Singapore. It is usually held in the month of March.

In an effort to keep the age-old tradition alive, Clarke Quay is holding regular opera shows here at Gas Lamp Square, on every Wednesday, Thursday, and Friday, at 7:45 pm. You are welcomed to take photographs of the performance. You may if you wish come as close as possible to the opera stage to take pictures. Those who are interested in opera makeup may come at 6:30 pm to see the artistes doing their own makeup at the opera stage and take pictures of them. And those who want to take pictures with the performers or talk to them are most welcomed to do so after the performance at 8:30 pm. Our performers are effectively bilingual: they speak good English and Mandarin and they have been with the Chinese Theatre Circle to almost half the world.

[Conclusion]

Tonight, we will be performing the excerpt called "None Gives Way on the Wedding Night," an episode taken from the very famous Cantonese opera called The Arrogant Princess. It's a very hilarious piece of opera excerpt, telling the story of the arrogance of a princess, so

much so that she refused to give way to the prince consort on her wedding night. Well, you'll see how things go. And with subtitles on both sides of the stage, English on your right and Chinese on your left, we believe you should be able to enjoy the show. And now, ladies and gentlemen, please put your hands together to welcome our two young artistes this evening from the Chinese Theatre Circle, Joanna Seetoh Hoi Siang and Garrett Khong Yew Cheong in this excerpt called "None Gives Way on the Wedding Night" from The Arrogant Princess.

While the audience applauded, the percussion ensemble played a rhythmic segment, later joined by the melodic group, followed by the entrance of the actor and actress. The play lasted for about forty minutes, after which the members of the audience were invited to take photographs with the performers.

The performance event at Clarke Quay constructs a specific notion about traditional Chinese street opera in Singapore. The introductory speech presents an interesting image of Chinese street opera in Singapore and deserves closer analysis.

The main section of the speech is repeated prior to every performance; only the introduction and sometimes the conclusion vary. The introduction begins by welcoming visitors to Clarke Quay. It then proceeds to validate the authenticity of the performance by emphasizing its continuity with traditional or customary practices. Compare the slightly different version below with the one above:

Good evening ladies and gentlemen, welcome to Clarke Quay Festival Village. We apologize for the delay in opening the show; it's due to the rain. And because of the rain, we are putting our orchestra on the stage. In fact, this is the traditional way of the orchestra layout of a Chinese opera stage: the percussionist on your left and the wind and string instruments on your right. With the help of subtitles this evening, with English on your right and Chinese on your left, we hope you'll be able to follow the story. Whilst the projectionists are preparing for the projectors and the subtitles, let me say a few words this evening.

While it has been the usual practice of the Chinese Theatre Circle to position the orchestra in front and below the stage during their performances at Clarke Quay to enable the audience to have a closer view of the instruments, there were occasions when the orchestra is placed on the stage. For whatever reasons this is done, the concept of "tradition" is emphasized, as revealed in the two speech excerpts above, and likewise, for the description of the musical prelude. On some occasions when the orchestra was placed below the stage, Leslie Wong introduced the musicians after his general introduction, in a manner that called for applause from the audience: for instance, he would stress that the lead musicians are from operatic institutions in the Guangdong province in China, or that the lead percussionist is the "most experienced Cantonese opera percussionist in Singapore" (recorded on Thursday, November 27, 1997). Thus, in addition to emphasizing traditional aspects of the performance event, it seemed evident that Wong attempted to establish symbolic aspects of authenticity (with performers from Mainland China) and performance quality (with the orchestra being led by the "most experienced" percussionist).

The main section begins by acknowledging the sponsors and performers of the "Traditional Chinese Street Opera" performance series, namely Clarke Quay Singapore and the Singapore Tourist Promotion Board (renamed as Singapore Tourism Board in November 1997). Chinese street opera is proclaimed as a phenomenon that existed in the past: "The Chinese street opera *was* a very popular street entertainment" (my emphasis), which implies that street opera no longer exists or is not as popular in Singapore today. Furthermore, the sentence implies that the series of performance by the Chinese Theatre Circle in Clarke Quay is the

only extant form of Chinese street opera in Singapore. Chinese street opera is then localized within the history of Clarke Quay and contextualized as a form of entertainment during religious and festive seasons. No reference whatsoever is given to the ongoing street performances by professional opera troupes that were, and continues to be presented almost every night in multiple locations around Singapore.

The speech then goes on to introduce the Chinese Theatre Circle as "Singapore's premier Cantonese opera group" and "a professional arts company," one that boasts numerous performances worldwide (a selection being listed in alphabetical order), won many awards, and organizes the annual Chinese Opera Festival to "preserve and promote" Chinese opera. Besides implying that Chinese Theatre Circle is the only opera group that performs "Traditional Chinese Street Opera" in Singapore today, in this section of the speech, Chinese street opera is being practiced by a "professional arts company" that specializes in Cantonese opera. It is important to note that the Chinese Theatre Circle started as an amateur opera group in 1981, and was designated a "non-profit professional" company by the National Arts Council in 1995.

Chinese street opera is now being revived and nurtured as an art form, by a Cantonese opera group that has achieved honours and recognition both locally and in many foreign countries. The paragraph beginning with "in an effort to keep the age-old tradition alive" addresses the audience directly and positions the whole performance event as a tourist attraction, or rather, as a conspicuous consumption of the exotic and traditional. The audience is invited to take photographs of the performance, observe opera make-up and converse with the performers. The performers of the "Traditional Chinese Street Opera" as defined by the Chinese Theatre Circle are young and bilingual, proficient in both English and Mandarin, and as if to validate their artistry, have performed worldwide with the company.

In sum, this speech suggests that traditional Chinese street opera in Singapore is a historical phenomenon that no longer exists in Singapore today. It is only through the efforts of the Chinese Theatre Circle, supported by Clarke Quay Singapore and the Singapore Tourism Board, and visitors to Clarke Quay who make up the audience, that Chinese street opera is being preserved, promoted, and secularized in the form of Cantonese opera. Furthermore, any religious and ritual connotations that have traditionally characterized Chinese street opera in Singapore are effectively obliterated through the performance event itself. In the new form of presentation, traditional Chinese street opera in Singapore today is performed by artists who are educated, who have performed in both local and foreign contexts, and who possess a level of artistry that is honoured in Singapore.

REPRESENTING CHINESE STREET OPERA

As mentioned above, Chinese street opera is performed by professional opera troupes almost everyday in Singapore today, and usually in religious contexts where it is known as *choushenxi* (thanksgiving performance), a social phenomenon that has continued since the early days of the Chinese immigrants. Very often, several troupes perform in different venues at the same time. By excluding references to these professional troupes and their performances, the "Traditional Chinese Street Opera" event at Clarke Quay attempts to construct and define new notions of traditional Chinese street opera in contemporary Singapore.

The performance is shaped as an "authentic" representation of traditional Chinese street opera through references to traditional operatic practices. In this sense, it alludes to

Edward Bruner's first meaning of authenticity with an emphasis on "mimetic credibility" (Bruner 1994: 399). By referencing historical aspects of attending Chinese opera performances and the traditional placement of the instrumental ensembles, the "Traditional Chinese Street Opera" event draws its authenticity from general practices of Chinese opera, thus making itself more "credible and convincing" (ibid.). Yet, while certain features are emphasized as customary, other "inauthentic" elements are conveniently obscured. One such example is the use of backdrop. Professional troupes always feature several changes of backdrops, which depict images such as a court, garden, and temple among others, in a single performance. The performance by the Chinese Theatre Circle at Clarke Quay, however, has a stationary backdrop that features a fairy and the organization's Chinese name, Dunhuang Jufang—both images unrelated to any plays it performs. To be sure, there are certain constraints in such cultural performances for tourists, and it is not my intention to pinpoint which element is or is not "authentic." Rather, it may be more useful to consider the processes through which "authenticity" is acquired, which I shall discuss below.

One of the objectives of the Chinese Theatre Circle was to familiarize its audience with Chinese opera through its didactic approaches, thus demystifying the genre. This is achieved in the following ways: (1) locating it in a middle/upper-class, modernized entertainment location; (2) merging the performance with the crowd by holding make-up demonstrations and photo-taking sessions in the audience area; (3) verbally introducing the performance and projecting the script and its translation; and (4) constructing it as a purely secular event. . These methods differ markedly from the everyday Chinese street opera performances by professional troupes, which take place in residential areas and function solely as a religious/

ritual event. One might say that while conventional street opera is distanced from its audience, the "Traditional Chinese Street Opera" event at Clarke Quay is consciously "bringing Chinese opera to the people" (to paraphrase one of Chinese Theatre Circle's community projects that began in 1984; see www.ctcopera.com.sg).

Providing projections of the script and its translation is one way to familiarize the audience with the performance. This raises an interesting issue on the ethnicity/genre of Chinese street opera in Singapore. The two predominant types of Chinese street opera performed by professional troupes in Singapore today are Chaozhou and Fujian operas. Cantonese opera, on the other hand, is limited to occasional performances during the Hungry Ghost Festival (seventh month of the lunar calendar), organized by local agents who engage overseas performers for lead roles and local performers for minor roles (Lai 1986: 27).

I noted above that the announcement placed on the opera stage at Clarke Quay reads: "Traditional Chinese Street Opera" in English and "street Cantonese opera (jietou yueju)" in Chinese characters. An immediate question arises: To what extent does Cantonese opera represent the Chinese street opera tradition in Singapore? Interestingly, in the planning of the "Traditional Chinese Street Opera" event at Clarke Quay, the Singapore Tourism Board had invited several amateur Chinese opera troupes of different genres to perform for the event, but apparently, only the Chinese Theatre Circle was able to undertake it (personal communication). In other words, it is not so much an issue of which genre appropriately represents the street opera tradition in Singapore, but simply to have a visual display of street opera appropriate for the tourist context. Projecting the Chinese script and its translation surely enhances the effectiveness of the event, but it also diminishes the significance of ethnicity in the Chinese street opera tradition in

Singapore. With the Chinese script, anyone who reads Chinese can understand the performance regardless of the language used, while the English translations cater to most of the visitors to Clarke Quay. Through its performance in a tourist context, the "Traditional Chinese Street Opera" event transcends ethnic differentiations of Chinese opera to foreground "street opera" as a genre in itself.[5]

The event's credibility is further generated by framing itself as part of an evolutionary trajectory of Chinese street opera in Singapore. The performance suggests that while traditional street opera used to be a communal, festive event, especially during religious occasions, it is now preserved, promoted, and developed as a secular art form. The absence of references to the everyday street opera performances and other operatic genres renders an exclusive image for the event. Traditional Chinese street opera in Singapore has now become an object of artistic pursuit, exclusive to an elite community of educated and widely travelled practitioners.

The performers at Clarke Quay are young and bilingual, as emphasized in the introductory speeches. The event's emphasis on the young and bilingual attributes of the performers at Clarke Quay has two implications: (1) that it is unusual to be young and bilingual and to be involved in Chinese street opera performance, and (2) that Chinese street opera has become less of an outmoded tradition, but has been developed into an "in" tradition which the educated, younger generation of Singaporeans are actively promoting. The kind of traditional Chinese street opera promoted in Clarke Quay and by other amateur troupes is different from that practiced by professional opera troupes in both the past and today in Singapore. In this way, the tradition of Chinese street opera is appropriated by an elite community to create and establish its group identities to the public through performance. Through the production of an event promoted as "Traditional

Chinese Street Opera," Chinese Theatre Circle and Clarke Quay not only construct a new image for Chinese street opera, but also present and affirm new status, knowledge, and power to appropriate and resignify a tradition that is generally recognized as the domain of another community.

As an upscale site for entertainment catering mainly to young Singaporeans and visitors to Singapore, Clarke Quay spatially enhances the "Traditional Chinese Street Opera" performance event as an exclusive circumstance. Chinese street opera is projected as an event purely for secular entertainment, not unlike that of the merry-go-round. The performance event locates street opera within the continuum of activities that is out of the everyday life, creating a marked contrast to professional Chinese street opera, where the majority of its practitioners perform for a living. The embodiment of tradition in the performance event within the modern context of Clarke Quay enhances the experience of a phenomenon that is unusual and ephemeral, yet real and compelling.

SOUNDSCAPE AND CULTURAL AUTHENTICITY

The soundscape of the "Traditional Chinese Street Opera" performance at Clarke Quay comprises a range of performative elements, such as the instrumental prelude and accompaniment, narratives and songs, introductory remarks, visual aspects of the opera stage, costumes and make-up of performers, and activities such as the make-up demonstration and photo-taking sessions. This soundscape draws its meanings and values from the Clarke Quay setting, and simultaneously enhances Clarke Quay as a modern historical site. In other words, the interactions between the performance of the "Traditional Chinese Street Opera" event and Clarke Quay as a public space produce a certain sense of authenticity.

Thus far, we have outlined at least two factors that may have contributed to creating such authentic aura at Clarke Quay. First, the introductory speech before the performance claims that what the audience is viewing preserves original aspects of the street opera tradition (Bruner's third meaning of authenticity; see Bruner 1994: 400). Second, the context of Clarke Quay, with its history, architecture, spatial organization, and activities, produces its own authenticity and further enhances that of the performance, just as the performance constitutes the emergent meanings of the locale. In this way, Clarke Quay is somewhat similar to the New Salem Historic Site in its "verisimilitude" and "genuineness" (Bruner's first and second meanings of authenticity; ibid: 399).

The authenticity of Clarke Quay as a soundscape defined by the "Traditional Chinese Street Opera" performance may also be attributed to marketing strategies in tourist brochures. *The Singapore Visitor*, a weekly guide for tourists in Singapore, introduces Clarke Quay and its street opera performance in the following manner:

> It seems that Clarke Quay has always been "the" place to be for fun ... even 100 years ago when it was known as "Festival Quay." Religious and cultural festivals were celebrated here, complete with street performers. Clarke Quay is bringing back these days and recapturing the "spirit" of traditional street entertainment with Chinese "Wayang" (street opera) which you can enjoy every Wednesday, Thursday and Friday at 7:45 pm. (Singapore Visitor 1997)

The "Entertainment Delights" section in *New Asia Singapore: Mature Travellers* highlights the street opera performance as follows:

> Of the cultural shows, one of the most memorable has to be the Chinese street opera or "wayang." An iridescent display of vibrance and movements, the performances take place in the evenings (Wednesdays, Thursdays and

Fridays) at Clarke Quay throughout the year. (Singapore Tourism Board 1997: 21)

In an article titled "Street Theatre," published in *Changi: The Magazine*, a publication distributed to passengers entering or leaving the Singapore Changi Airport, Clarke Quay's "Traditional Chinese Street Opera" is contextualized in a nostalgic rhetoric of a decline of tradition:

> It is sad that this ancient art is dying in Singapore but you can still happen [to chance] upon a vibrant street performance in Chinatown during Chinese holidays or catch a scaled down show at tourist venues.
> Chinese Opera performances are staged every Thursday and Friday evening at the Gas Lamp Square in Clarke Quay by the Chinese Theatre Circle. This is a professional Cantonese Opera group established to preserve and promote Chinese opera, drama, dance and music. Translations can be provided for English speakers. (Singapore Changi Airport 1997: 21)

As with the introductory speech preceding performances, the above publications position the "Traditional Chinese Street Opera" event at Clarke Quay in terms of its originality ("bringing back these days . . ."), and the survival of a declining tradition in contemporary Singapore. While the event is recognized as a cultural show performed at a tourist venue, the "authenticity" discourse is not diminished. On the contrary, the event's authenticity is enhanced despite, or perhaps because of, its focus on cultural tourism.

Unlike tourists attending concerts of traditional Naxi music in Lijiang County in northwest Yunnan province who may be able to juxtapose their experiences of modern traditions with the more conservative Naxi music to form their opinions on the latter's "authenticity" (Rees 1998), local and foreign tourists at Clarke Quay are not likely to be exposed to conventional street opera performances by professional troupes, which

generally take place in relatively private areas. For them then, "Traditional Chinese Street Opera" at Clarke Quay is likely their sole point of reference. Yet, how does the case of cultural tourism in Clarke Quay create and sustain its own authenticity?

I suggest that Clarke Quay's "Traditional Chinese Street Opera" event achieves its authenticity because its soundscape embodies broader meanings and values of national culture in contemporary Singapore. The event's authenticity depends on context as a "place"—Clarke Quay, within the Chinatown vicinity, in a rapidly modernizing country. Its sense of authenticity is also derived from the more subtle performative context—specific performance practices (such as the introductory speech to the performance), types of performing institutions and support, parity between tradition and modernity (such as the performers' ability to excel in Cantonese opera and be young, educated, and bilingual). Indeed, the evolutionary trajectory in which the event is marketed and performed affirms an authenticity defined in terms of its propensity to credibly adapt itself to new contexts (see Duggan 1997).[6]

If the Clarke Quay Adventure attraction described above covers Singapore's history in a ride, we might also regard Clarke Quay as a microcosm of contemporary Singapore. The confluence of the modern and traditional, the Western and Asian at Clarke Quay reflect a prevailing trend in Singapore today described as "cultural cosmopolitanism" (Koh 1989: 723). Viewed in this way, Clarke Quay as a tourist locale is "a showcase of post-modernism: a concoction of something 'native' and something borrowed, something old and something new" (Leong 1997a: 530). Yet even in such a context, I suggest that cultural authenticity is further enhanced rather than "eclipsed by estrangement" (ibid.).

The authenticity of "Traditional Chinese Street Opera" at Clarke Quay is sustained by feeding off a broader notion of culture in Singapore today, just as it simultaneously constitutes it. Its authenticity emerges from its viability in current cultural aesthetics and values in Singapore, and its relevance is derived because of its novelty, not its traditionalism (see Taruskin 1988: 152). It highlights Singapore's perpetual concern for salvaging cultural heritage for the purposes of displaying its history to Singaporeans and tourists in Singapore, a concern that is mapped onto the very structure and process of Clarke Quay as a public space.[7] To paraphrase Clifford Geertz, we might say that "Traditional Chinese Street Opera" at Clarke Quay is "a story we tell us about ourselves" (Geertz 1973: 448): it provides a meta-commentary upon matters concerning the role of cultural traditions amidst processes of modernization in Singapore, and the planning of culture and the arts around this concern. In this soundscape, tourism and culture are constitutive of each other.[8] The ability to control this soundscape translates into a capacity to shape new interpretive frameworks of culture (see Friedland and Boden 1994: 28–29).

NOTES

1. This essay is adapted from a more detailed chapter published in *Chinese Street Opera in Singapore* (Lee 2009). For an overview of space, politics, and arts in Singapore, see Lee (1995).
2. For studies on tourism and local cultures, see Deitch (1989), Duggan (1997), and Dunbar-Hall (2001).
3. Chaozhou and Fujian communities in Singapore are primarily immigrants, or descendants of immigrants, from the Guangdong and Fujian provinces in south China.
4. The first series ended on December 31, 1996 and because it proved to be a popular attraction, it was instituted again in 1997, this time increasing to three performances a week. In 1998, performances were reduced to twice a week and the series ended shortly afterwards.
5. See Leong (1997b) on tourism and its implications on ethnicity in Singapore.
6. This approach to "authenticity" alludes to Paul Gilroy's conception of "music as a *changing* rather than an unchanging same" (Gilroy 1993: 101; emphasis in original).
7. For an overview of heritage marketing, see Dominguez (1986).
8. See Picard (1997) for an analysis of how Balinese cultural identities have developed through tourism.

Conclusions

Relocating Public Space

Zachary P. Neal

In the preceding readings and essays we have tried to capture the essence of public space, as it is viewed in three different ways. Public space sometimes appears as a *facilitator for civic order* by providing a location for public life to play out, especially through interactions with both friends and strangers that foster the formation of social bonds. Other times, public space appears as a *site for power and resistance*, where conflict can occur between different groups that each assert their right to use the space. In still other cases, public space appears as *a stage for art, theatre, and performance* that allows individuals and groups to express themselves in formal and informal ways.

Of course, any particular public space might play several of these roles at once. For example, when a political protest takes place on a public plaza, the space is clearly functioning as a site of resistance. But at the same time the protestors may be expressing themselves through song, through painted banners, or simply through their dress, thus using the space as a stage. Moreover, as the protestors interact with one another, they not only assert their beliefs, but also may form new friendships or run into old acquaintances, using the space as a social facilitator.

While these various ways of thinking about how public space works are useful, it is also important to take a step back from the models and ask: What is happening to public space? However public space might work, and whatever it might be used for, how is public space changing? Are public spaces taking different forms than before, or do they appear in different locations than in the past? And most critically, is there more public space, or are we losing our public spaces and at the same time our public lives?

FOR DISCUSSION

How do you think public space is changing (a) in the way it is used, (b) in where it is located, and (c) in how much of it there is?

THE LOSS OF PUBLIC SPACE

Much of the writing on public space and public life features a narrative of loss. Scholars lament the fact that there are fewer parks and fewer people in the parks that remain. This loss has been connected to the rise of such things as the automobile, the suburb, and the Internet, but more generally to the emergence of an increasingly individualistic and inwardly focused society. As Robert Putnam famously noted, although more and more people are bowling, they are increasingly bowling alone.

The connection between the loss of public space and a loss of public life and sociability is clear. Public spaces provide sites for the many types of person-to-person interaction that constitutes public life: civic, antagonistic, artistic. But, as such spaces disappear or become less open, so too do the opportunities to engage in these activities. Some of the readings in this book have discussed the loss of particular public spaces through exclusion: People's Park in California (Mitchell), Bryant Park in New York (Zukin), and the Central district in Hong Kong (Law). But a number of broad trends in the loss of public space have been observed. In some cases, spaces that formerly were, or under other circumstances would have been, public are being privatized and appropriated for the exclusive use of only certain individuals. In other cases, spaces are being constructed that only create the illusion of publicness and openness. Finally, with a retreat from public life, once vibrant public spaces are being abandoned, while new ones are distributed unevenly across the landscape, creating inequalities of accessibility.

One of the most common forms of privatization of space can be observed in the emergence of gated communities. Gated communities often look like any other residential community, but they are surrounded by barriers that prevent access to the community's streets, sidewalks, parks, and other amenities by non-residents. In politically unstable areas gated communities provide security to residents, but in most cases they primarily provide exclusivity and status. Although gated communities feature many of the same physical spaces as non-gated communities, their role as public spaces are often not the same. Chance encounters with strangers on the sidewalk, especially those that over time establish a sense of community and belonging, cannot occur because strangers are not permitted to use the sidewalks. Political protests are unlikely to take place in the community's parks because no one but the community's own residents would see them. And the use of these spaces for artistic expression can be severely limited by the rules and regulations of the Home Owners Association. While gated communities, and the loss of public space they represent, was initially a consequence of the affluence found in economically advanced Western nations, the residential form has rapidly spread worldwide.

Gated communities are clear examples of non-public spaces, but still other problems and other notions of loss arise because they create the illusion of being public spaces. Residents can live private lives acting as if they are participating in public life, but the public life and public space in gated communities is inauthentic. Similar issues of the inauthenticity of public space arise outside of gated communities as well, but often are so well masked that they go unnoticed. The ancient Greek Agora, the open air marketplace of ideas and goods, is a classic example of a public space. But it has been recreated in Las Vegas as the Forum Shops, a shopping mall decorated with faux-classical architecture and complete with an arched ceiling painted and lighted to resemble the sky. Shoppers are embedded in an illusory public space; it looks like someone could at any moment deliver a speech on the evils of capitalism or begin drawing on the "pavement" in colored chalk. But in reality the well-staffed private security guards would quickly swoop in and escort the individual away. On a superficial level, strolling through the Forum Shops may look and feel like public life, but in fact it is merely individualized consumerism packaged to look like public life. The trouble with such inauthentic public spaces is that they divert attention from more genuine public spaces, and from the more interactive public life they make possible.

Thus, while some public space is lost to privatization, other public space is lost to neglect when it is abandoned in favor of public-looking private space. With all this loss, one might be surprised that there are any public spaces left at all. Certainly new public spaces are being created all the time, but this paradoxically points to yet a third chapter in the "loss of public space" narrative. These new public spaces are not evenly spread across cities and neighborhoods, but tend to be concentrated in certain areas, especially those with the most money and power. When a low income neighborhood's park is abandoned by residents or is slowly taken over by drug dealers or the homeless, the result is usually closure and demolition, not restoration and revitalization. However, unused public property in a high-rent district is often a prime target for the creation of a "pocket park," or if large enough a public fountain, plaza, or museum. This uneven distribution of new public spaces creates situations where public space may be open, but not accessible. And, perhaps, not even open if those living near the space attempt to preserve it for their exclusive use. Thus, even the creation of public space can lead to its loss.

FOR DISCUSSION

Have you lost any public spaces that were important to you (e.g. the park you played in as a child)? How did you and others confront that loss?

THE RECOVERY OF PUBLIC SPACE

A narrative of loss, drawing on these and other mechanisms, can be found in so much of the scholarship on public space that it frequently goes unquestioned. Is it really true that public space is being lost? Perhaps not. Certainly some specific public spaces have been lost to forces like privatization, but much of public space is just being relocated as attitudes, technologies, and practices change. This section looks ahead, seeking to recover public space from the pervasive narrative of its alleged loss. As the way public life is lived changes, we need to look for public space in different ways and in different places. Conceptions of the public are constantly being redefined, and thus notions of where and what counts as public space is changing. The edges of public space are also being redrawn as ideas about the nature of space shift from the physical to the virtual and electronic. And even traditional public spaces are being redesigned by forward-thinking socially and environmentally conscious new architects.

Redefining the Public

Public space was defined at the beginning of this book as "all areas that are open and accessible to all members of the public in a society in principle, though not necessarily in practice." Most discussions of the loss of public space revolve around claims that its openness and accessibility are in decline. However, this is particularly difficult to establish because the very idea of "the public"—the people for whom public space is supposed to be open and accessible—is continuously being redefined, and more importantly being expanded. As conceptions of the public are redefined and expanded, public space is gained not lost; it actually becomes more open, or at least open to a wider range of individuals. Recall, although the classical Greek agora was technically open and accessible, its openness was restricted to that narrow sliver of the population recognized as the public (i.e. male citizens). But, as marginalized others including women, slaves, and non-citizens have gained acceptance as legitimate members of the public over the centuries, public spaces have become increasingly open to them as well.

How does this process of redefinition of both the public and public space work? One possibility is James Holston's (1995) notion of *insurgent citizenship*, or the attempt to assert one's right to be recognized as a member of the public. In some cases, the group seeking recognition has always been present and marginalized (e.g. the homeless), while in others, new arrivals into the city seek an opportunity to participate in public life (e.g. immigrants). The common thread, however, is that when these groups demand a place in the larger public, this insurgence disrupts established understandings of the social order and of how space should be allocated and used. Holston suggests that the sites of insurgent citizenship—immigrant enclaves, homeless encampments in parks, etc.—provide opportunities to re-ask the question: *Who* should have access to *where*? In answering this question, which inevitably is a tug-of-war struggle between the hegemonic and insurgent citizens, conceptions of both the public and public space get redefined.

Margaret Crawford has described Los Angeles street vendors as an instance of insurgent citizenship that is forcing a redefinition of both the public and public space. Street vending is illegal, and thus an impermissible use of public space. Additionally, most street vendors are undocumented immigrants, and thus not members of the politically sanctioned public. However, despite their doubly illegal status, immigrant street vendors "are becoming a political as well as an economic presence in the city" (Crawford 1995: 7) visible on many corners and incorporating themselves into the fabric of the community and into public life. This continued presence and activity has started to practically, though not yet legally, redefine where public space is, what it can be used for, and by whom.

Public space can be expanded and gained, therefore, as the public is redefined, and especially as formerly excluded groups are incorporated into wider conceptions of who the public is. But is it always necessary for formerly excluded groups to be incorporated into a single conception of the public? Scholars like Iris Young (1990) and Kurt Iveson (1998) have proposed a multi-public model public space that says "no." Their approach suggests that there should be multiple, simultaneous conceptions of the public, rather than just a single, homogenous conception. On this view, the vibrancy of public space results from recognizing, for example, that undocumented workers constitute a separate "public" that is distinct, that brings its own unique values to public life, and that should have a right to public space without needing to conform to a single definition of the public. Thus, for the multi-public model, the future of public space depends on accommodating not simply "all members of the public," but "all members of all publics." In doing so, public space is enriched and expanded not simply through a redefinition of the public, but through the celebration of difference and diversity in several definitions of the public.

FOR DISCUSSION

Do you think public space is really opening up to a wider range of people? Is it possible that public space is becoming less open in terms of how it can be used, but more open in terms of who can use it? Is this trade-off worth it?

Redrawing the Border

One way to recover public space from the narrative of loss and to find new and emerging public spaces is to redefine precisely what is meant by "the public." A second way to identify new kinds of public space is to redraw the borders of space itself. This entire book has been focused on *public space*, but in that short phrase, what does the word "space" really mean? The definition of public space offered in the first chapter starts off: "Public space includes all areas," but what are "areas"? Where is the edge of this thing we're trying to understand? In all the preceding readings, space was simply assumed to be a physical construct, and thus public space was an actual location on the Earth that one could travel to and stand in. But technological advances have made an exclusively physical conception of space and public space obsolete. There are, of course, still physical public spaces, but now there are also virtual public spaces.

In its early years, the Internet was thought of as a new type of media, the next step in the progression from book to radio to television. However, examining how and for what activities the Internet is used quickly made it clear that the Internet is less like a new type of media and more like a location. Indeed, despite some obvious differences, in a number of ways websites are very similar to actual physical places. Individuals interact with one another by "visiting" a website. Particular sites can either be public, like a blog, or private, like a company's inventory database. And, to get from one site to another, one frequently passes through other intermediate sites that are related via a series of hypertext links, and just like walking through a new city occasionally stumbles onto an unexpected new site, acting as a sort of virtual *flâneur*.

Adopting this metaphor of the Internet as a type of place, scholars like Jean Camp and Y. T. Chien (2000) have noted that the Internet has come to be used as a public space in a range of different ways. Traditional types of public space like libraries, schools, and marketplaces can be found online and are used in much the same way as their physical counterparts. But even the new types of public space that have emerged online frequently "work" like the public spaces described in the three sections of this book. Chat rooms, message boards, and other sites that allow users to engage in conversations facilitate the formation of social bonds, both on- and offline, and thus provide a framework for civil order similar to streets, parks, and coffee shops. Sites maintained by governments, political parties, and interest groups provide an opportunity for power to be exercised electronically by distributing their message to the virtual world. Moreover, activities like website vandalism, or Denial-of-Service (DoS) attacks that render a website inaccessible, mean that nearly any part of the Internet can be a space of resistance.

Perhaps the most visible function of the Internet as a public space, however, is as a stage for art, theatre, and performance. Websites like YouTube allow users to post video clips of themselves, quite literally providing a public stage for expression. Individuals' personal pages on social networking sites like Facebook and MySpace provide opportunities to directly document the facets of one's identity, including physical appearance, musical preferences, and even what one is doing at the moment. The Internet has also served as a platform for entire virtual worlds (e.g. Second Life), in which users construct avatars of themselves that interact with other users' avatars in a domain purposefully meant to resemble an actual physical world.

Compared to other public spaces like the plaza or park or street, the Internet is in its infancy. And although it shares many features of, and often works like, other kinds of public spaces, there are also some key differences. As a result, questions remain about the role of the Internet as a public space. First, the Internet is more public than even the most open of traditional public spaces, and even private areas of the Internet are not completely private. Therefore, viewing the Internet as a public space is challenged by the lack of private space and of privacy; can public space exist if private space does not? Second, although the Internet may be open, it may not be fully accessible. The accessibility of traditional public spaces depended on mobility, but the accessibility of virtual public spaces depends on equipment, and therefore the requirements for the Internet to be a truly public space may present unique challenges. Finally, some have questioned whether the Internet can really function as a public space at all, and more specifically, whether the interactions that occur on the Internet serve to foster connectedness and community or isolation and loneliness.

FOR DISCUSSION

Do you think a virtual public space can work just as well as physical public space as (a) a facilitator of civil order, (b) a site of power and resistance, and (c) a stage for art, theatre, and performance? What are the pros and cons of combining physical and virtual public spaces, like providing Wireless Internet (WiFi) in a public park?

Redesigning the Space

A final way to recover public space from the narrative of loss is to consider the quality of the spaces that remain. Certainly some formerly public spaces are being privatized or demolished, but many of the remaining public spaces are being redesigned and revitalized. And as today's architects and planners redesign public spaces, or even when they design new ones, there is a much greater focus on creating spaces that can fulfill the purposes of public space.

In 2004 the Van Alen Institute in New York showcased a number of new designs for public spaces aimed at making them work better. The plaza had always been a grand public space, but in recent decades they came to look more like empty cement boxes. But the plaza is being reborn. In Genoa the Ponte Parodi places the traditional plaza in the middle of the city's harbor, surrounded by water and water-related activities. At the same time, in London the plaza has moved indoors at a new City Hall that features spiraling ramps (not staircases, for truly accessible public space) that lead to "London's Living Room," a 7,000 square foot gallery with panoramic views of the river. Moreover, this redesigning of public space is not restricted to wealthy cities and mega-projects. In Rio de Janeiro, work has begun to construct pathways for pedestrians and emergency vehicles that will connect the *favelas* or shantytowns to the rest of the city, and to city services. With the introduction of even basic services like garbage collection and police patrol, these streets not only provide access, but also have come to function as social spaces where residents can interact with one another and build pride in their community.

Danish architect Jan Gehl has been at the forefront of this movement toward public spaces that are more public. He found that while cities generally have excellent data on things like traffic patterns and parking, they pay very little attention to the quality of life in the city, especially from the pedestrian's point of view. Thus, in a comprehensive study of the public spaces in Adelaide, Australia, he documented how the existing areas worked (or didn't), and what was needed to make them work better. Central among his findings was that "the key to establishing lively and safe public spaces is pedestrian traffic and pedestrian activities" (Gehl Architects APS 2002: 10). Public spaces are of limited value in what he called the "invaded city" that is overrun by vehicular traffic and in the "abandoned city" that has freeways and parking lots but no pedestrians. Thus, in seeking to make the city more pedestrian friendly, even minor details of minor public spaces were significant. For example, Gehl suggested that bus shelters and trash cans be placed on the same side of the sidewalk to create an uninterrupted walking path and view of the landscape.

Many of these innovations in public space design have been collected for the benefit of communities by non-profit organizations that serve as resources for the improvement of public space. The Project for Public Space (PPS), one of the larger such organizations, was founded in 1975 by Fred Kent, who had worked as a research assistant to William Whyte during the street life project that culminated in the reading in this book. The PPS performs a range of functions, including serving as a virtual public space itself by hosting an online discussion forum. Beyond this, they assist communities with the redevelopment of their own public spaces, and serve as an excellent source of additional information for those interested in public space.

FOR DISCUSSION

How would you redesign the public spaces you use to make them more useful, open, or vibrant? When existing public spaces get redesigned, who should get to participate in the design process?

CONCLUSION

Much has been written about how we are losing our public spaces. But is this really the case? As conceptions of the public are redefined and expanded, public spaces are increasingly open to a wider range of people. As technological advances make new ways of communicating possible, the borders of what counts as public spaces are being redrawn; now public space can be created out of thin air, and by nearly anyone. And as greater attention is focused on public space generally, new and existing public spaces are being redesigned to be more public and more useful. So perhaps public space is not vanishing at all, but actually growing. In any case, what is clear is that public space is being relocated. We must start to look for and think about public space in new ways, because it is starting to appear in places it once did not: on water, over railroads, under highways, and inside electrons.

Toolkits for Interrogating Public Space

Anthony M. Orum and Zachary P. Neal

The three models that we have identified and used as a means of organizing our anthology provide ways to think about the nature and uses of public space by people and social institutions. The various selections here also provide cogent and useful examples of how thoughtful writers have tried to make sense of public space. But all this work can only be productive, we believe, if it promotes further empirical inquiries of its own. Although collectively there are a set of lessons and insights available in our anthology, they should be viewed only as the beginning, and not the conclusion, of work on public space. If this work is to endure, it must produce new and imaginative ways to engage in research on public space, probing it for new and important empirical discoveries.

Thus, we try here in this brief summary of our anthology both to furnish a concise summary of the key analytic ideas contained within each of the models, as well as the questions that these models establish for further empirical research. We believe that these questions illuminate a path for further inquiries.

A TOOLKIT FOR THE STUDY OF PUBLIC SPACE AS CIVIL ORDER

Those writers and scholars who study public space as civil order attend to the way that social relationships develop in public space, and the nature of those relationships. The world in their eyes is constructed on the foundations of how people get along with one another, and the ways in which the built environment, including parks, streets and sidewalks, may facilitate extensive as well as incidental social contacts. And they believe that, ultimately, the world is a good place, or at least it can be so, provided that people of varying kinds and types can regularly come in contact with both friends and strangers in public.

There are special questions that then flow from this perspective: What kinds of social relationships develop among people in public? Where do such relationships occur? Do the streets and sidewalks, even meeting halls of an area, help to promote such relationships, or do they impede them? What goes on in larger public spaces such as parks? Who are the people who engage in these relationships: are they all alike, or different? Do they act in large groups, or just in small ones? How long do such interactions occur? And in what ways do these actions promote the civil order of a community or society?

Such questions as these flow naturally from the perspective that students of public space use to construct their sense of the world in public. They look not for chaos but for order, and they believe the world is a naturally ordered place, though, like Anderson, they may seek to explain how such order comes about. This is, in the end, a very powerful and productive view that is based on a variety of empirical sightings of public space. But it is, of course, only one view.

A TOOLKIT FOR STUDYING PUBLIC SPACE AS THE SPACE OF POWER AND RESISTANCE

The view of public space as power and domination has become an increasingly popular view among social scientists. And, we believe, it has happened with very good reason. As terrorism has expanded across the globe, one can easily embrace this dark and sinister view about the workings of institutions and the actual freedom of the public to congregate in open spaces. The world, in fact, has become more intensely dangerous, and the powers of the state clearly intrude more than ever before in our everyday lives.

This view of public space also invokes its own set of particular questions. Is the amount of public space, like parklands or sidewalks, actually diminishing? To what extent are those people of privilege and wealth turning to gated communities to protect themselves from the world outside them? Is access to public spaces actually open; and are the rights of all people accommodated in the use of those spaces? What role does the state play in defining who can, and who cannot, occupy public space—and how precisely does it play that role? To what extent are public spaces configured in ways that do not accommodate all the members of the public? And do members of the public actually believe and act in ways to justify the conclusion that their rights to public space are infringed upon?

These and other questions represent the productive lines of inquiry that come from this manner of thinking of public space. Compared to the view of public space as civil order, moreover, such inquiries take a top-down, or structural, view of the world. They ask about broad political and social tendencies, and they inquire especially into the ways that the actions of institutions like the government limit and constrain the public space that is available, in fact, to the public, in general. One might even say that proponents of this line of argument routinely assume that people in public are effectively rendered powerless and impotent by their own social institutions, a claim not open to empirical examination and disproof, but rather the fundamental premise from which all further inquiry ensues.

A TOOLKIT FOR STUDYING PUBLIC SPACE AS ART, THEATRE AND PERFORMANCE

Like the other two perspectives, this model of public space also provides us with a toolkit of questions and elements on which we can focus our attention. In general, one will examine the symbolic side to public space with this model, and so one will direct attention precisely to the ways in which such space is represented, particularly in the form of art, theatre and other types of performance.

What kinds of performance take place in public spaces? Are they forms like mural art or musical forms of performance? What is actually said or performed, and who engages in these performances? Where are the public spaces in which such performances take place? Who are the people who engage in these performances, and where they do they come from? And, when queried, what do people say about their own performances and how they think of themselves?

These, then, are the kinds of questions one can pursue in using this model, and thereby achieve yet another angle on understanding a particular community and its people by observing its public space and what happens therein.

SOME FINAL REFLECTIONS AND CONCLUSIONS

Public space, that space such as parks, sidewalks and plazas that we all, in principle, share, has become a matter of increasing interest and concern to social scientists. The reasons are rather obvious: such space is not only open to the public, but it is also open and available to the eyes and ears of social science. By examining what happens and unfolds in such areas, we are in a position to provide broader interpretations of the workings of people, institutions and communities, and to do so in a way that relies on firsthand evidence of relationships, not indirect evidence that might come by way of such social science tools as that of social surveys.

We have argued here that there are at least three perspectives that are available to social scientists who want to study and understand public space. The first views public space as civil order, and argues that the relationships that unfold in places like parks and sidewalks provide insight into the nature of civil order. To the extent that people interact often and the composition of such groups is broad and diverse, the civil order of the community, or society, is understood as vital and substantial. Where, however, there is very limited interaction in public, and where the people that interact are of uniform character, there the civil order is seen as diminished and weaker than in the first instance.

But there is an alternative way for viewing public space, that which we have referred to as the perspective that views public space as the space of power and domination. This view claims that the major institutions of modern society, particularly those of private property and the modern state, are relentlessly infringing on the rights of all people to have access to public space. Citizens, from this perspective, are being exploited by the major institutions of modern society, and such exploitation is especially evident in the ways that public space is becoming increasingly privatized and otherwise unavailable to the public. At the same time, those who take this view argue that even those spaces which are public, like sidewalks and parks, are the object of close surveillance and social control by authorities, guards and cameras, so that the space which appears to be open and accessible is actually not so at all.

And, finally, there is a third model of public space, that sees such space as the site of theatre and performance, whether music, murals or other forms of cultural expression. More and more public space is coming to be defined and to be represented by such material forms, and thus this furnishes a significant perspective that one can employ in order to understand both people and institutions. While there are rich and varied forms of such cultural expression, social scientists have not yet developed a means to explore and interpret such forms, apart from providing very full and interesting descriptions—which, of course, are absolutely essential to understanding these forms. But, we have insisted, it also is important to provide concepts that allow us to penetrate the descriptions themselves—to talk about such things as the centrality of particular performances in public space and other similar elements.

These three views have their proponents and are built upon alternative bodies of evidence, we have argued, but they are substantially different from one another in the tone of their arguments—one, for instance, takes a bright view, the other a dark view—of how public space operates today. They also promote their own lines of inquiry, and lead to their own specific manner of investigation, but, because they emphasize different sets of facts and different ways of looking at those facts, observations assembled for one view cannot refute another perspective. For this reason, we have claimed they represent models of space and society, models that are self-contained and self-enclosed.

In addition, it is easily seen that each view leads to a different set of normative implications, a different political attitude. The bright view of public space, that which sees it as civil order, encourages people and groups to promote greater vitality in the operation of parks and sidewalks, to build community from the bottom up, as it were. The dark view of public space, however, encourages people to resist and protest the inroads of major modern institutions, much in the way that Don Mitchell observes in the activities of the homeless people "taking over" parks and other public lands. And, of course, the view of public space as theatre and performance encourages one to foster the development and creation of such spaces precisely because they permit people to achieve a sense of collective identity therein.

Finally, because these views represent alternative ways to conceive of public space, they can also be seen as complementary to one another. In fact, we would insist that if one wishes to understand public space and, by implication, the people and institutions in which such space is embedded, all three perspectives provide in tandem the deepest and richest understanding of such space. Together they will permit one to unearth not only the social dynamics at work in public space, but also the often invisible hand of power that crafts, shapes and limits such space. And, of course, by employing the model of public space as art and performance, one also will be able to unearth the stories that people tell themselves along with the nature of the specific identities they hold important.

REFERENCES AND FURTHER READING

Abbas, A. 1997a. *Hong Kong: Culture and the Politics of Disappearance*. Hong Kong: Hong Kong University Press.

——. 1997b. Hong Kong: Other Histories, Other Politics. *Public Culture*, 9: 293–313.

Abelson, E. S. 1989. *When Ladies Go A-Thieving: Middle-Class Shoplifters in the Victorian Department Store*. Oxford: Oxford UniversityPress.

Appadurai, A. 1990. Disjuncture and Difference in the Global Cultural Economy. *Public Culture* 2: 1–24.

——. 1996. *Modernity at Large: Cultural Dimensions of Globalization*. Minneapolis, MN: University of Minnesota Press.

Arendt, H. [1958] 1998. *The Human Condition*, 2nd edition. Chicago, IL: University of Chicago Press.

Asian Migrant Centre and Migrant forum in Asia. 2000. *Asian Migrant Yearbook*. Hong Kong: AMC and MFA.

Auchard, E. 1991. How Did it Happen? A Protest Diary. *East Bay Express* August 9, 1991: 1, 18–23.

Banerjee, T. 2001. The Future of Public Space: Beyond Invented Streets and Reinvented Places. *Journal of the American Planning Association* 67: 9–24.

Barnett, J. 1982. *An Introduction to Urban Design*. New York: Harper & Row.

Benjamin, W. 2002. *The Arcades Project*, edited by Rolf Tiedmann, translated by Howard Eiland and Kevin McLaughlin. New York: Belknap Press.

Berger, J. 1985. Manhattan. In *The Sense of Sight*, pp. 61–67. New York: Pantheon.

Bernstein, I. 1990. *The New York City Draft Riots: Their Significance for American Society and Politics in the Age of the Civil War*. Oxford: Oxford University Press.

Biederman, D. A. and Nager, A. R. 1981. Up From Smoke: A New, Improved Bryant Park? *New York Affairs* 6: 97–105

Bishop, K. 1991. Vouchers Route Money to the Needy Separating Hustlers from the Homeless. *New York Times* July 26, 1991: A10.

Blair, K. 1980. *The Clubwoman as Feminist: True Womanhood Redefined, 1868–1914*. New York: Holmes & Meier.

Blakely, E. and Snyder, M. G. 1999. *Fortress America: Gated Communities in the United States*. Washington, DC: Brookings Institute Press.

Blodgett, G. 1976. Frederick Law Olmsted: Landscape Architecture as Conservative Reform. *Journal of American History* 62: 869–889.

Blumin, S. 1990. George G. Foster and the Emerging Metropolis. In *New York by Gas-Light and Other Urban Sketches* by George G. Foster, ed. Stuart Blumin, pp. 1–62. Berkeley: University of California Press.

Boudreau, J. 1991. The People Grudgingly Give In on Park. *Contra Costa Times* August 2, 1991: A3.

Boyer, C. 1992. Cities for Sale: Merchandising History at South Street Seaport. In *Variations on a Theme Park: The New American City and the End of Public Space*, ed. M. Sorkin, pp. 181–204. New York: Hill and Wang.

Boyer, M. C. 1985. *Manhattan Manners*. New York: Rizzoli Press.

Brain, D. 1991. Practical Knowledge and Occupational Control: The Professionalization of Architecture in the United States. *Sociological Forum* 6: 239–268.

Brecher, C. and Horton, R. D. 1993. *Power Failures: New York City Politics and Policy Since 1960*. New York: Oxford University Press.

Breitbart, M., Holton, W. et al. 1993. *Creating a Sense of Place in Urban Communities*. Boston, MA: UrbanArts.

Bruner, E. M. 1994. Abraham Lincoln as Authentic Reproduction: A Critique of Postmodernism. *American Anthropologist* 92: 397–415.

Calhoun, C. 1989. Tiananmen, Television and the Public Sphere: Internationalization of Culture and the Beijing Spring of 1989. *Public Culture* 2: 54–71.

——. 1992. *Habermas and the Public Sphere*. Cambridge, MA: MIT Press.

Camp, J. and Chien, Y. T. 2000. The Internet as Public Space: Concepts, Issues, and Implications in Public Policy. *Computers and Society* September: 13–19.

Carpignano, P., Andersen, R., Aronowitz, S., and Difazio, W. 1990. Chatter in the Age of Electronic Reproduction: Talk Television and the "Public Mind." *Social Text* 25/26: 33–55.

Carr, S., Francis, M., Rivlin, L. G., and Stone, A. M. 1992. *Public Space*. New York: Cambridge University Press.

Cheah, P. and Robbins, B. 1998. *Cosmopolitics: Thinking and Feeling beyond the Nation*. Minneapolis, MN: University of Minnesota Press.

Chua, B. H. 1992. Decoding the Political in Civic Spaces: An Interpretive Essay. In *Public Space: Design, Use and Management*, ed. B. H. Chua and N. Edwards, pp. 55–68. Singapore: Centre for Advanced Studies and Singapore University Press.

Clifford, J. 1998. Mixed feelings. In *Cosmopolitics: Thinking and Feeling beyond the Nation*, ed. P. Cheah and B. Robbins. Minneapolis, MN: University of Minnesota Press.

Commonwealth of Pennsylvania. 1890. *General Report of the Commissioners Appointed to Revise and Codify the Laws Relating to the Relief, Care and Maintenance of the Poor in the Commonwealth of Pennsylvania*. Harrisburg: Meyer's Printing House.

Conkling, M. C. 1857. *The American Gentleman's Guide to Politeness and Fashion*. New York.

Constable, N. 1997. *Maid to Order in Hong Kong: Stories of Filipina Workers*. Ithaca, NY: Cornell University Press.

"Conversation with Architect," April 28, 1972. From archives of William H. Whyte, at the Project for Public Space.

Cooper, M. and Chaifant, H. 1984. *Subway Art*. New York: Holt, Rinehart and Winston.

Cope, M. 1996. Weaving the Everyday: Identity, Space, and Power in Lawrence, Massachusetts, 1920–1939. *Urban Geography* 17: 179–204.

Cornett, L. 1993. Beyond Open Space: Answers Come Hard. *Boulder (Colorado) Daily Camera* September 26, 1993: A9.

Cowling, M. 1989. *The Artist as Anthropologist*. Cambridge: Cambridge University Press.

Cranz, G. 1982. *The Politics of Park Design: A History of Urban Parks in America*. Cambridge: MIT Press.

Crawford, M. 1992. The World in a Shopping Mall. In *Variations on a Theme Park: The New American City and the End of Public Space*, ed. M. Sorkin, pp. 3–30. New York: Hill and Wang.

——. 1995. Contesting the Public Realm: Struggles over Public Space in Los Angeles. *Journal of Architectural Education* 49: 4–9.

Cresswell, T. 1996. *In Place/Out of Place: Geography, Ideology, and Transgression*. Minneapolis: University of Minneapolis Press.

Crilley, D. 1993. Megastructures and Urban Change: Aesthetics, Ideology and Design. In *The Restless Urban Landscape*, ed. P. Knox, pp. 127–164. Englewood Cliffs, New Jersey: Prentice Hall.

Cuthbert, A. and McKinnell, K. 1997. Ambiguous Space, Ambiguous Rights: Corporate Power and Social Control in Hong Kong. *Cities* 14: 295–311.

Darnton, R. 1984. *The Great Cat Massacre and Other Episodes in French Cultural History*. New York: Basic Books.

Davis, M. 1987. Chinatown, Part Two? The Internationalization of Downtown Los Angeles. *New Left Review* 164 (July–August).

——. 1990. *City of Quartz: Excavating the Future in Los Angeles*. New York: Verso.

——. 1992. Fortress Los Angeles: The Militarization of Urban Space. In *Variations on a Theme Park: The New American City and the End of Public Space*, ed. M. Sorkin, pp. 154–180. New York: Hill and Wang.

Davis, S. G. 1986. *Parades and Power: Street Theater in Nineteenth-Century Philadelphia*. Berkeley: University of California Press.

de Certeau, M. 1984. *The Practice of Everyday Life*. Berkeley: University of California Press.

Decorum: A Practical Treatise on Etiquette and Dress in the Best American Society. 1878. New York.

Deitch, L. I. 1989. The Impact of Tourism on the Arts and Crafts of the Indians of the Southwestern United States. In *Hosts and Guests: The Anthropology of Tourism*. Second edition, ed. Valene L. Smith, pp. 223–235. Philadelphia, PA: University of Pennsylvania Press.

Deutsche, R. 1990. Architecture of the Evicted. *Strategies: A Journal of Theory, Culture and Politics* 3: 159–183.

——. 1992. Art and Public Space: Questions of Democracy. *Social Text* 33: 34–53.

Dickinson, J. 1998. In Its Place: Site and Meaning in Richard Serra's Public Sculpture. In *Philosophy and Geography III: Philosophies of Place*, ed. Andrew Light and Jonathan M. Smith. New York: Rowman and Littlefield.

Dijkstra, L. 2000. Public Spaces: A Comparative Discussion of the Criteria for Public Space. In *Constructions of Public Space: Research in Urban Sociology*. Vol. 5, ed. Ray Hutchinson, 1–22. Stamford, CT: JAI.

Dominguez, V. R. 1986. The Marketing of Heritage. *American Ethnologist* 3: 546–555

Domosh, Mona. 1996. *Invented Cities: The Creation of Landscape in 19th-Century New York and Boston*. New Haven: Yale University Press.

Dorgan, M. 1985. Hippies Moved from Street to Berkeley Dump. *San Jose Mercury-News* January 31, 1985: B12.

Drucker, J. 1994. "Thanks for Nothing: Homeless Sue Boss." *New York Observer* November 21.

Drummond, L. 2000. Street Scenes: Practices of Public and Private Space in Urban Vietnam. *Urban Studies* 37: 2377–2391.

Duany, A. and Plater-Zyberk, E. 1994. *Downcity Providence: Master Plan for a Special Time.* Plan 1A of the Area Plan Series of Providence 2000.

Duggan, B. J. 1997. Tourism, Cultural Authenticity, and the Native Crafts Cooperative: The Eastern Cherokee Experience. In *Tourism and Culture: An Applied Perspective*, ed. Erve Chambers, pp. 31–57. New York: State University of New York Press.

Dunbar-Hall, P. 2001. Culture, Tourism and Cultural Tourism: Boundaries and Frontiers in Performances of Balinese Music and Dance. *Journal of Intercultural Studies* 22: 173–187.

Duncan, J. 1990. *The City as Text: The Politics of Landscape Interpretation in the Kanyan Kingdom.* Cambridge: Cambridge University Press.

Duncan, N. 1996. Renegotiating Gender and Sexuality in Public and Private Spaces. In *BodySpace*, ed. N. Duncan, pp. 127–145. London: Routledge.

Ellington, G. 1869. *The Women of New York or the Under-World of the Great City.* New York: New York Book Co.

Enloe, C. 1989. *Bananas, Beaches and Bases: Making Feminist Sense of International Politics.* London: Pandora Press.

Fieden, D. 1992. "Midtown Bonds Spark BID Controversy." *Crain's New York Business* April 6, 1992: 1, 30.

Fimrite, P. and Wilson, Y. 1992. Intruder Slain at Home of UC Chancellor. *San Francisco Chronicle* August 26, 1992: A1, A11.

Fisher, S. and Davis, K. 1993. *Negotiating at the Margins: The Gendered Discourses of Power and Resistance.* New Brunswick, NJ: Rutgers University Press.

Flusty, S. 1994. *Building Paranoia: The Proliferation of Interdictory Space and the Erosion of Spatial Justice.* Los Angeles: Los Angeles Forum for Architecture and Urban Design.

Foster, G. G. [1856] 1990. *New York by Gas-light and Other Urban Sketches.* Berkeley: University of California Press.

Fraser, N. 1989. *Unruly Practices: Power, Discourse, and Gender in Contemporary Social Theory.* Minneapolis: University of Minnesota Press.

——. 1990. Rethinking the Public Sphere: A Contribution to Actually Existing Democracy. *Social Text* 25/26: 56–79.

——. 1992. Rethinking the Public Sphere: A Contribution to the Critique of Actually Existing Democracy. In *Habermas and the Public Sphere*, ed. Craig Calhoun, pp. 109–142. Cambridge: MIT Press.

Freeman, R. G. 1994. *The Free Negro in New York City in the Era before the Civil War.* New York: Garland Publishing.

Friedan, B. J. and Sagalyn, L. B. 1989. *Downtown, Inc.: How America Rebuilds Cities.* Cambridge, MA: MIT Press.

Friedland, R. and Boden, D. 1994. Nowhere: An Introduction to Space, Time and Modernity. In *NowHere: Space, Time and Modernity*, ed. Roger Friedland and Deirdre Boden, pp. 1–60. Berkeley and Los Angeles, CA: University of California Press.

Fyfe, N. 2004. Zero Tolerance, Maximum Surveillance? Deviance, Difference and Crime Control in the Late Modern City. In *The Emancipatory City? Paradoxes and Possibilities*, ed. Loretta Lees, pp. 40–58. Thousand Oaks, CA: Sage.

Fyfe, N. R. and Bannister, J. 1998. The Eyes Upon the Street: Closed Circuit Television Surveillance and the City. In *Images of the Street: Planning, Identity and Control in Public Space*, ed. Nicholas R. Fyfe, pp. 254–276. New York: Routledge.

Gans, H. 2006. Jane Jacobs: Toward an Understanding of "Death and Life of Great American Cities." *City and Community* 5: 213–215.

Garreau, J. 1991. *Edge City: Life on the New Frontier.* New York: Doubleday.

Gastil, R. W. and Ryan, Z. 2004. *Open: New Designs for Public Spaces.* New York: Van Allen Institute.

Geertz, C. 1973. *The Interpretation of Cultures: Selected Essays.* New York: Basic Books.

Gehl Architects APS. 2002. *Public Spaces and Public Life: City of Adelaide 2002.* (Available at http://www.adelaidecitycouncil.com/adccwr/publications/reports_plans/public_spaces_public_life.pdf)

Gehl, J. 2002. Pedestrian Cities. In *Metropolis Magazine*, August/September. (Available electronically at http://www.metropolismag.com/html/content_0802 /ped/index_b.html)

George, M. 1993. Handout Coupons May Foil Begging for Booze, Smokes. *Denver Post* March 2, 1993: B4.

Gibson, K., Law, L., and McKay, D. 2001. Beyond Heroes and Victims: Filipina Contract Migrants, Economic Activism and Class Transformations, *International Feminist Journal of Politics* 3: 365–386.

Gilroy, P. 1993. *The Black Atlantic: Modernity and Double Consciousness.* Cambridge, MA: Harvard University Press.

Glazer, N. 1992. "Subverting the Context": Public and Space and Public Design. *Public Interest* 109: 3–21.

Goheen, P. 1994. Negotiating Access to Public Space in Mid-Nineteenth-Century Toronto. *Journal of Historical Geography* 24: 430–49.

Gonzalez, J. L. III. 1998. *Philippine Labour Migration: Critical Dimensions of Public Policy.* Singapore: Institute of Southeast Asian Studies.

Goodsell, C. T. 2003. The Concept of Public Space and

Its Democratic Manifestations. *The American Review of Public Administration* 33: 361–383.

Goss, J. 1988. The Built Environment and Social Theory: Towards an Architectural Geography. *Professional Geographer* 40: 392–403.

——. 1992. Modernity and Postmodernity in the Retail Landscape. In *Inventing Places*, ed. K. Anderson and F. Gale, pp. 159–177. Melbourne: Longman Scientific.

——. 1993. The "Magic of the Mall": An Analysis of Form, Function, and Meaning in the Retail Built Environment. *Annals of the Association of American Geographers* 83: 18–47.

——. 1996. Disquiet on the Waterfront: Nostalgia and Utopia in the Festival Marketplace. *Urban Geography* 17: 221–47.

Gottdiener, M., Collins, C., and Dickens, D. R. 2000. *Las Vegas: The Social Production of An All American City*. New York: Blackwell.

Grannis, R. 1998. The Importance of Trivial Streets: Residential Streets and Residential Segregation. *American Journal of Sociology* 103: 1530–1564.

Greenberg, K. 1990. The Would-Be Science and Art of Making Public Spaces. *Architecture et Comportment/Architecture and Behaviour* 6: 323–338.

Habermas, J. [1962] 1989. *The Structural Transformation of the Public Sphere: An Inquiry into a Category of Bourgeois Society*. Translated by Thomas Burger. Cambridge, MA: MIT Press.

Hales, L. 2004. At Columbus Circle, Going Round and Round Over a Building's Fate. *The Washington Post*, May 29.

Hammack, D. 1987. *Power and Society: Greater New York at the Turn of the Century*. New York: Columbia University Press.

Hampton, K. and Wellman, B. 2003. Neighboring in Netville: How the Internet Supports Community and Social Capital in a Wired Suburb. *City and Community* 2: 277–311.

Harris, B. 1988. Homeless and their Neighbors. *Oakland Tribune* February 22, 1988: B12.

Hartley, J. 1992. *The Politics of Pictures: The Creation of the Public in the Age of Popular Media*. London: Routledge.

Harvey, D. 1973. *Social Justice and the City*. Baltimore: Johns Hopkins University Press.

——. 1989. *The Condition of Postmodernity: An Enquiry into the Origins of Social Change*. Oxford: Basil Blackwell.

——. 1992. Social Justice, Postmodernism and the City. *International Journal of Urban and Regional Research* 16: 588–601.

——. 1993. From Space to Place and Back Again: Reflections on the Condition of Postmodernity. In *Mapping the Futures: Local Cultures Global Change*, ed. J. Bird, B. Curtis, T. Putnam, G. Robertson, and L. Tickner, pp. 3–29. London: Routledge.

Hayden, D. 1988. Placemaking, Preservation and Urban History. *Journal of Architectural Education* 41: 45–51.

Henderson, T. 2000. Pity, South *China Morning Post*, 20 February, 2000: 10.

Hershkovitz, L. 1993. Tiananmen Square and the Politics of Place. *Political Geography* 12: 395–420.

Hillis, K. 1994. The Virtue of Becoming a No-Body. *Ecumene* 1: 177–196.

Holston, J. 1995. Spaces of Insurgent Citizenship. *Planning Theory* 13: 35–51.

Howell, P. 1993. Public Space and the Public Sphere: Political Theory and the Historical Geography of Modernity. *Environment and Planning D: Society and Space* 11: 303–322.

How to Behave: A Pocket Manual of Republican Etiquette. 1872. New York.

Huxtable, A. L. 1970. Tale of a Few Cities—Everywhere. *The New York Times*, March 9.

Ignatiev, N. 1995. *How the Irish Became White*. New York: Routledge.

International Union of Public Transport. 1988. Metro and Architecture: Buildings and Public Transport. *Revue of the International Union of Public Transport* 36.

Iveson, K. 1998. Putting the Public Back into Public Space. *Urban Policy and Research* 16: 21–33.

Jacobs, J. 1961. *Death and Life of Great American Cities*. New York: Vintage Books.

Jaher, F. C. 1982. *The Urban Establishment: Upper Strata in Boston, New York, Charleston, Chicago, and Los Angeles*. Urbana: University of Illinois Press.

Jen, G. n.d. The Great World Transformed. *Boston Contemporary Writers*. Boston, MA: UrbanArts.

Jordan, S. 1987. *Public Art, Public Controversy: Tilted Arc on Trial*. New York: American Council for the Arts.

Judd, D. and Fainstein, S. 1999. *The Tourist City*. New Haven, CT: Yale University Press.

Kahn, B. 1991a. People's Park: Is the Fight Over? *East Bay Express* March 22, 1991: 2, 28.

——. 1991b. Activists and Homeless Haggle Over Future of People's Park. *East Bay Express* June 14, 1991: 3, 29–30.

——. 1991c. Who's in Charge Here? University Bulldozer Rolls While Council is Out of Town. *East Bay Express* August 9, 1991: 1, 11–13.

Kasson, J. 1990. *Rudeness and Civility: Manners in 19th-Century America*. New York: Hill and Wang.

Kayden, J. S., New York City Department of City Planning, and Municipal Art Society. 2000. *Privately Owned Public Space: The New York City Experience*. New York: John Wiley.

Keith, M. and Pile, S. 1993. *Place and the Politics of Identity*. London: Routledge.

Koh, T. A. 1989. Culture and The Arts. In *Management*

of Success: The Moulding of Modern Singapore, ed. Kernial Singh Sandhu and Paul Wheatley, pp. 710–748. Singapore: Institute of Southeast Asian Studies.

Koopman, J. 1991. People's Park Protestors Brace for Today. *Contra Costa Times* August 3, 1991: A1, A13.

Kowinski, W. 1985. *The Malling of America: An Inside Look at the Great Consumer Paradise*. New York: William Morrow.

Kramer, J. 1992. "Whose Art is it?" *The New Yorker* December 21, 1992: 80–109.

Lai, W. Y. 1986. *Modernization of a Cultural Tradition: A Case Study of Cantonese Opera in Singapore*. Singapore: Academic Exercise, Department of Sociology, National University of Singapore.

Law, L. 2000. *Virtual Activism: New Political Spaces for Transnational Migrants*. Paper presented at the *International Conference on Transnational Communities in the Asia-Pacific Region: Comparative Perspectives*, Singapore, August.

——. 2001. Home Cooking: Filipino Women and Geographies of the Senses in Hong Kong. *Ecumene* 8: 264–283.

——. 2002. Sites of Transnational Activism: Filipino NGOs in Hong Kong. In *Gender Politics in the Asia Pacific Region*, ed. B. Yeoh, P. Teo, and S. Huang, pp. 205–222. London: Routledge.

Lee, T. S. 2009. *Chinese Street Opera in Singapore*. Champaign, IL: University of Illinois Press.

Lee, W. C. 1995. *Space, Spaces and Spacing*. Singapore: The Substation.

Lees, L. 1998. Urban Renaissance and the Street: Spaces of Control and Contestation. In *Images of the Street: Planning, Identity and Control in Public Space*, ed. Nicholas R. Fyfe, pp. 236–253. New York: Routledge.

Lefebvre, H. 1991. *The Production of Space*, translated by D. Nicholson-Smith. Oxford: Basil Blackwell.

——. 1996. *Writings on Cities*, translated and edited by Eleonore Kofman and Elizabeth Lebas. Oxford: Blackwell. [see especially Chapter 14, "The Right to the City."]

Leighninger, R. D. 1996. Cultural Infrastructure: The Legacy of New Deal Public Space. *Journal of Architectural Education* 49: 226–236.

Leo, J. 1994. Cities Finally Acting to Restore Public Order. Syndicated Column, Universal Press.

Leong, W. T. 1997a. Culture and the State: Manufacturing Traditions for Tourism. In *Understanding Singapore Society*, ed. Ong Jin Hui, Tong Chee Kiong, and Tan Ern Ser, pp. 513–534. Singapore: Times Academic Press. Originally published in 1989 in *Critical Studies in Mass Communication* 6: 355–375.

——. 1997b. Commodifying Ethnicity: State and Ethnic Tourism in Singapore. In *Tourism, Ethnicity, and the State in Asian and Pacific Societies*, ed. Michel Picard and Robert E. Wood, pp. 71–98. Honolulu, HI: University of Hawai'i Press.

Levine, H. 1987. Homeless Shelter Closes. *San Francisco Examiner* May 11, 1987: C1.

Lockwood, C. 1976. *Manhattan Moves Uptown*. New York: Barnes and Noble.

Lofland, L. 1998. *The Public Realm: Exploring the City's Quintessential Social Territory*. New York: Aldine de Gruyter.

Los Angeles Times. 1988. Eviction of Homeless in Berkeley Sparks Melee. March 17, 1988: I3.

——. 1989a. Rally at Berkeley Erupts into Riot. May 21, 1989: I3.

——. 1989b. S.F. Clears Park's Tent City of Structures, Not People. July 21, 1989: I3.

——. 1990. Compassion for the Homeless Wearing Thin in Bay Area. July 20, 1990: A1.

——. 1991a. Berkeley Bastion. March 13, 1991: A3.

——. 1991b. Temper Tantrums Over Dystopian Nightmare. August 7, 1991: A10.

——. 1992. Play Replaces Protest at People's Park. March 31, 1992: A3.

Low, S. 2000. *On the Plaza: The Politics of Public Space and Culture*. Austin, TX: University of Texas Press.

Low, S. and Smith, N. 2006. *The Politics of Public Space*. New York: Routledge.

Low, S., Taplin, D., and Scheld, S. 2005. *Rethinking Urban Parks: Public Space and Cultural Diversity*. Austin, TX: University of Texas Press.

Lowenthal, D. 1985. *The Past is a Foreign Country*. Cambridge: Cambridge University Press.

Lyford, J. 1982. *The Berkeley Archipelago*. Chicago: Regnery Gateway.

Lynch, A. 1991a. Council Recess Adds to "People's Park" Woes. *San Francisco Chronicle* August 6, 1991: B1.

——. 1991b. What They're Saying About People's Park. *San Francisco Chronicle* August 7, 1991: A11–A12.

——. 1991c. Police Arrest Protestors at New Volleyball Courts. *San Francisco Chronicle* August 9, 1991: 1, 20.

Lynch A. and Dietz, D. 1991. Fewer Recruits for People's Park Wars. *San Francisco Chronicle* August 2, 1991: A1, A20.

Lynch, K. 1981. *A Theory of Good City Form*. Cambridge, MA: MIT Press.

——. [1972] 1990. The Openness of Open Spaces. In *City Sense and City Design: Writings and Projects of Kevin Lynch*, ed. T. Banerjee and M. Southworth, pp. 396–412. Cambridge, MA: MIT Press.

Mair, A. 1986. The Homeless and the Post-Industrial City. *Political Geography Quarterly* 5: 351–368.

Maitland, B. 1985. *Shopping Malls: Planning and Design*. London: Nichols.

Mandelbaum, S. J. 1965. *Boss Tweed's New York*. New York: John Wiley.

Mann, P. S. 1994. *Micro-Politics: Agency in Postfeminist Era*. Minneapolis: University of Minneapolis Press.

Mara, P. 1981. *L'Art Dans le Metro*. Brussels: Societe Transport Intercommunaux Brusselois.

Marcuse, P. 1988. Neutralizing Homelessness. *Socialist Review* 18: 69–96.

Marston, S. 1990. Who are "The People": Gender, Citizenship, and the Making of the American Nation. *Environment and Planning D: Society and Space* 8: 449–458.

Martin, E. W. 1868. *The Secrets of the Great City*. Philadelphia: Jones Brothers.

Masschaele, J. 2002. The Public Space of the Marketplace in Medieval England. *Speculum* 77: 383–421.

May, M. 1993. Telegraph Ave. Shoppers Report Retail Revival. *The Bay Guardian* January 9, 1993: 9.

McCabe, J. D. Jr. 1872. *Lights and Shadows of New York Life*. Reprinted by Andre Deutsch, London, 1971.

McDowell, L. 1999. *Gender, Identity and Place: Understanding Feminist Geographies*. Cambridge: Polity Press.

McKenzie, E. 1994. *Privatopia: Homeowner Associations and the Rise of Residential Private Government*. New Haven, CT: Yale University Press.

Meehan, J. 1995. *Feminists Read Habermas: Gendering the Subject of Discourse*. New York: Routledge.

Miles, M. 1989. *Art for Public Places: Critical Essays*. Hampshire, U.K.: Winchester School of Art.

Mitchell, D. 1992a. Iconography and Locational Conflict from the Underside: Free Speech, People's Park and the Politics of Homelessness in Berkeley, California. *Political Geography* 11: 152–169.

——. 1992b. Land and Labor: Worker Resistance and the Production of Landscape in Agricultural California Before World War II. Unpublished PhD Dissertation, Department of Geography, Rutgers University.

——. 1995. The End of Public Space? People's Park, Definitions of the Public and Democracy. *Annals of the Association of American Geographers* 85: 108–133.

——. 2000. *Cultural Geography: A Critical Introduction*. Oxford: Blackwell.

——. 2003. *The Right to the City: Social Justice and the Fight for Public Space*. New York: Guilford Press.

Mitchell, D. and Staeheli, L. 2006. Clean and Safe? Property Redevelopment, Public Space, and Homelessness in Downtown San Diego. In *The Politics of Public Space*, ed. Setha Low and Neil Smith, pp. 143–176. New York: Routledge.

Morgan, E. 1988. *Inventing the People: The Rise of Popular Sovereignty in England and America*. New York: W.W. Norton.

Morris, J. [1988] 1997. *Hong Kong*. London: Penguin.

Morse, L. G. 1927. Recollections of the Draft Riots of 1863 New York City. New York Historical Society, miscellaneous documents.

Mott, F. L. 1957. *A History of American Magazines*. Cambridge: Harvard University Press.

National Committee on the Causes and Prevention of Violence. *To Establish Justice. To Ensure Domestic Tranquility (Final Report)*, Washington D. C. 1969.

Naughton, E. 1992. Is Cyberspace a Public Forum? Computer Bulletin Boards and State Action. *The Georgetown Law Journal* 81: 409–441.

Negt, O. and Kluge, A. 1993. *Public Sphere and Experience, toward an Analysis of the Bourgeois and Proletarian Public Sphere*. Minneapolis: University of Minneapolis Press.

New York Times. 1969. Plazas, Nice for Strollers, Give Builders Problems. August 24, 1969: 8.

——. 1988a. A Playground Derelicts Can't Enter. August 20, 1988: A31.

——. 1988b. 29 Trying to Feed Homeless are Arrested in San Francisco. August 30, 1988: A14.

——. 1989a. Violence Flares at Berkeley Park During Event Marking 60's Battle. May 21, 1989: 1, 26.

——. 1989b. New Message to the Homeless: Get Out. August 3, 1989: A14.

——. 1989c. For the Homeless Public Spaces Are Growing Smaller. October 1, 1989: E5.

——. 1991a. Deal is Struck on Fate of Park and Protest Site. March 10, 1991: 1, 39.

——. 1991b. The Public's Right to Put a Padlock on Public Space. June 3, 1991: B1.

——. 1991c. Idealism to Decay to Volleyball at People's Park. July 5, 1991: A8.

——. 1992a. Trial to Be a Test on Homeless Living in Parks. June 14, 1992: 1, 40.

——. 1992b. Judge Orders "Safe Zones" for Homeless. November 18, 1992: A10.

Olmstead, F. L. 1902. *Public Parks: Being Two Papers Read before the American Social Science Association in 1870 and 1880, Entitled, Respectively, Public Parks and the Enlargement of Towns, and, a Consideration of the Justifying Value of a Public Park*. Brookline, MA. (Available electronically at http://books.google.com/ books?id=vWIAAAAAYAAJ)

Ong, A. 1997. 'A Better Tomorrow?' The Struggle For Global Visibility. *Sojourn* 12: 192–225.

Oral History Department. 1990. *Recollections: People and Places*. Singapore: Singapore Oral History Department.

Picard, M. 1996. *Bali: Cultural Tourism and Touristic Culture*. Translated by Diana Darling. Singapore: Archipelago Press, Editions Didier Millet. Originally published in 1992 in French as *Bali: Tourisme Culturel et culture touristique*. Paris: Editions L'Harmattan.

——. 1997. Cultural Tourism, Nation-Building, and Regional Culture: The Making of a Balinese Identity. In *Tourism, Ethnicity, and the State in Asian and Pacific Societies*, ed. Michel Picard and Robert E. Wood, pp. 181–214. Honolulu: University of Hawaii Press.

Poovey, M. 1988. *Uneven Developments: The Ideological Work of Gender in Mid-Victorian England*. Chicago: University of Chicago Press.

Putnam, R. 2000. *Bowling Alone: The Collapse and Revival of American Community*. New York: Simon and Schuster.

Raven, A. 1989. *Art in the Public Interest*. Ann Arbor, MI: UMI Research Press.

Rees, H. 1998. 'Authenticity' and the Foreign Audience for Traditional Music in Southwest China. *Journal of Musicological Research* 17: 135–161.

Reynolds, J. 1993. Introduction, in Wilfred Holton et al., *Creating a Sense of Place in Urban Communities*. Boston, MA: UrbanArts.

Riemans, P. and Lovink, G. 2002. Local Networks: Digital City Amsterdam. In *Global Networks, Linked Cities*, ed. Saskia Sassen, pp. 327–346. New York: Routledge.

Ripton-Turner, C. 1887. *A History of Vagrants and Vagrancy and Beggars and Begging*. London: Chapman Hill.

Rivlin, G. 1991a. People's Park: Construction Zone. *East Bay Express* August 2, 1991: 3, 27.

——. 1991b. Appropriate Force? Reports of Police-inflicted Injuries Continue to Flow in. *East Bay Express* August 9, 1991: 1, 13–18.

Robbins, B. 1990. Intellectuals in Decline? (review of Russell Jacoby's *The Last Intellectuals: American Culture in the Age of Academe*). *Social Text* 25/26: 254–259.

——. 1998. Introduction Part I: Actually Existing Cosmopolitanism. In *Cosmopolitics: Thinking and Feeling beyond the Nation*, ed. P. Cheah and B. Robbins, pp. 1–19. Minneapolis, MN: University of Minnesota Press.

Roberts, C. 1994. Girding the Globe: The Boundaries Between People and Countries are Being Erased by Telecommunications. *Boulder (Colorado) Daily Camera* February 10, 1994: C1.

Rorabaugh, W. 1989. *Berkeley at War: The 1960s*. New York: Oxford University Press.

Rosenzweig, R. and Blackmar, E. 1992. *The Park and the People: A History of Central Park*. Ithaca, NY: Cornell University Press.

Rowe, S. and Wolch, J. 1990. Social Networks in Time and Space: Homeless Women in Skid Row, Los Angeles. *Annals of the Association of American Geographers* 80: 184–204.

Rowell, M. 1999. *Brancusi v. United States: The Historic Trial, 1928*. Paris: Adam Biro.

Ruddick, S. 1990. Heterotopias of the Homeless: Strategies and Tactics of Placemaking in Los Angeles. *Strategies: A Journal of Theory, Culture, and Politics* 3: 184–201.

Rules of Etiquette and Home Culture. 1893. Chicago and New York.

Schafer, R. M. 1994. *The Soundscape: Our Sonic Environment and the Tuning of the World*. Rochester, VT: Destiny Books. Originally published in 1977 as *The Tuning of the World*. New York: Knopf.

Scheer, R. 1969. The Dialectics of Confrontation: Who Ripped Off the Park? *Ramparts* 8 (August): 42–53.

Scheiner, S. 1965. *Negro Mecca: A History of the Negro in New York City, 1865–1920*. New York: New York University Press.

Scherzer, K. 1992. *The Unbounded Community: Neighborhood Life and Social Structure in New York City, 1830–1875*. Chapel Hill: Duke University Press.

Schlachter, E. 1993. Cyberspace, the Free Market and the Free Market Place of Ideas: Recognizing Differences in Computer Board Functions. *Hastings Communications and Entertainment Law Journal* 16: 87–150.

Scobey, D. 1992. Anatomy of the Promenade: The Politics of Bourgeois Sociability in Nineteenth-Century New York. *Social History* 17: 203–227.

Scott, J. 1985. *Weapons of the Weak: Everyday Forms of Peasant Resistance*. New Haven: Yale University Press.

Sennett, R. [1977] 1992. *The Fall of Public Man*. New York: Knopf.

Siegel, F. 1992. Reclaiming our Public Spaces. *City Journal* (Spring): 35–45.

Simmel, G. [1903] 1964. The Metropolis and Mental Life. In *The Sociology of Georg Simmel*, translated by Kurt H. Wolff, pp. 409–424. New York: The Free Press.

Singapore Changi Airport. 1997. *Changi: The Magazine* (The Bi-Monthly Companion Magazine for Singapore Changi Airport). Issue 9 (Feb/Mar). London: Highbury House Communications PLC.

Singapore Tourism Board. 1997. *New Asia Singapore: Mature Travellers*. Singapore: Singapore Tourism Board.

Singapore Visitor. 1997. *The Singapore Visitor: The Weekly Guide to Help You Enjoy Your Stay*. Issue No. 1100/97 (June 7–13). Singapore: Creations & Communications (Private) Limited.

Slatin, P. 1993. Al Fresco Dining Facing Grand Central? *New York Times* (August 22).

Smith, M. H. 1868. *Sunshine and Shadow in New York*. Hartford.

Smith, N. 1989. Tompkins Square Park. *The Portable Lower East Side* 6(2): 1–28.

——. 1992a. Contours of a Spatialized Politics: Homeless

Vehicles and the Production of Geographical Scale. *Social Text* 33: 55–81.

——. 1992b. New City, New Frontier: The Lower East Side as Wild, Wild West. In *Variations on a Theme Park: The New American City and the End of Public Space*, ed. M. Sorkin, pp. 61–93. New York: Hill and Wang.

——. 1993. Homeless/Global: Scaling Places. In *Mapping the Futures: Local Cultures Global Change*, ed. J. Bird, B. Curtis, T. Putnam, G. Robertson, and L. Tickner, pp. 87–119. London: Routledge.

Smith-Rosenberg, C. 1985. *Disorderly Conduct: Visions of Gender in Victorian America*. Oxford: Oxford University Press.

Snider, A. 1992. Intruder Slain in House of UC Chief. *Contra Costa Times* August 26, 1992: A1, A12.

Soja, E. 1989. *Postmodern Geographies: The Reassertion of Space in Critical Social Theory*. London: Verso.

Sorkin, M. 1992. *Variations on a Theme Park: The New American City and the End of Public Space*. New York: Hill and Wang.

Spann, E. 1981. *The New Metropolis: New York City, 1840–1857*. New York: Columbia University Press.

Squires, J. 1994. Private Lives, Secluded Places: Privacy as Political Possibility. *Environment and Planning D: Society and Space* 12: 387–402.

Stallone, S. 1993. People's Park Protestor Sues UC Over Search. *The Bay Guardian* January 6, 1993: 9.

Stern, S. 1987. Activists Seek a Solution Beyond Shelters. *Oakland Tribune* February 22, 1987: D10.

Straits Times. 1996. Complete Opera Lessons at CC [Community Centre]. July 30.

Sunstein, C. 2001. *Republic.com*. Princeton, NJ: Princeton University Press.

Tafuri, M. 1979. The Disenchanted Mountain: The Skyscraper and the City. In Giorgio Ciucci, et al., *The American City*. Cambridge, Mass: MIT Press.

Talk with Mel Kaufman 1/8/72. 1972. From the archives of William H. Whyte, Project for Public Space.

Taruskin, R. 1988. The Pastness of the Present and the Presence of the Past. In *Authenticity and Early Music: A Symposium*, ed. Nicholas Kenyon, pp. 137–207. Oxford: Oxford University Press.

U.S. Supreme Court. 1983. *Perry Education Association v. Perry Local Educators' Association*. 460 U.S. 37.

Vaness, A. 1993. Neither Homed nor Homeless: Contested Definitions and the Personal Worlds of the Poor. *Political Geography* 12: 319–340.

Veness, A. 1995. Designer Shelter as Models and Makers of Homelessness in Urban America. *Urban Geography* 15: 150–167.

Wallace, M. 1989. Mickey Mouse History: Portraying the Past at Disney World. In *History Museums in the United States: A Critical Assessment*, ed. W. Leon and R. Rosenzweig, pp. 158–180. Urbana: University of Illinois Press.

Wang, Z. C. 1990. *Gen de Xilie Zhi Er [The 'Roots' Series 2]*. Singapore: Sinmin Ribao and Seng Yew Book Store.

Webster, C., Glasze, G., and Frantz, K. 2002. Theme Issue: The Global Spread of Gated Communities. *Environment and Planning B* 29: 3.

Werbner, P. 1998. Diasporic Political Imaginaries: A Sphere of Freedom or a Sphere of Illusions? *Communal/Plural* 6: 11–31.

Weyergraf-Serra, C. and Buskirk, M. 1991. *Tilted Arc. See The Destruction of Tilted Arc: Documents*. Cambridge, MA: MIT Press.

Wharton, E. [1920] 1968. *The Age of Innocence*. New York: Charles Scribner's Sons.

——. [1905] 1984. *The House of Mirth*. New York: Bantam Books.

White, S. 1991. *Somewhat More Independent: The End of Slavery in New York City, 1770–1810*. Athens, GA: University of Georgia Press.

Whyte, W. H. 1980. *The Social Life of Small Urban Spaces*. Washington, DC: Conservation Foundation.

——. 1988. *City: Rediscovering the Center*. New York: Doubleday.

Will, G. 1987. Living on the Street: Mentally Ill Homeless Contribute to Community Decay. Syndicated Column, Washington Post Writer's Group.

Wilson, A. 1992. *The Culture of Nature: North American Landscape from Disney to the Exxon Valdez*. Oxford: Basil Blackwell.

Wilson, E. 1991. *The Sphinx in the City: Urban Life, the Control of Disorder, and Women*. Berkeley: University of California Press.

Winchester, H., Kong, L., and Dunn, K. 2002. *Landscape: Ways of Imagining the World*. Melbourne: Longman.

Winter, J. 1993. *London's Teeming Streets 1830–1914*. London: Routledge.

Wolfe, T. 1981. *From Bauhaus to Our House*. New York: Pocket Books.

Wolfson, H. 1992. New York Bets on BIDs. *Metropolis* (April): 15, 21.

Yasmeen, G. 1996. Plastic-Bag Housewives and Post-Modern Restaurants? Public and Private in Bangkok's Foodscape. *Urban Geography* 17: 526–544.

Yeoh, B. and Huang, S. 1998. Negotiating Public Space: Strategies and Styles of Female Domestic Workers in Singapore. *Urban Studies* 35: 583–602.

Young, I. M. 1990. *Justice and the Politics of Difference*. Princeton, NJ: Princeton University Press.

Zukin, S. 1991. *Landscapes of Power: From Detroit to Disney World*. Berkeley: University of California Press.

——. 1995. *Cultures of Cities*. Cambridge, MA: Blackwell.

INDEX